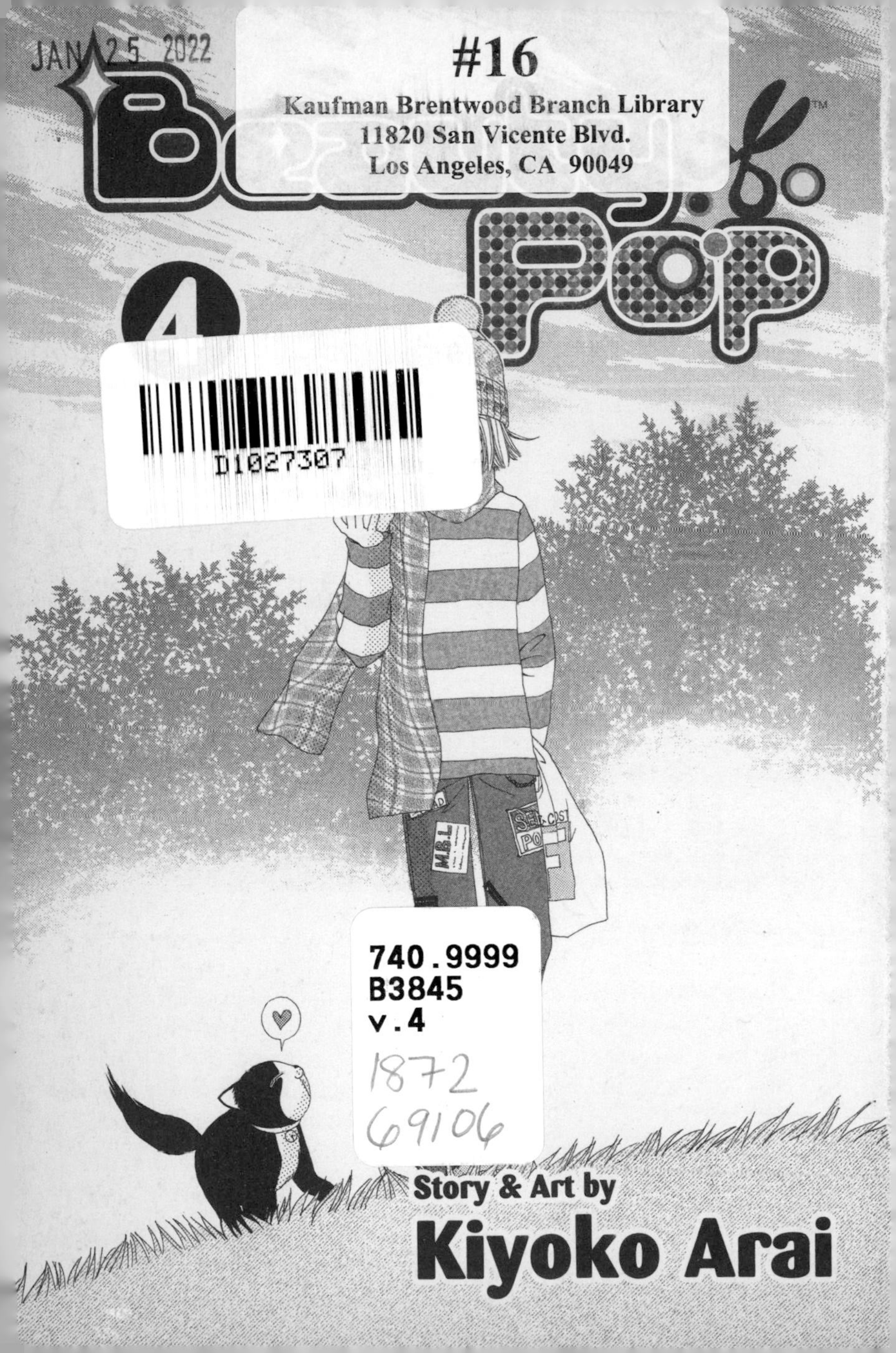

Pop
4
Story & Art by
Kiyoko Arai

Beauty Pop

Characters

4

KIRI KOSHIBA

◀ She's absentminded and seems self-centered, but she really cares for her friends. Kiri has exceptional haircutting techniques.

KEI MINAMI

NAIL ART

AROMATHERAPY

IORI MINAMOTO

SHOGO NARUMI

MAKEUP

HAIR

KAZUHIKO OCHIAI

Story So Far ✂

At Kiri's school there are three boys who created a club called the Scissors Project, and they are famous for doing makeovers on girls. Kiri had a haircut battle with Narumi, a member of the Scissors Project, and won! Since then, Narumi's hot-tempered rivalry has become a nuisance to Kiri. But when the Scissors Project is challenged to a beauty battle, Kiri ends up helping out...?!

CONTENTS

Beauty Pop.....3
Recent Events Manga Theater.....64, 96, 128, 190

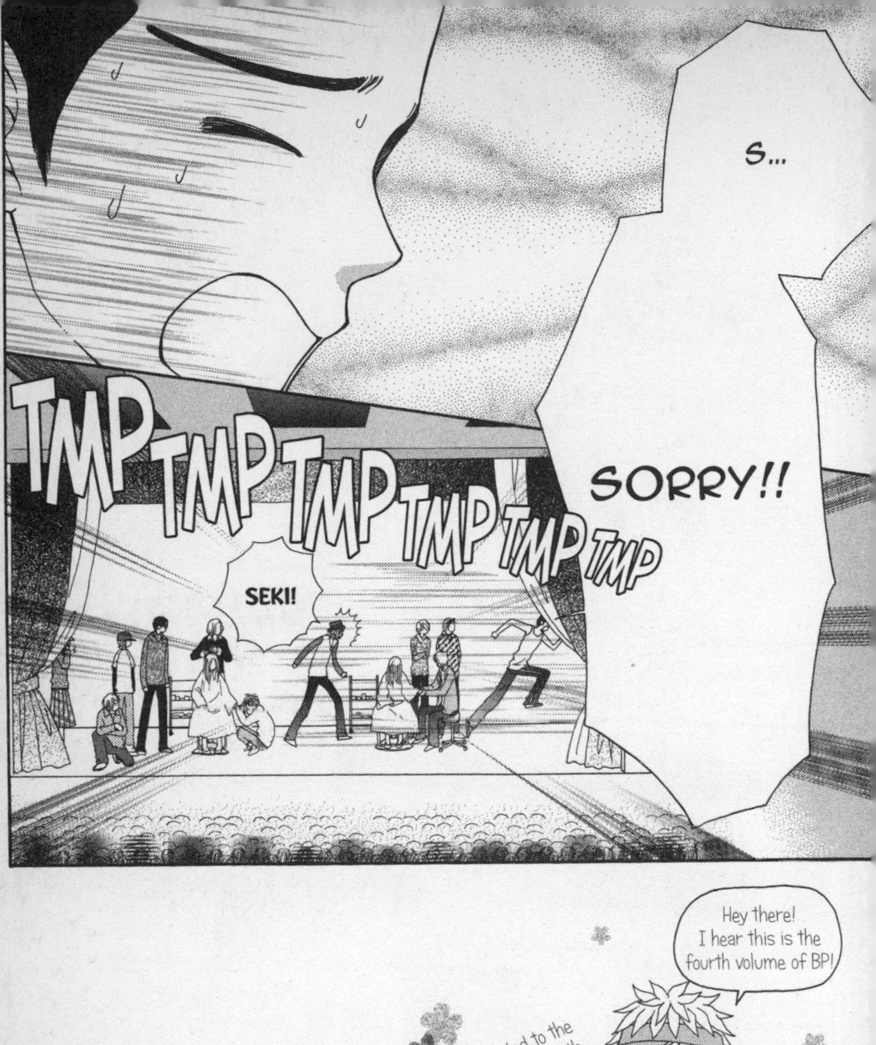
S...
SORRY!!
TMP TMP TMP TMP TMP TMP
SEKI!

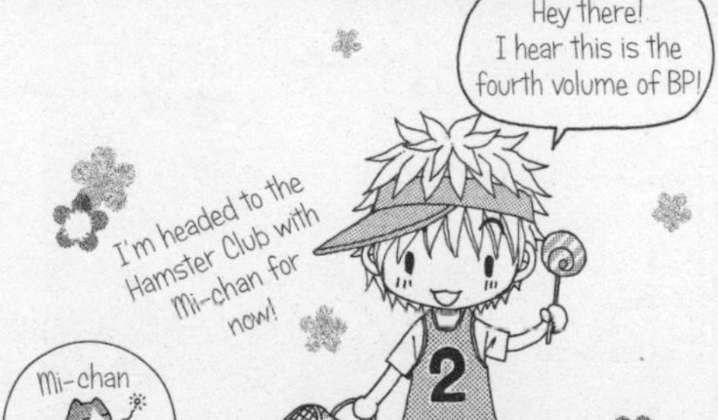
Hey there! I hear this is the fourth volume of BP!
I'm headed to the Hamster Club with Mi-chan for now!
Mi-chan

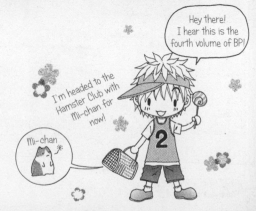

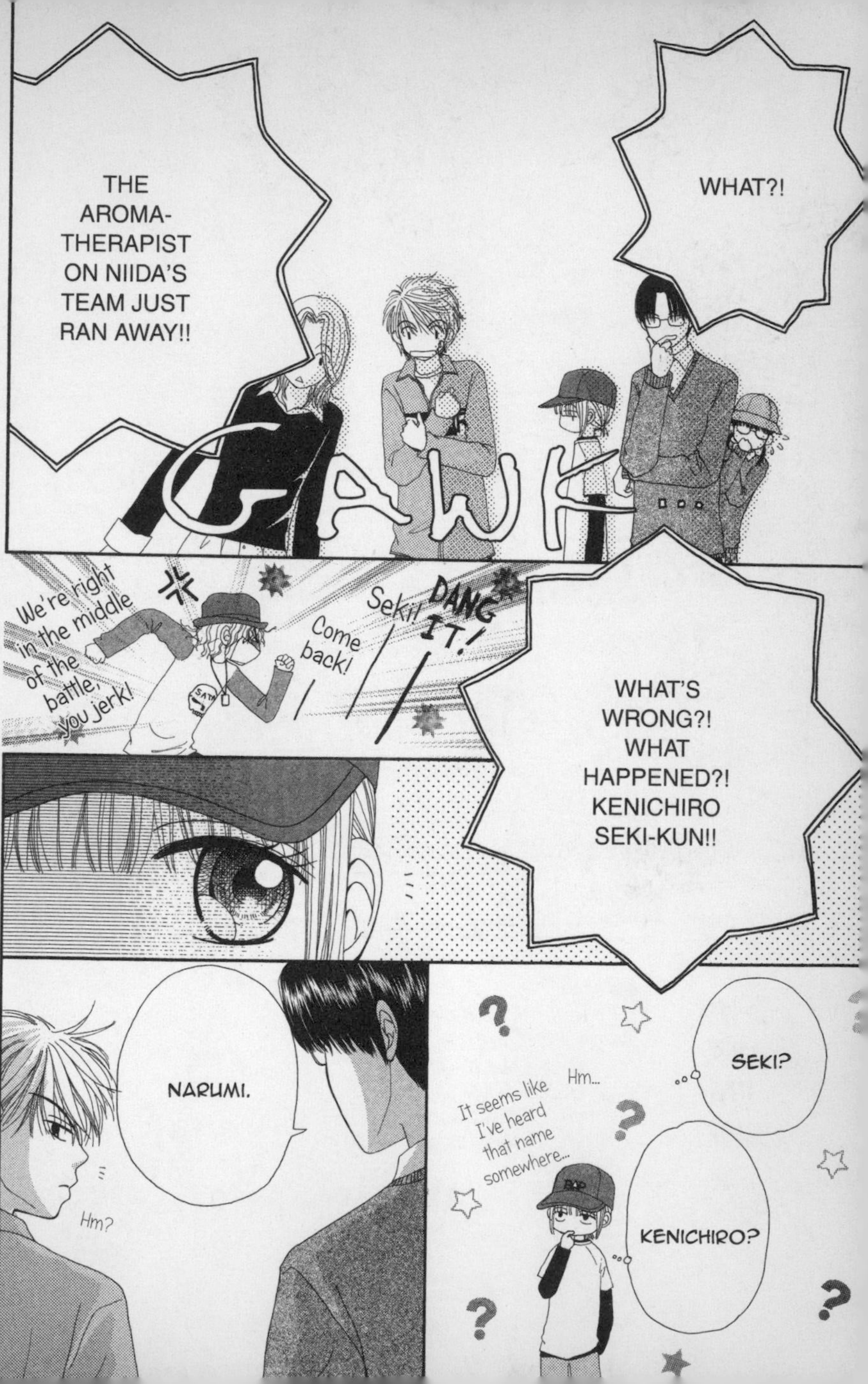

WHAT?!
THE AROMA-THERAPIST ON NIIDA'S TEAM JUST RAN AWAY!!
GAWK
...
WHAT'S WRONG?! WHAT HAPPENED?! KENICHIRO SEKI-KUN!!
DANG IT!
Seki! Come back!
We're right in the middle of the battle, you jerk!
SEKI?
Hm...
It seems like I've heard that name somewhere...
KENICHIRO?
NARUMI.
Hm?

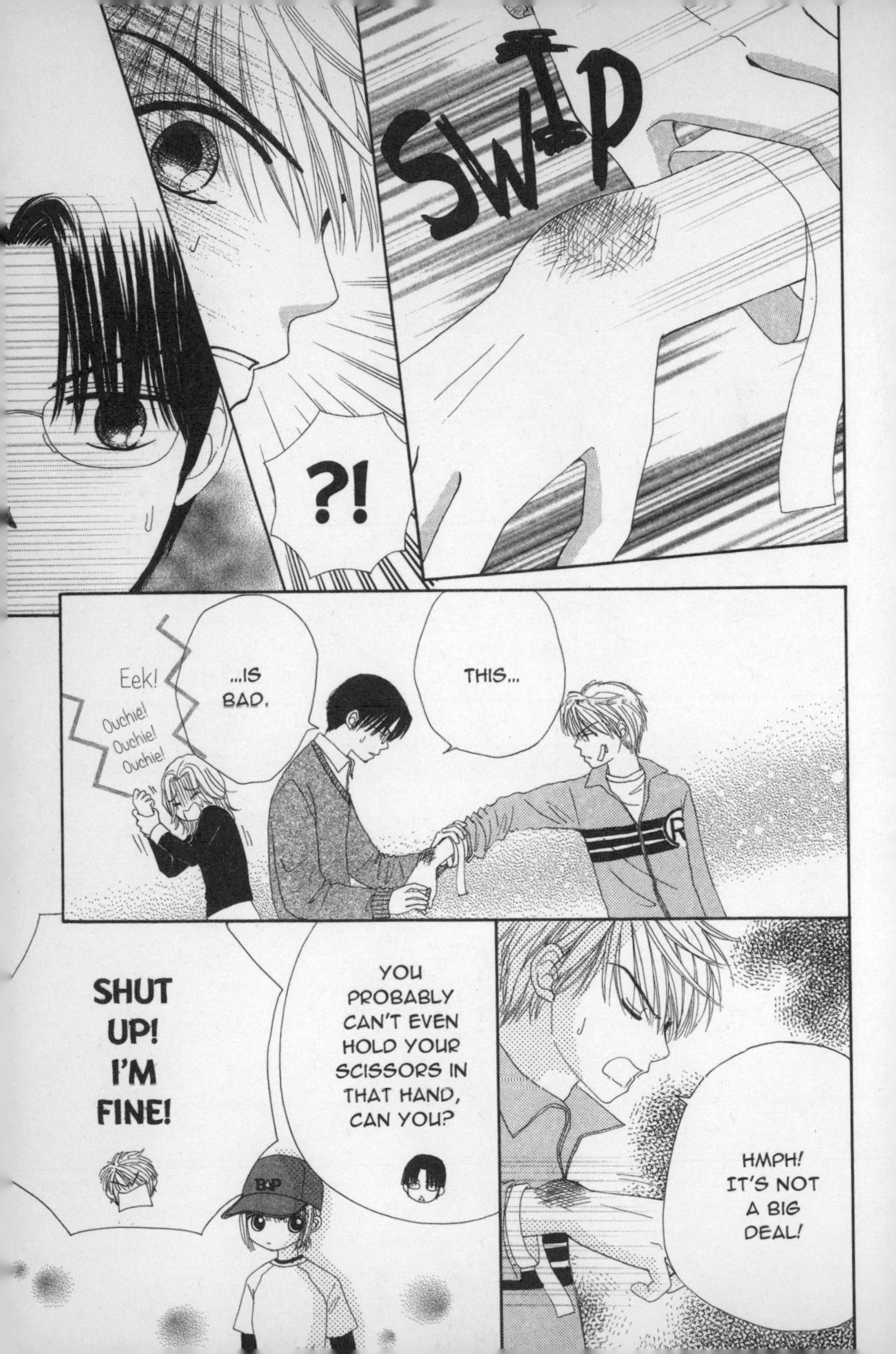
SWIP
?!
THIS...
...IS BAD.
Eek!
Ouchie! Ouchie! Ouchie!
HMPH! IT'S NOT A BIG DEAL!
YOU PROBABLY CAN'T EVEN HOLD YOUR SCISSORS IN THAT HAND, CAN YOU?
SHUT UP! I'M FINE!

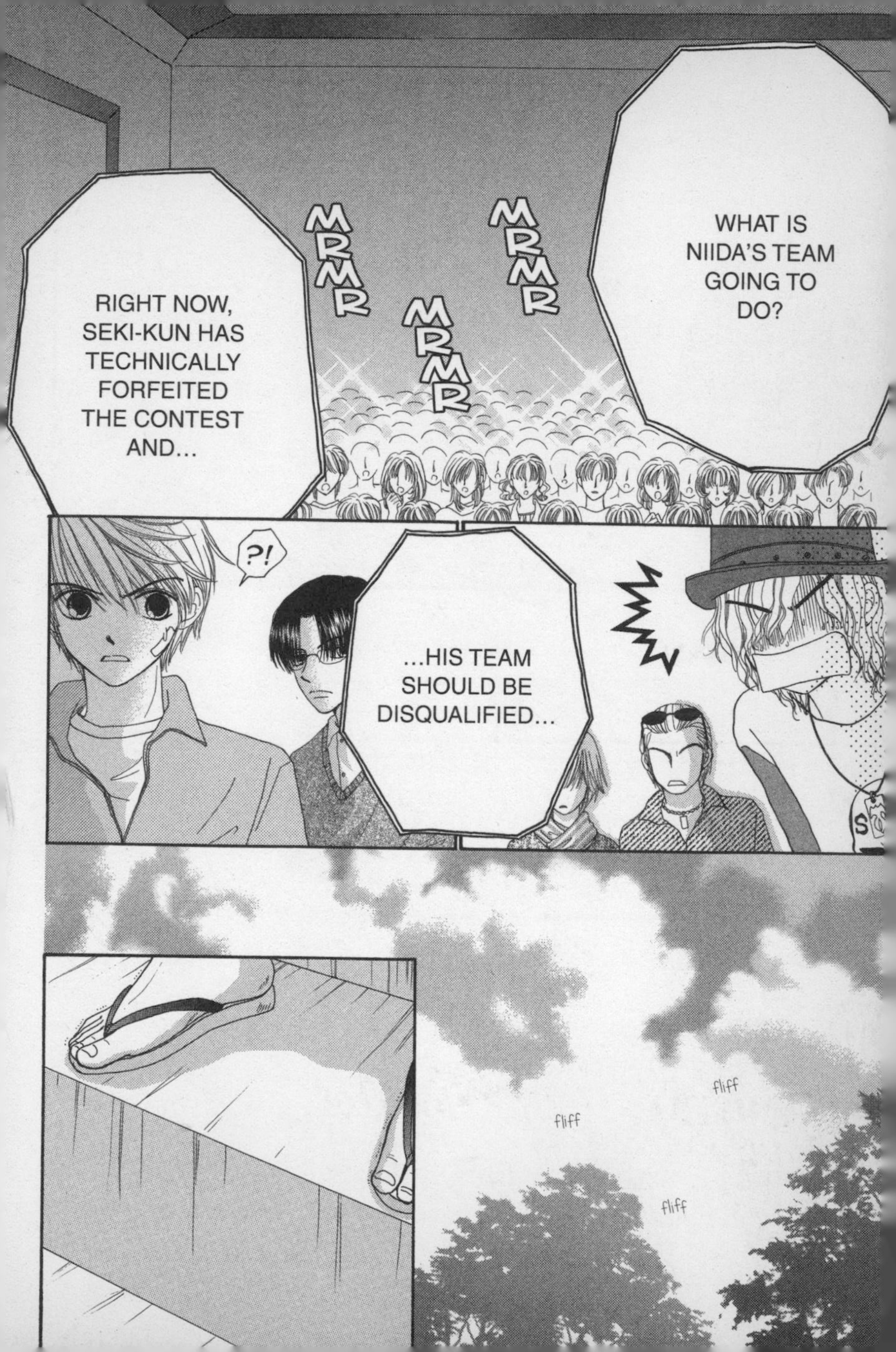
WHAT IS NIIDA'S TEAM GOING TO DO?
MRMR
MRMR
MRMR
RIGHT NOW, SEKI-KUN HAS TECHNICALLY FORFEITED THE CONTEST AND...
...HIS TEAM SHOULD BE DISQUALIFIED...
?!
fliff
fliff
fliff

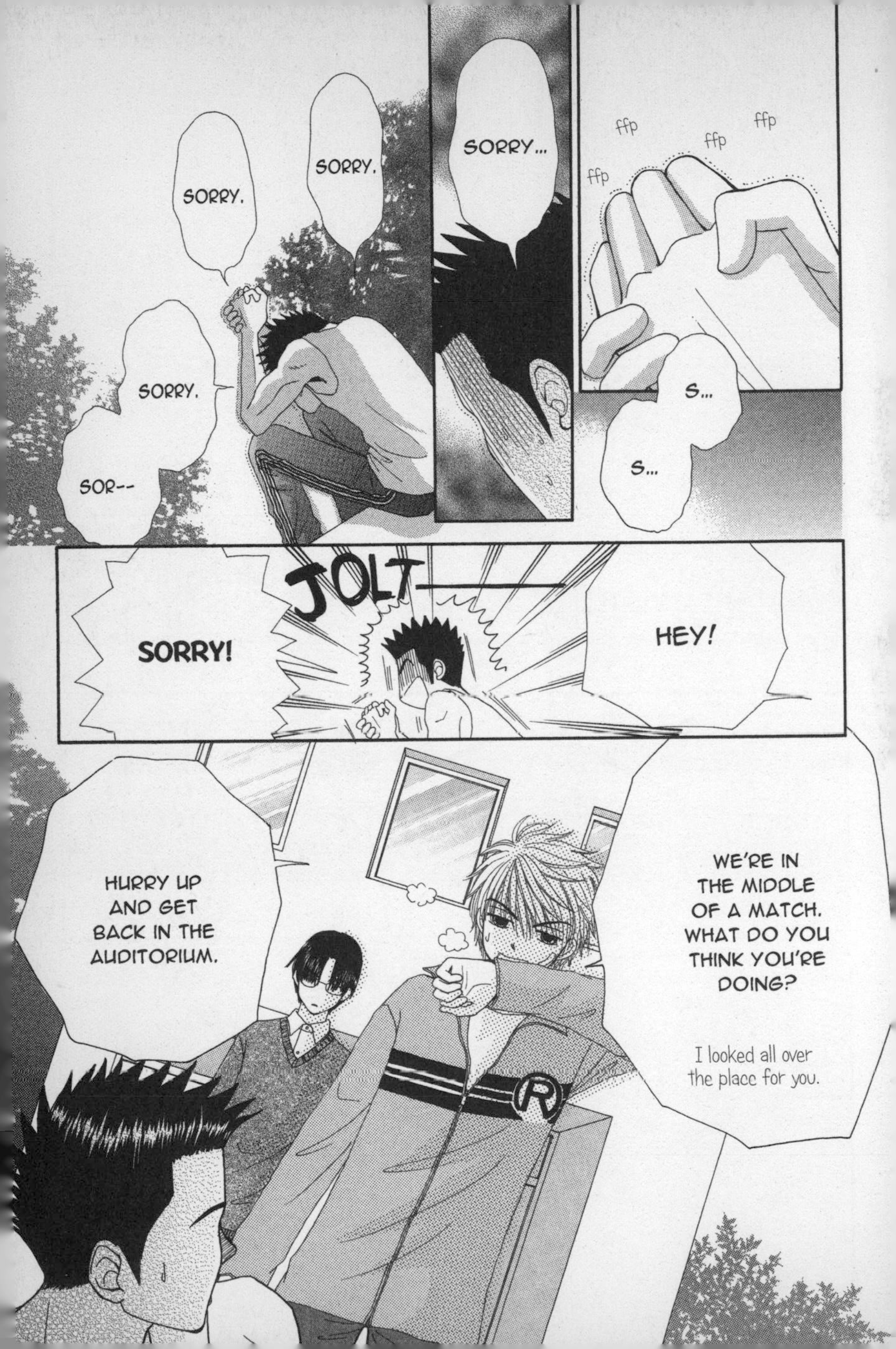
ffp
ffp
ffp
ffp
S...
S...
SORRY...
SORRY.
SORRY.
SORRY.
SOR--
HEY!
JOLT
SORRY!
WE'RE IN THE MIDDLE OF A MATCH. WHAT DO YOU THINK YOU'RE DOING?
I looked all over the placc for you.
HURRY UP AND GET BACK IN THE AUDITORIUM.

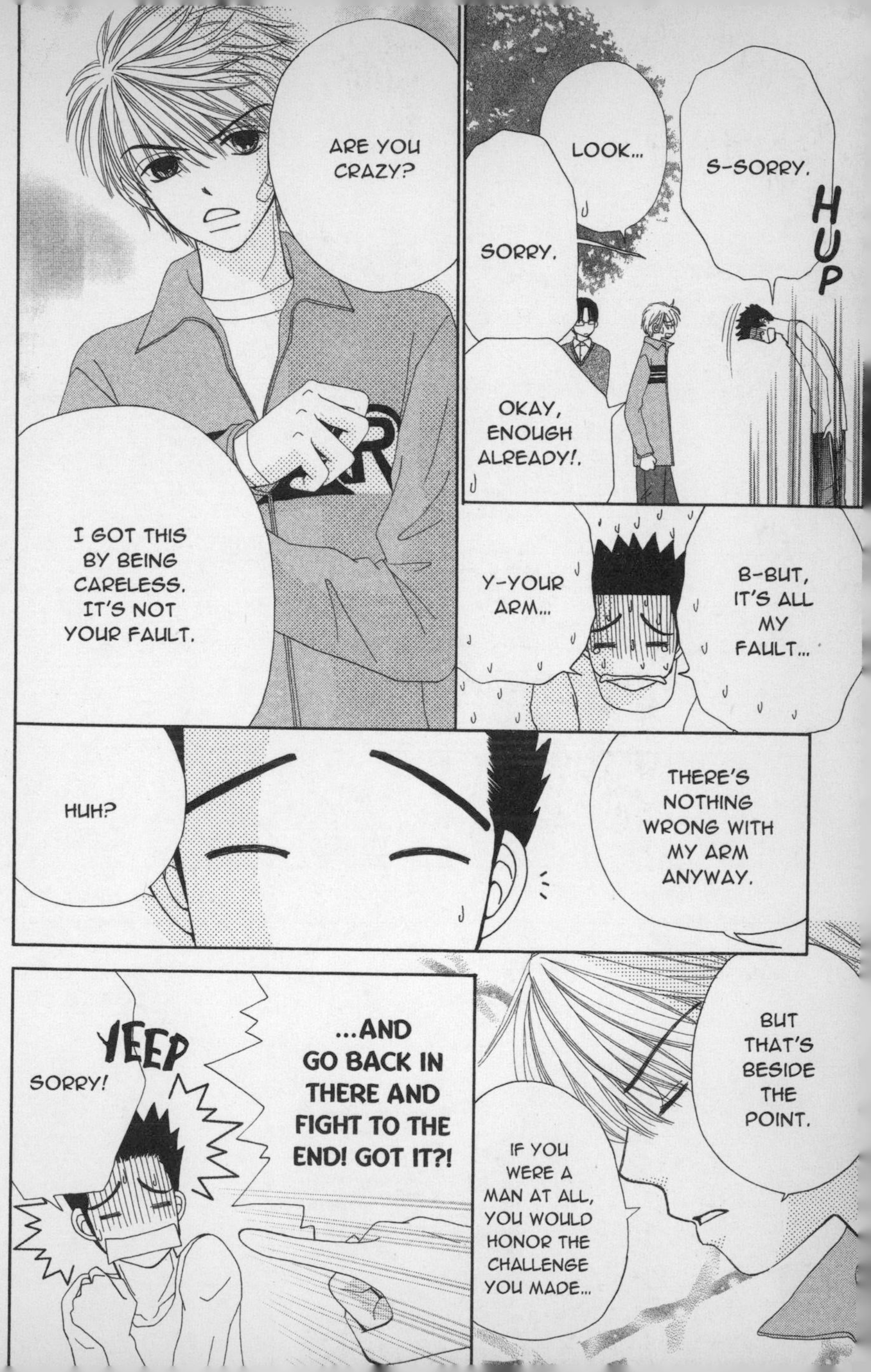
S-SORRY.
HUP
LOOK...
SORRY.
OKAY, ENOUGH ALREADY!.
B-BUT, IT'S ALL MY FAULT...
Y-YOUR ARM...
ARE YOU CRAZY?
I GOT THIS BY BEING CARELESS. IT'S NOT YOUR FAULT.
THERE'S NOTHING WRONG WITH MY ARM ANYWAY.
HUH?
BUT THAT'S BESIDE THE POINT.
IF YOU WERE A MAN AT ALL, YOU WOULD HONOR THE CHALLENGE YOU MADE...
...AND GO BACK IN THERE AND FIGHT TO THE END! GOT IT?!
YEEP
SORRY!

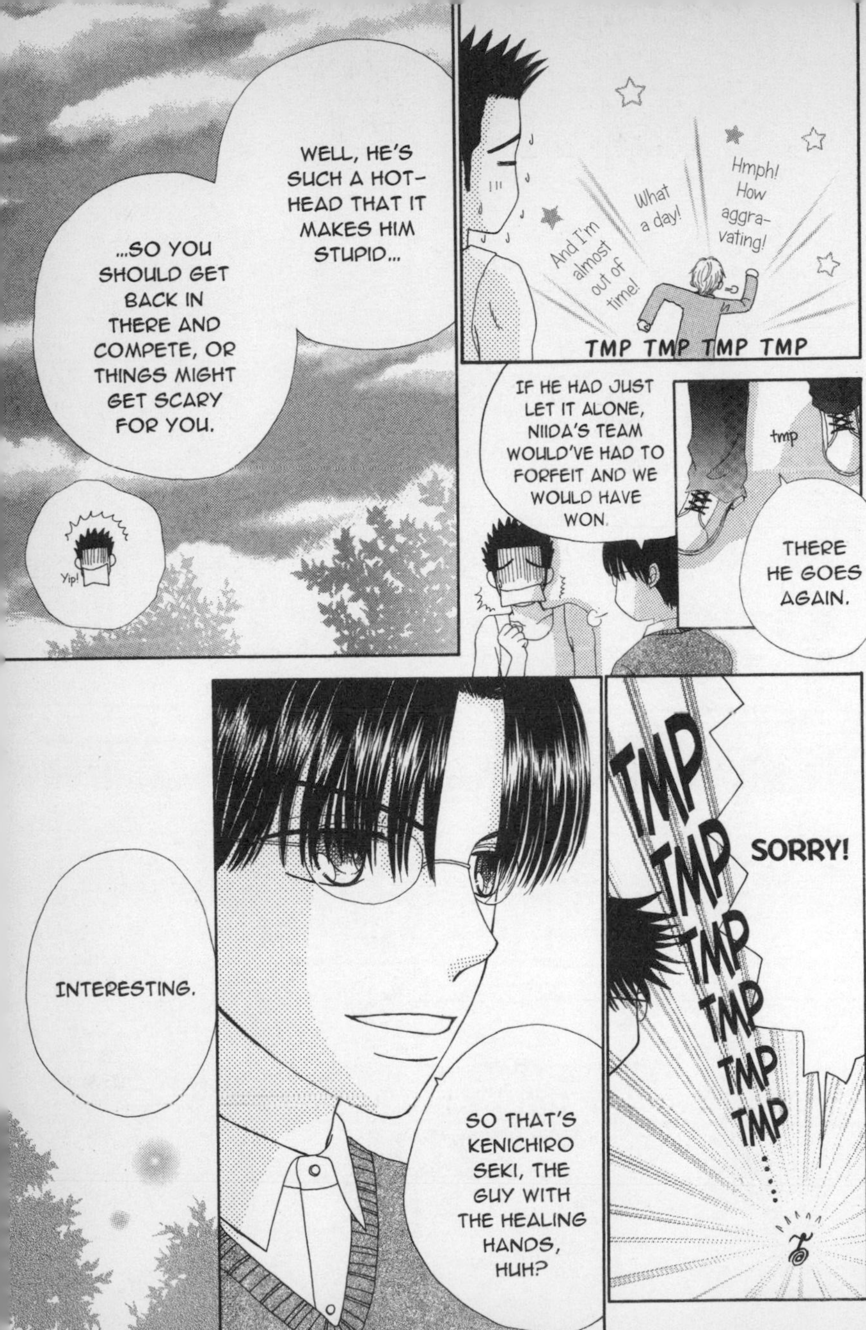
Hmph! How aggra-vating!
What a day!
And I'm almost out of time!
TMP TMP TMP TMP
tmp
THERE HE GOES AGAIN.
IF HE HAD JUST LET IT ALONE, NIIDA'S TEAM WOULD'VE HAD TO FORFEIT AND WE WOULD HAVE WON.
WELL, HE'S SUCH A HOT-HEAD THAT IT MAKES HIM STUPID...
...SO YOU SHOULD GET BACK IN THERE AND COMPETE, OR THINGS MIGHT GET SCARY FOR YOU.
Yip!
TMP TMP TMP TMP TMP TMP TMP
SORRY!
SO THAT'S KENICHIRO SEKI, THE GUY WITH THE HEALING HANDS, HUH?
INTERESTING.

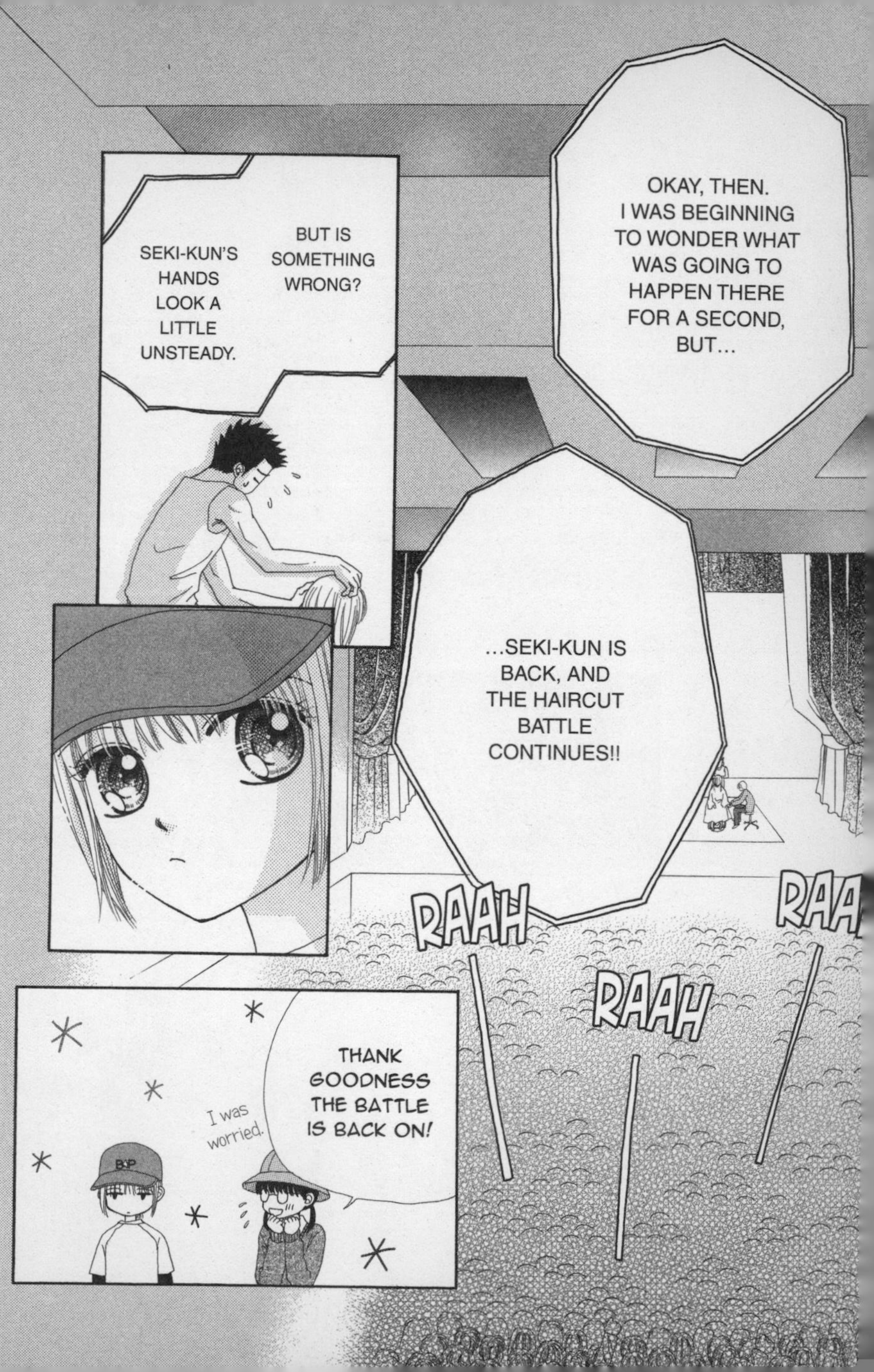
OKAY, THEN. I WAS BEGINNING TO WONDER WHAT WAS GOING TO HAPPEN THERE FOR A SECOND, BUT...
...SEKI-KUN IS BACK, AND THE HAIRCUT BATTLE CONTINUES!!
RAA
RAAH
RAAH
BUT IS SOMETHING WRONG?
SEKI-KUN'S HANDS LOOK A LITTLE UNSTEADY.
THANK GOODNESS THE BATTLE IS BACK ON!
I was worried.

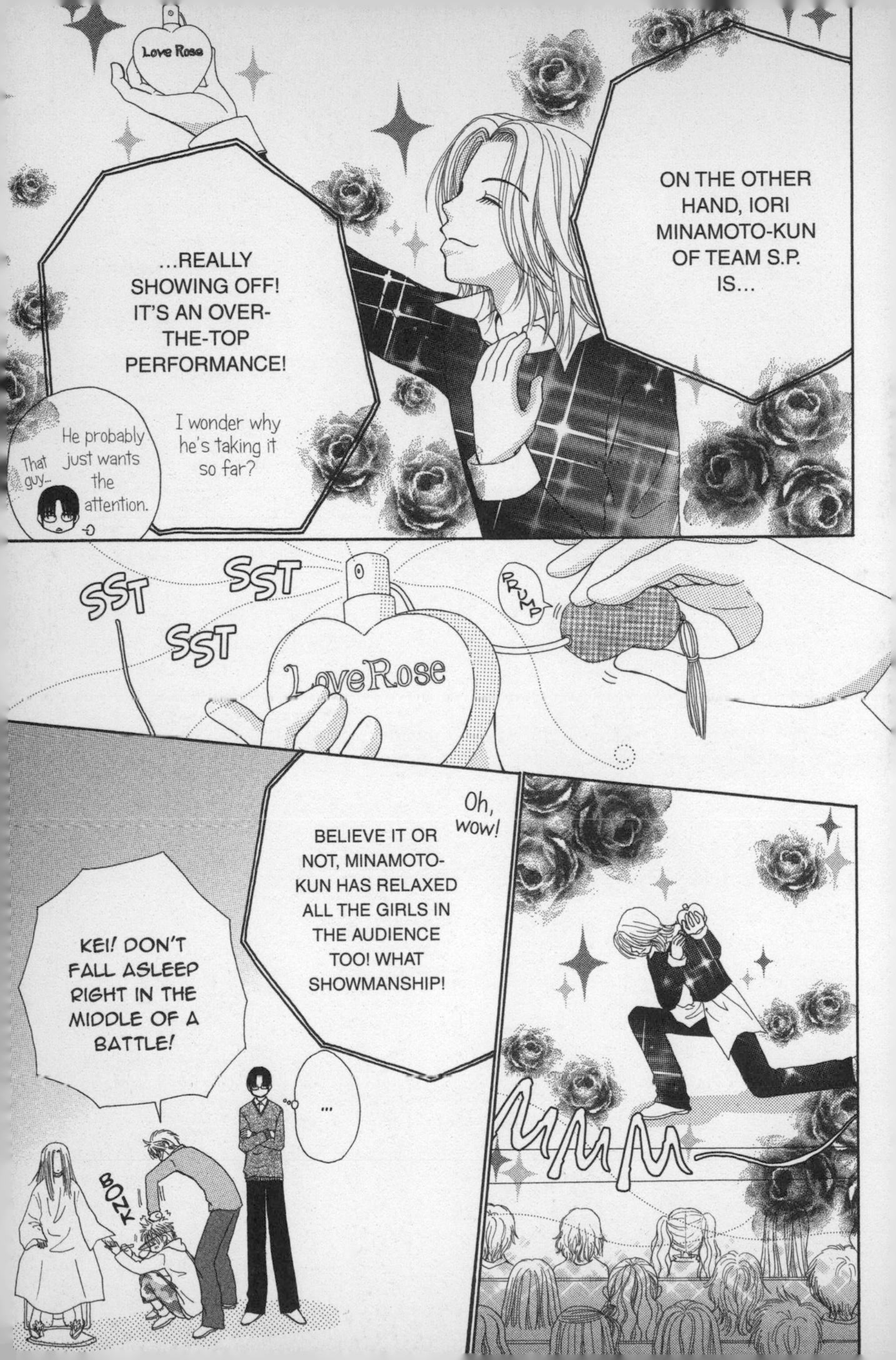
ON THE OTHER HAND, IORI MINAMOTO-KUN OF TEAM S.P. IS...
...REALLY SHOWING OFF! IT'S AN OVER-THE-TOP PERFORMANCE!
I wonder why he's taking it so far?
He probably just wants the attention.
That guy...
PRUMP
SST
SST
SST
LoveRose
MMM
Oh, wow!
BELIEVE IT OR NOT, MINAMOTO-KUN HAS RELAXED ALL THE GIRLS IN THE AUDIENCE TOO! WHAT SHOWMANSHIP!
...
KEI! DON'T FALL ASLEEP RIGHT IN THE MIDDLE OF A BATTLE!
BONK

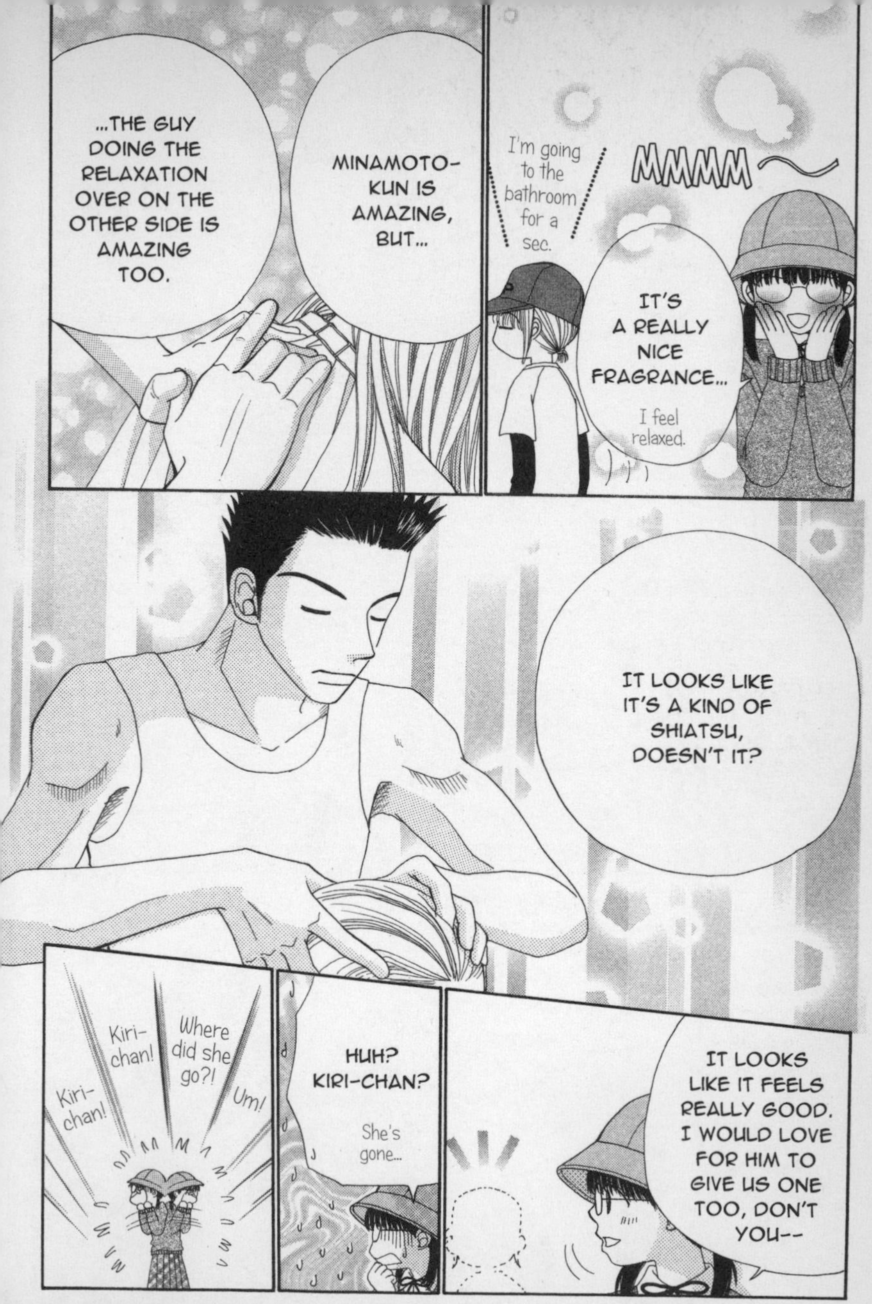
MMMM~
I'm going to the bathroom for a sec.
IT'S A REALLY NICE FRAGRANCE...
I feel relaxed.
MINAMOTO-KUN IS AMAZING, BUT...
...THE GUY DOING THE RELAXATION OVER ON THE OTHER SIDE IS AMAZING TOO.
IT LOOKS LIKE IT'S A KIND OF SHIATSU, DOESN'T IT?
IT LOOKS LIKE IT FEELS REALLY GOOD. I WOULD LOVE FOR HIM TO GIVE US ONE TOO, DON'T YOU--
HUH? KIRI-CHAN?
She's gone...
Where did she go?!
Um!
Kiri-chan!
Kiri-chan!

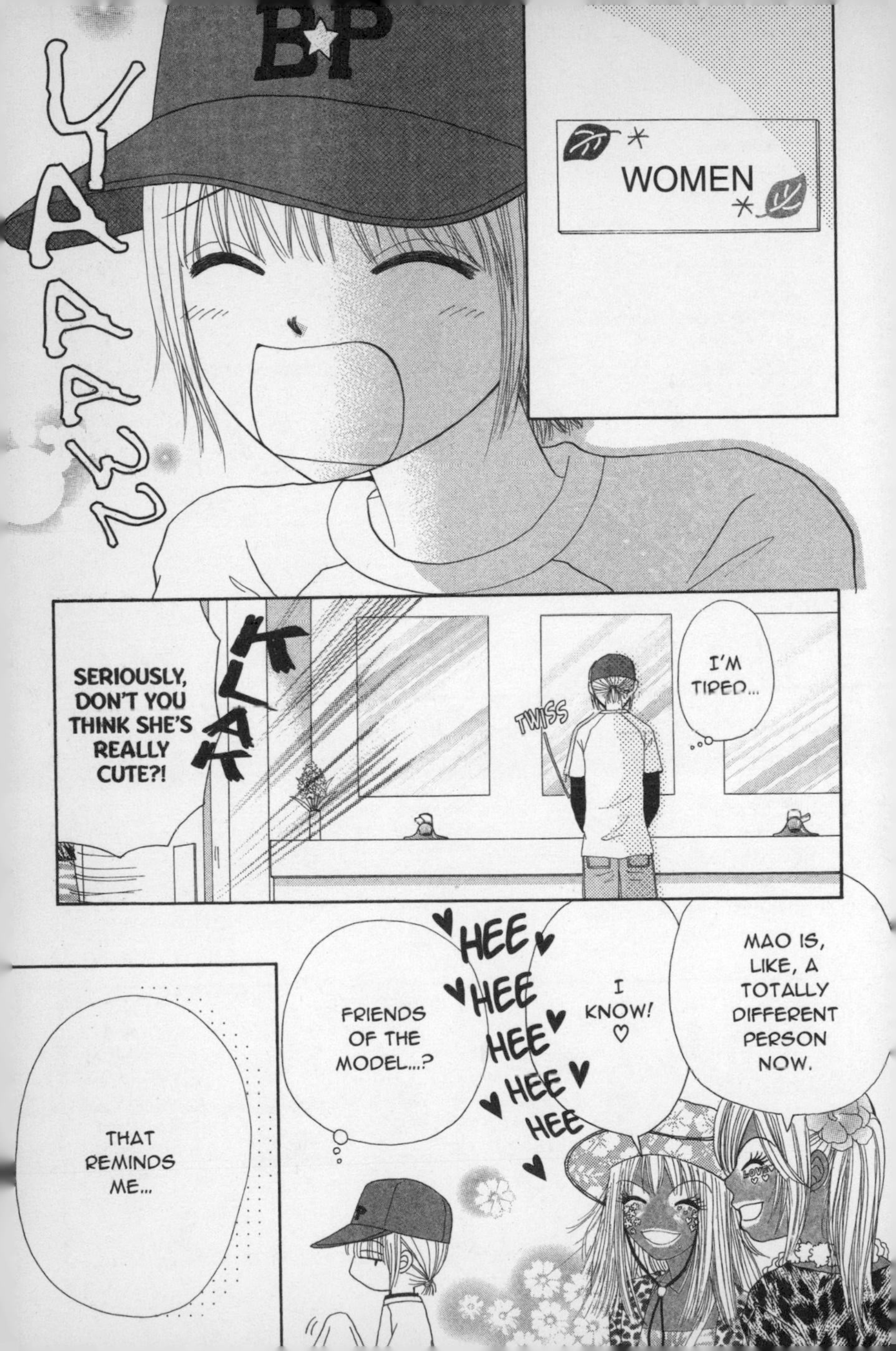
WOMEN
YAAA
I'M TIRED...
TWISS
KLAK
SERIOUSLY, DON'T YOU THINK SHE'S REALLY CUTE?!
MAO IS, LIKE, A TOTALLY DIFFERENT PERSON NOW.
I KNOW! ♡
HEE HEE HEE HEE HEE
FRIENDS OF THE MODEL...?
THAT REMINDS ME...

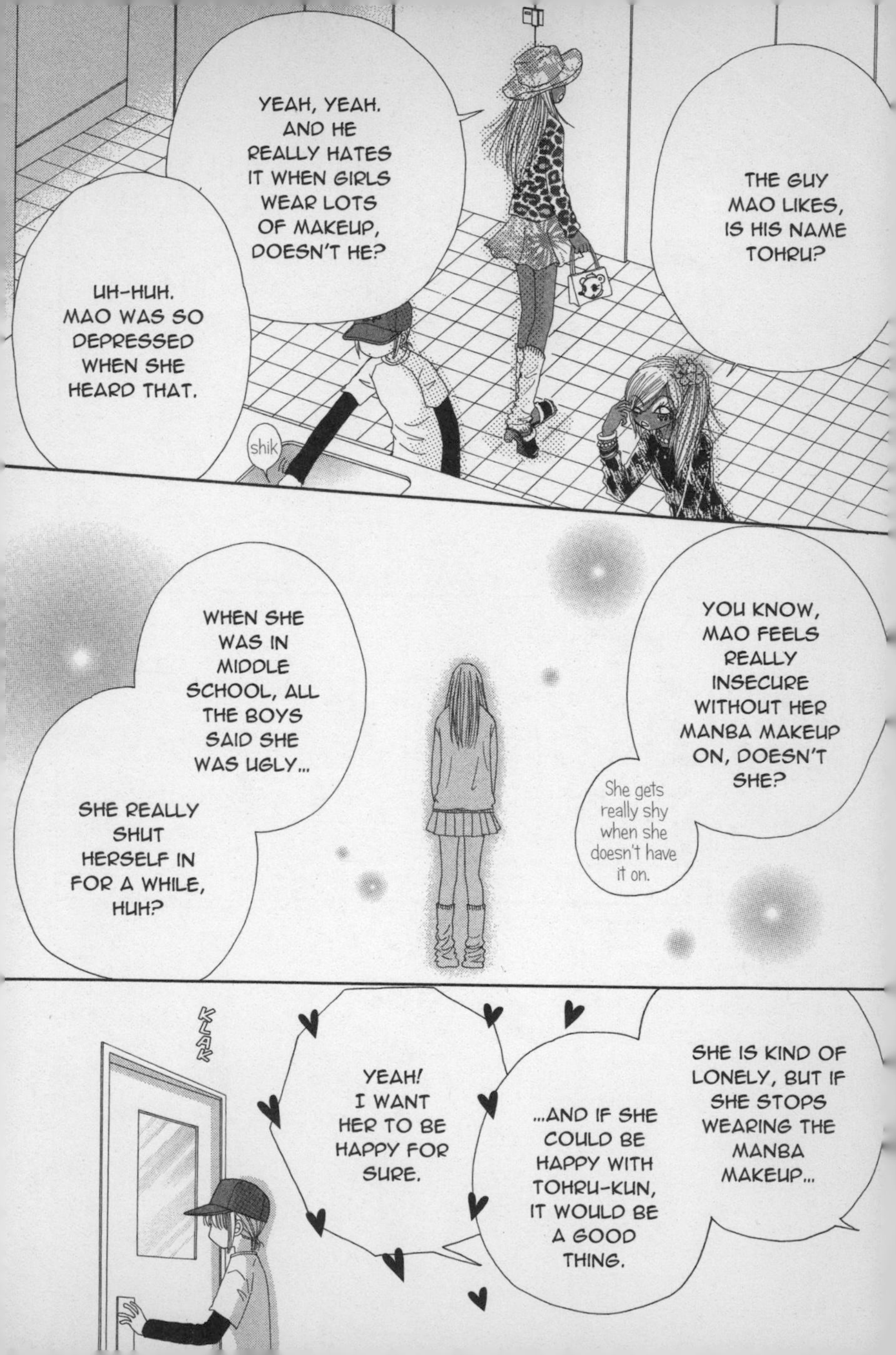

THE GUY MAO LIKES, IS HIS NAME TOHRU?
YEAH, YEAH. AND HE REALLY HATES IT WHEN GIRLS WEAR LOTS OF MAKEUP, DOESN'T HE?
UH-HUH. MAO WAS SO DEPRESSED WHEN SHE HEARD THAT.
shik
YOU KNOW, MAO FEELS REALLY INSECURE WITHOUT HER MANBA MAKEUP ON, DOESN'T SHE?
She gets really shy when she doesn't have it on.
WHEN SHE WAS IN MIDDLE SCHOOL, ALL THE BOYS SAID SHE WAS UGLY...
SHE REALLY SHUT HERSELF IN FOR A WHILE, HUH?
SHE IS KIND OF LONELY, BUT IF SHE STOPS WEARING THE MANBA MAKEUP...
...AND IF SHE COULD BE HAPPY WITH TOHRU-KUN, IT WOULD BE A GOOD THING.
YEAH! I WANT HER TO BE HAPPY FOR SURE.
KLAK

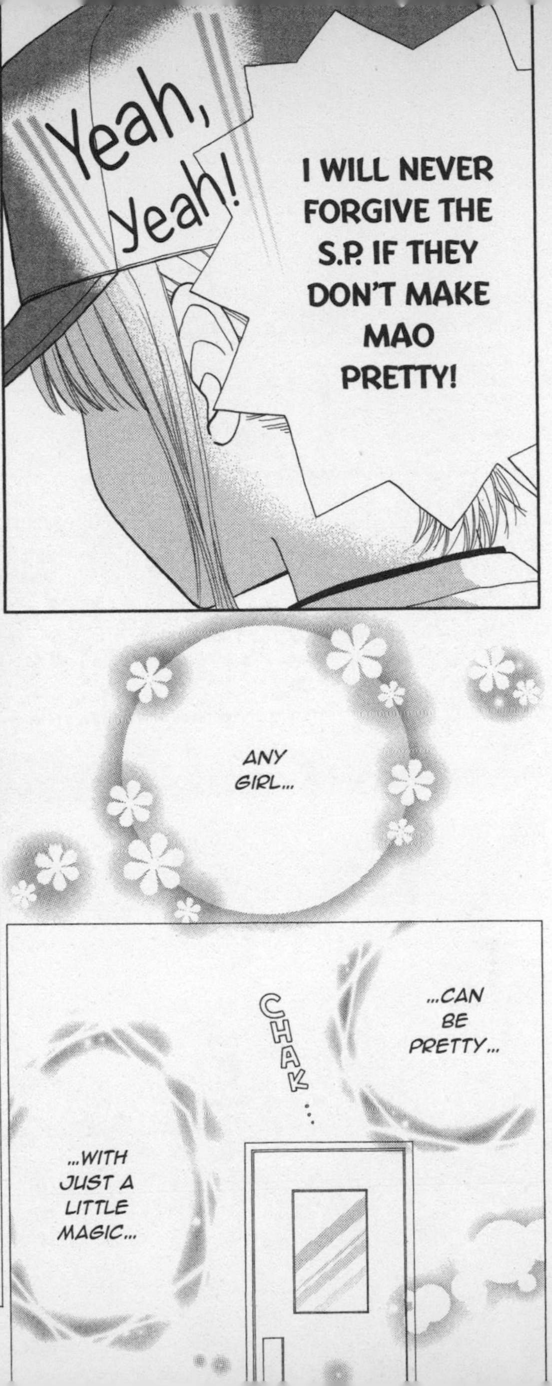
I WILL NEVER FORGIVE THE S.P. IF THEY DON'T MAKE MAO PRETTY!
Yeah, Yeah!
ANY GIRL...
...CAN BE PRETTY...
CHAK...
...WITH JUST A LITTLE MAGIC...

K's Club Talk

Lately, when I'm drawing B.P., I always think about how many more characters there are now. Really, drawing all of them is hard work. Sometimes there are more than 20 people on one page! Drawing the manuscript really takes a lot of time. And on top of all that, there are a whole bunch of characters--not just the main characters--who talk a lot.

Blabbermouth Army

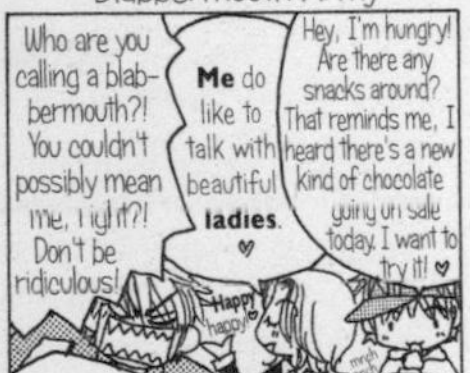
Hey, I'm hungry! Are there any snacks around? That reminds me, I heard there's a new kind of chocolate going on sale today. I want to try it! ♥
Me do like to talk with beautiful **ladies**. ♥
Who are you calling a blab-bermouth?! You couldn't possibly mean me, right?! Don't be ridiculous!
Happy happy♥
mgh mgh
Huh? How bizarre that I would be called talkative. I speak as little as possible, and only when necessary.
Wow, that's amazing! I'm in the group! Yeah! Amazing!
klik klik
Yeah, yeah!
Heh
Well now, Narumi's days of being number one are over. It's my time now. This is the era of Niida!
S-Sorry. Was I talking too much? Sorry!
Haha

This is what it's like, so when I write out the dialogue, there are lots and lots of words to put in. I have no idea how much I've had to cut so far... Sometimes when I get really stressed, I get the urge to just erase all of them really fast with my eraser. Really, these people are loud... ♪♪♪ (I know that I'm the one who created them, but... ♪)

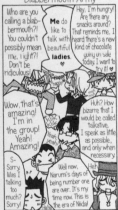

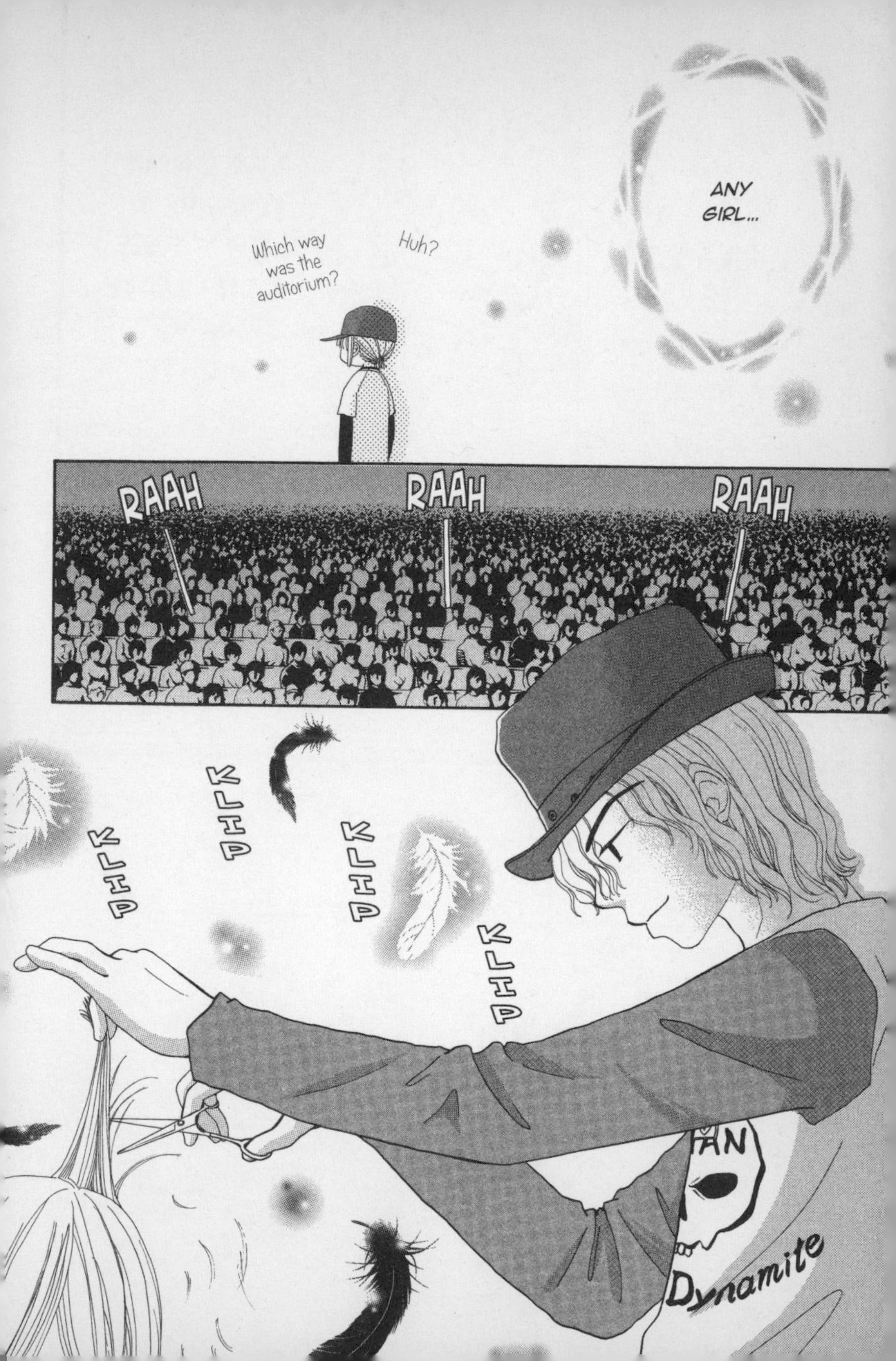
ANY GIRL...
Huh?
Which way was the auditorium?
RAAH
RAAH
RAAH
KLIP
KLIP
KLIP
KLIP
Dynamite

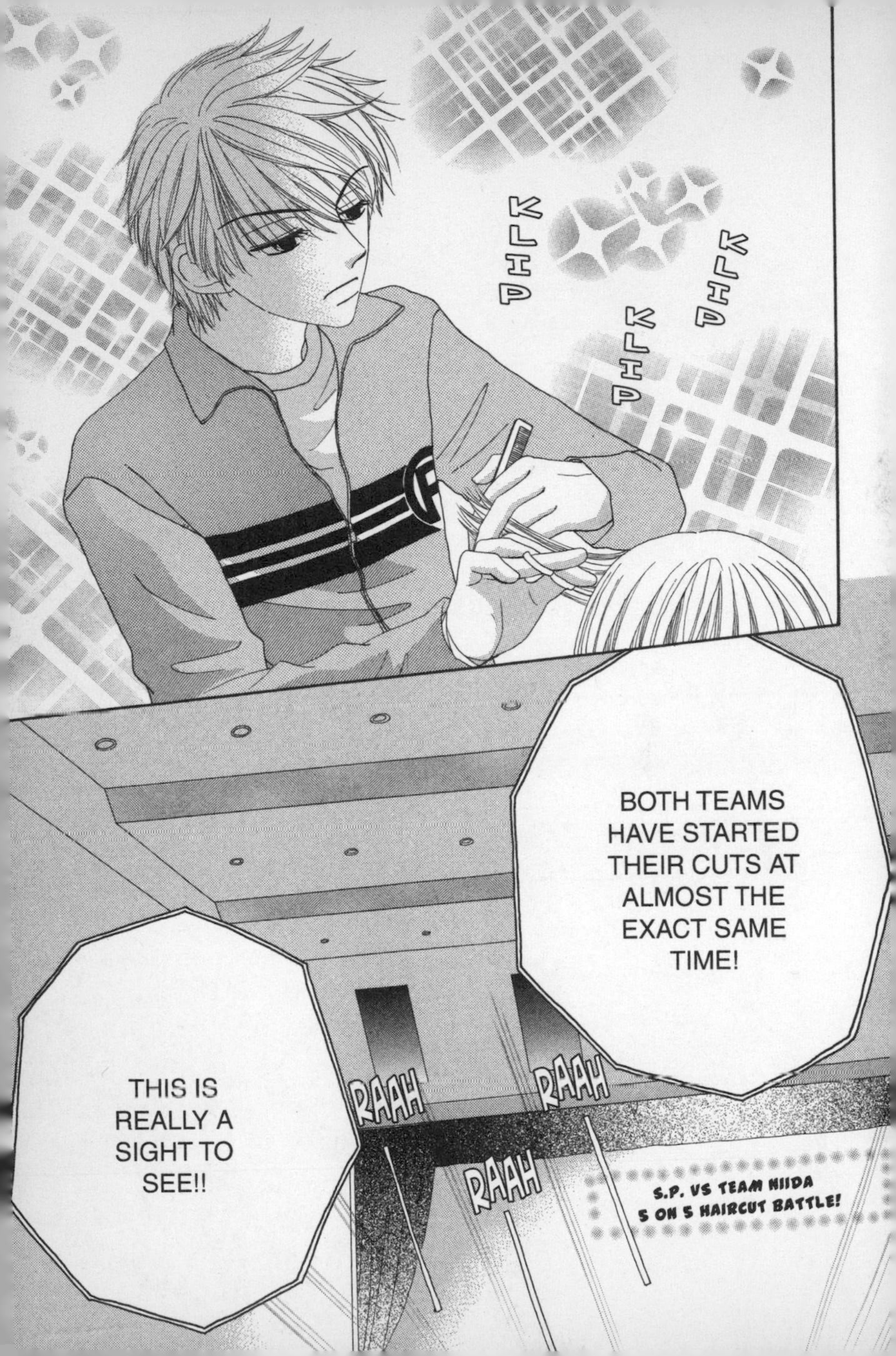
KLIP
KLIP
KLIP
BOTH TEAMS HAVE STARTED THEIR CUTS AT ALMOST THE EXACT SAME TIME!
RAAH
RAAH
RAAH
S.P. VS TEAM NIIDA
5 ON 5 HAIRCUT BATTLE!
THIS IS REALLY A SIGHT TO SEE!!

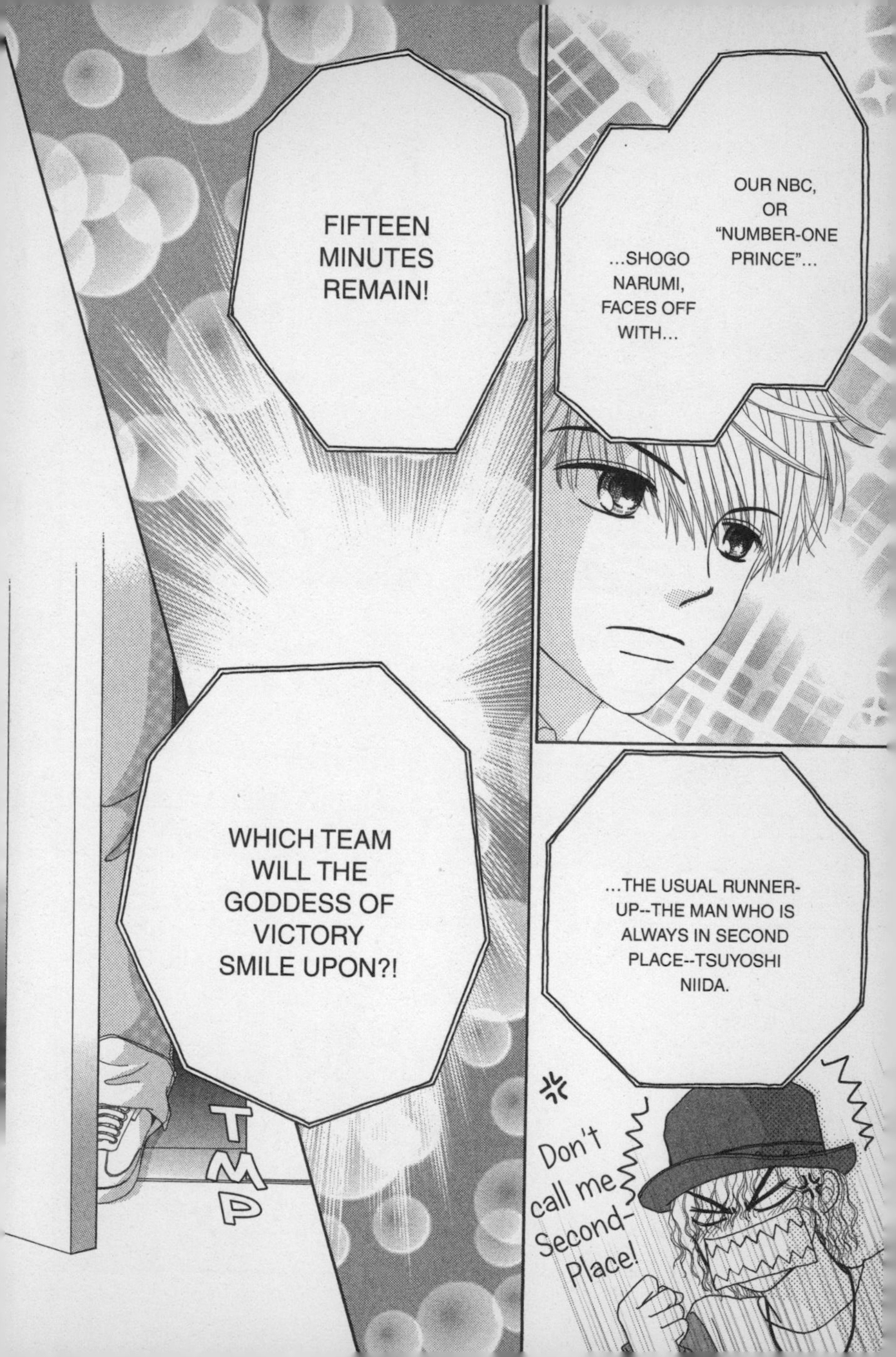
OUR NBC, OR "NUMBER-ONE PRINCE"...
...SHOGO NARUMI, FACES OFF WITH...
...THE USUAL RUNNER-UP--THE MAN WHO IS ALWAYS IN SECOND PLACE--TSUYOSHI NIIDA.
Don't call me Second-Place!
FIFTEEN MINUTES REMAIN!
WHICH TEAM WILL THE GODDESS OF VICTORY SMILE UPON?!
TMP

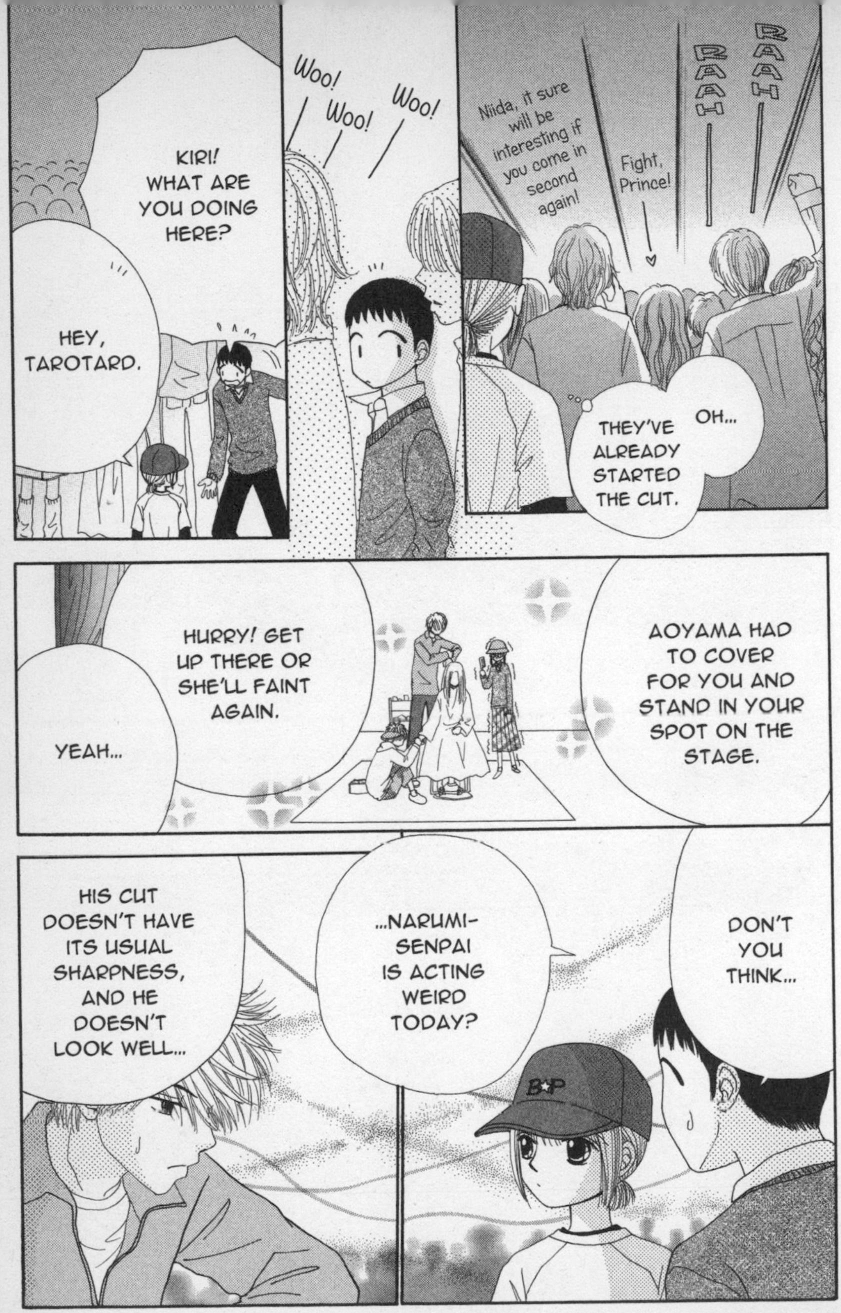
RAAH
RAAH
Fight, Prince!
Niida, it sure will be interesting if you come in second again!
OH...
THEY'VE ALREADY STARTED THE CUT.
Woo!
Woo!
Woo!
KIRI! WHAT ARE YOU DOING HERE?
HEY, TAROTARD.
AOYAMA HAD TO COVER FOR YOU AND STAND IN YOUR SPOT ON THE STAGE.
HURRY! GET UP THERE OR SHE'LL FAINT AGAIN.
YEAH...
DON'T YOU THINK...
...NARUMI-SENPAI IS ACTING WEIRD TODAY?
HIS CUT DOESN'T HAVE ITS USUAL SHARPNESS, AND HE DOESN'T LOOK WELL...

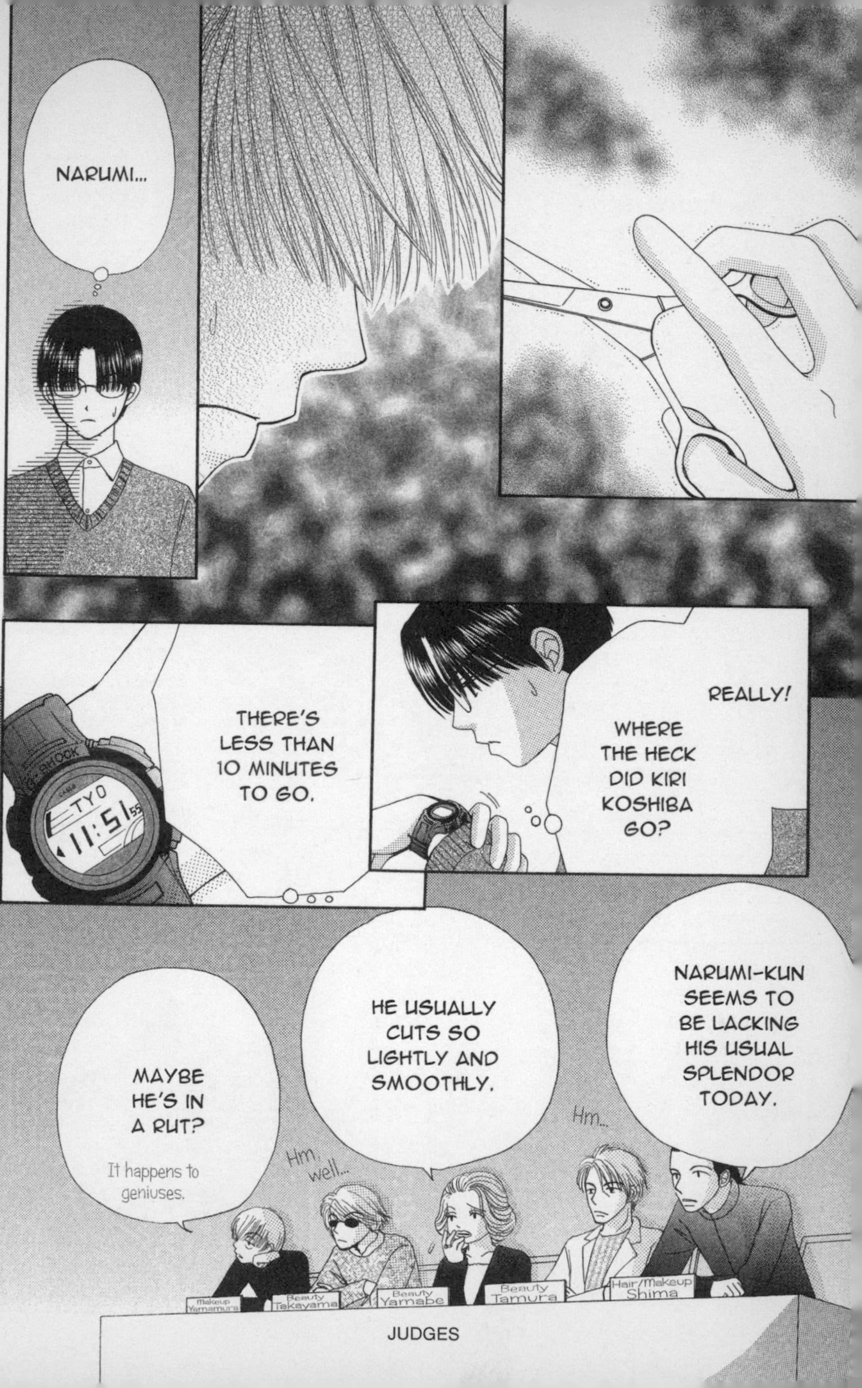
NARUMI...
REALLY!
WHERE THE HECK DID KIRI KOSHIBA GO?
THERE'S LESS THAN 10 MINUTES TO GO.
NARUMI-KUN SEEMS TO BE LACKING HIS USUAL SPLENDOR TODAY.
Hm...
HE USUALLY CUTS SO LIGHTLY AND SMOOTHLY.
Hm, well...
MAYBE HE'S IN A RUT?
It happens to geniuses.
Hair/Makeup Shima
Beauty Tamura
Beauty Yamabe
Beauty Takayama
Makeup Yamamura
JUDGES

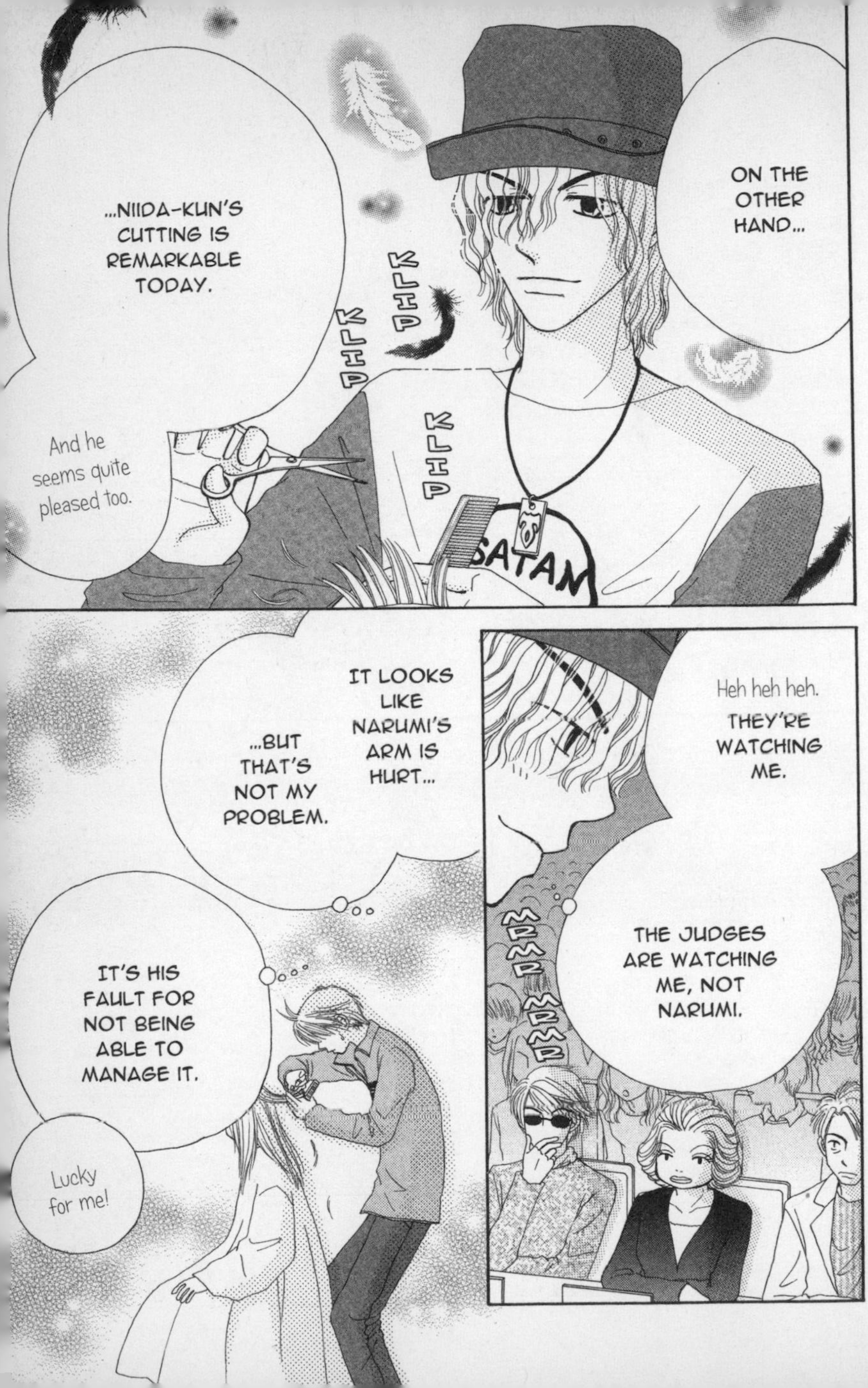
ON THE OTHER HAND...
...NIIDA-KUN'S CUTTING IS REMARKABLE TODAY.
KLIP
KLIP
KLIP
And he seems quite pleased too.
SATAN
Heh heh heh.
THEY'RE WATCHING ME.
THE JUDGES ARE WATCHING ME, NOT NARUMI.
MRMR MRMR
IT LOOKS LIKE NARUMI'S ARM IS HURT...
...BUT THAT'S NOT MY PROBLEM.
IT'S HIS FAULT FOR NOT BEING ABLE TO MANAGE IT.
Lucky for me!

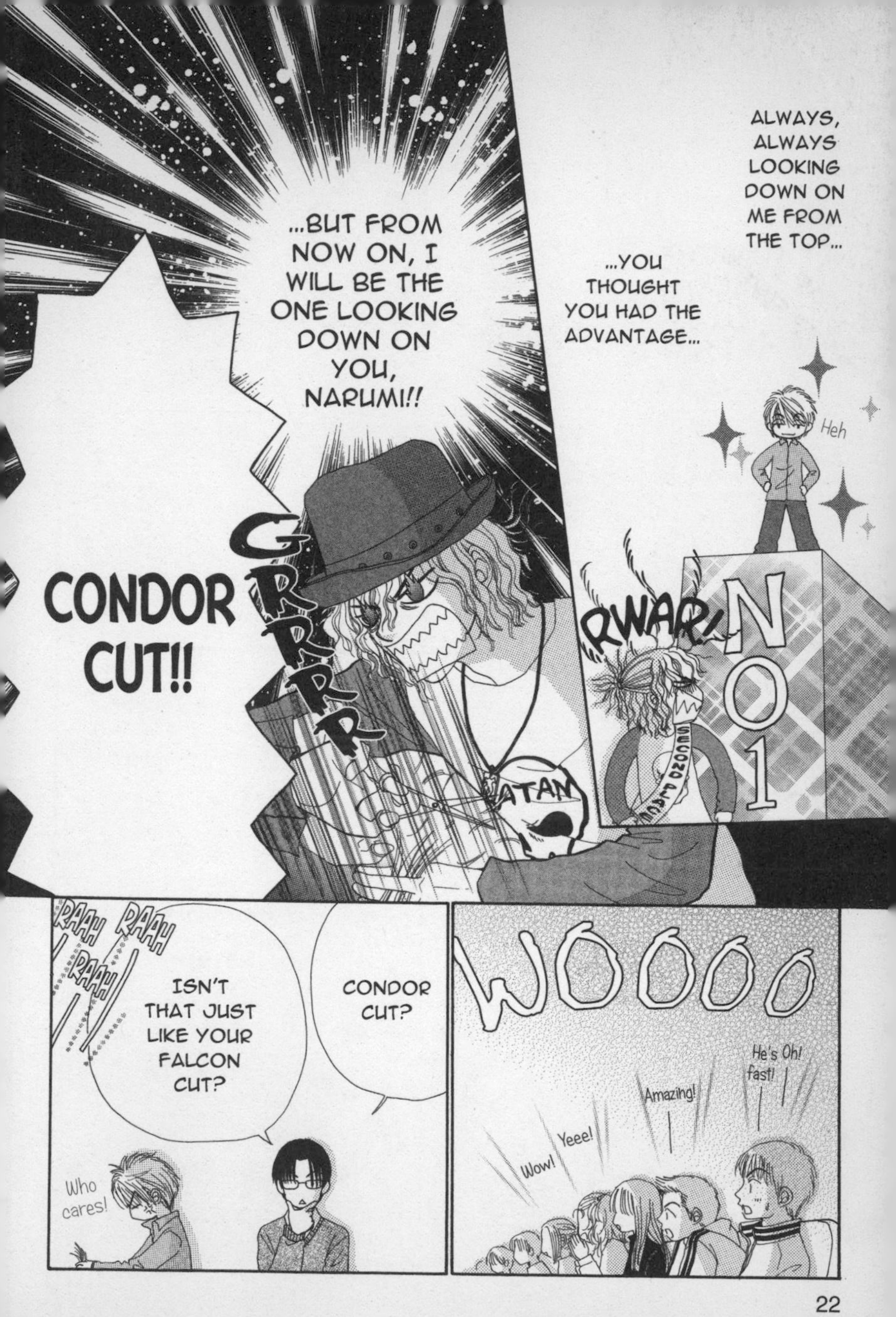
ALWAYS, ALWAYS LOOKING DOWN ON ME FROM THE TOP...
...YOU THOUGHT YOU HAD THE ADVANTAGE...
Heh
...BUT FROM NOW ON, I WILL BE THE ONE LOOKING DOWN ON YOU, NARUMI!!
NO 1
RWAR!
GRRRR
CONDOR CUT!!
WOOOO
Oh!
He's fast!
Amazing!
Yeee!
Wow!
CONDOR CUT?
ISN'T THAT JUST LIKE YOUR FALCON CUT?
RAAH RAAH RAAH
Who cares!

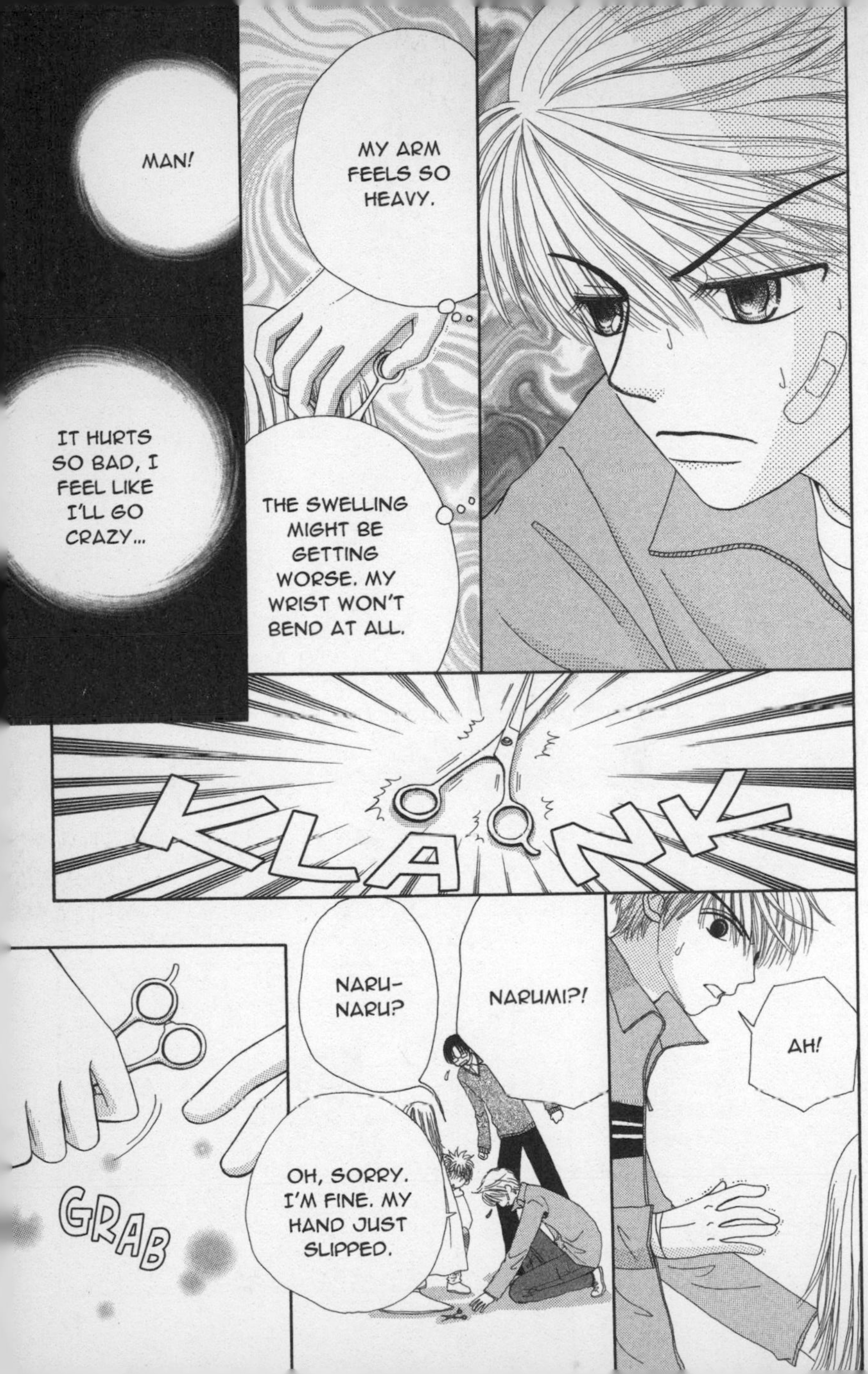

MY ARM FEELS SO HEAVY.
THE SWELLING MIGHT BE GETTING WORSE. MY WRIST WON'T BEND AT ALL.
MAN!
IT HURTS SO BAD, I FEEL LIKE I'LL GO CRAZY...
KLANK
AH!
NARUMI?!
NARU-NARU?
OH, SORRY. I'M FINE. MY HAND JUST SLIPPED.
GRAB

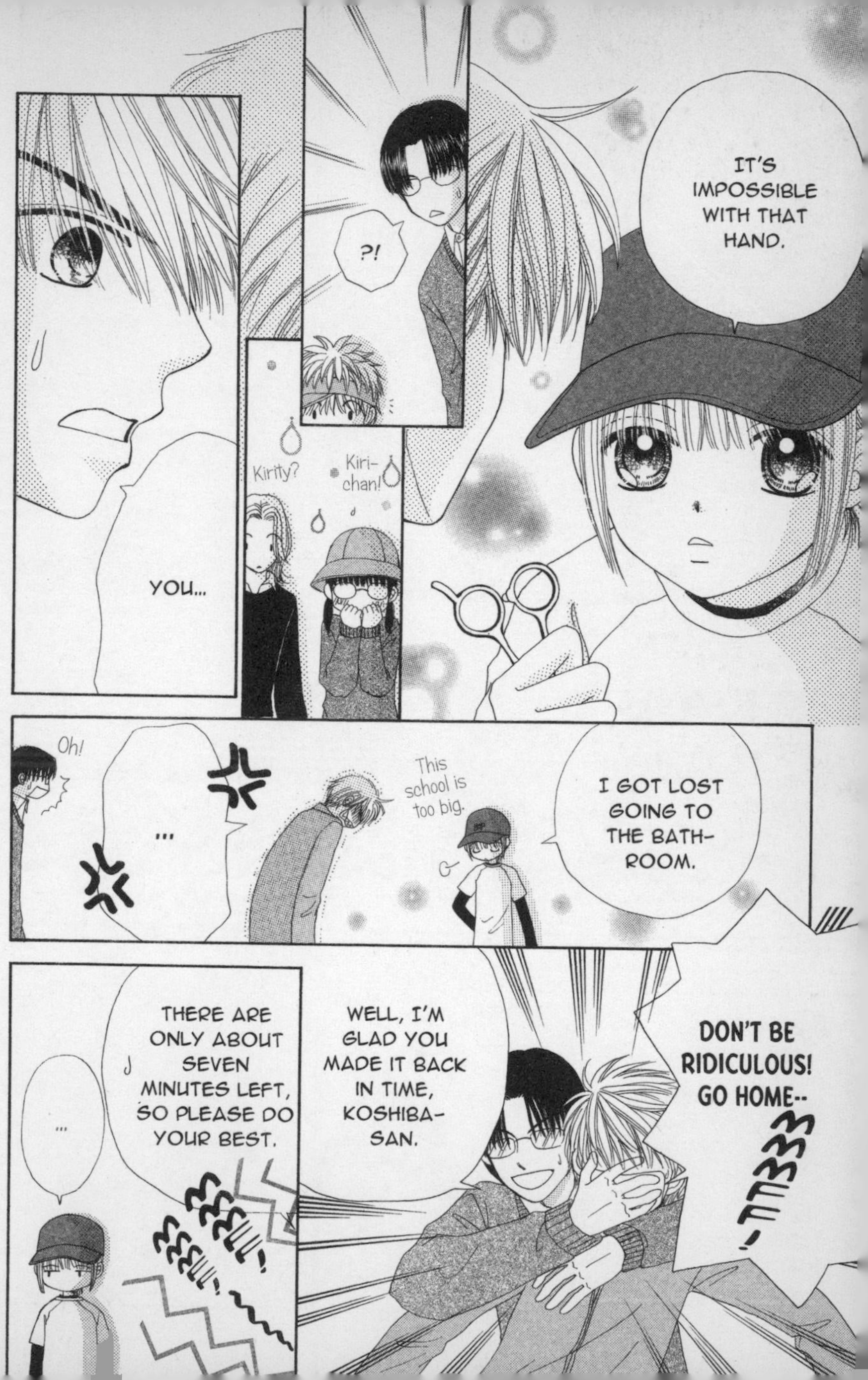

IT'S IMPOSSIBLE WITH THAT HAND.
?!
Kiri-chan!
Kirity?
YOU...
I GOT LOST GOING TO THE BATH-ROOM.
This school is too big.
...
Oh!
DON'T BE RIDICULOUS! GO HOME--
WELL, I'M GLAD YOU MADE IT BACK IN TIME, KOSHIBA-SAN.
THERE ARE ONLY ABOUT SEVEN MINUTES LEFT, SO PLEASE DO YOUR BEST.
...

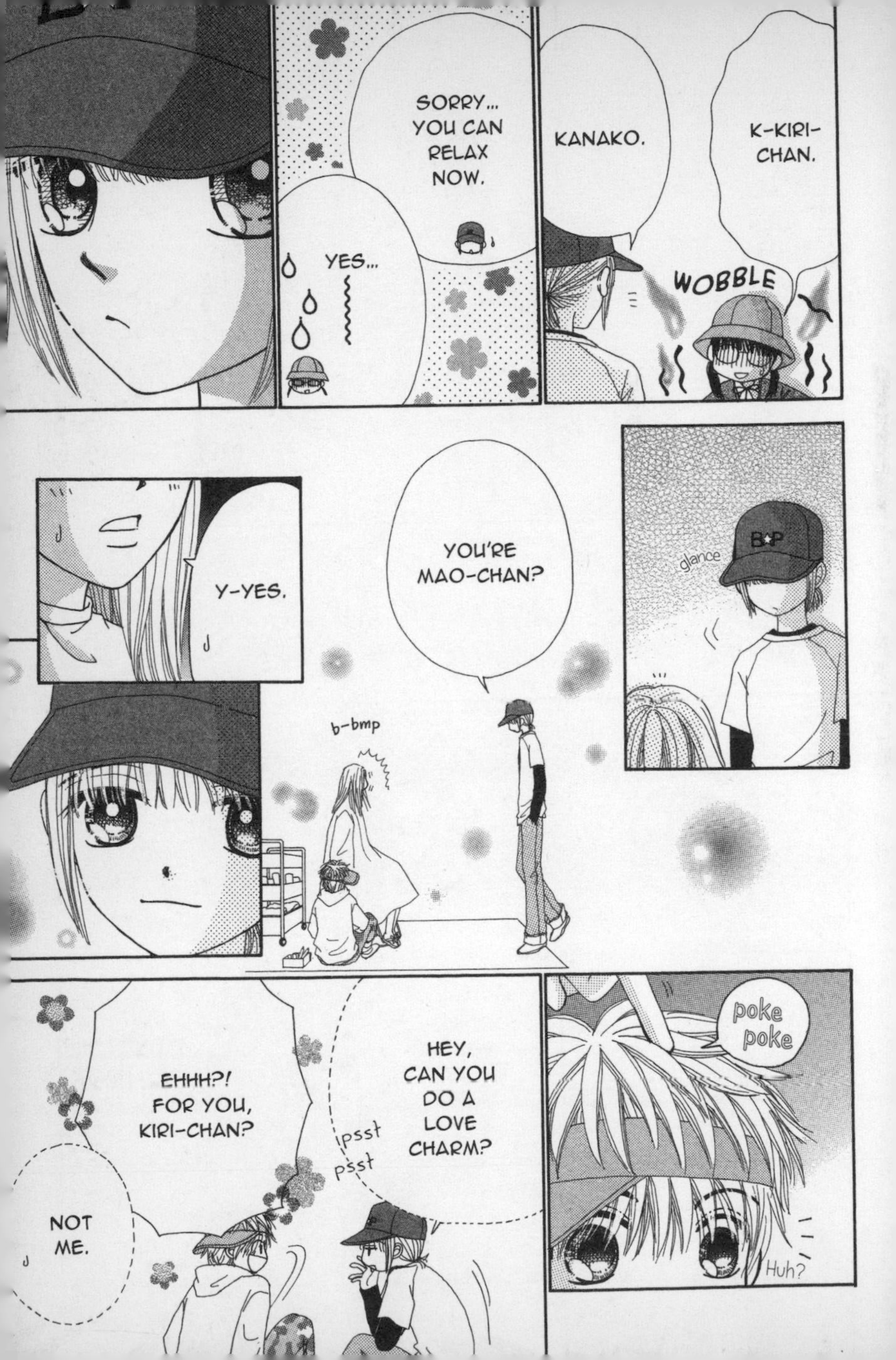
K-KIRI-CHAN.
KANAKO.
WOBBLE
SORRY... YOU CAN RELAX NOW.
YES...
glance
YOU'RE MAO-CHAN?
b-bmp
Y-YES.
poke poke
Huh?
HEY, CAN YOU DO A LOVE CHARM?
psst psst
EHHH?! FOR YOU, KIRI-CHAN?
NOT ME.

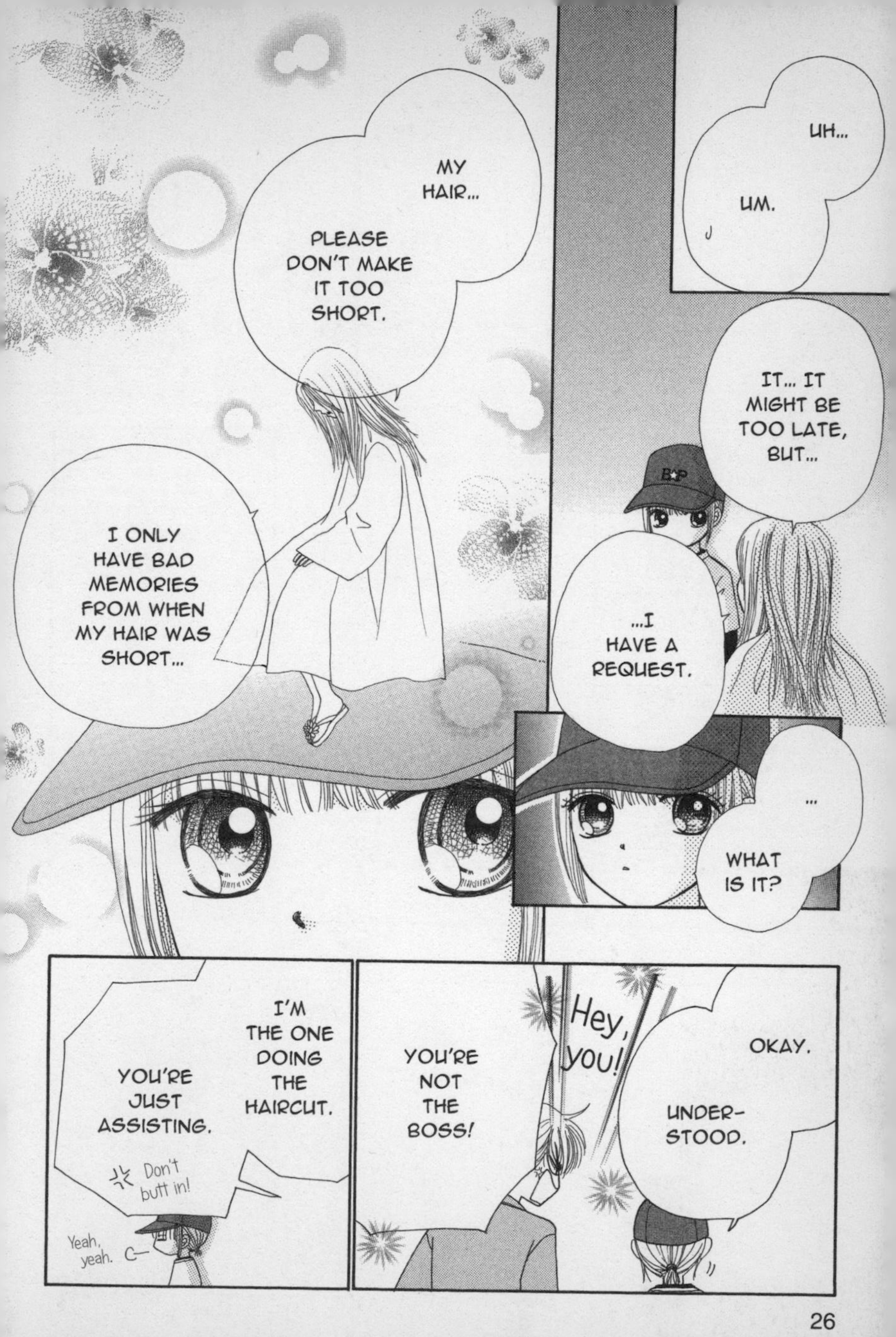
UH... UM.
IT... IT MIGHT BE TOO LATE, BUT...
...I HAVE A REQUEST.
... WHAT IS IT?
MY HAIR... PLEASE DON'T MAKE IT TOO SHORT.
I ONLY HAVE BAD MEMORIES FROM WHEN MY HAIR WAS SHORT...
OKAY. UNDERSTOOD.
Hey, you!
YOU'RE NOT THE BOSS!
I'M THE ONE DOING THE HAIRCUT.
YOU'RE JUST ASSISTING.
Don't butt in!
Yeah, yeah.

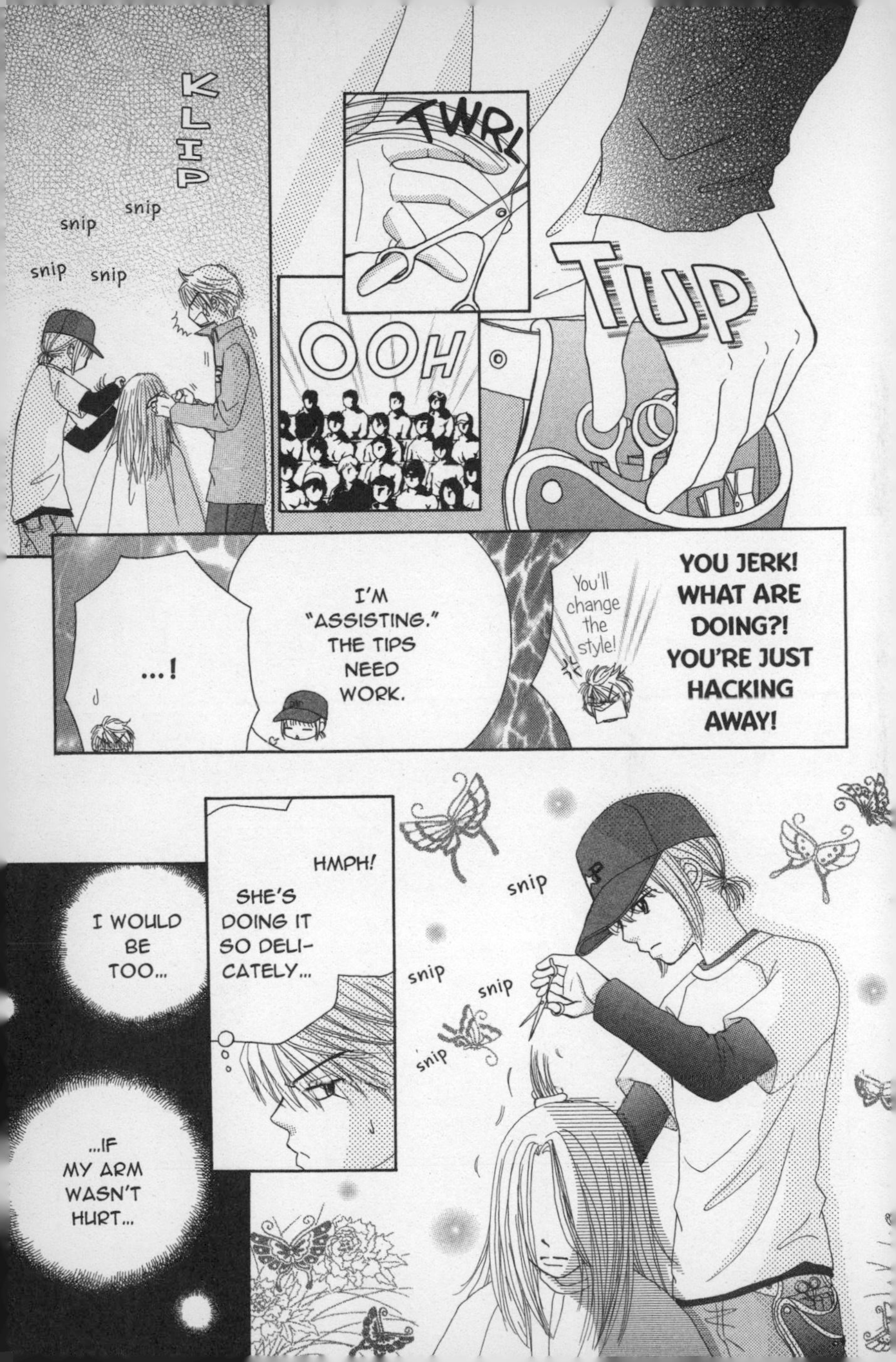
TUP
TWRL
OOH
KLIP
snip snip snip snip
YOU JERK! WHAT ARE DOING?! YOU'RE JUST HACKING AWAY!
You'll change the style!
I'M "ASSISTING." THE TIPS NEED WORK.
...!
snip
snip
snip
snip
HMPH!
SHE'S DOING IT SO DELI-CATELY...
I WOULD BE TOO...
...IF MY ARM WASN'T HURT...

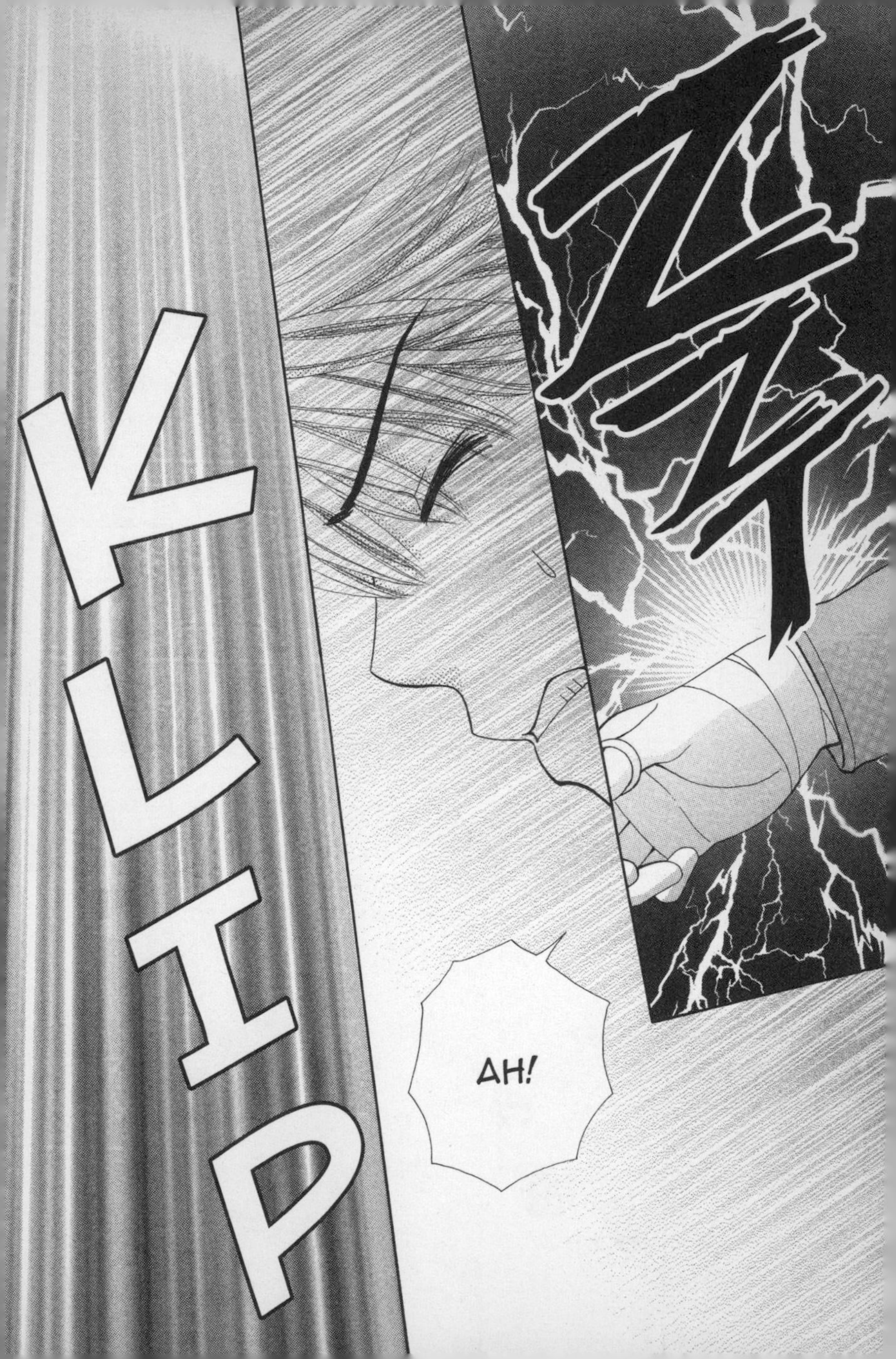
ZZZT
AH!
KLIP

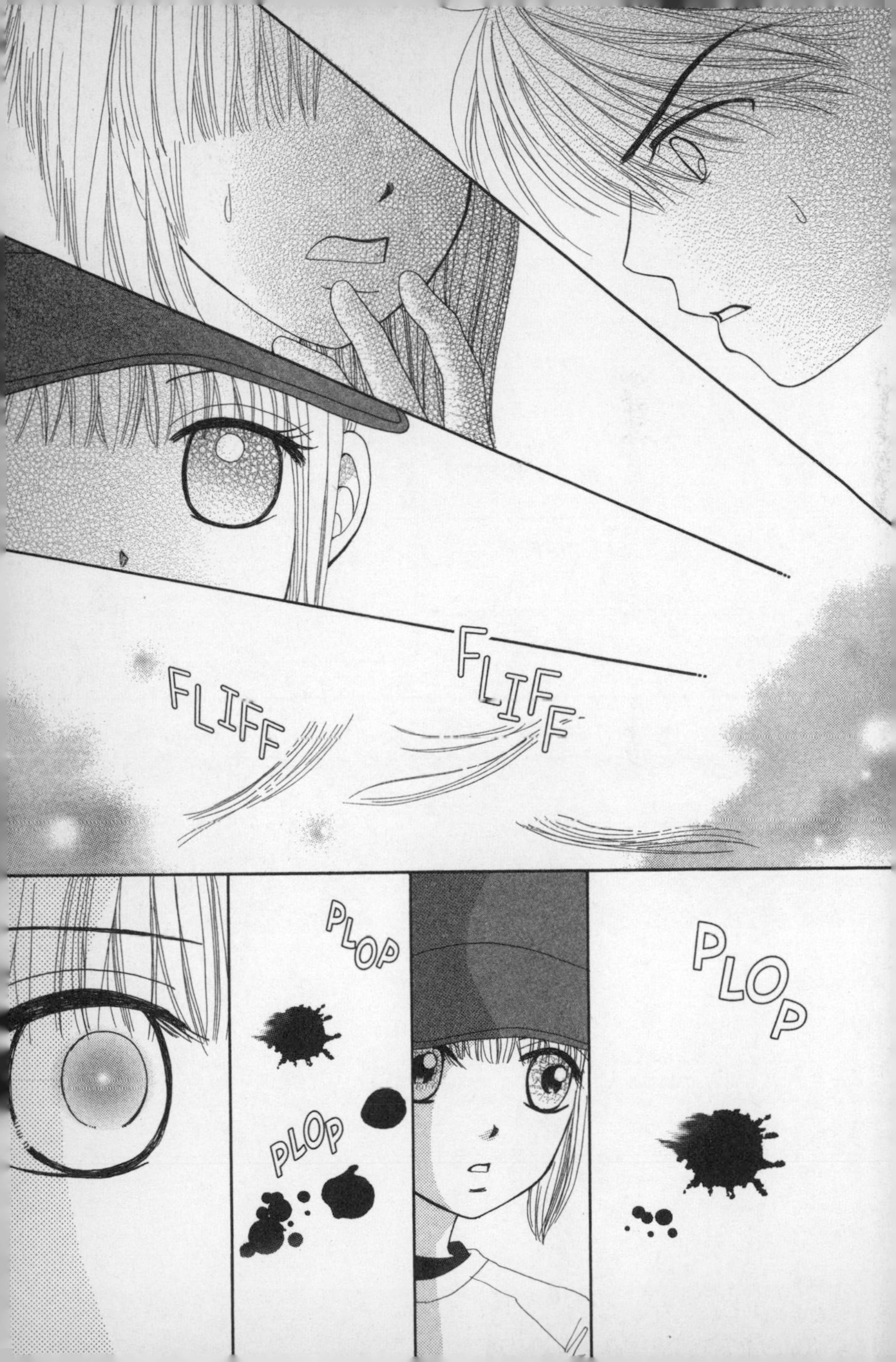
FLIFF
FLIFF
PLOP
PLOP
PLOP

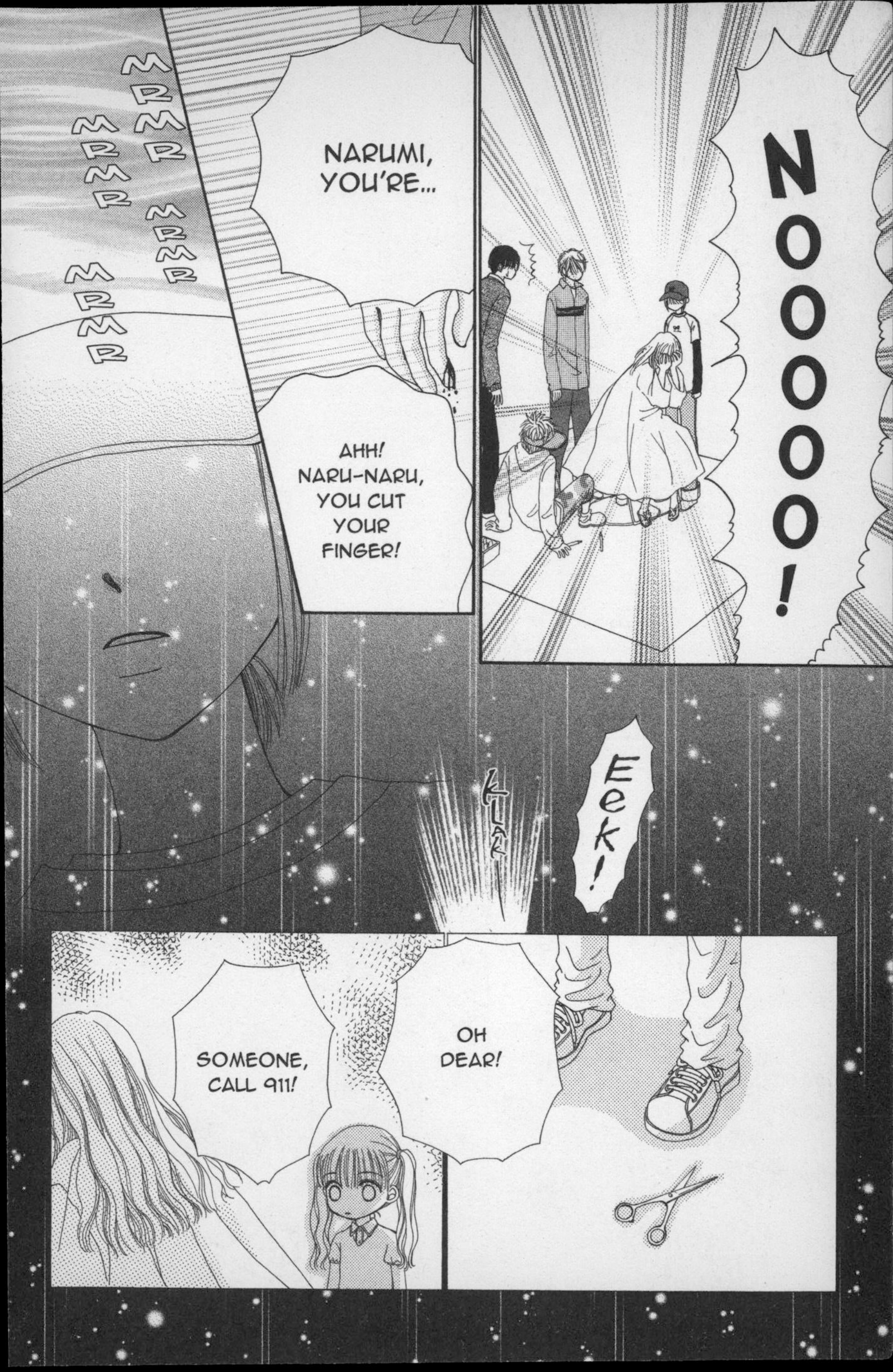
NOOOOO!
NARUMI, YOU'RE...
AHH! NARU-NARU, YOU CUT YOUR FINGER!
MRMR MRMR MRMR MRMR
Eek!
KLAK
OH DEAR!
SOMEONE, CALL 911!

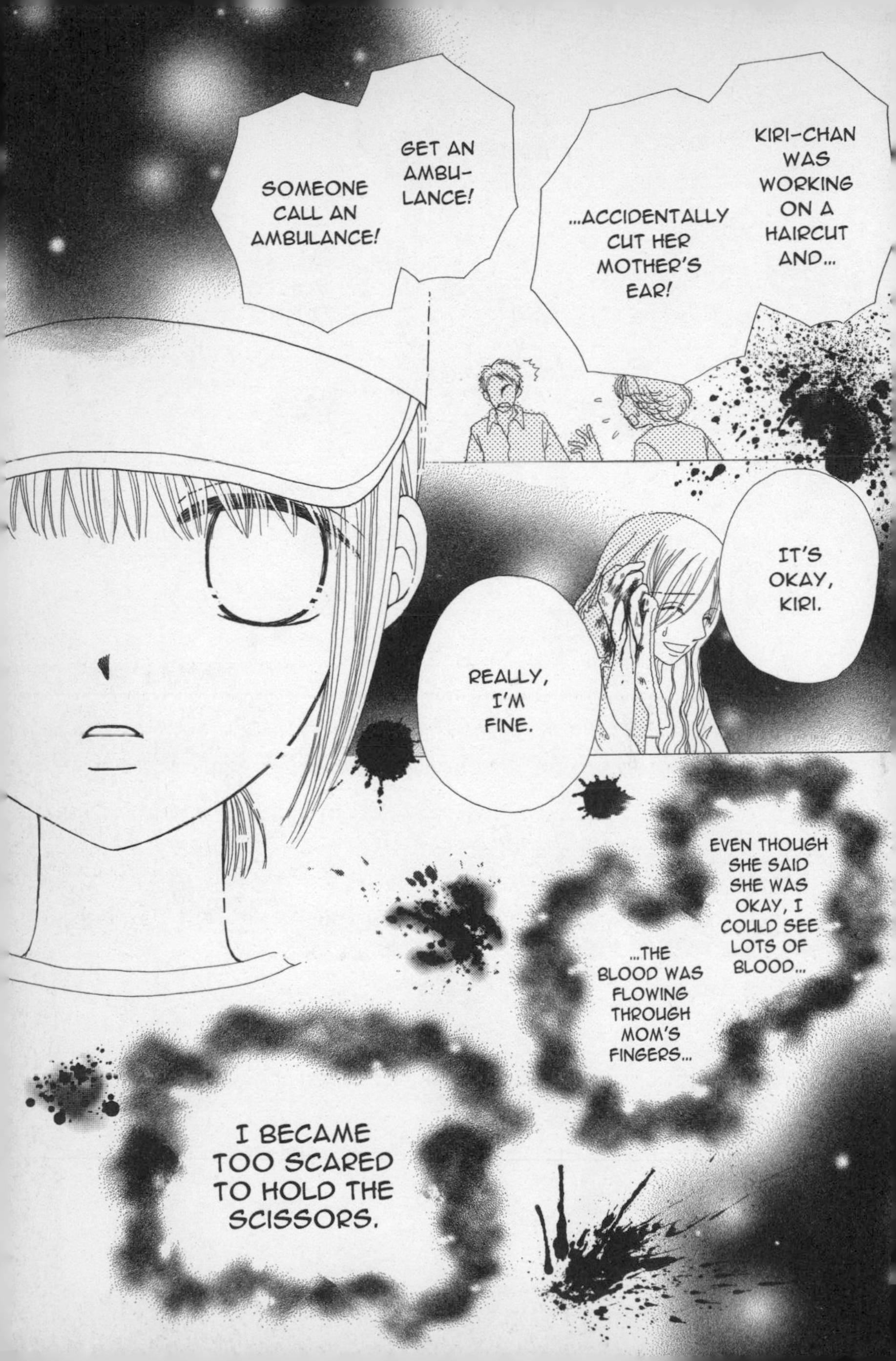
KIRI-CHAN WAS WORKING ON A HAIRCUT AND...
...ACCIDENTALLY CUT HER MOTHER'S EAR!
GET AN AMBU-LANCE!
SOMEONE CALL AN AMBULANCE!
IT'S OKAY, KIRI.
REALLY, I'M FINE.
EVEN THOUGH SHE SAID SHE WAS OKAY, I COULD SEE LOTS OF BLOOD...
...THE BLOOD WAS FLOWING THROUGH MOM'S FINGERS...
I BECAME TOO SCARED TO HOLD THE SCISSORS.

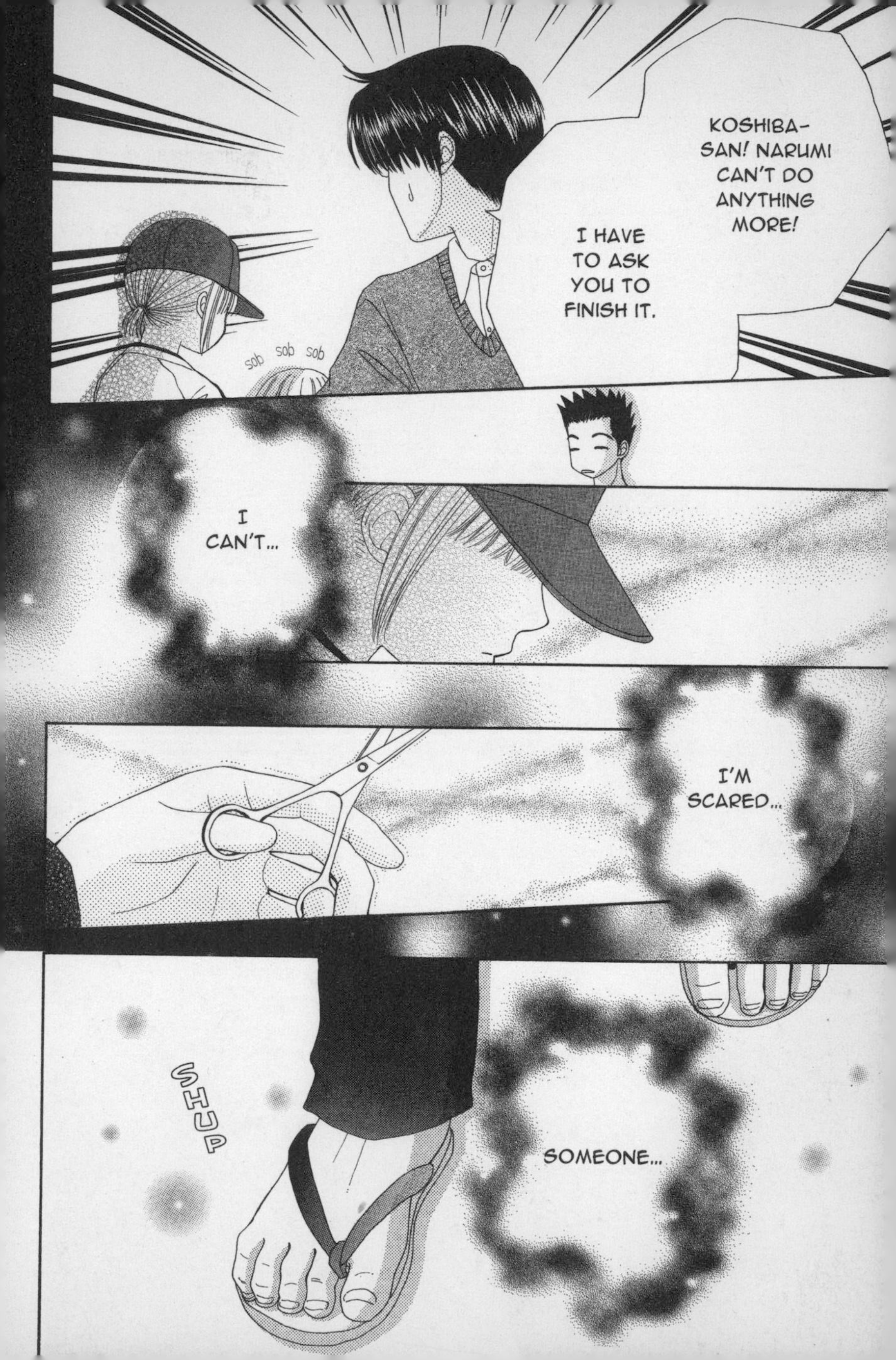
KOSHIBA-SAN! NARUMI CAN'T DO ANYTHING MORE!
I HAVE TO ASK YOU TO FINISH IT.
sob sob sob
I CAN'T...
I'M SCARED...
SOMEONE...
SHUP

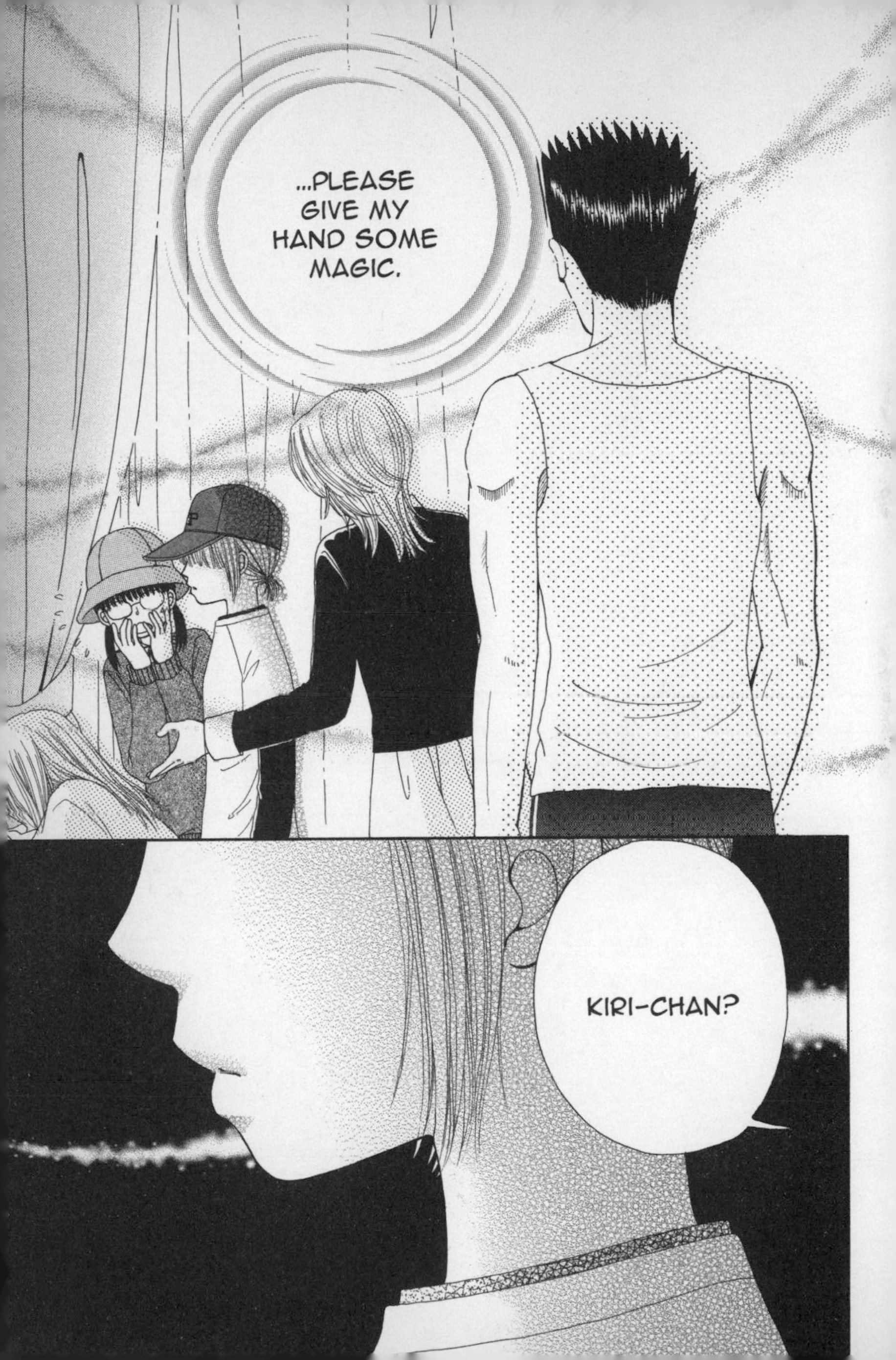
...PLEASE GIVE MY HAND SOME MAGIC.
KIRI-CHAN?

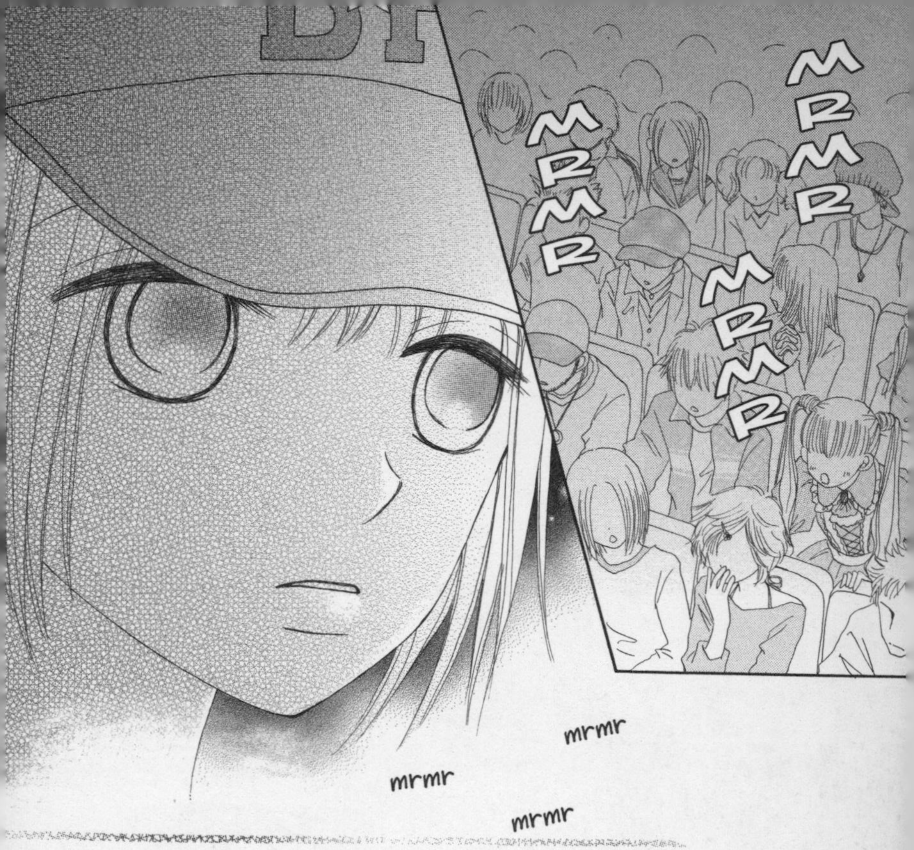
MRMR
MRMR
MRMR
mrmr
mrmr
mrmr

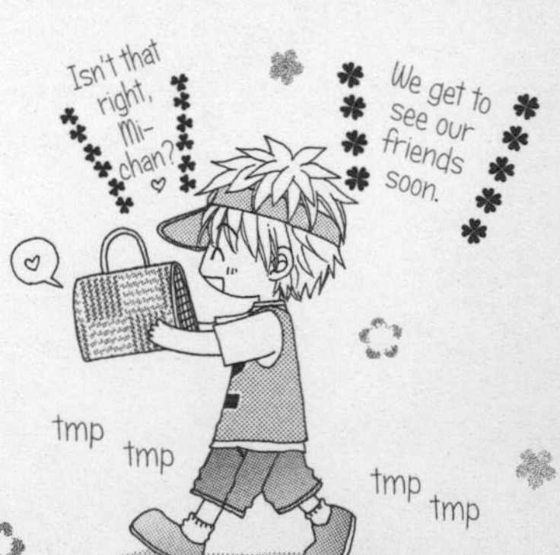
We get to see our friends soon.
Isn't that right, Mi-chan? ♡
tmp tmp
tmp tmp

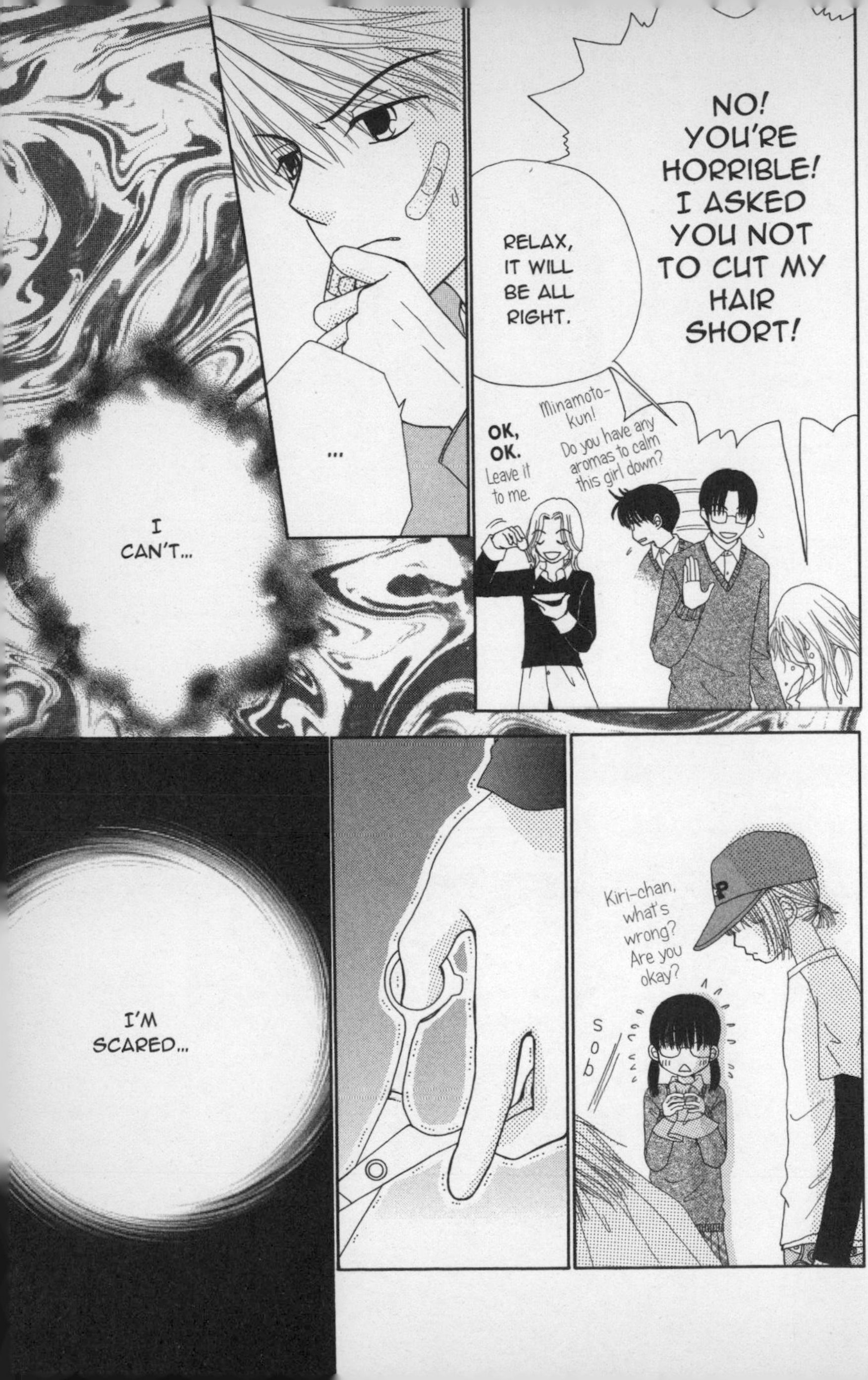
NO! YOU'RE HORRIBLE! I ASKED YOU NOT TO CUT MY HAIR SHORT!
RELAX, IT WILL BE ALL RIGHT.
Minamoto-kun! Do you have any aromas to calm this girl down?
OK, OK. Leave it to me.
...
I CAN'T...
Kiri-chan, what's wrong? Are you okay?
sob
I'M SCARED...

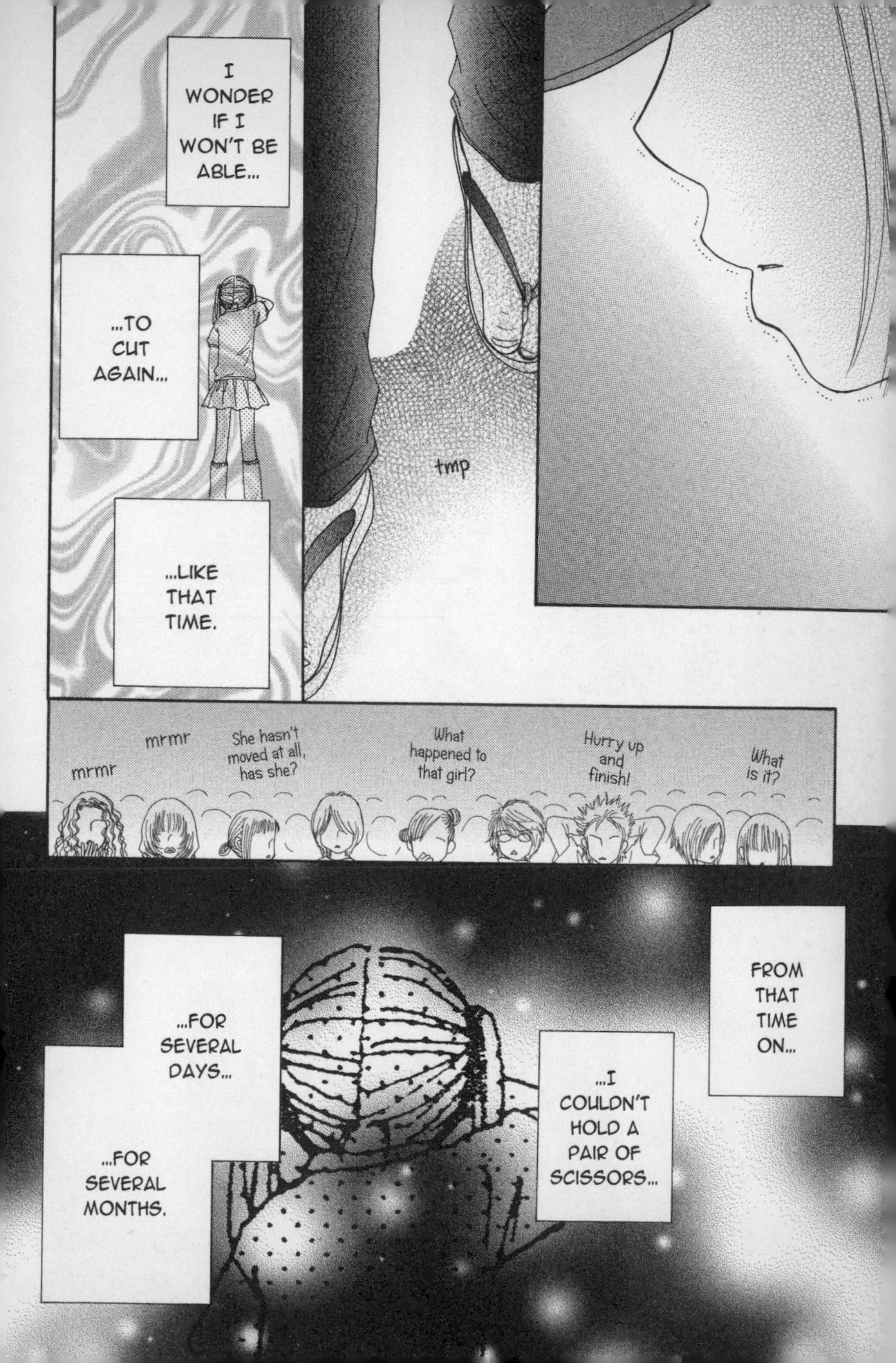
tmp
I WONDER IF I WON'T BE ABLE...
...TO CUT AGAIN...
...LIKE THAT TIME.
What is it?
Hurry up and finish!
What happened to that girl?
She hasn't moved at all, has she?
mrmr
mrmr
FROM THAT TIME ON...
...I COULDN'T HOLD A PAIR OF SCISSORS...
...FOR SEVERAL DAYS...
...FOR SEVERAL MONTHS.

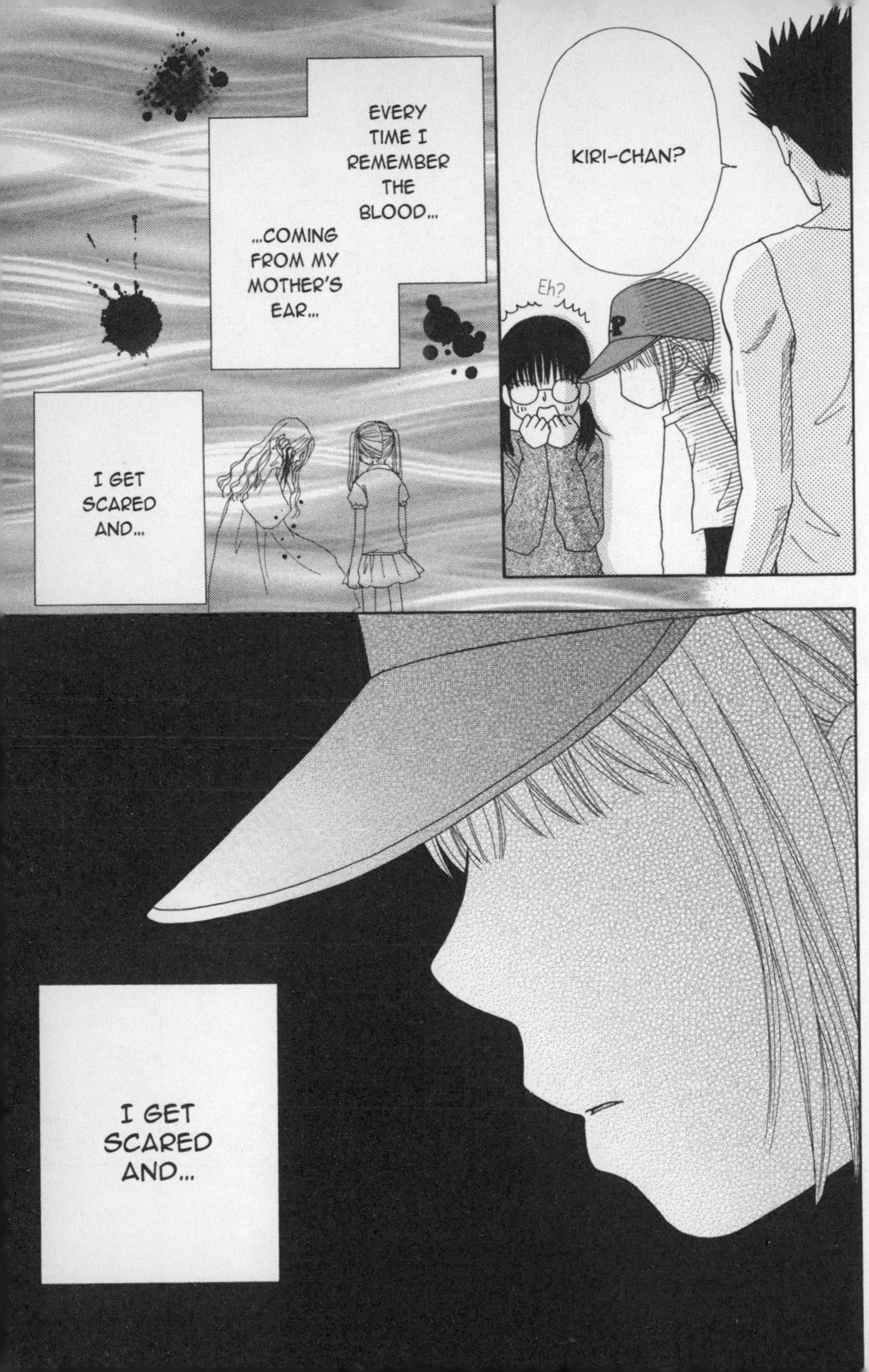
KIRI-CHAN?
Eh?
EVERY TIME I REMEMBER THE BLOOD...
...COMING FROM MY MOTHER'S EAR...
I GET SCARED AND...
I GET SCARED AND...

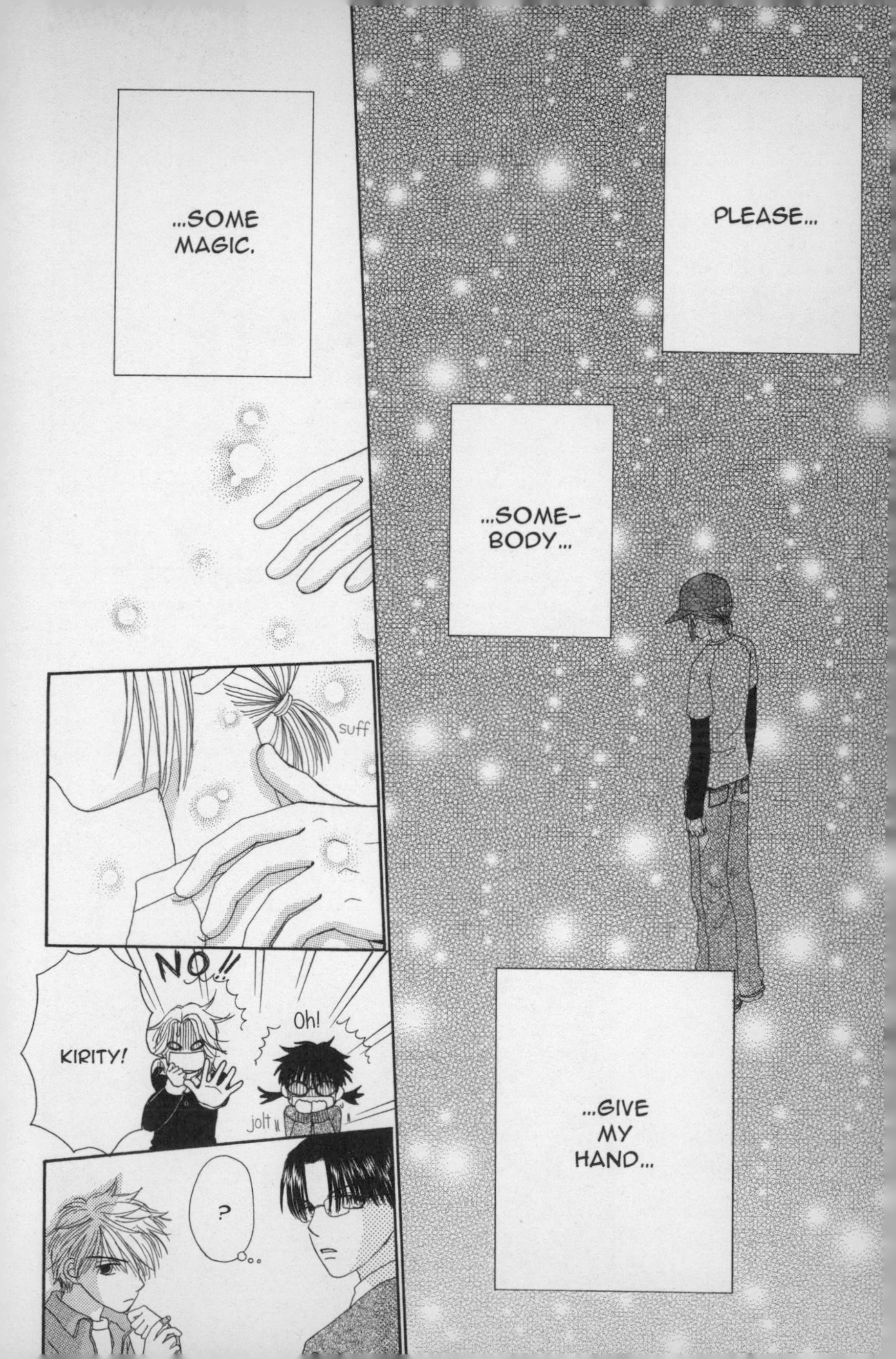
PLEASE...
...SOME-BODY...
...GIVE MY HAND...
...SOME MAGIC.
suff
NO!!
Oh!
KIRITY!
jolt
?

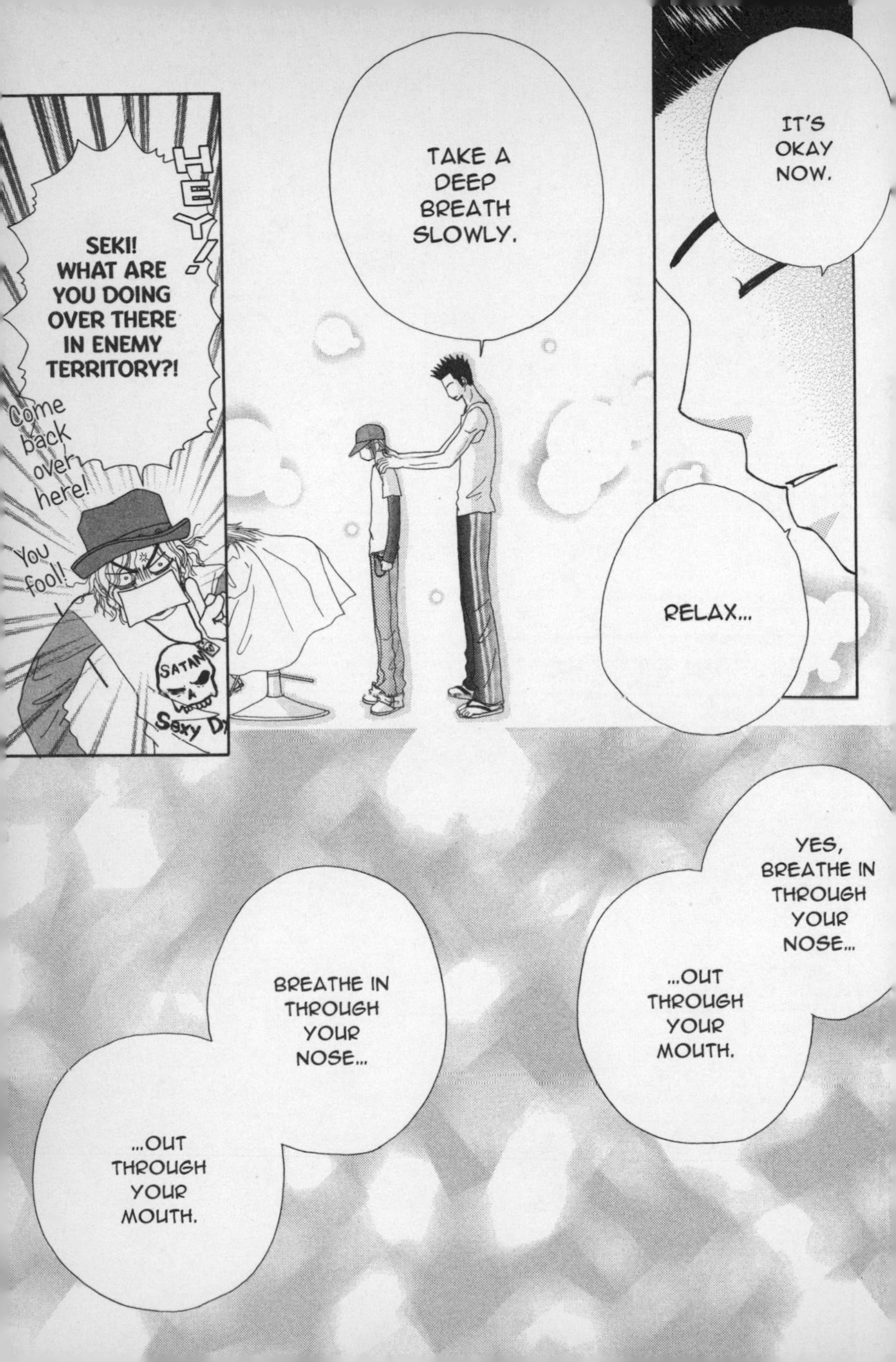
IT'S OKAY NOW.
RELAX...
TAKE A DEEP BREATH SLOWLY.
HEY!!
SEKI! WHAT ARE YOU DOING OVER THERE IN ENEMY TERRITORY?!
Come back over here!
You fool!
SATAN
Sexy Dx
YES, BREATHE IN THROUGH YOUR NOSE...
...OUT THROUGH YOUR MOUTH.
BREATHE IN THROUGH YOUR NOSE...
...OUT THROUGH YOUR MOUTH.

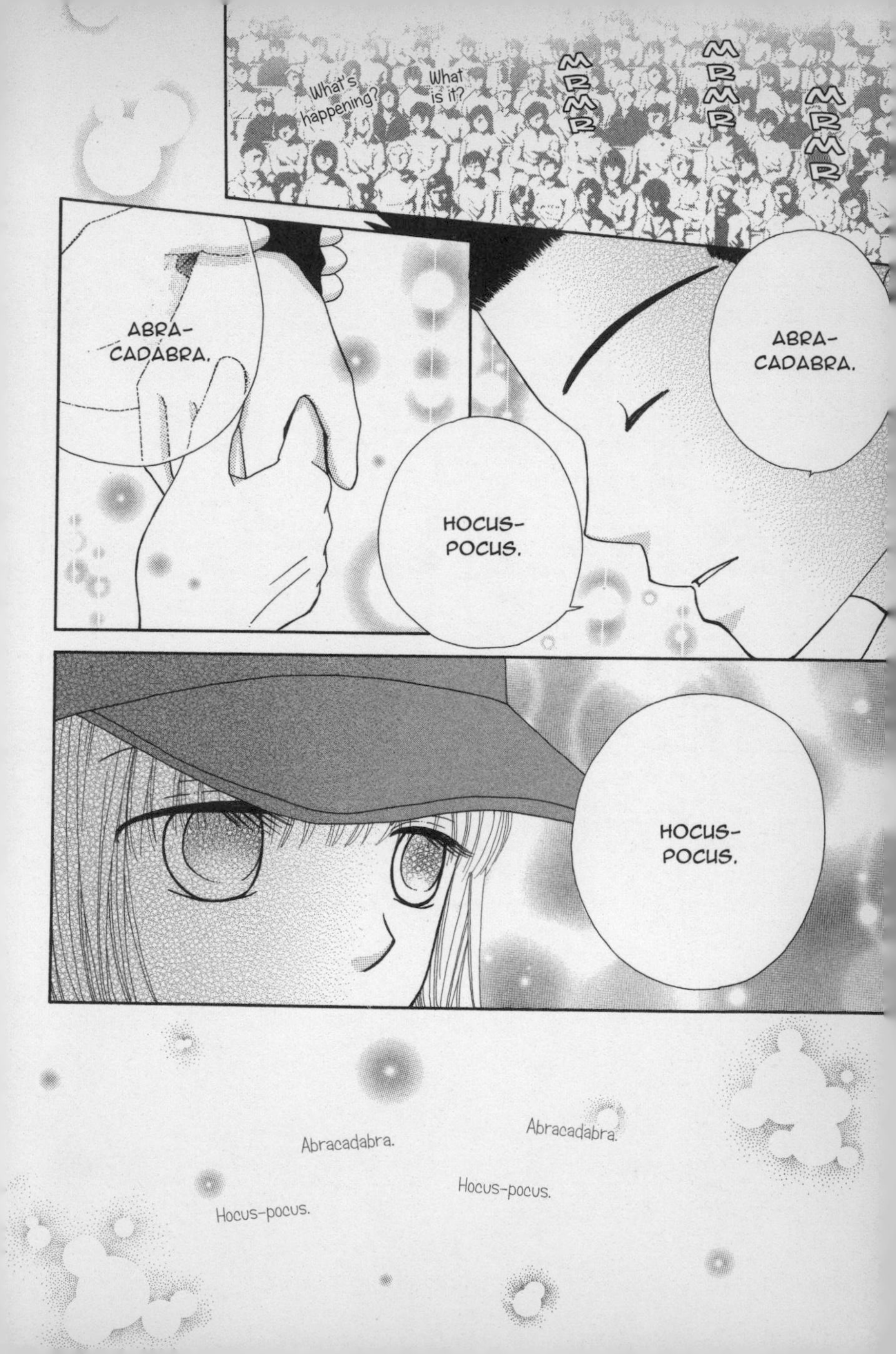
MRMR
MRMR
MRMR
What is it?
What's happening?
ABRA-CADABRA.
HOCUS-POCUS.
ABRA-CADABRA.
HOCUS-POCUS.
Abracadabra.
Abracadabra.
Hocus-pocus.
Hocus-pocus.

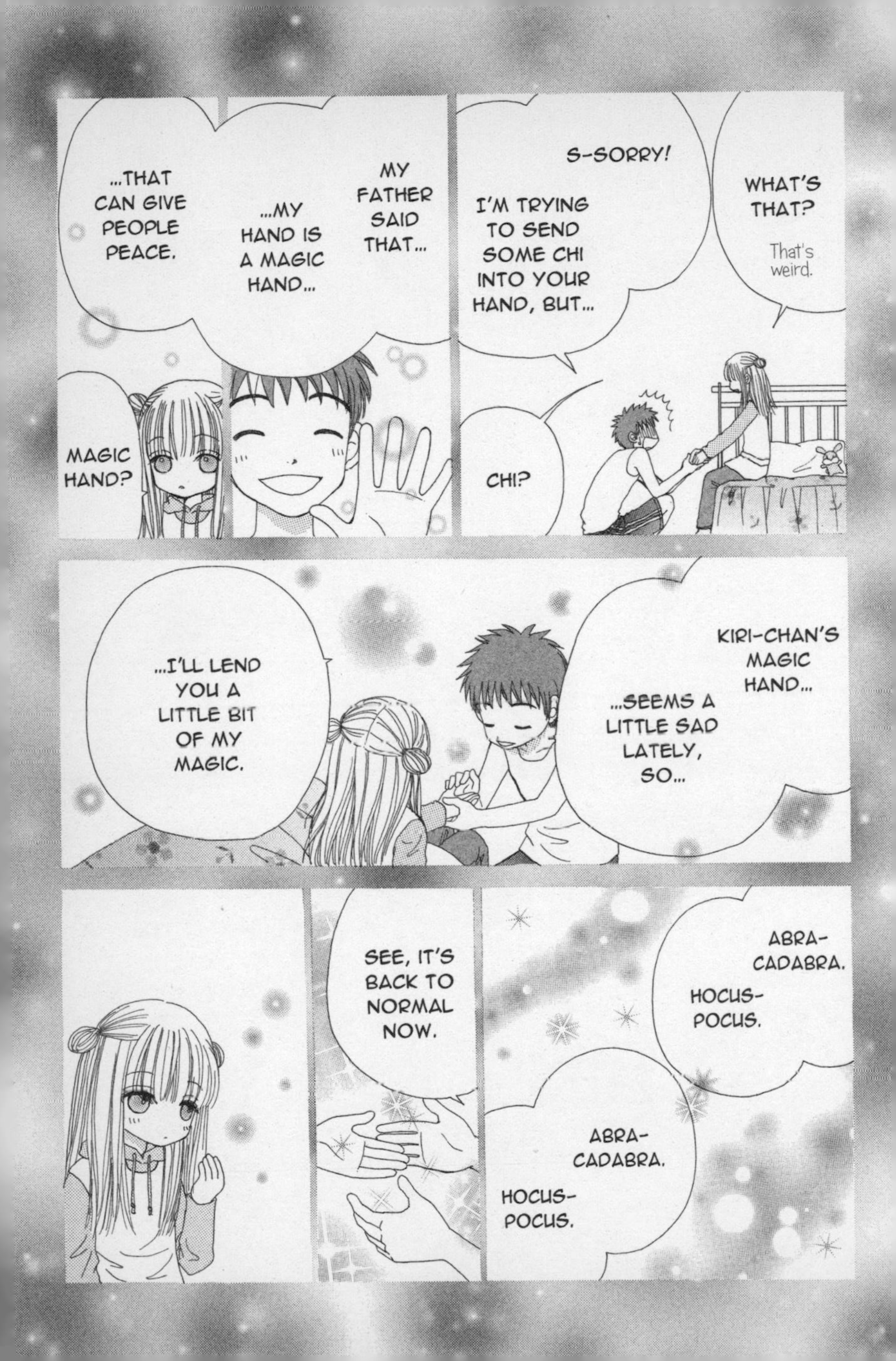
WHAT'S THAT?
That's weird.
S-SORRY!
I'M TRYING TO SEND SOME CHI INTO YOUR HAND, BUT...
CHI?
MY FATHER SAID THAT...
...MY HAND IS A MAGIC HAND...
...THAT CAN GIVE PEOPLE PEACE.
MAGIC HAND?
KIRI-CHAN'S MAGIC HAND...
...SEEMS A LITTLE SAD LATELY, SO...
...I'LL LEND YOU A LITTLE BIT OF MY MAGIC.
ABRA-CADABRA.
HOCUS-POCUS.
ABRA-CADABRA.
HOCUS-POCUS.
SEE, IT'S BACK TO NORMAL NOW.

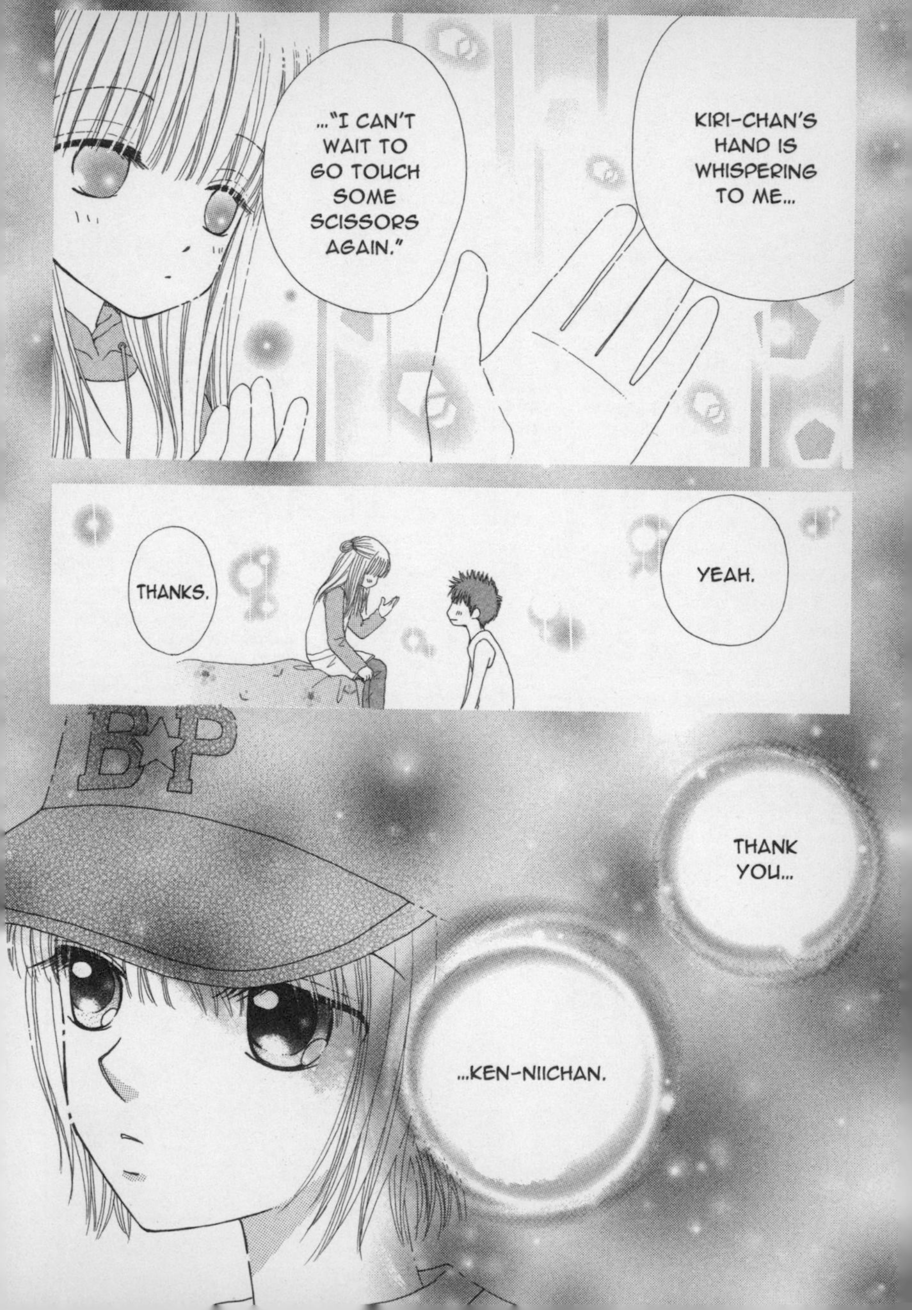
KIRI-CHAN'S HAND IS WHISPERING TO ME...
..."I CAN'T WAIT TO GO TOUCH SOME SCISSORS AGAIN."
YEAH.
THANKS.
THANK YOU...
...KEN-NIICHAN.

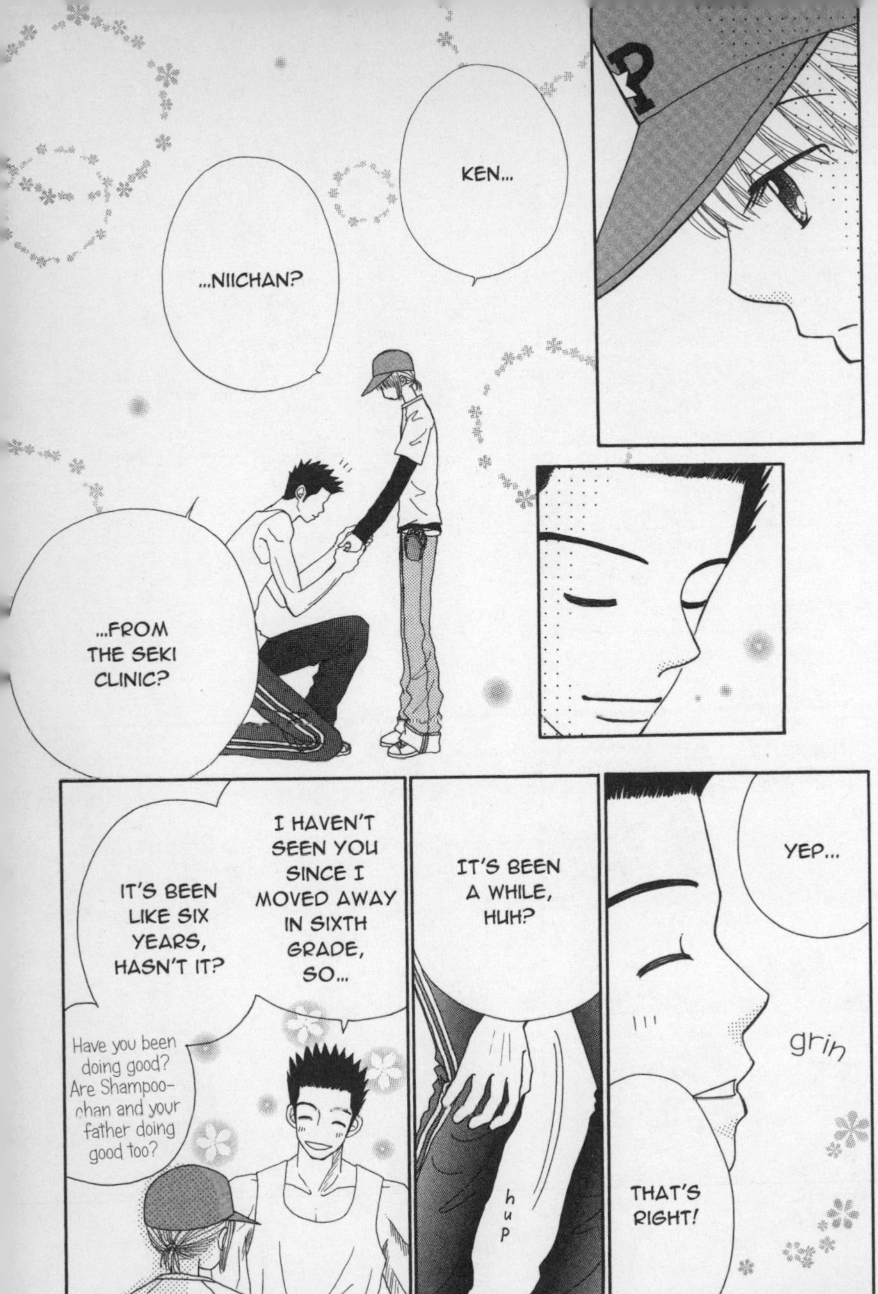
KEN...
...NIICHAN?
...FROM THE SEKI CLINIC?
YEP...
grin
THAT'S RIGHT!
IT'S BEEN A WHILE, HUH?
hup
I HAVEN'T SEEN YOU SINCE I MOVED AWAY IN SIXTH GRADE, SO...
IT'S BEEN LIKE SIX YEARS, HASN'T IT?
Have you been doing good? Are Shampoo-chan and your father doing good too?

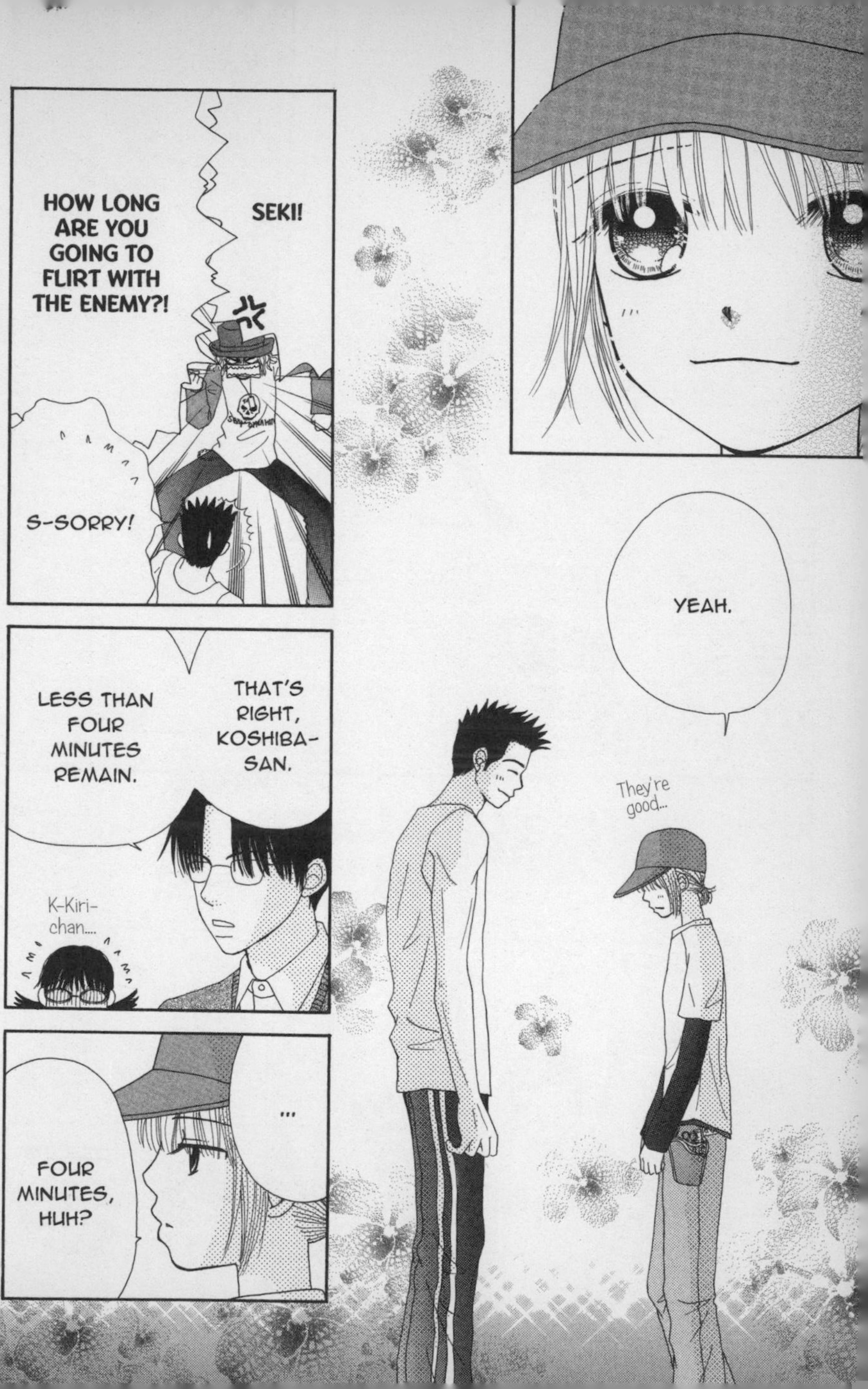
YEAH.
They're good...
SEKI!
HOW LONG ARE YOU GOING TO FLIRT WITH THE ENEMY?!
S-SORRY!
THAT'S RIGHT, KOSHIBA-SAN.
LESS THAN FOUR MINUTES REMAIN.
K-Kiri-chan....
...
FOUR MINUTES, HUH?

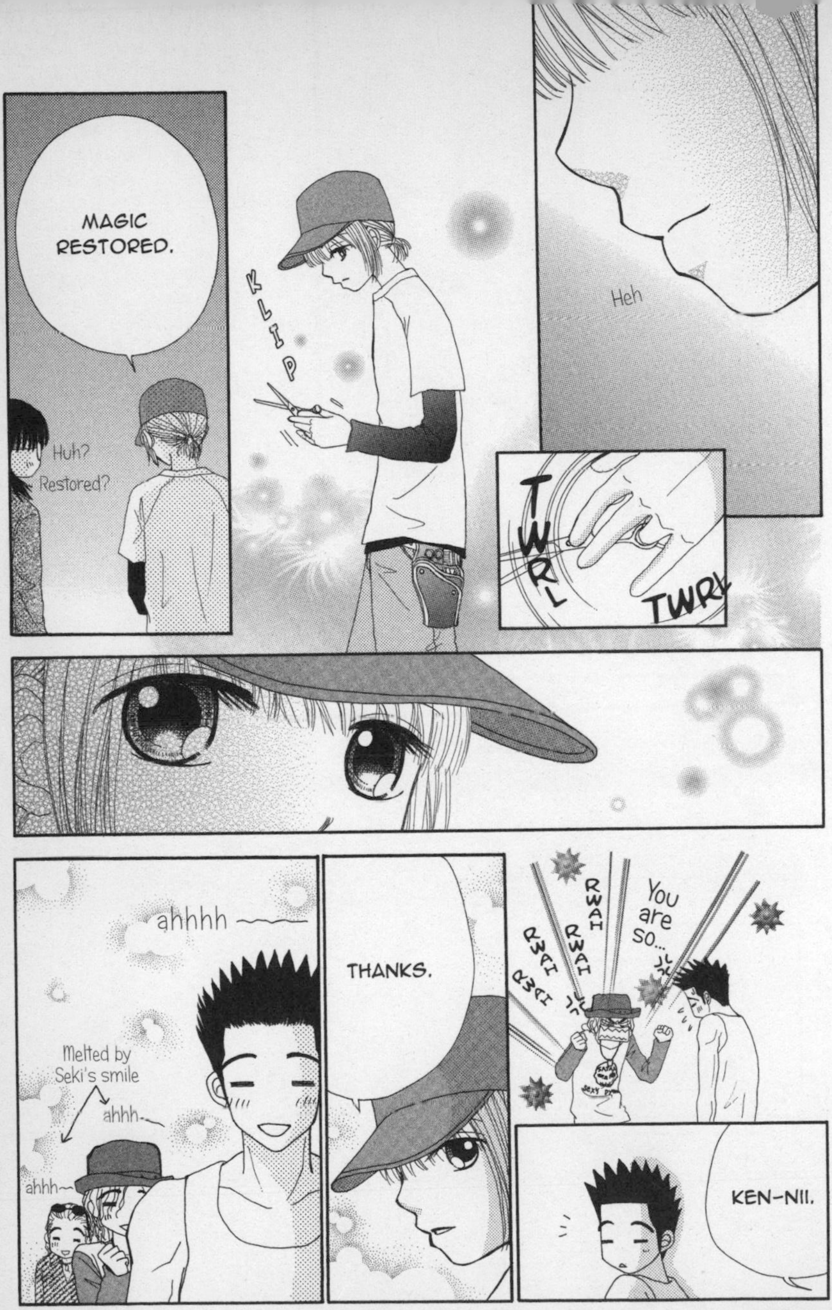
Heh
TWRL
TWRL
KLIP
MAGIC RESTORED.
Huh? Restored?
You are so...
RWAH
RWAH
KEN-NII.
THANKS.
ahhhh
Melted by Seki's smile
ahhh
ahhh

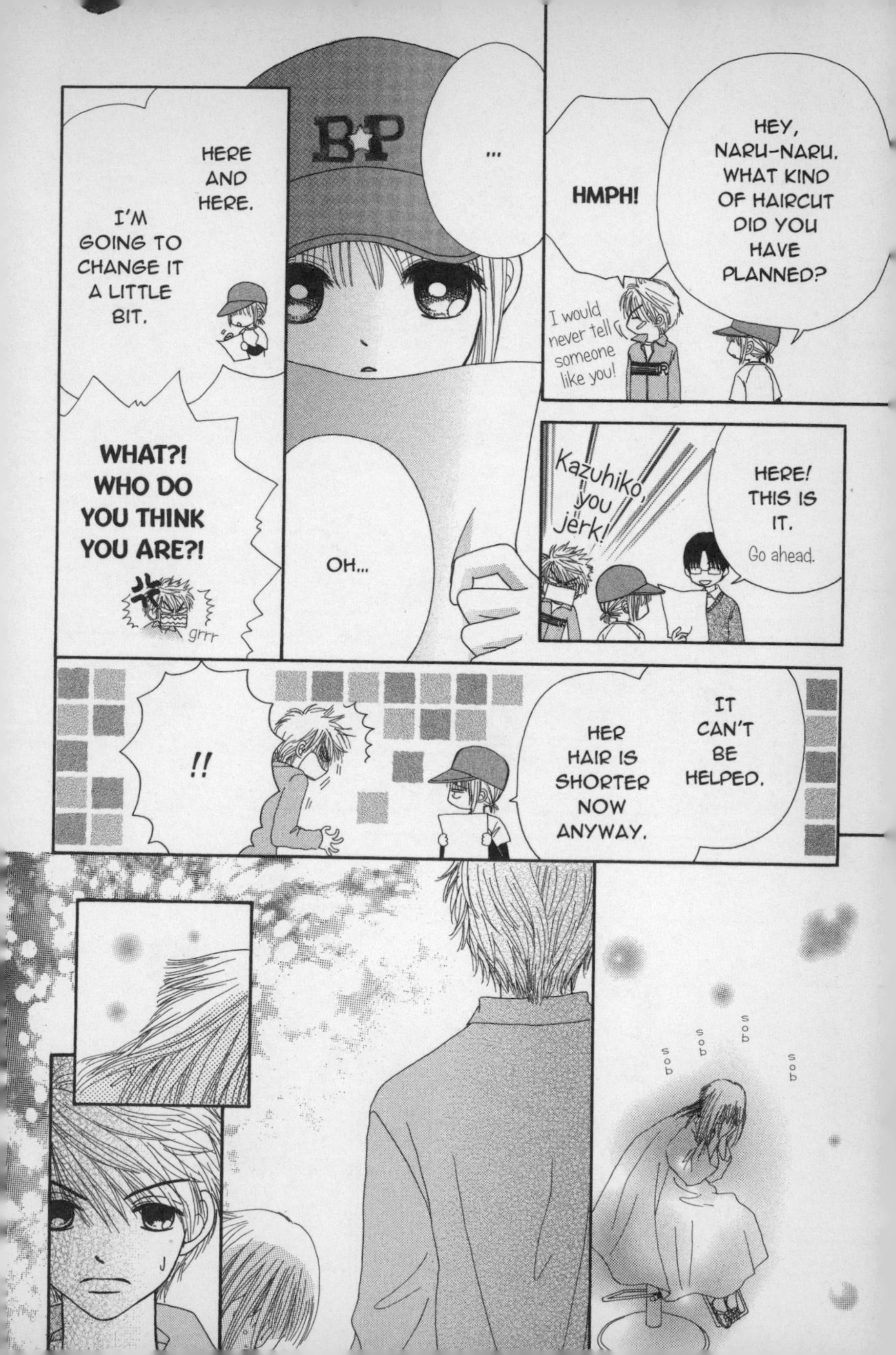
HEY, NARU-NARU. WHAT KIND OF HAIRCUT DID YOU HAVE PLANNED?
HMPH!
I would never tell someone like you!
HERE! THIS IS IT.
Go ahead.
Kazuhiko, you jerk!
...
OH...
HERE AND HERE.
I'M GOING TO CHANGE IT A LITTLE BIT.
WHAT?! WHO DO YOU THINK YOU ARE?!
grrr
IT CAN'T BE HELPED.
HER HAIR IS SHORTER NOW ANYWAY.
!!
sob
sob
sob
sob

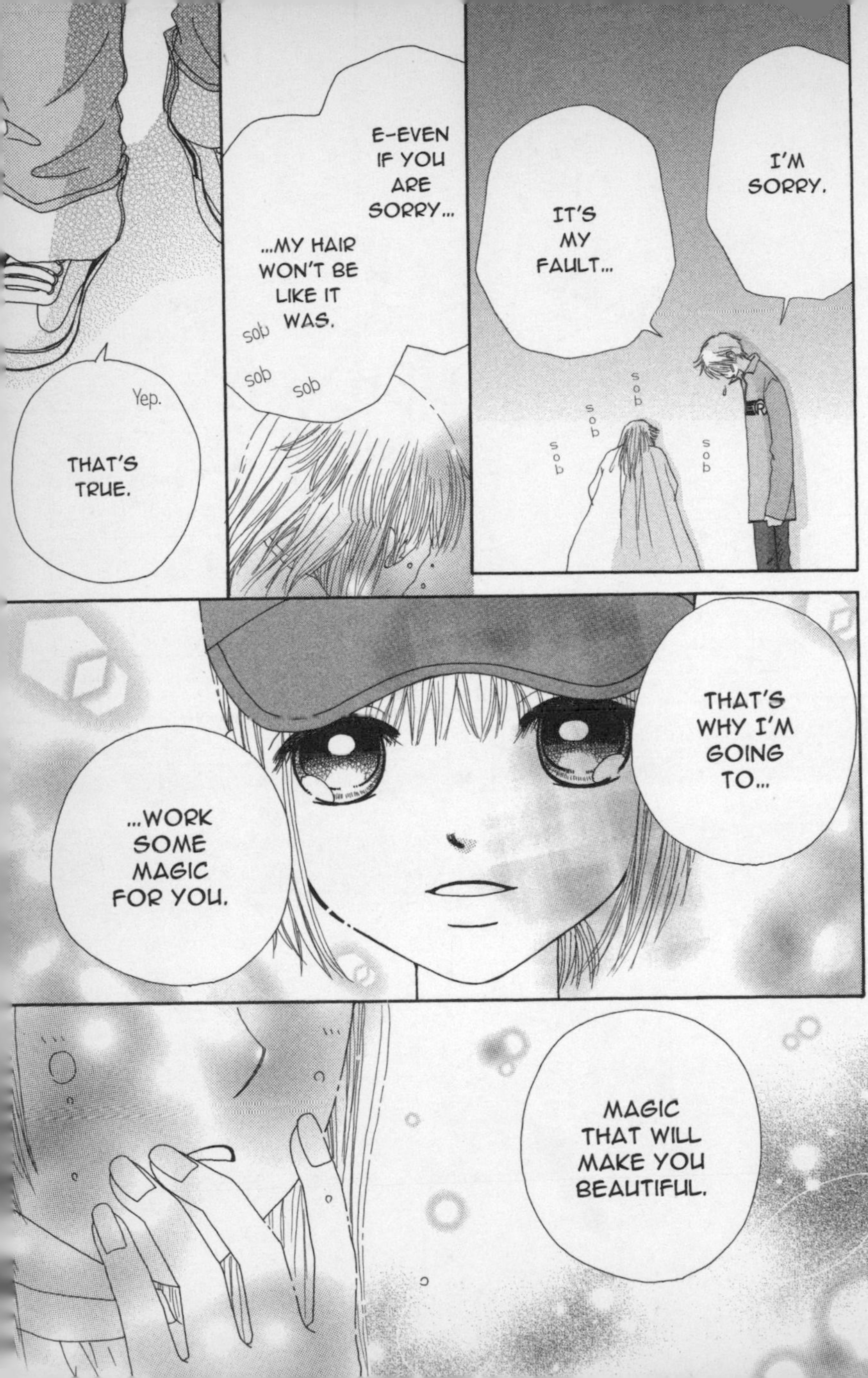
I'M SORRY.
IT'S MY FAULT...
sob
sob
sob
sob
E-EVEN IF YOU ARE SORRY...
...MY HAIR WON'T BE LIKE IT WAS.
sob
sob
sob
Yep.
THAT'S TRUE.
THAT'S WHY I'M GOING TO...
...WORK SOME MAGIC FOR YOU.
MAGIC THAT WILL MAKE YOU BEAUTIFUL.

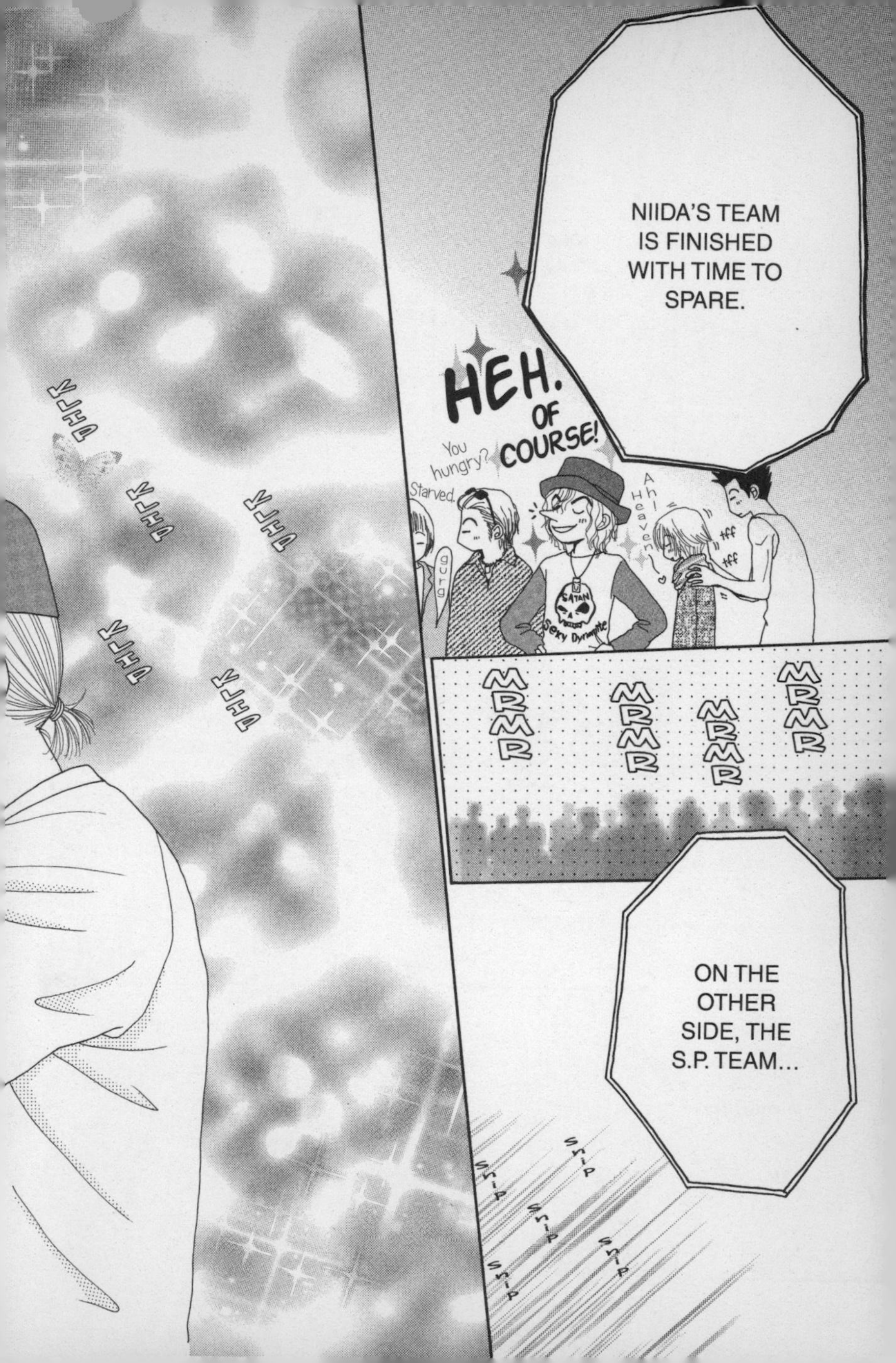

NIIDA'S TEAM IS FINISHED WITH TIME TO SPARE.
HEH. OF COURSE!
You hungry?
Starved.
gurg
Ah! Heaven~
fff
fff
SATAN
Sexy Dynamite
MRMR
MRMR
MRMR
MRMR
ON THE OTHER SIDE, THE S.P. TEAM...
snip
snip
snip
snip
snip
FLAP
FLAP
FLAP
FLAP
FLAP

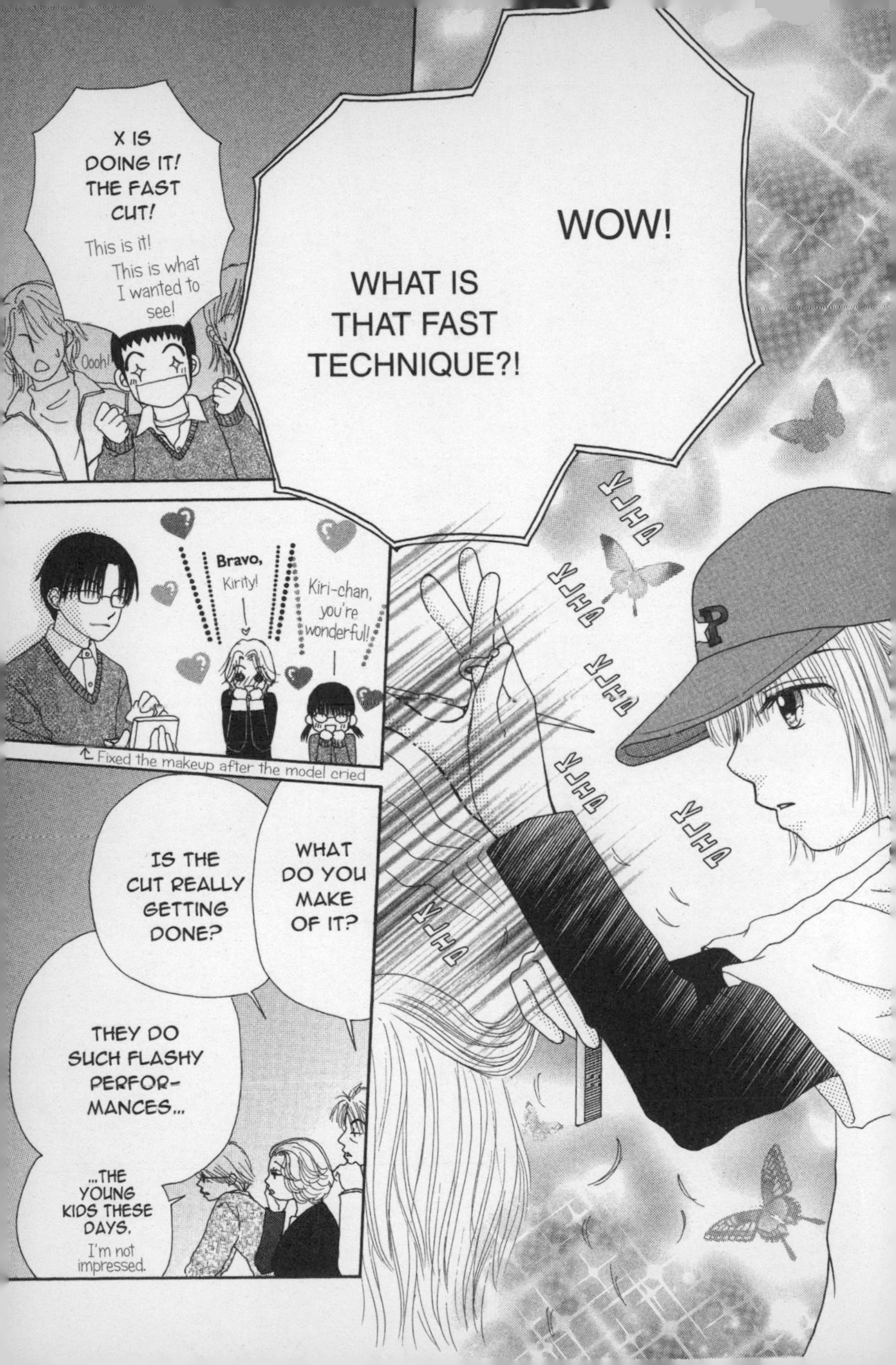
WOW!
WHAT IS THAT FAST TECHNIQUE?!
X IS DOING IT! THE FAST CUT!
This is it! This is what I wanted to see!
Oooh!
Kiri-chan, you're wonderful!
Bravo, Kirity!
↑ Fixed the makeup after the model cried
WHAT DO YOU MAKE OF IT?
IS THE CUT REALLY GETTING DONE?
THEY DO SUCH FLASHY PERFOR-MANCES...
...THE YOUNG KIDS THESE DAYS.
I'm not impressed.

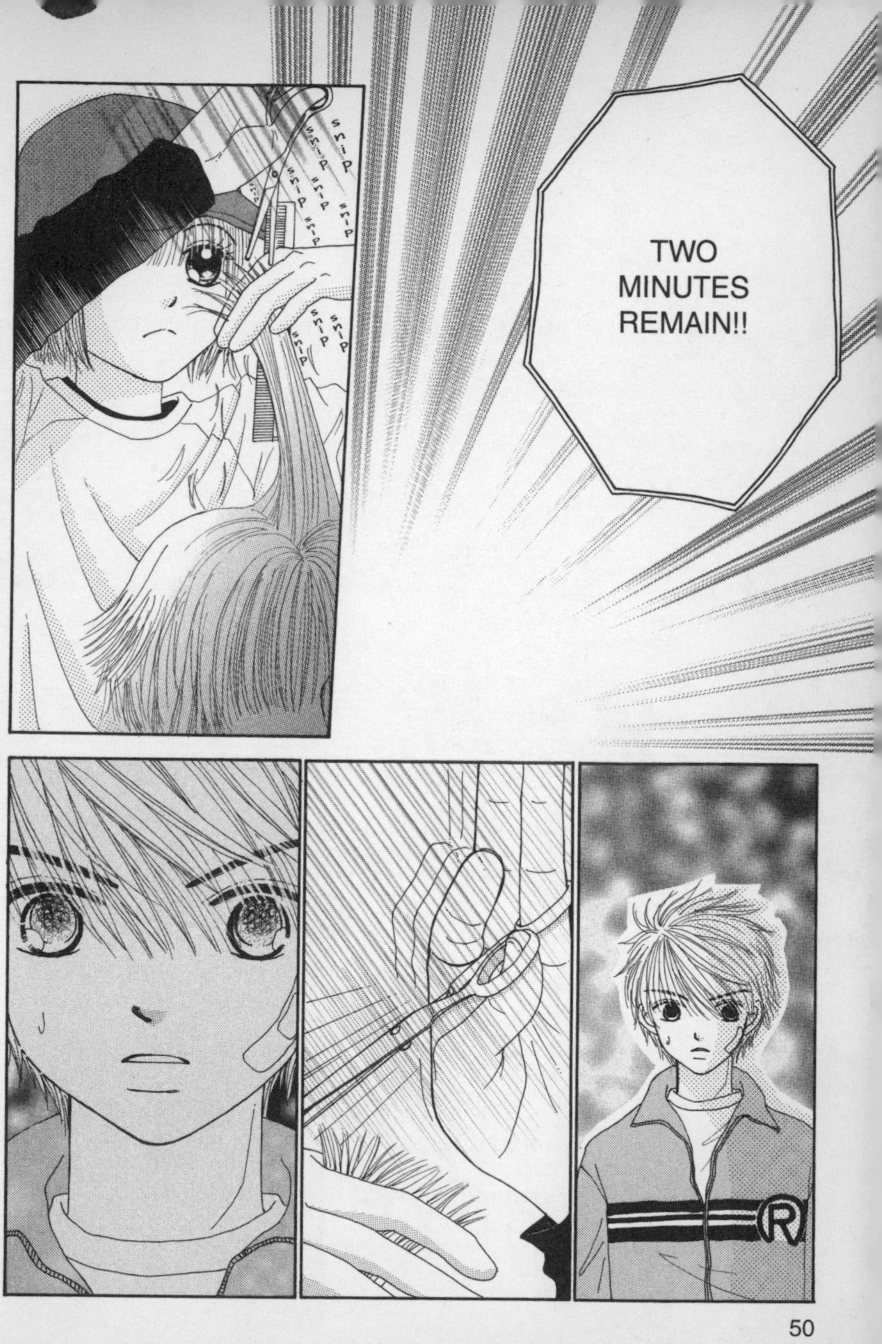
TWO MINUTES REMAIN!!
snip snip
snip snip snip
snip
snip snip snip

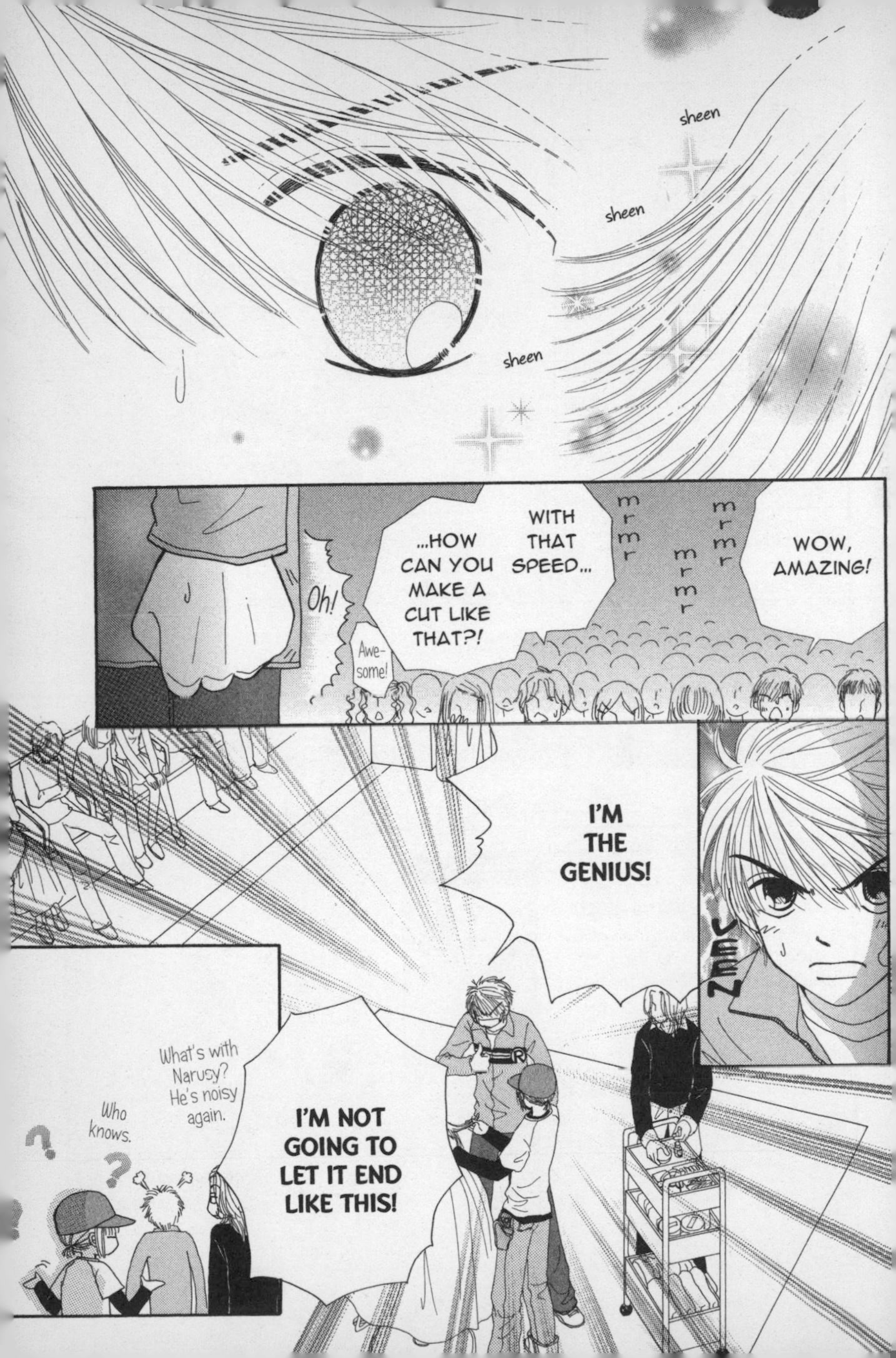
sheen
sheen
sheen
WOW, AMAZING!
mrmr
mrmr
mrmr
WITH THAT SPEED...
...HOW CAN YOU MAKE A CUT LIKE THAT?!
Oh!
Awe-some!
I'M THE GENIUS!
I'M NOT GOING TO LET IT END LIKE THIS!
What's with Narusy? He's noisy again.
Who knows.

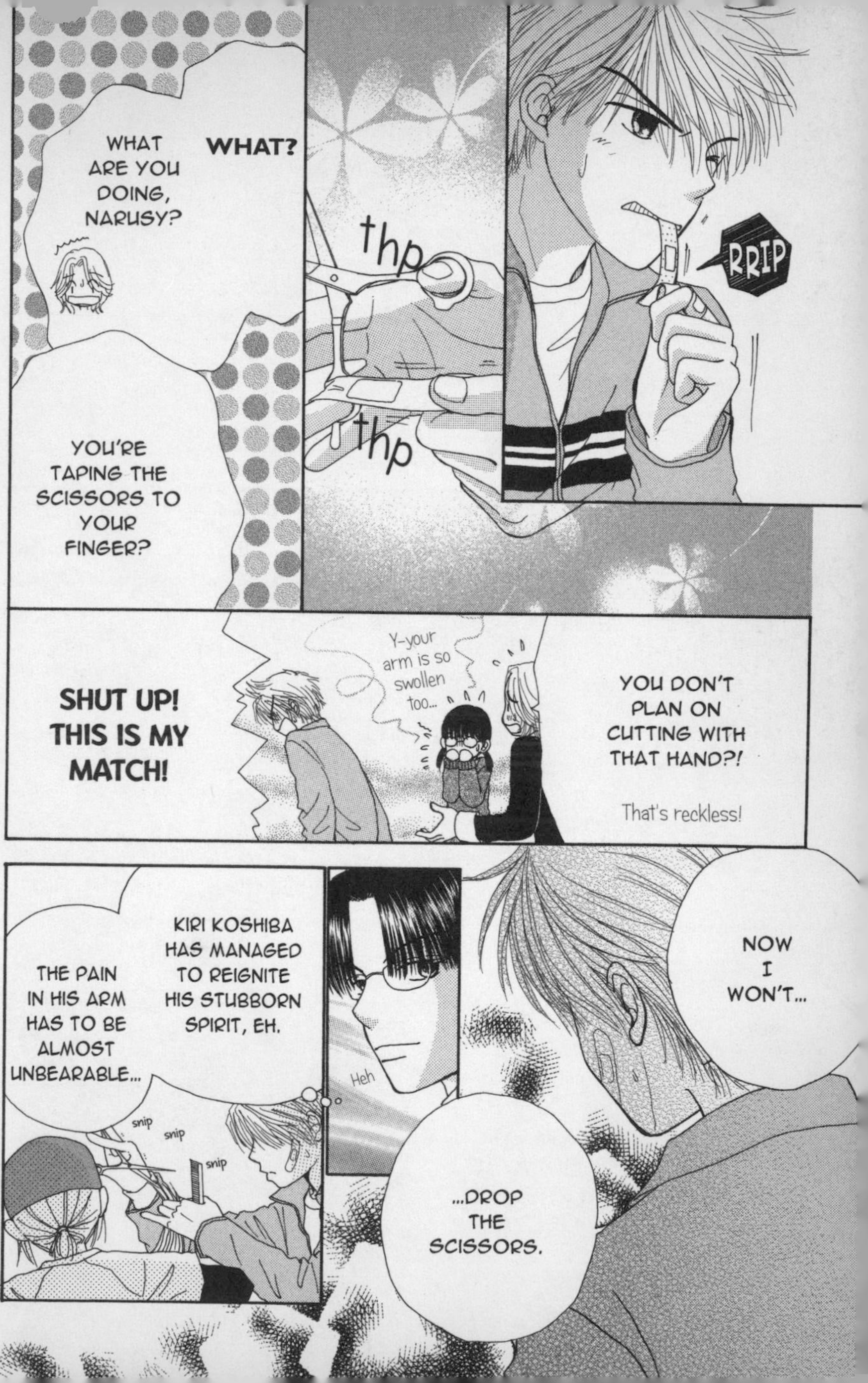
RRIP
thp
thp
WHAT?
WHAT ARE YOU DOING, NARUSY?
YOU'RE TAPING THE SCISSORS TO YOUR FINGER?
YOU DON'T PLAN ON CUTTING WITH THAT HAND?!
That's reckless!
Y-your arm is so swollen too...
SHUT UP! THIS IS MY MATCH!
NOW I WON'T...
...DROP THE SCISSORS.
KIRI KOSHIBA HAS MANAGED TO REIGNITE HIS STUBBORN SPIRIT, EH.
Heh
THE PAIN IN HIS ARM HAS TO BE ALMOST UNBEARABLE...
snip
snip
snip

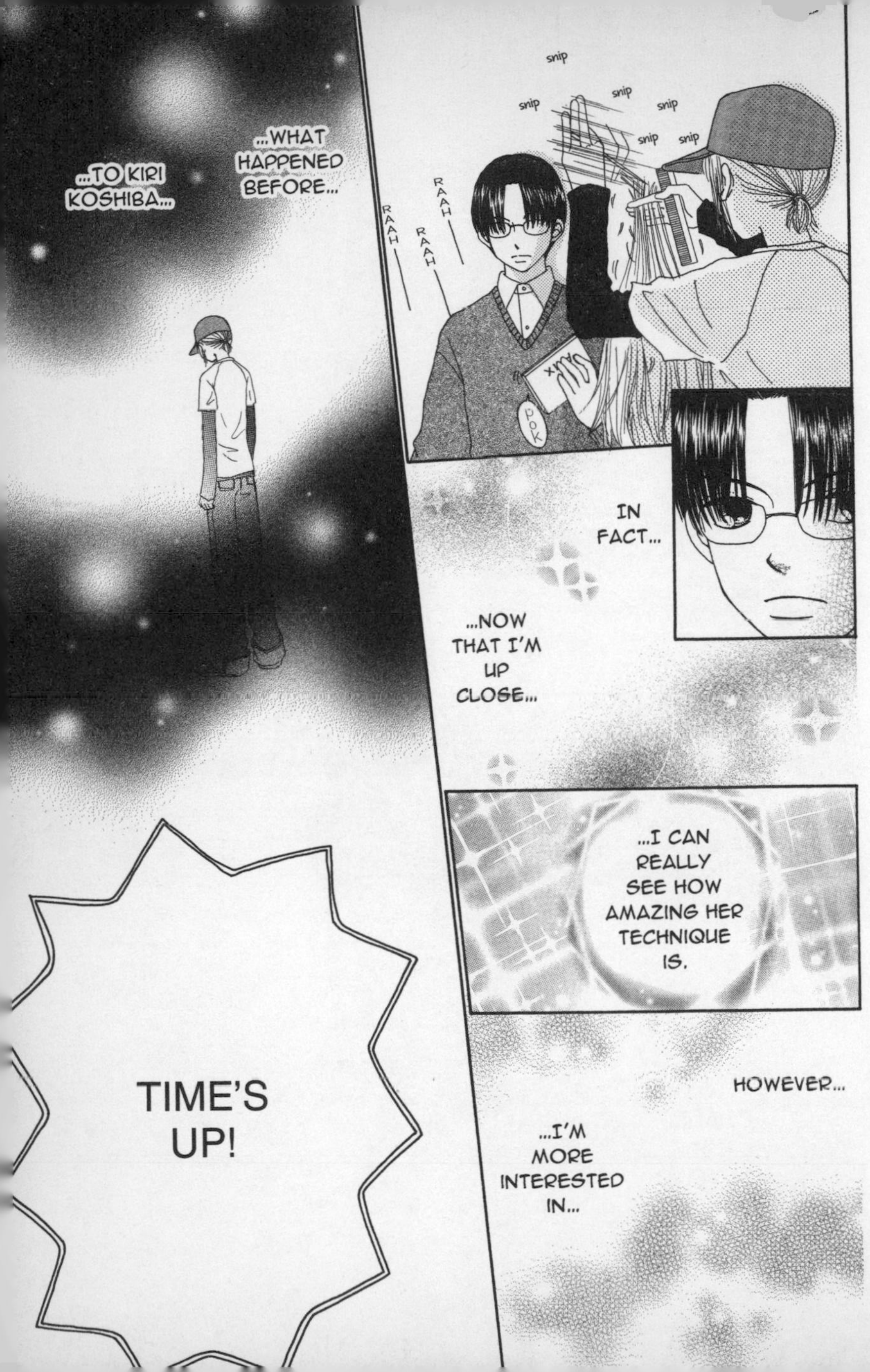
snip
snip
snip
snip
snip
snip
RAAH
RAAH
RAAH
pok
IN FACT...
...NOW THAT I'M UP CLOSE...
...I CAN REALLY SEE HOW AMAZING HER TECHNIQUE IS.
HOWEVER...
...I'M MORE INTERESTED IN...
...WHAT HAPPENED BEFORE...
...TO KIRI KOSHIBA...
TIME'S UP!

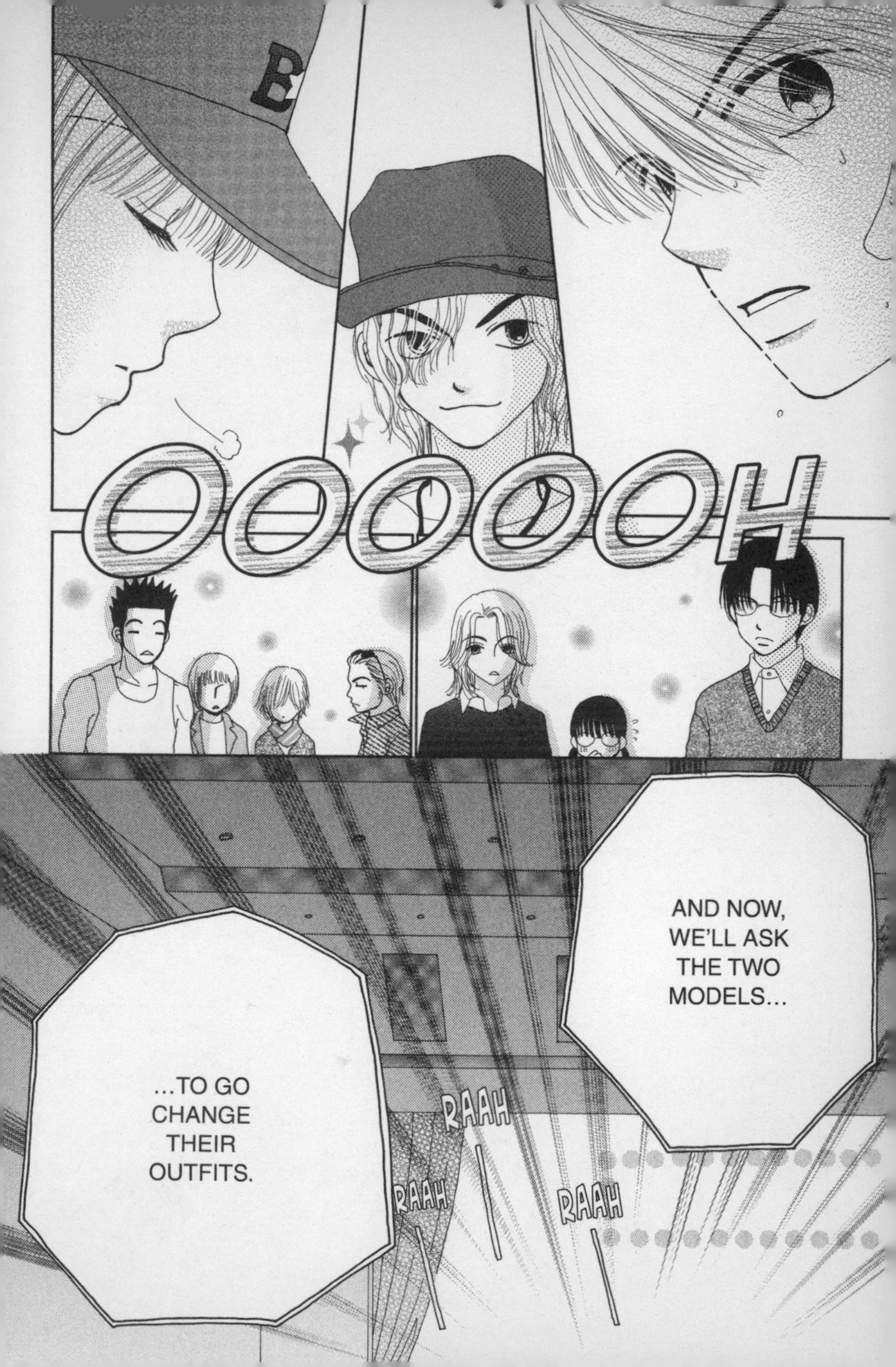
OOOOOH
AND NOW, WE'LL ASK THE TWO MODELS...
RAAH
...TO GO CHANGE THEIR OUTFITS.
RAAH
RAAH

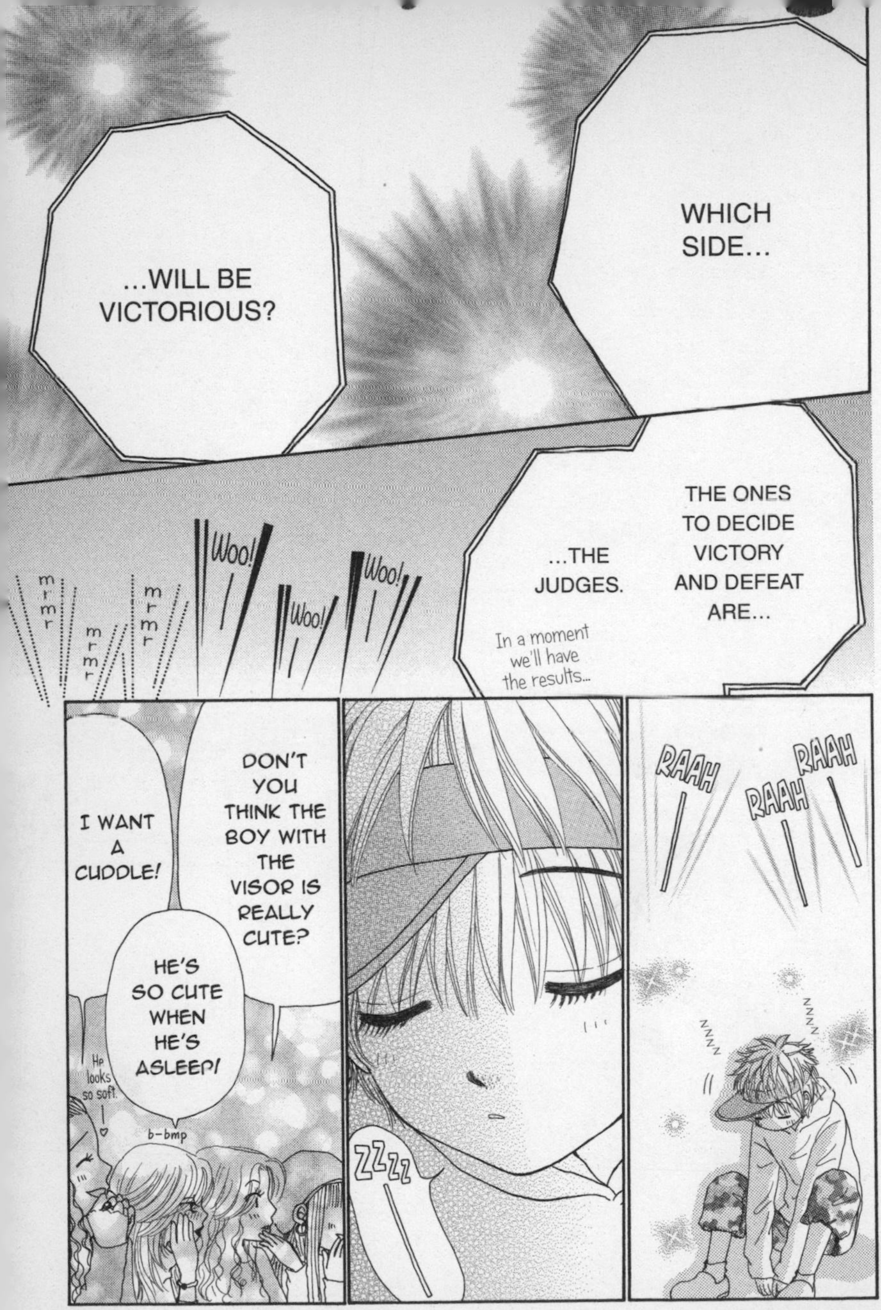
WHICH SIDE...
...WILL BE VICTORIOUS?
THE ONES TO DECIDE VICTORY AND DEFEAT ARE...
...THE JUDGES.
In a moment we'll have the results...
Woo!
Woo!
Woo!
mrmr
mrmr
mrmr
RAAH
RAAH
RAAH
ZZZZ
ZZZZ
ZZzz
DON'T YOU THINK THE BOY WITH THE VISOR IS REALLY CUTE?
I WANT A CUDDLE!
HE'S SO CUTE WHEN HE'S ASLEEP!
He looks so soft.
b-bmp

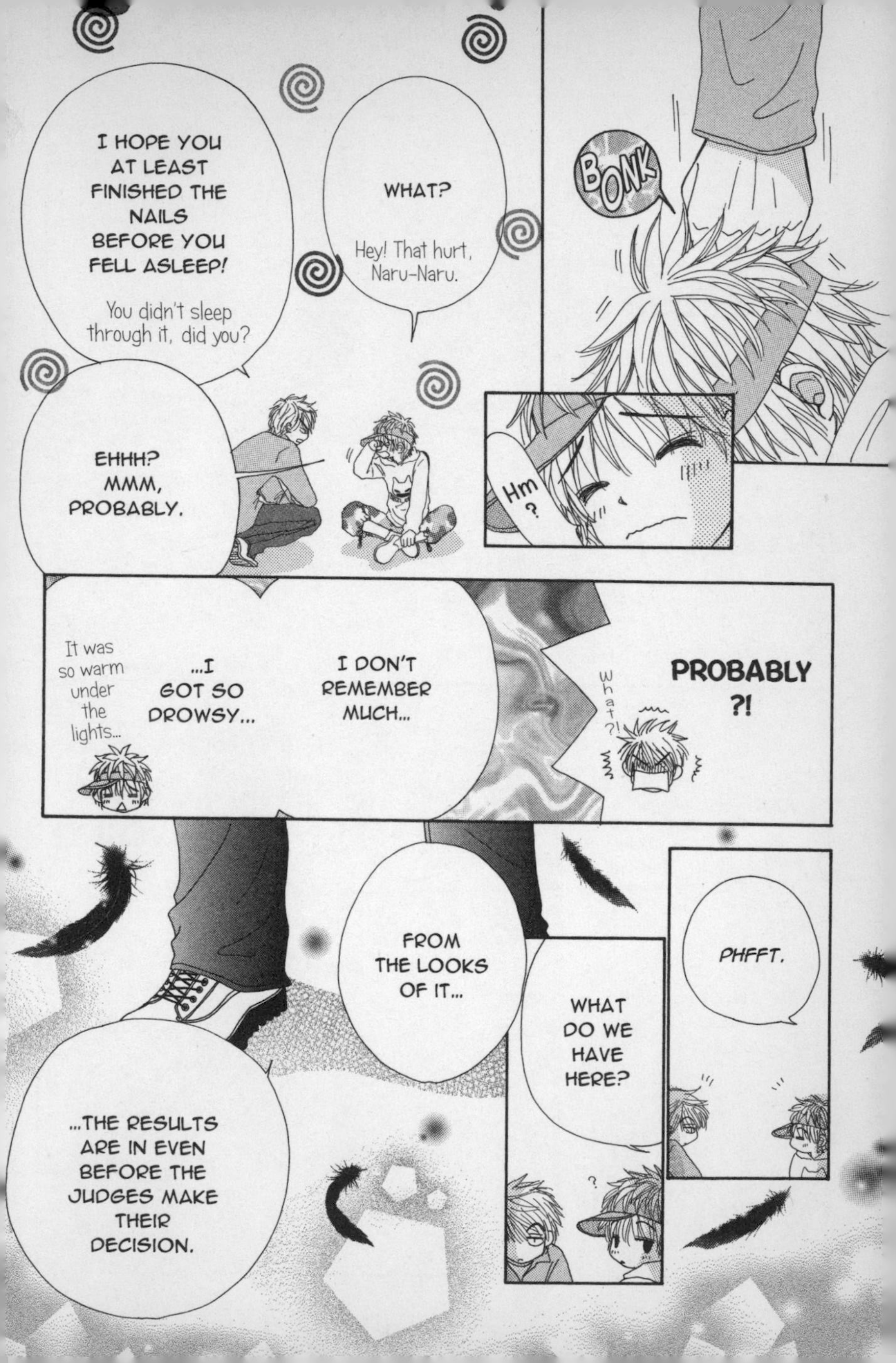

BONK
Hm?
WHAT?
Hey! That hurt, Naru-Naru.
I HOPE YOU AT LEAST FINISHED THE NAILS BEFORE YOU FELL ASLEEP!
You didn't sleep through it, did you?
EHHH? MMM, PROBABLY.
PROBABLY?!
What?!
I DON'T REMEMBER MUCH...
...I GOT SO DROWSY...
It was so warm under the lights...
PHFFT.
WHAT DO WE HAVE HERE?
?
FROM THE LOOKS OF IT...
...THE RESULTS ARE IN EVEN BEFORE THE JUDGES MAKE THEIR DECISION.

READ THIS WAY

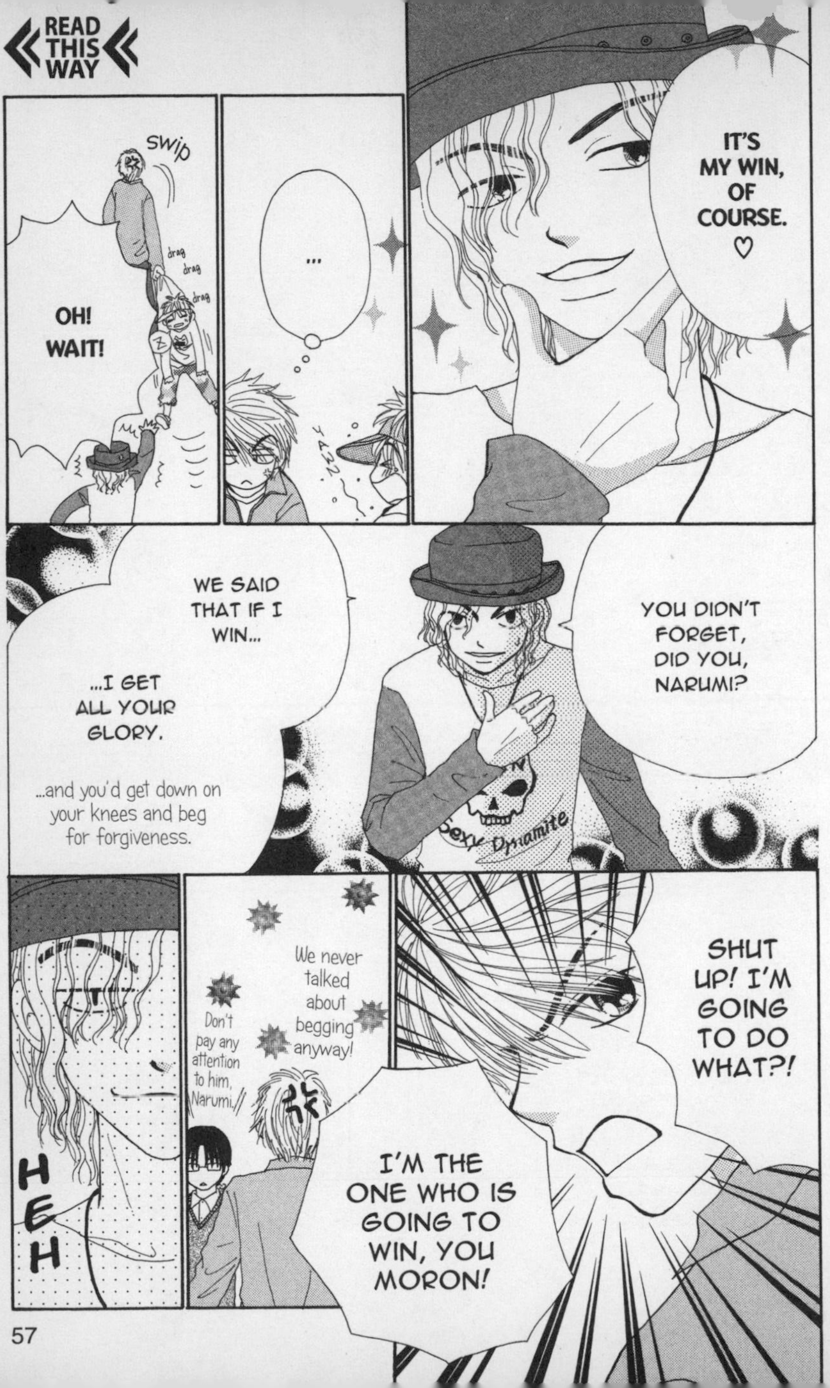
IT'S MY WIN, OF COURSE. ♡
...
swip
drag drag drag
OH! WAIT!
YOU DIDN'T FORGET, DID YOU, NARUMI?
WE SAID THAT IF I WIN...
...I GET ALL YOUR GLORY.
...and you'd get down on your knees and beg for forgiveness.
SHUT UP! I'M GOING TO DO WHAT?!
I'M THE ONE WHO IS GOING TO WIN, YOU MORON!
We never talked about begging anyway!
Don't pay any attention to him, Narumi.//
HEH

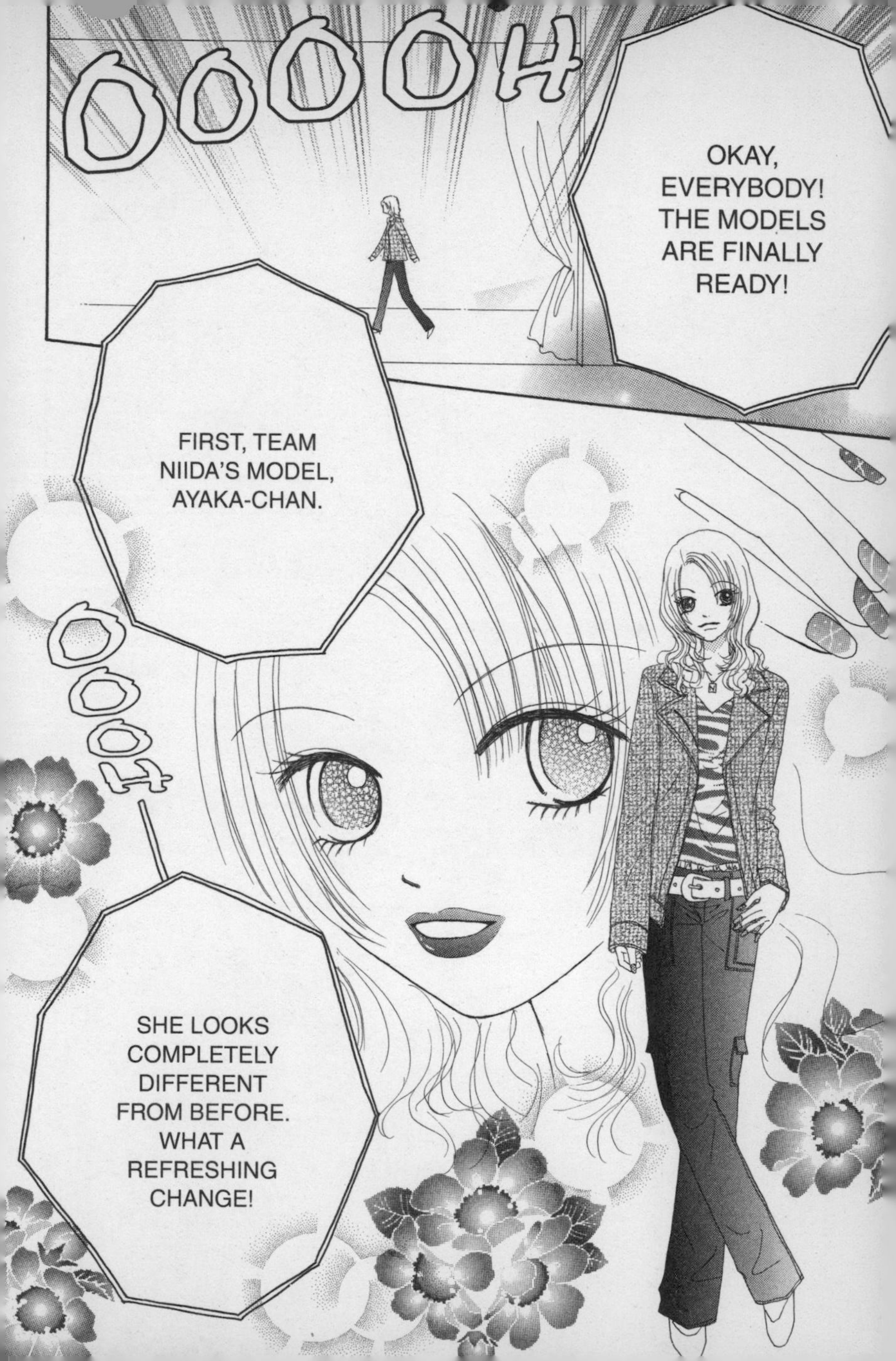
OKAY, EVERYBODY! THE MODELS ARE FINALLY READY!
OOOOH
FIRST, TEAM NIIDA'S MODEL, AYAKA-CHAN.
OOOOH
SHE LOOKS COMPLETELY DIFFERENT FROM BEFORE. WHAT A REFRESHING CHANGE!

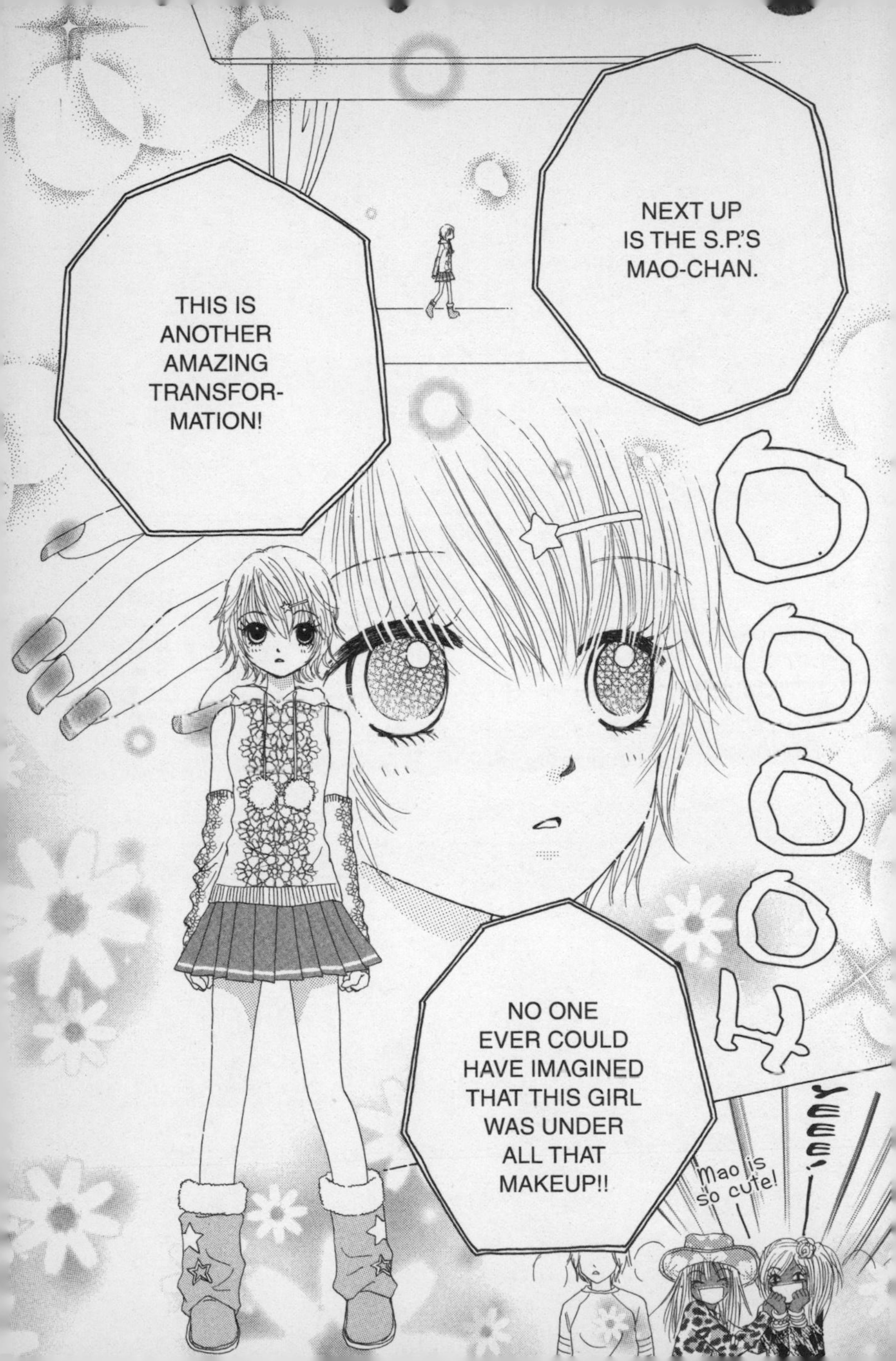
NEXT UP IS THE S.P.'S MAO-CHAN.
THIS IS ANOTHER AMAZING TRANSFOR-MATION!
OOOOH
NO ONE EVER COULD HAVE IMAGINED THAT THIS GIRL WAS UNDER ALL THAT MAKEUP!!
YEEES!
Mao is so cute!

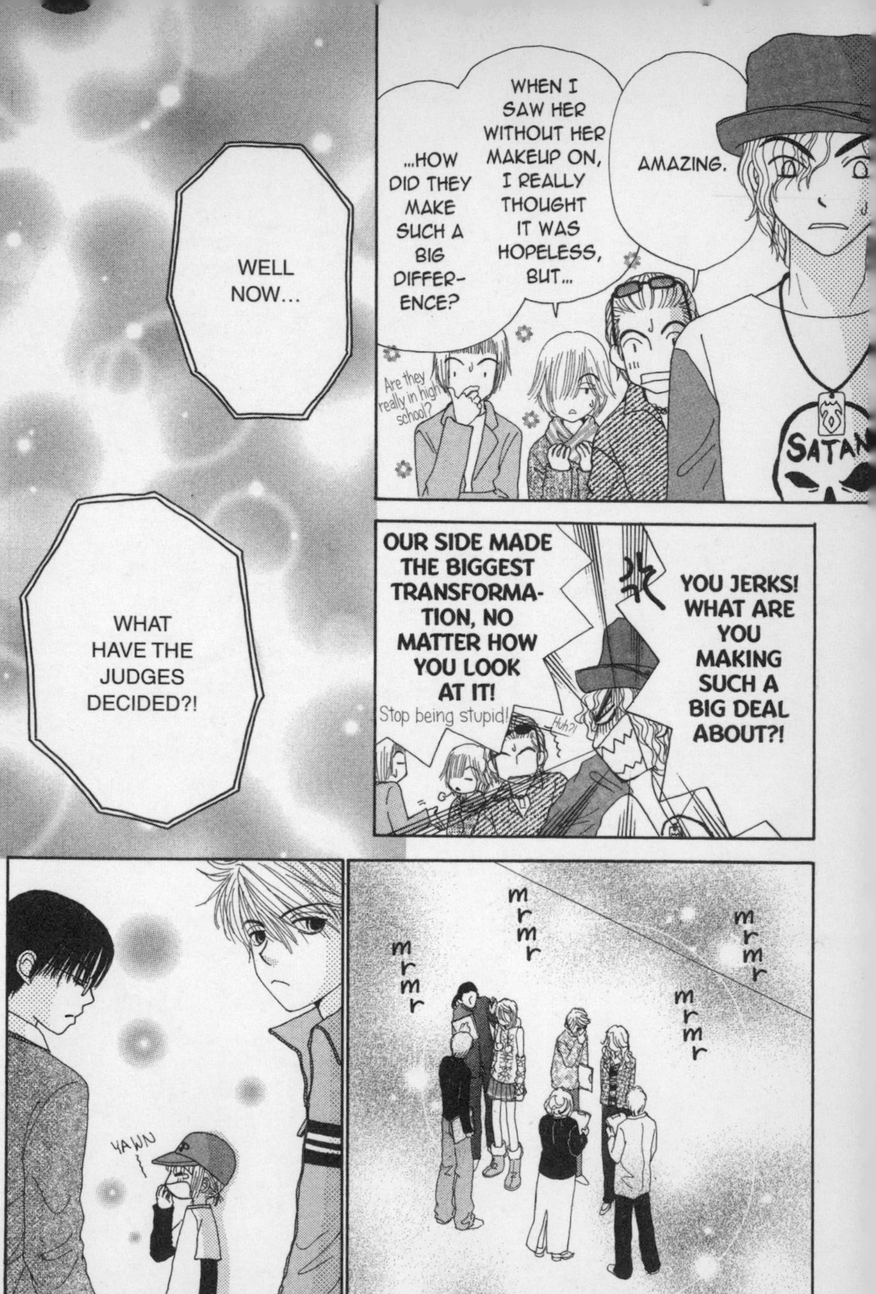
AMAZING.
WHEN I SAW HER WITHOUT HER MAKEUP ON, I REALLY THOUGHT IT WAS HOPELESS, BUT...
...HOW DID THEY MAKE SUCH A BIG DIFFER-ENCE?
Are they really in high school?
YOU JERKS! WHAT ARE YOU MAKING SUCH A BIG DEAL ABOUT?!
Huh?!
OUR SIDE MADE THE BIGGEST TRANSFORMA-TION, NO MATTER HOW YOU LOOK AT IT!
Stop being stupid!
WELL NOW...
WHAT HAVE THE JUDGES DECIDED?!
mrmr
mrmr
mrmr
mrmr
YAWN

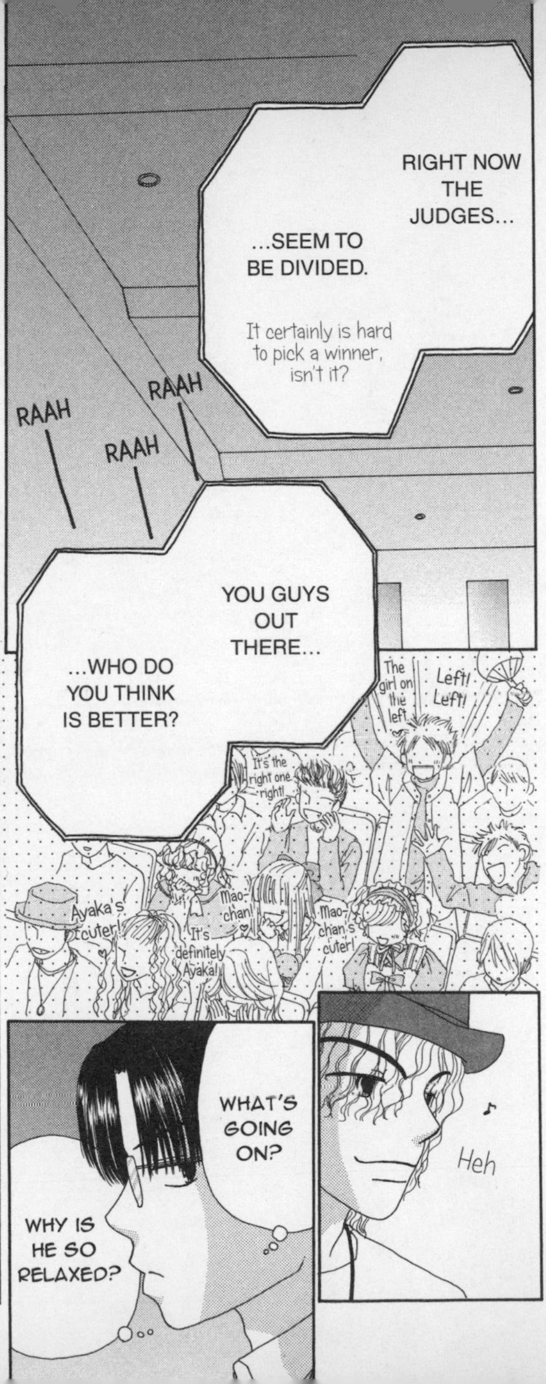
RIGHT NOW THE JUDGES...
...SEEM TO BE DIVIDED.
It certainly is hard to pick a winner, isn't it?
RAAH
RAAH
RAAH
YOU GUYS OUT THERE...
...WHO DO YOU THINK IS BETTER?
The girl on the left.
Left! Left!
It's the right one, right!
Mao-chan's cuter!
Mao-chan!
It's definitely Ayaka!
Ayaka's cuter!
Heh
WHAT'S GOING ON?
WHY IS HE SO RELAXED?

K's Club Talk

Ken-niichan is one of the characters who only shows up a little bit. Even so, he has gotten really popular.

☆Here's a letter from Natsuki-chan of Hiroshima prefecture:

> I love reading BP every chance I get. My mother is a BP fan too! She really likes Ken-niichan. She says she would be so happy if we had a Ken-niichan at our house so we'd be treated to a massage every day.

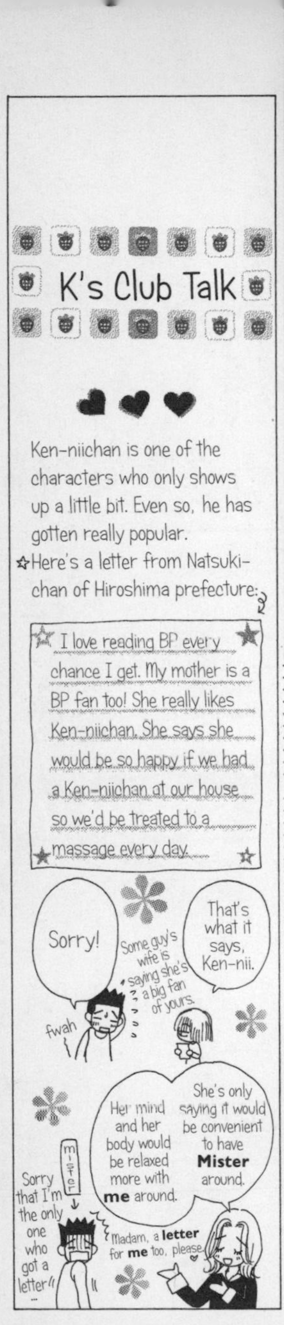
Sorry!
That's what it says, Ken-nii.
Some guy's wife is saying she's a big fan of yours.
fwah
She's only saying it would be convenient to have **Mister** around.
Her mind and her body would be relaxed more with **me** around.
mister
Sorry that I'm the only one who got a letter...
Madam, a **letter** for **me** too, please.

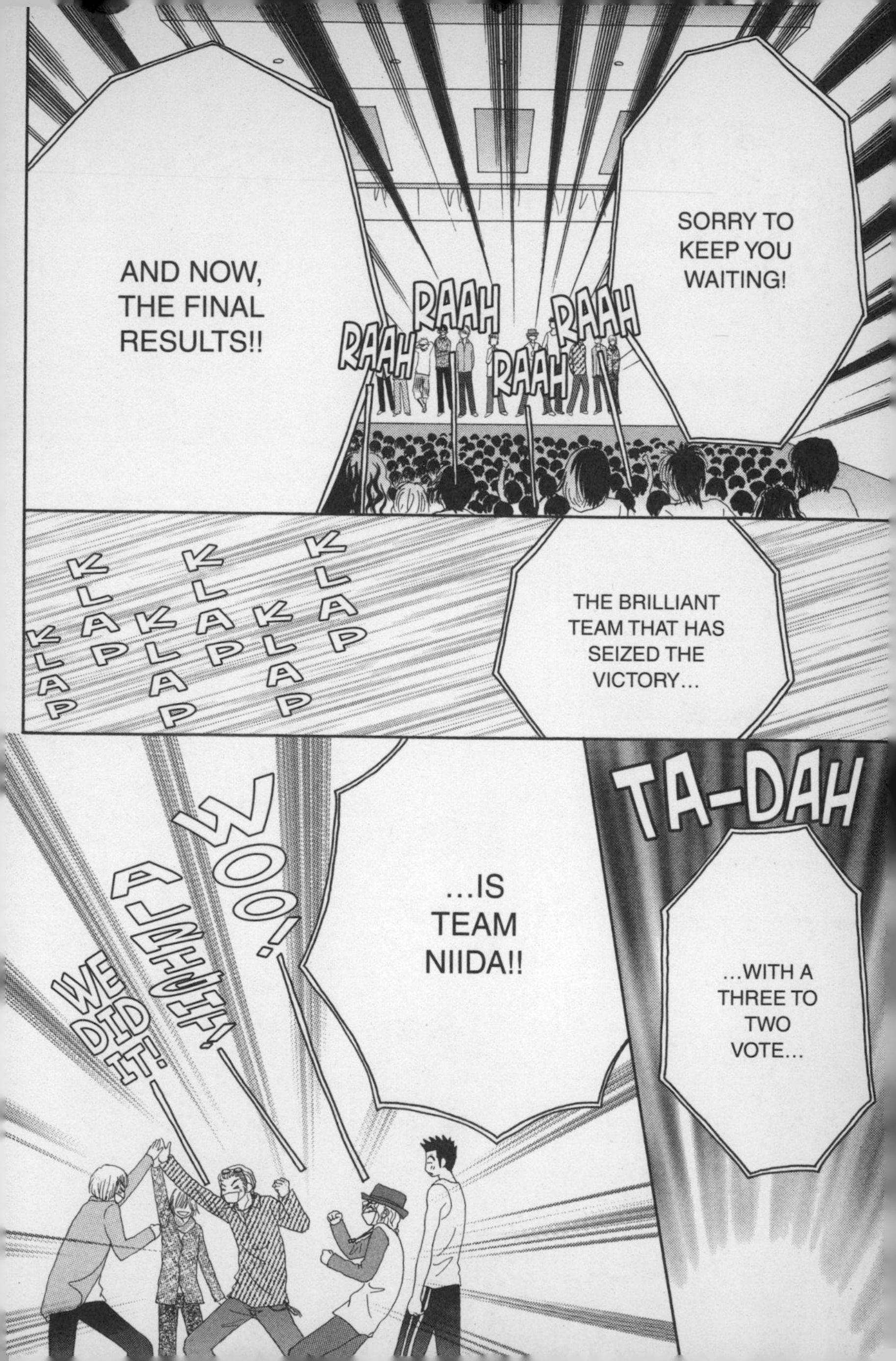
SORRY TO KEEP YOU WAITING!
AND NOW, THE FINAL RESULTS!!
RAAH
RAAH
RAAH
RAAH
THE BRILLIANT TEAM THAT HAS SEIZED THE VICTORY...
KLAP KLAP KLAP KLAP KLAP KLAP
TA-DAH
...WITH A THREE TO TWO VOTE...
...IS TEAM NIIDA!!
WOO!
ALRIGHT!
WE DID IT!

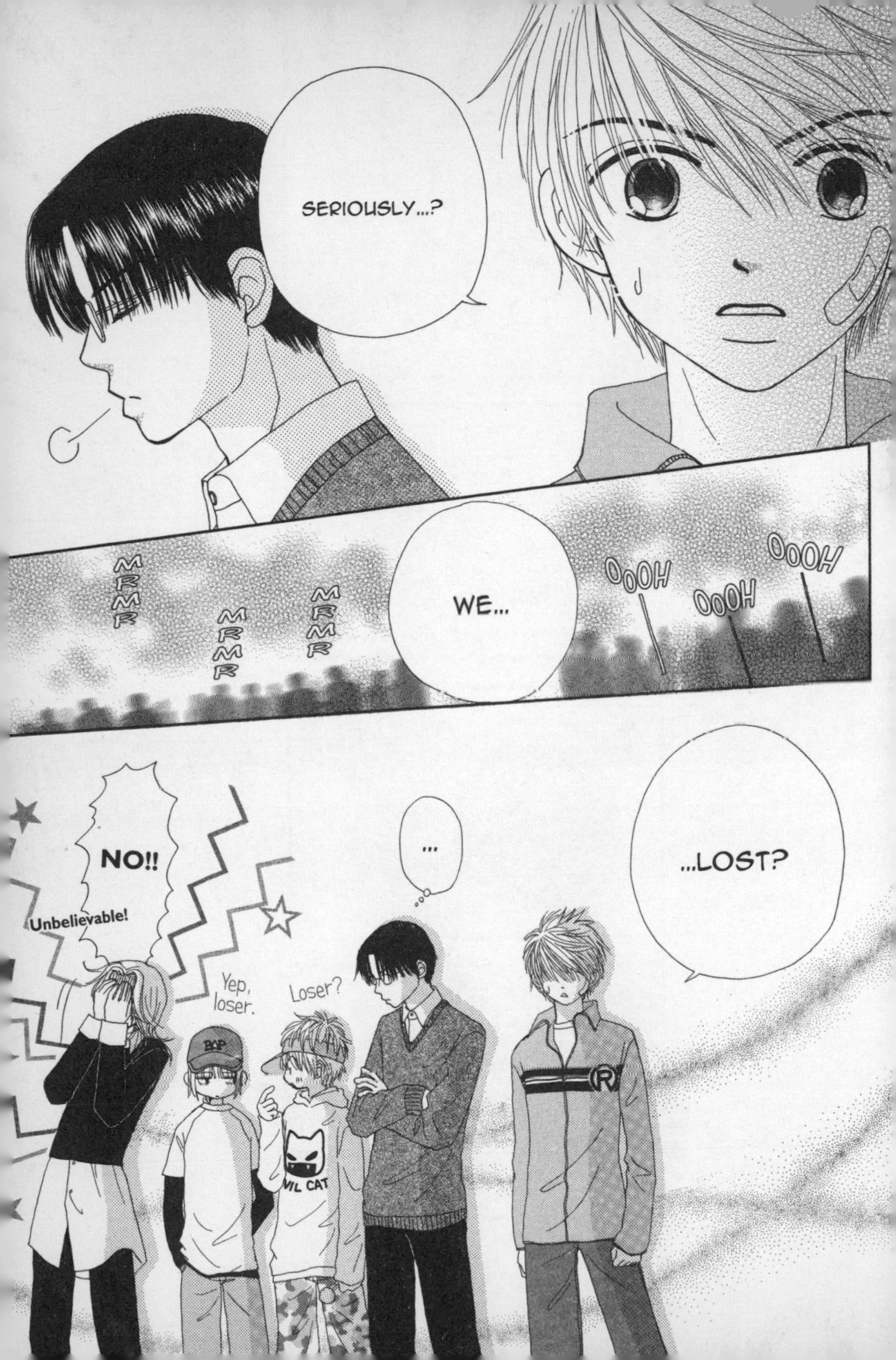
SERIOUSLY...?
OOOH
OOOH
OOOH
WE...
MRMR
MRMR
MRMR
...LOST?
...
Loser?
Yep, loser.
NO!!
Unbelievable!

MANGA THEATER ①

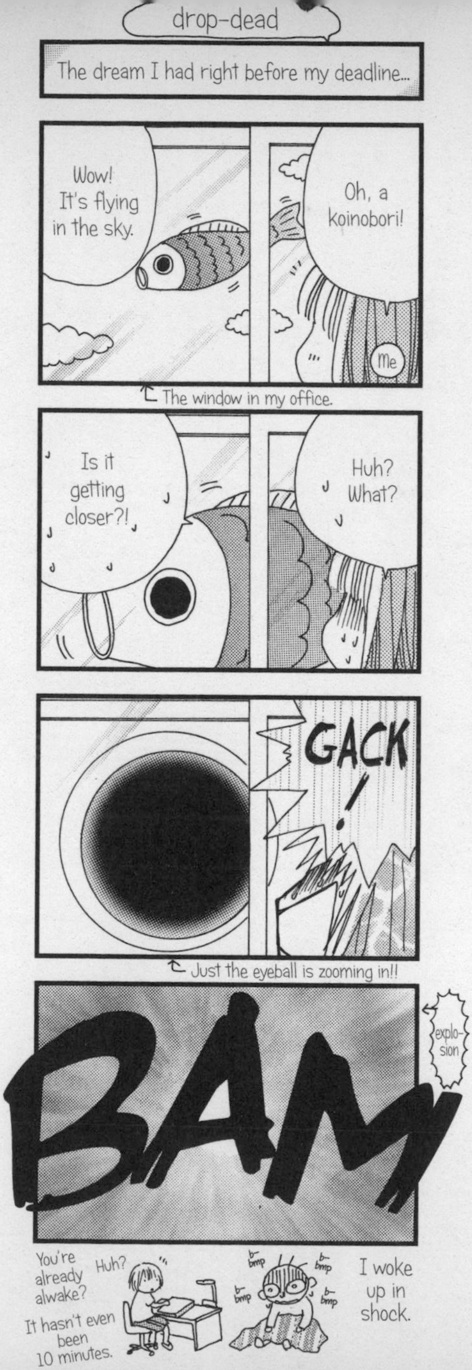
drop-dead
The dream I had right before my deadline...
Oh, a koinobori!
Wow! It's flying in the sky.
Me
The window in my office.
Huh? What?
Is it getting closer?!
GACK!
Just the eyeball is zooming in!!
explosion
BAM
I woke up in shock.
b-bmp
b-bmp
b-bmp
b-bmp
Huh?
You're already alwake?
It hasn't even been 10 minutes.

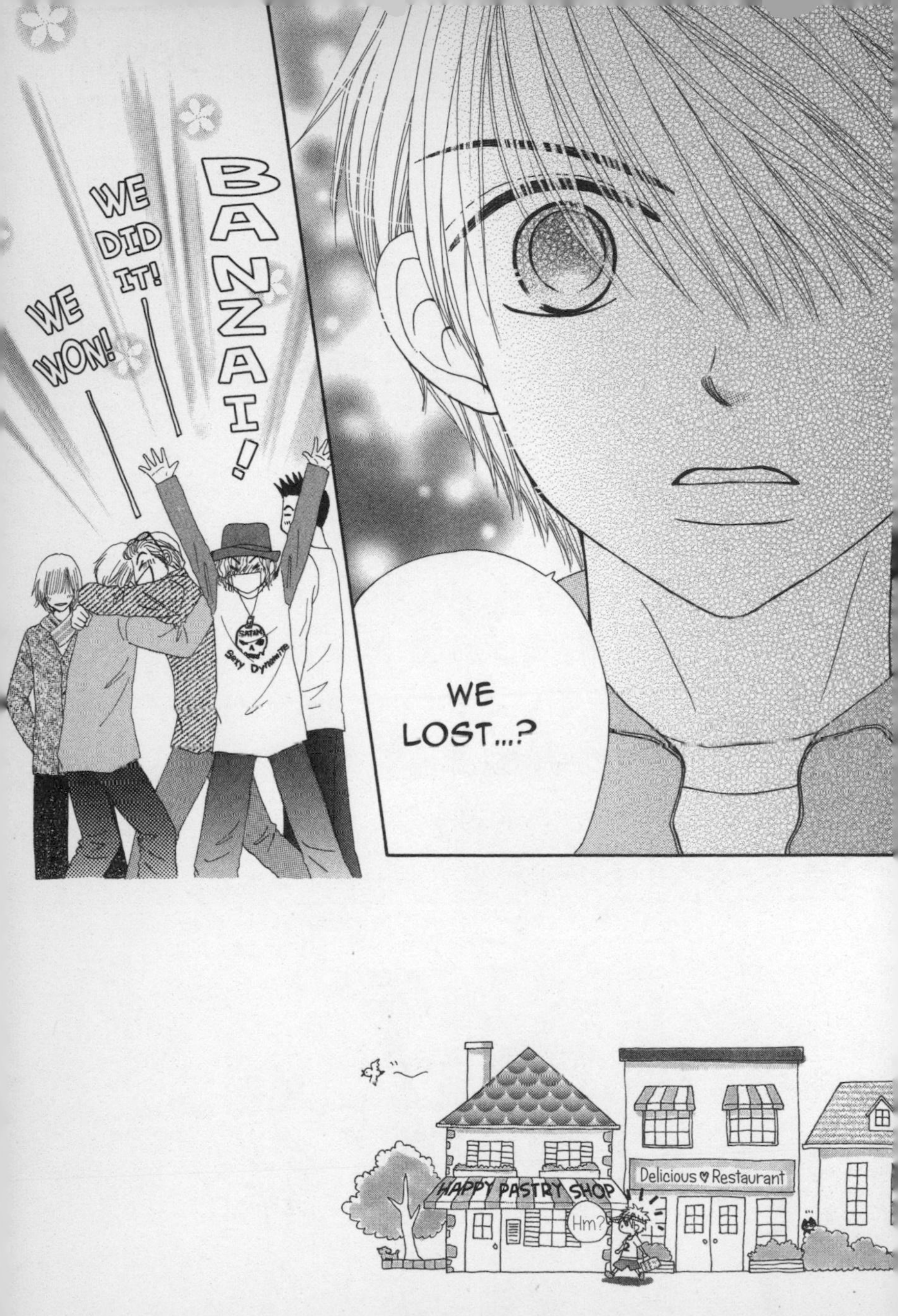
WE LOST...?
BANZAI!
WE DID IT!
WE WON!
HAPPY PASTRY SHOP
Hm?
Delicious ♥ Restaurant

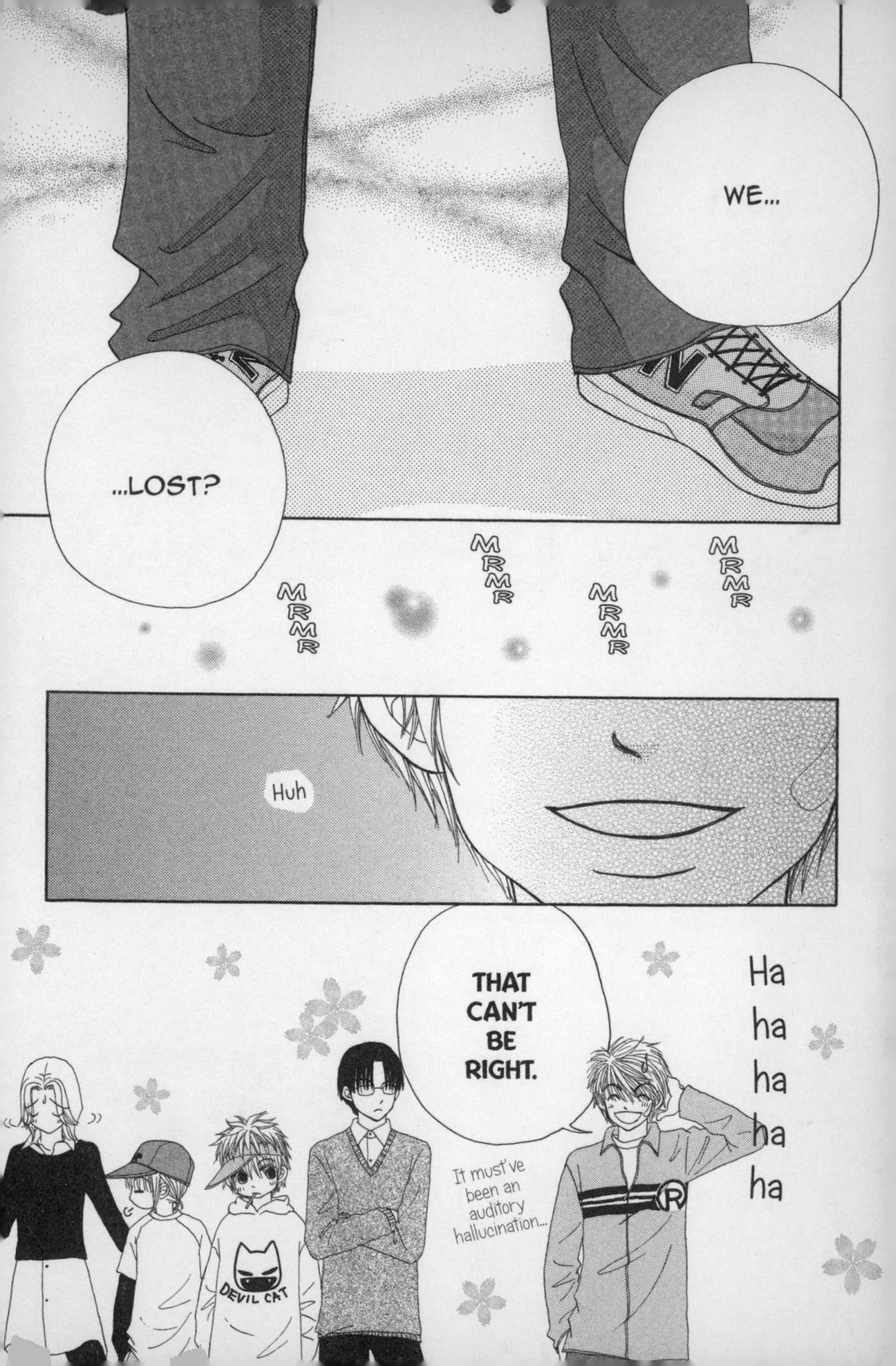
WE...
...LOST?
MRMR
MRMR
MRMR
MRMR
Huh
Ha ha ha ha ha
THAT CAN'T BE RIGHT.
It must've been an auditory hallucination...
DEVIL CAT

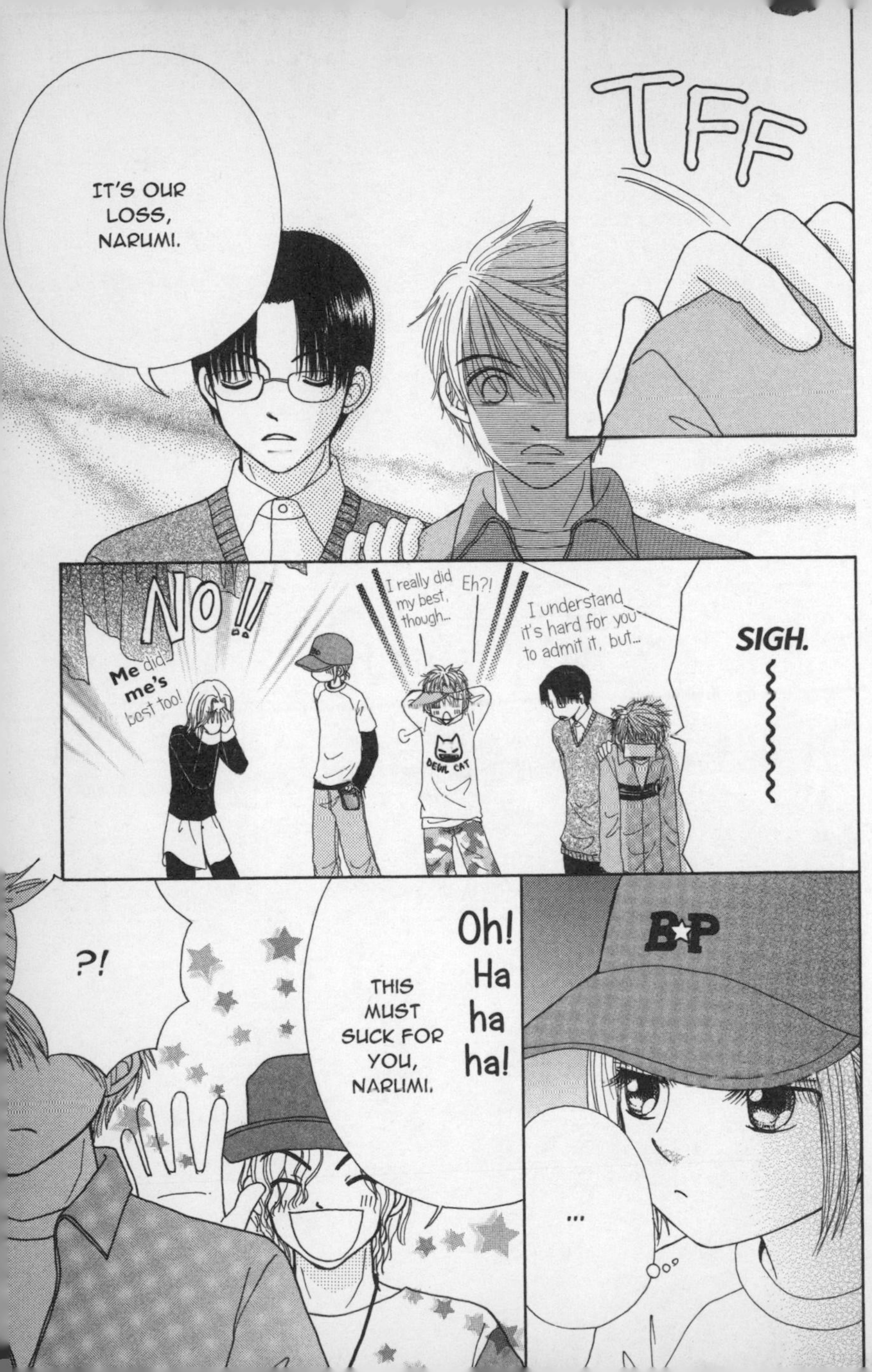

TFF
IT'S OUR LOSS, NARUMI.
SIGH.
I understand it's hard for you to admit it, but...
Eh?!
I really did my best, though...
NO!!
Me did me's best too!
B☆P
...
Oh! Ha ha ha!
THIS MUST SUCK FOR YOU, NARUMI.
?!

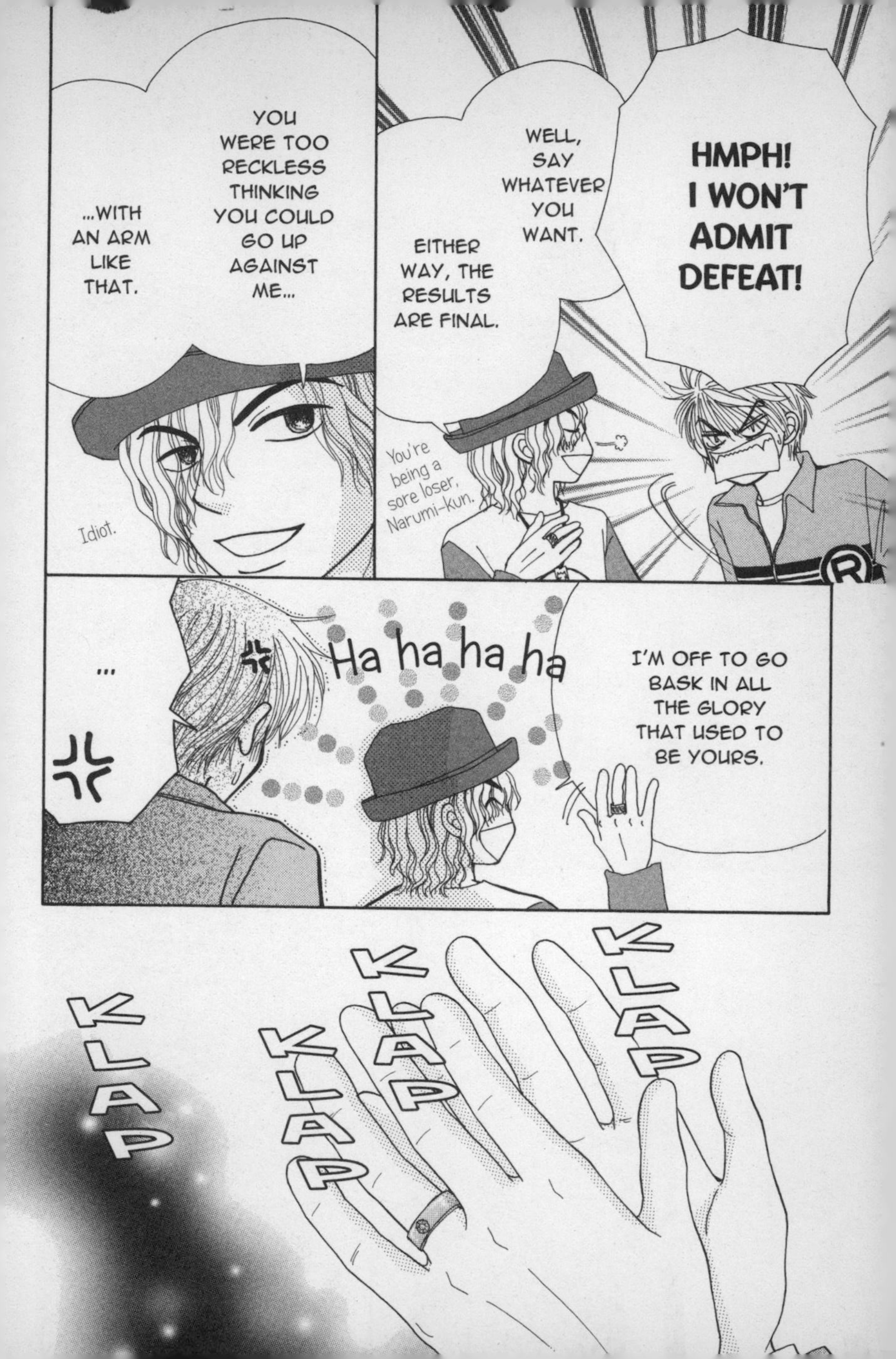
HMPH! I WON'T ADMIT DEFEAT!
WELL, SAY WHATEVER YOU WANT.
EITHER WAY, THE RESULTS ARE FINAL.
You're being a sore loser, Narumi-kun.
YOU WERE TOO RECKLESS THINKING YOU COULD GO UP AGAINST ME...
...WITH AN ARM LIKE THAT.
Idiot.
I'M OFF TO GO BASK IN ALL THE GLORY THAT USED TO BE YOURS.
Ha ha ha ha
...
KLAP
KLAP
KLAP
KLAP

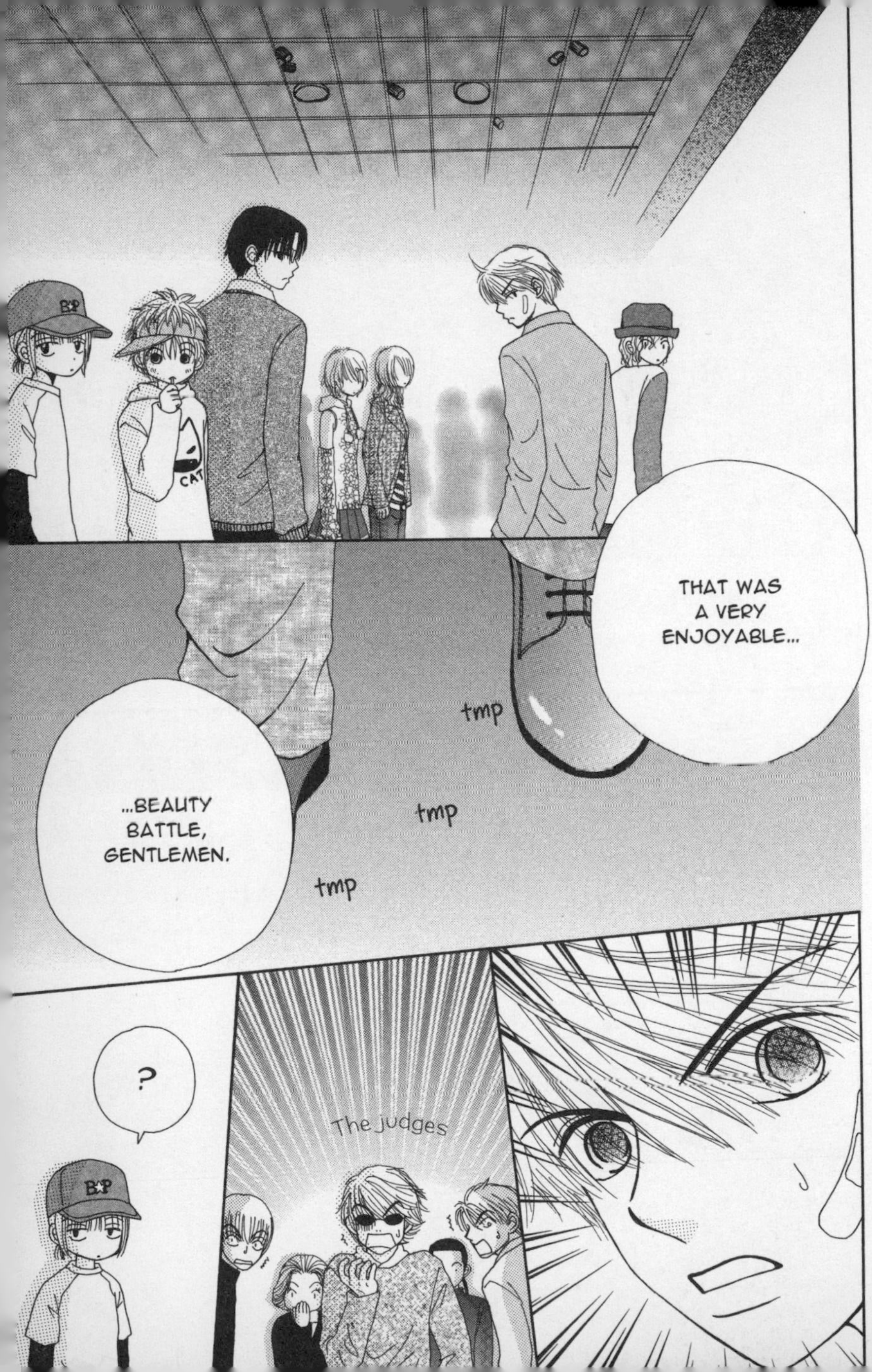
THAT WAS A VERY ENJOYABLE...
tmp
...BEAUTY BATTLE, GENTLEMEN.
tmp
tmp
The judges
?

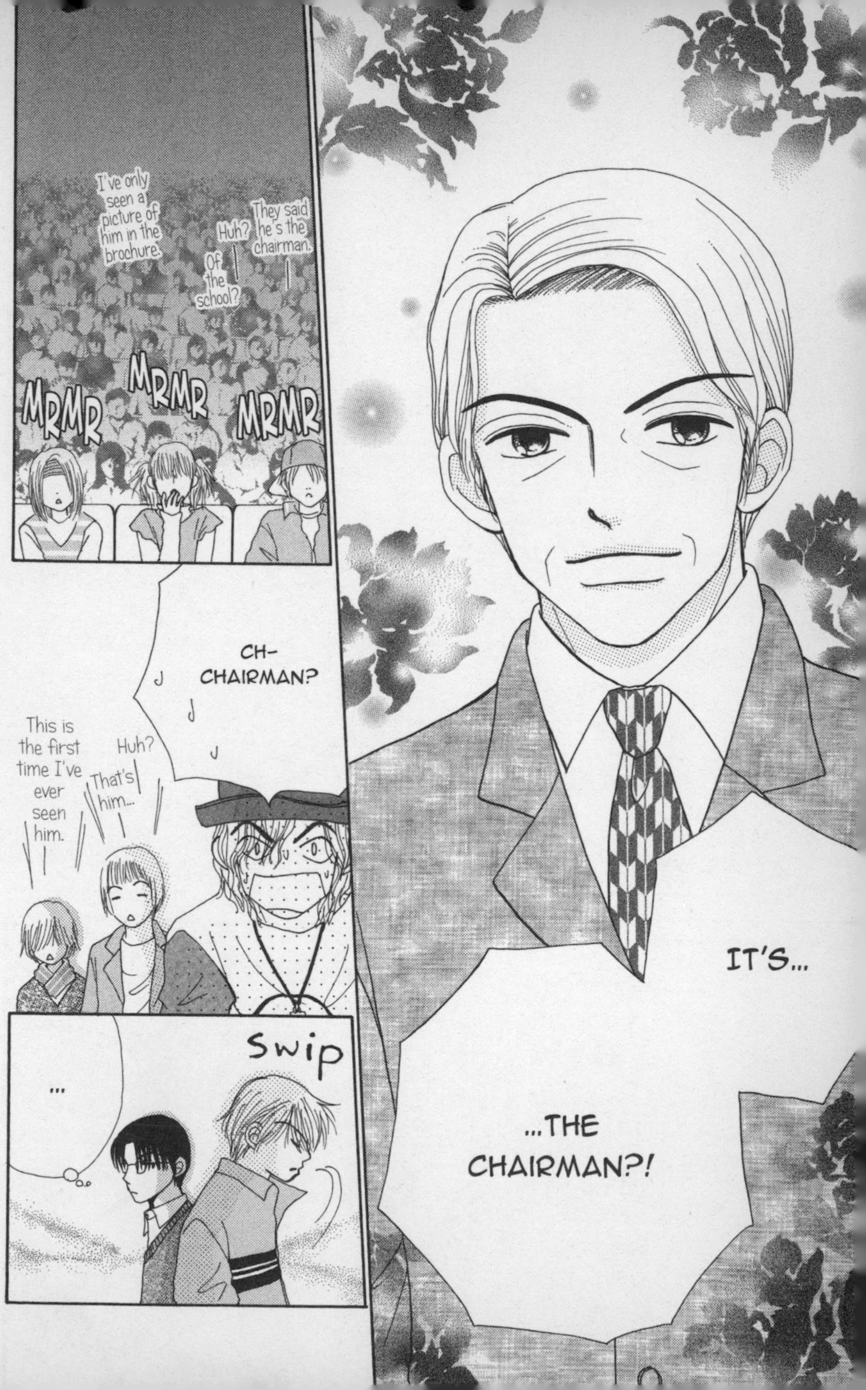
IT'S...
...THE CHAIRMAN?!
They said he's the chairman.
Huh?
Of the school?
I've only seen a picture of him in the brochure.
MRMR
MRMR
MRMR
CH-CHAIRMAN?
Huh? That's him...
This is the first time I've ever seen him.
Swip
...

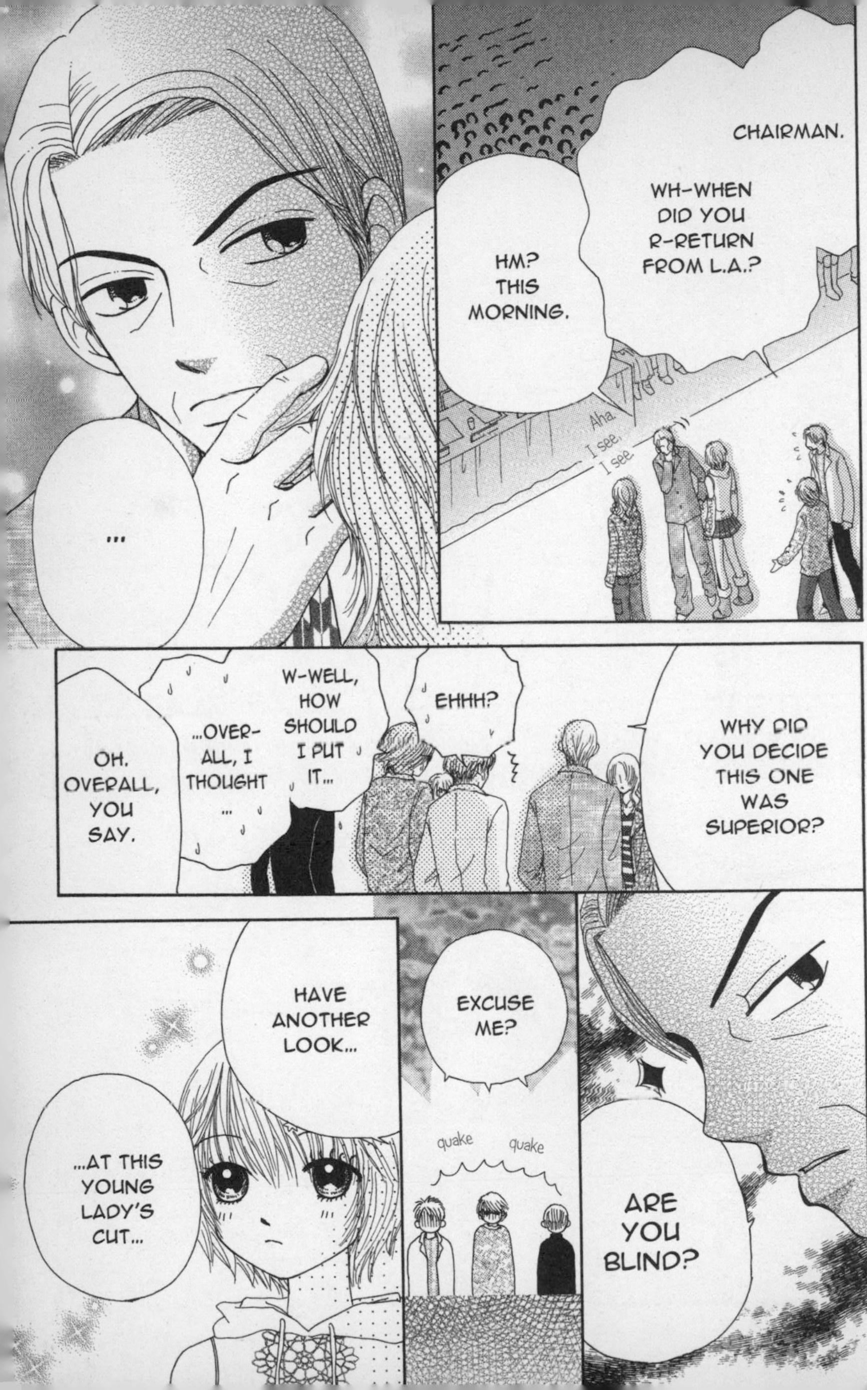
CHAIRMAN.
WH-WHEN DID YOU R-RETURN FROM L.A.?
HM? THIS MORNING.
Aha. I see. I see.
...
WHY DID YOU DECIDE THIS ONE WAS SUPERIOR?
EHHH?
W-WELL, HOW SHOULD I PUT IT...
...OVER-ALL, I THOUGHT ...
OH. OVERALL, YOU SAY.
ARE YOU BLIND?
EXCUSE ME?
quake quake
HAVE ANOTHER LOOK...
...AT THIS YOUNG LADY'S CUT...

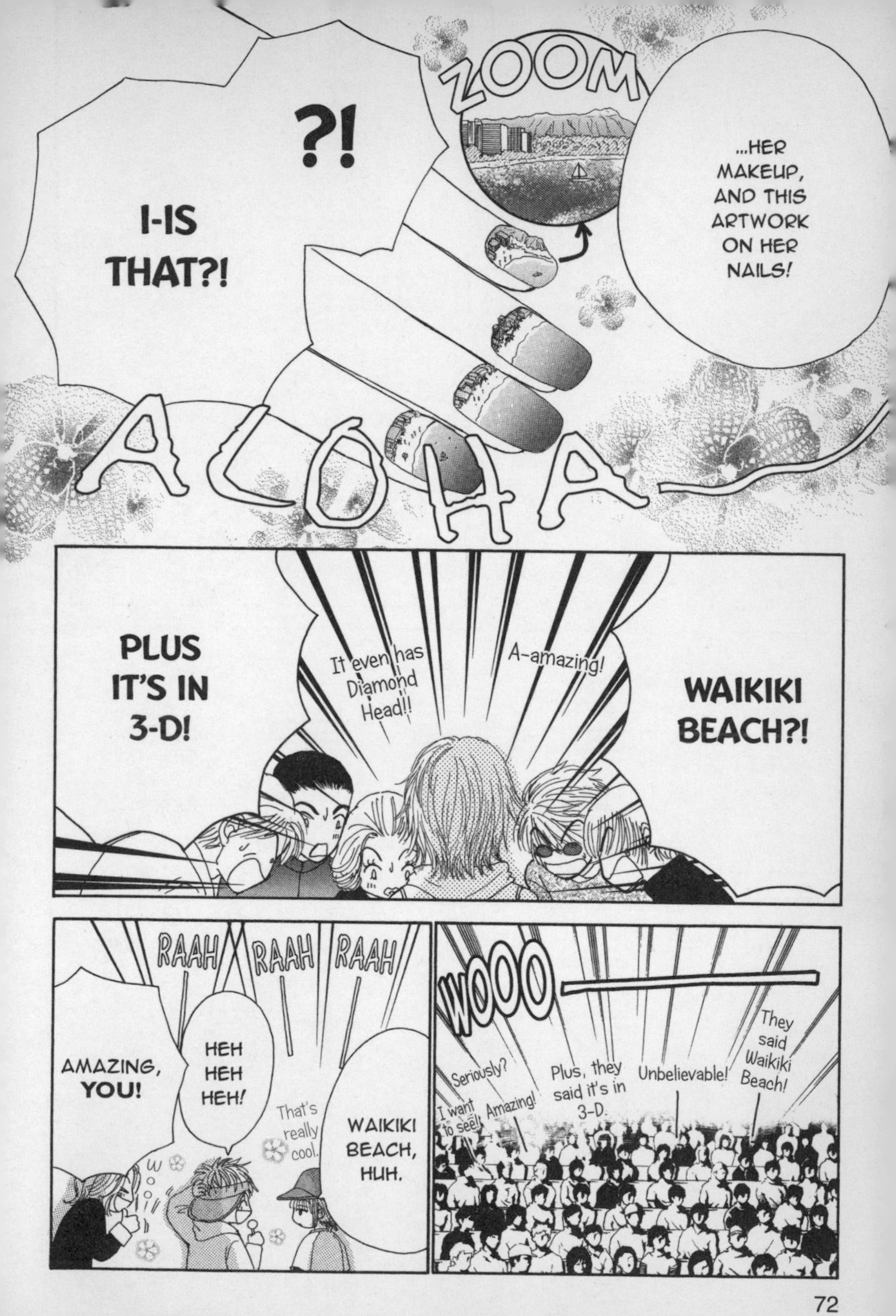
...HER MAKEUP, AND THIS ARTWORK ON HER NAILS!
ZOOM
?!
I-IS THAT?!
ALOHA
WAIKIKI BEACH?!
A-amazing!
It even has Diamond Head!!
PLUS IT'S IN 3-D!
WOOO
They said Waikiki Beach!
Unbelievable!
Plus, they said it's in 3-D.
Seriously?
Amazing!
I want to see!
RAAH
RAAH
RAAH
WAIKIKI BEACH, HUH.
That's really cool.
HEH HEH HEH!
AMAZING, YOU!

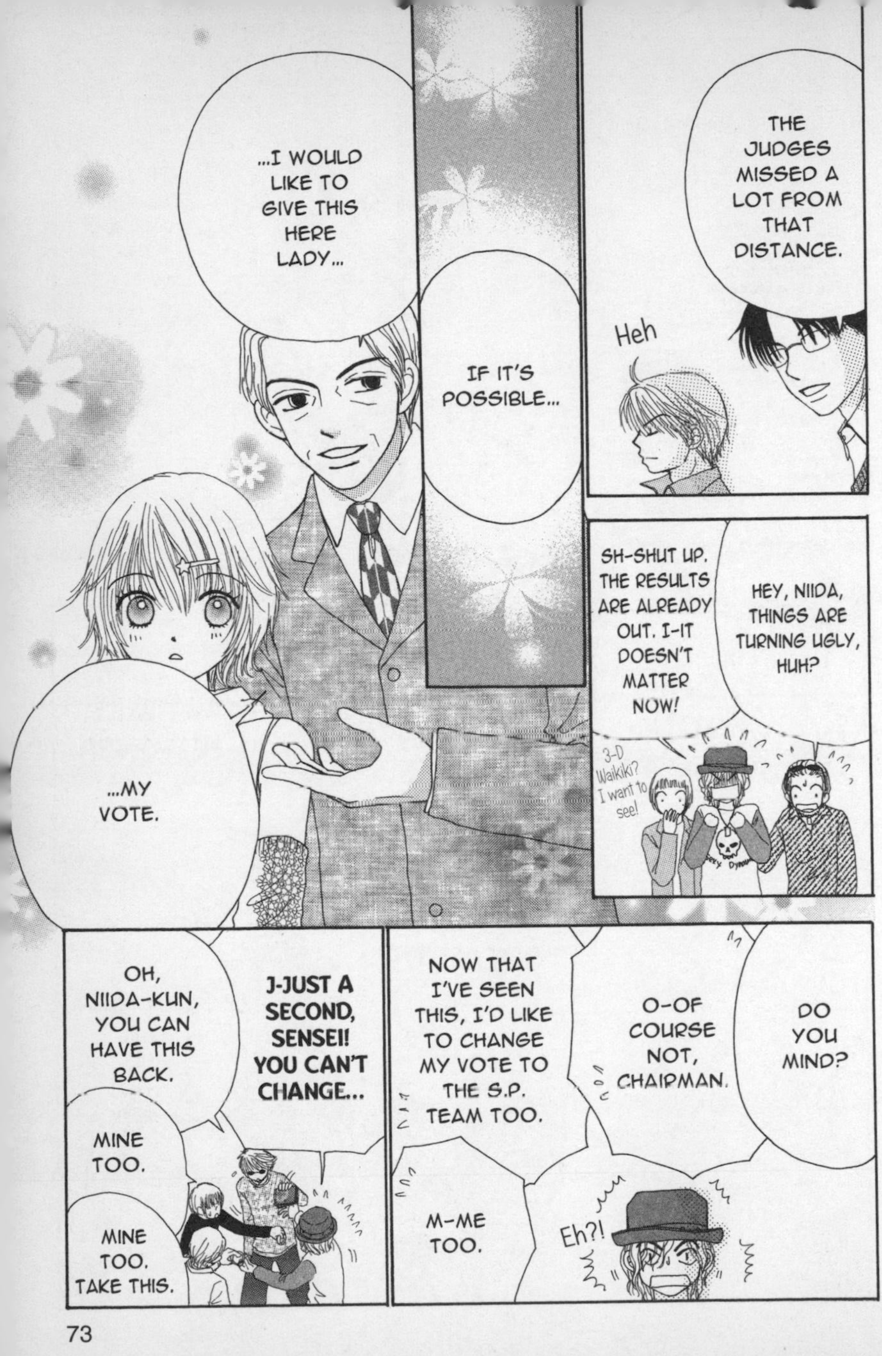
THE JUDGES MISSED A LOT FROM THAT DISTANCE.
Heh
HEY, NIIDA, THINGS ARE TURNING UGLY, HUH?
SH-SHUT UP. THE RESULTS ARE ALREADY OUT. I-IT DOESN'T MATTER NOW!
3-D Waikiki? I want to see!
IF IT'S POSSIBLE...
...I WOULD LIKE TO GIVE THIS HERE LADY...
...MY VOTE.
DO YOU MIND?
O-OF COURSE NOT, CHAIRMAN.
NOW THAT I'VE SEEN THIS, I'D LIKE TO CHANGE MY VOTE TO THE S.P. TEAM TOO.
Eh?!
M-ME TOO.
J-JUST A SECOND, SENSEI! YOU CAN'T CHANGE...
OH, NIIDA-KUN, YOU CAN HAVE THIS BACK.
MINE TOO.
MINE TOO. TAKE THIS.

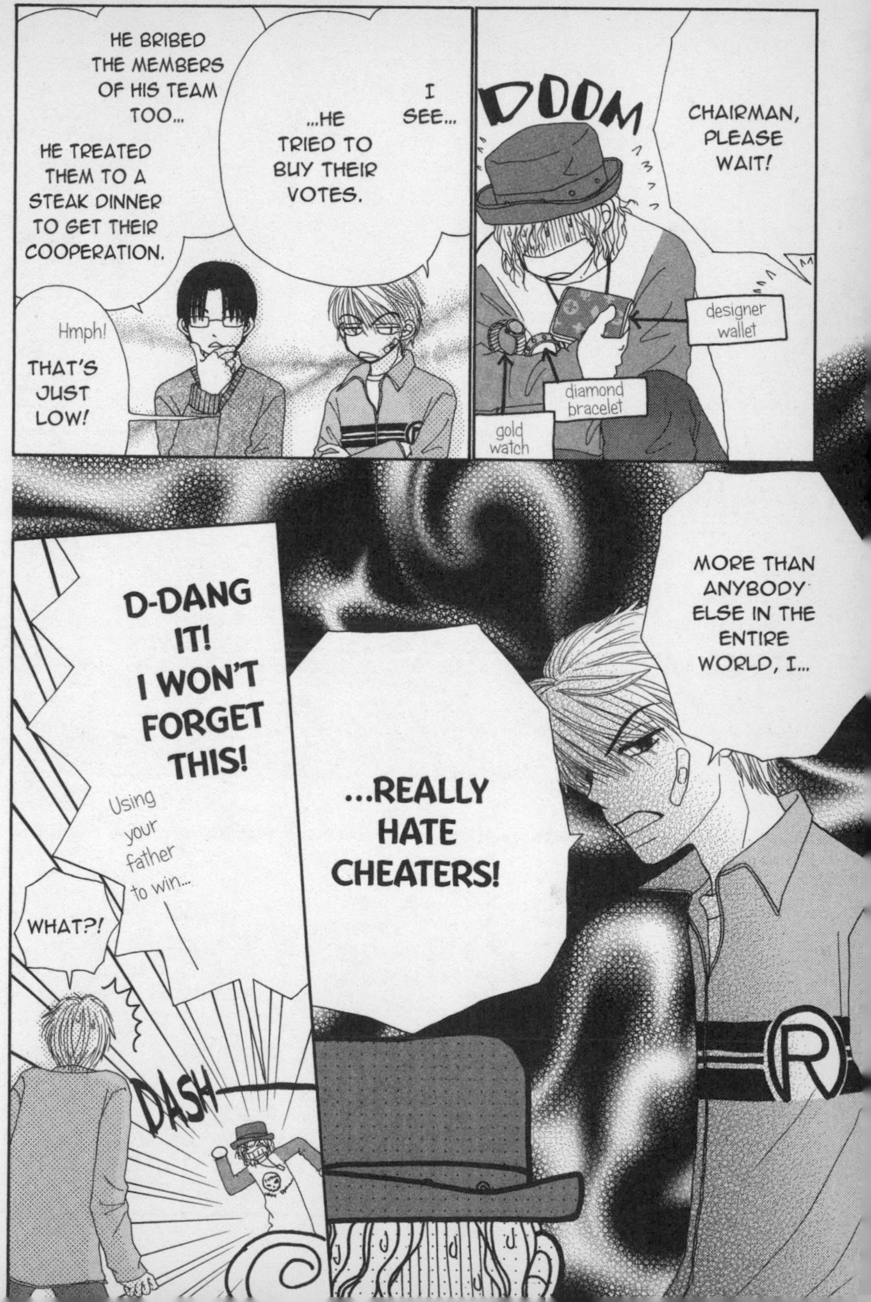
DOOM
CHAIRMAN, PLEASE WAIT!
designer wallet
diamond bracelet
gold watch
I SEE... ...HE TRIED TO BUY THEIR VOTES.
HE BRIBED THE MEMBERS OF HIS TEAM TOO...
HE TREATED THEM TO A STEAK DINNER TO GET THEIR COOPERATION.
Hmph! THAT'S JUST LOW!
MORE THAN ANYBODY ELSE IN THE ENTIRE WORLD, I...
...REALLY HATE CHEATERS!
D-DANG IT! I WON'T FORGET THIS!
Using your father to win...
WHAT?!
DASH

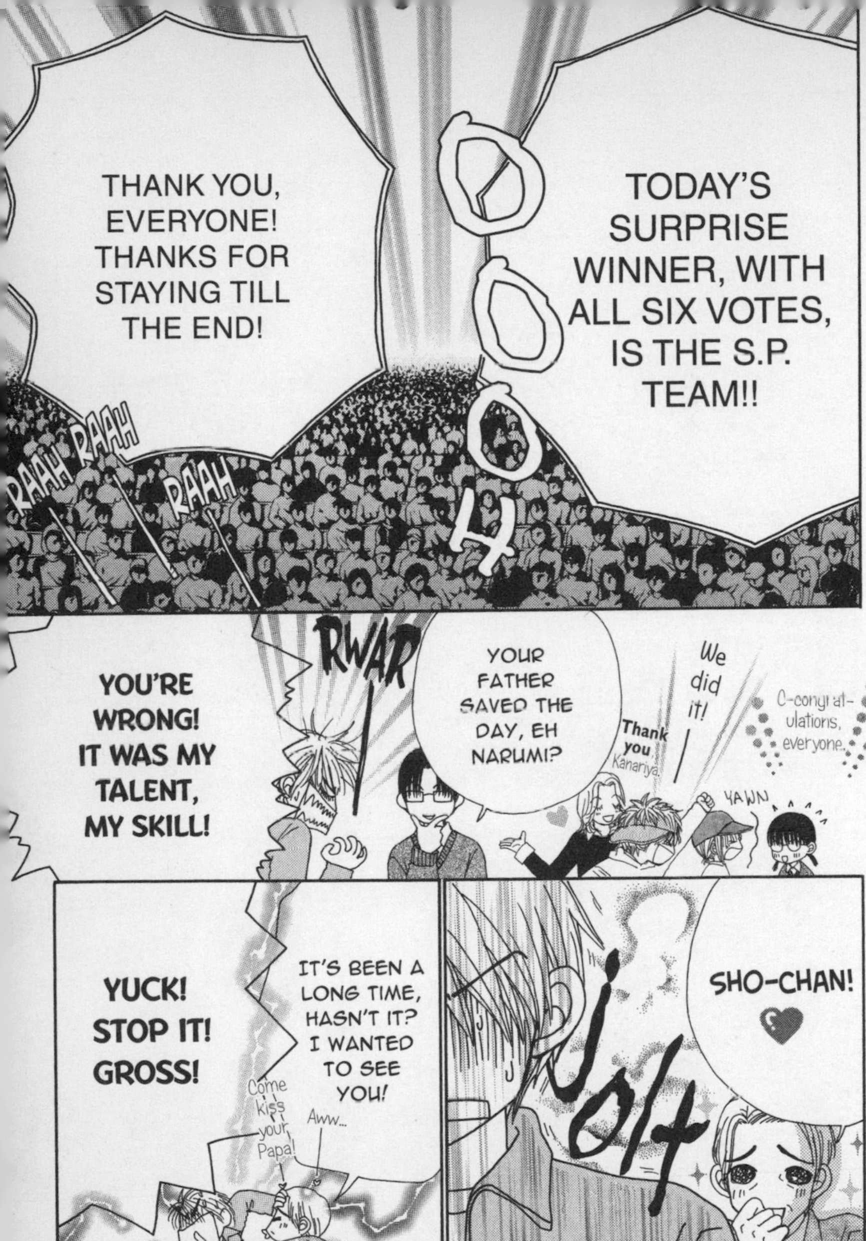
TODAY'S SURPRISE WINNER, WITH ALL SIX VOTES, IS THE S.P. TEAM!!
OOOH
THANK YOU, EVERYONE! THANKS FOR STAYING TILL THE END!
RAAH RAAH
RAAH
C-congratulations, everyone.
YAWN
We did it!
Thank you, Kanariya.
YOUR FATHER SAVED THE DAY, EH NARUMI?
RWAR
YOU'RE WRONG! IT WAS MY TALENT, MY SKILL!
SHO-CHAN!
Jolt
IT'S BEEN A LONG TIME, HASN'T IT? I WANTED TO SEE YOU!
Aww...
Come kiss your Papa!
YUCK! STOP IT! GROSS!

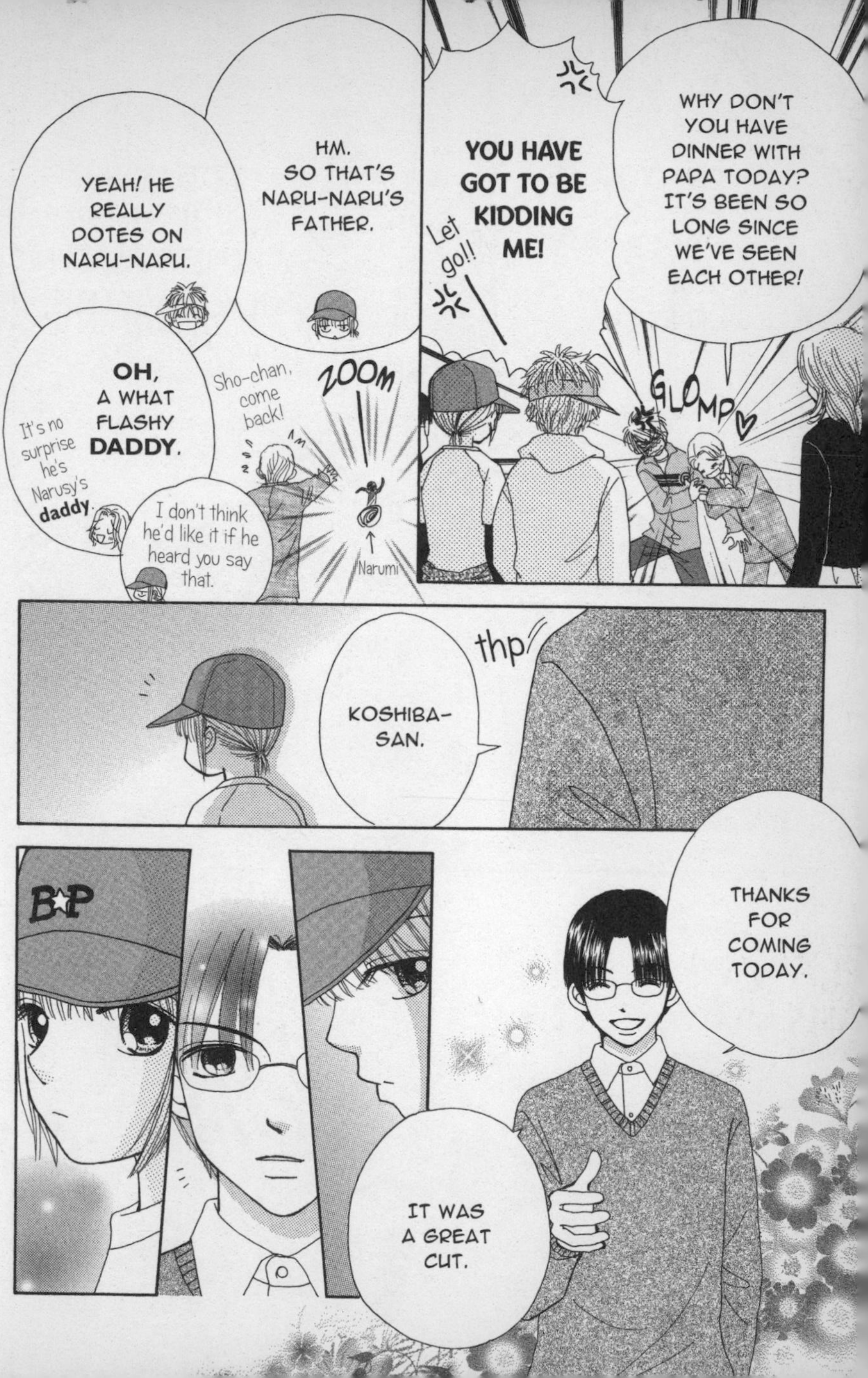

WHY DON'T YOU HAVE DINNER WITH PAPA TODAY? IT'S BEEN SO LONG SINCE WE'VE SEEN EACH OTHER!
YOU HAVE GOT TO BE KIDDING ME!
Let go!!
GLOMP
HM. SO THAT'S NARU-NARU'S FATHER.
YEAH! HE REALLY DOTES ON NARU-NARU.
Sho-chan, come back!
ZOOM
Narumi
OH, A WHAT FLASHY DADDY.
It's no surprise he's Narusy's daddy.
I don't think he'd like it if he heard you say that.
thp
KOSHIBA-SAN.
THANKS FOR COMING TODAY.
IT WAS A GREAT CUT.
B☆P

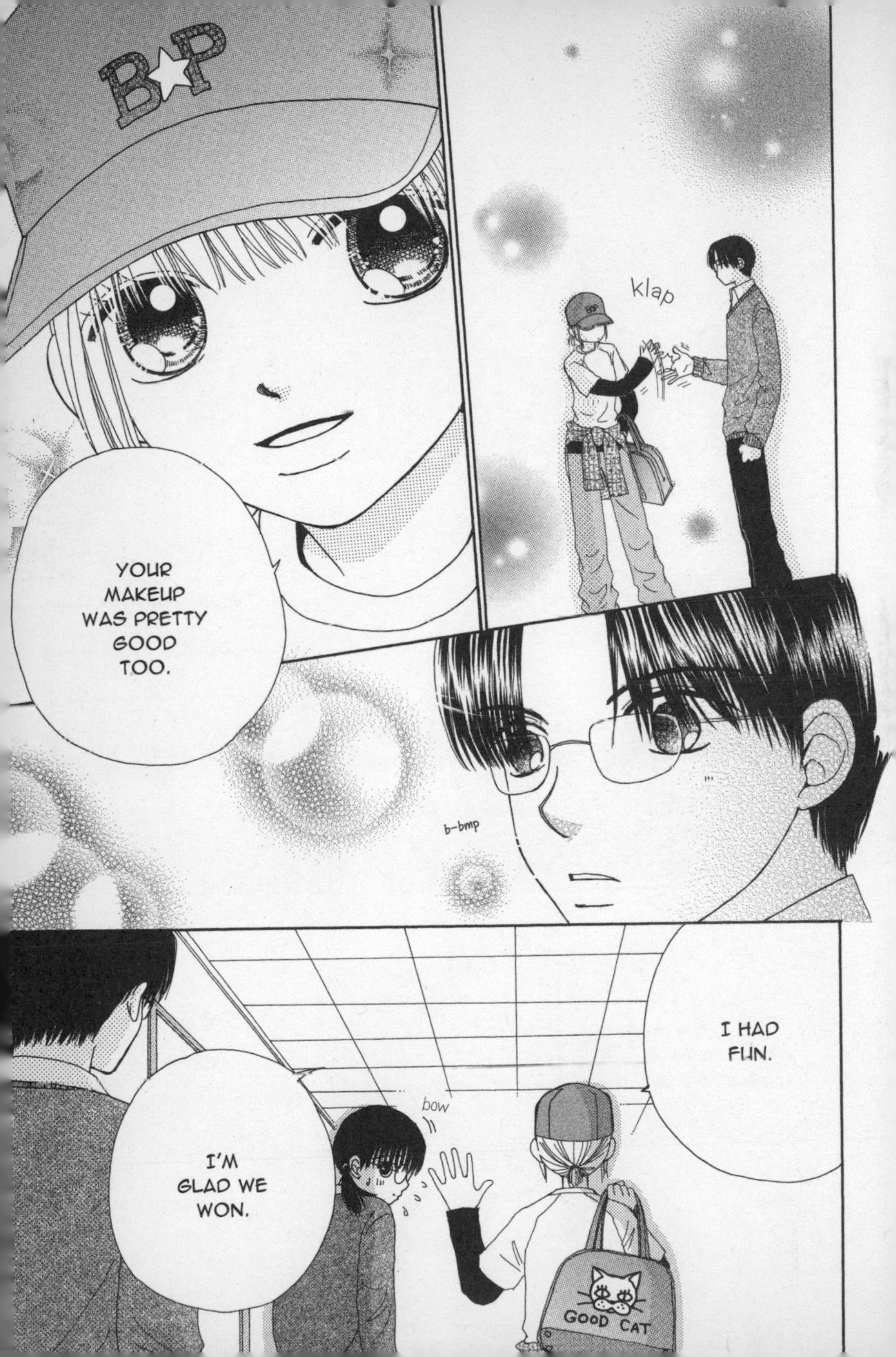
klap
YOUR MAKEUP WAS PRETTY GOOD TOO.
b-bmp
I HAD FUN.
bow
I'M GLAD WE WON.
GOOD CAT

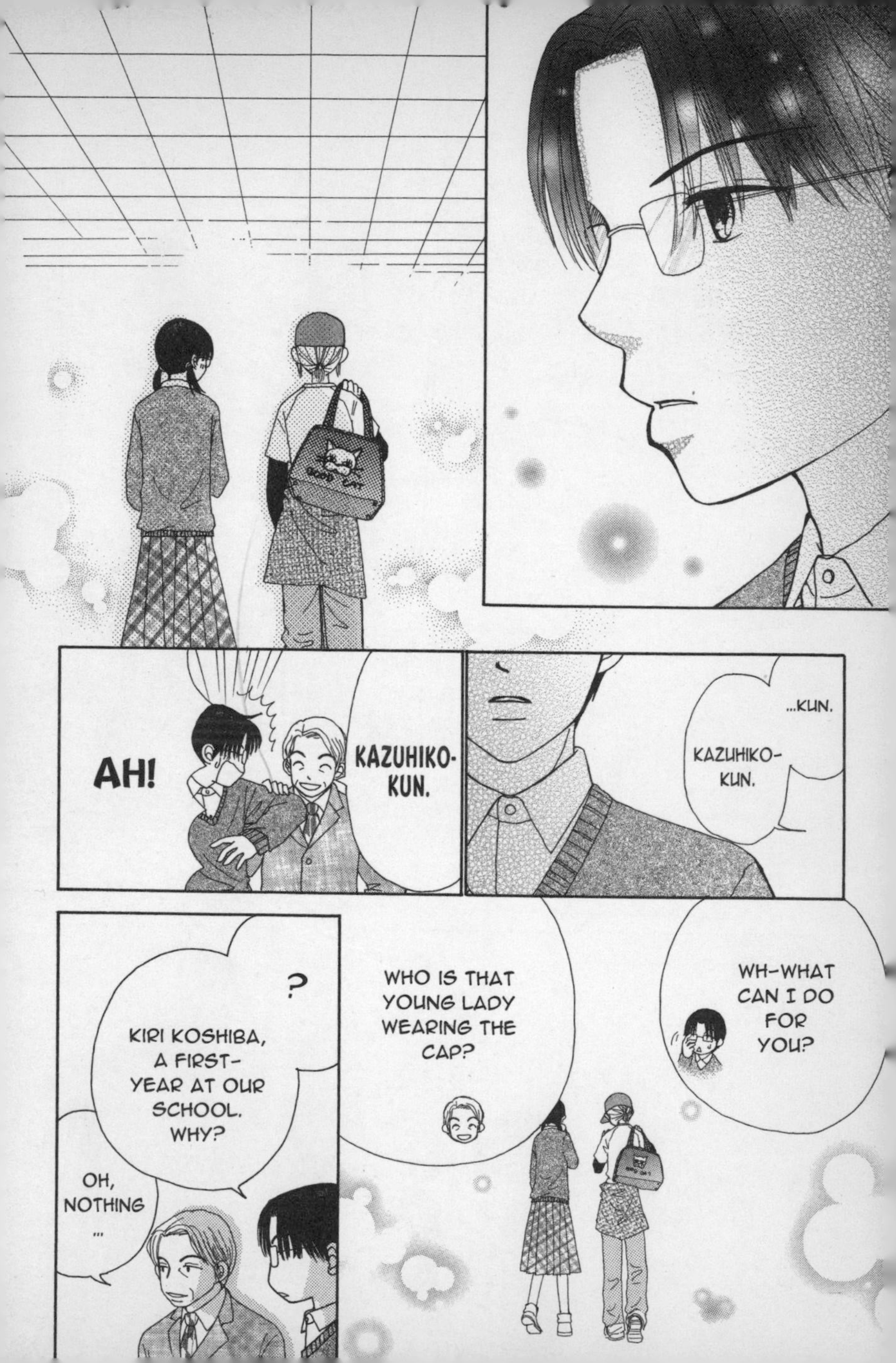
...KUN.
KAZUHIKO-KUN.
KAZUHIKO-KUN.
AH!
WH-WHAT CAN I DO FOR YOU?
WHO IS THAT YOUNG LADY WEARING THE CAP?
?
KIRI KOSHIBA, A FIRST-YEAR AT OUR SCHOOL. WHY?
OH, NOTHING ...

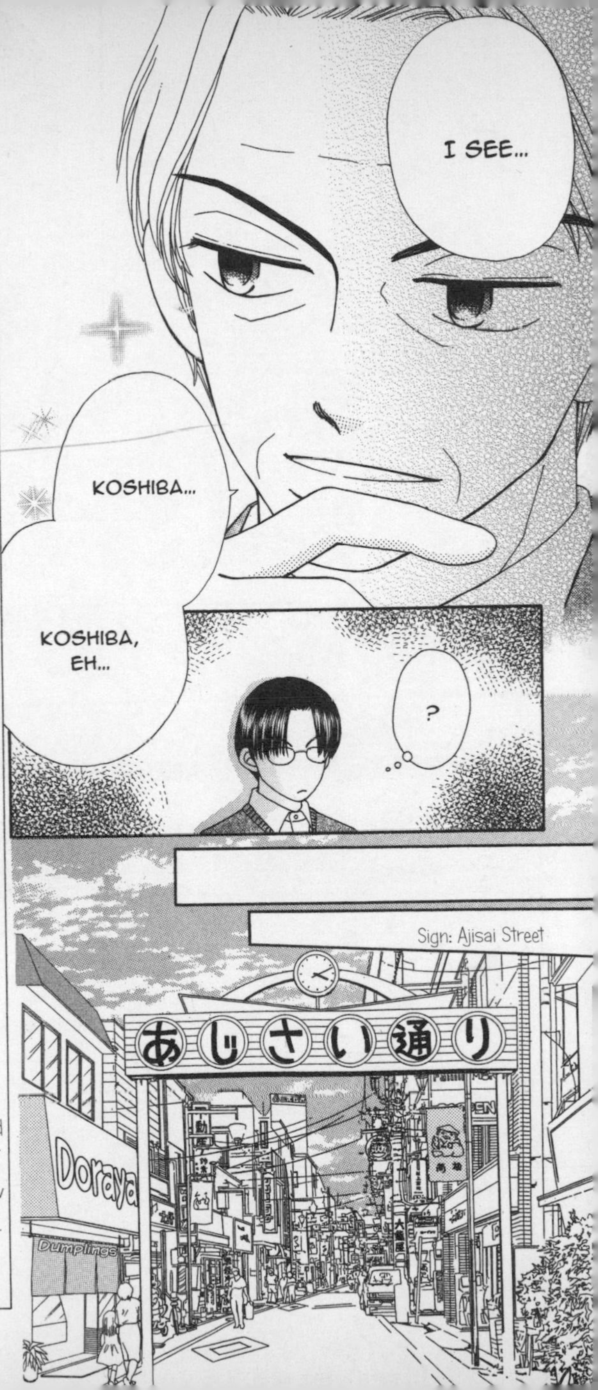
I SEE...
KOSHIBA...
KOSHIBA, EH...
?
Sign: Ajisai Street
あじさい通り
Doraya
Dumplings

K's Club Talk

In this episode, Kiri's father finds Kiri's scissors and thinks, "I guess I'll sharpen them for her." But in real life, beauticians have their scissors professionally sharpened whenever they start to get dull. I guess that's how their scissors are always sharp and ready to cut hair. I bought some beautician's scissors once and tried cutting my own hair. They really do cut so much better than regular scissors! It's amazing!! They're so sharp, it's almost scary. SHIK!! SHIK!!
And that reminds me... I tried twirling the scissors like they do and succeeded in cutting my finger really nicely. I know you are all really good kids, so please don't try twirling the scissors! It's really dangerous!!

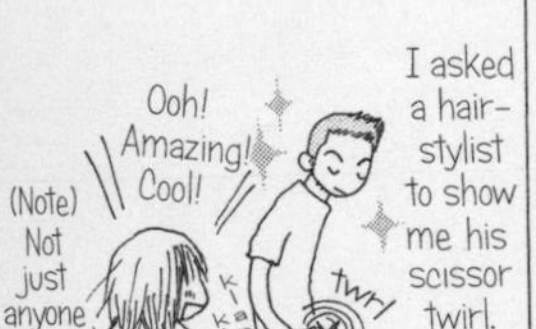
I asked a hair-stylist to show me his scissor twirl.
Ooh! Amazing! Cool!
(Note) Not just anyone can do it.
twirl
Klap Klap

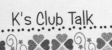

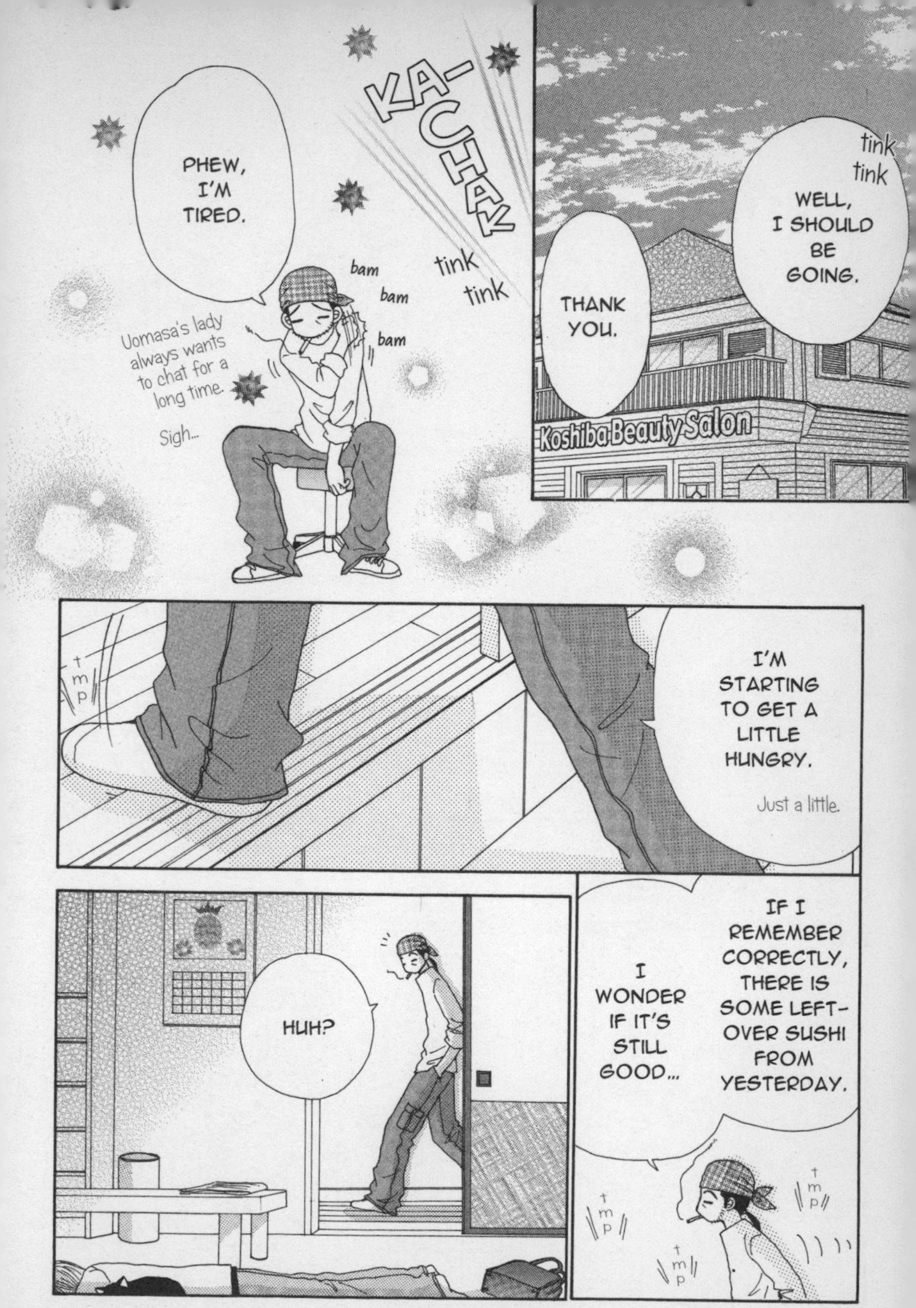

tink tink
WELL, I SHOULD BE GOING.
THANK YOU.
Koshiba Beauty Salon
KA-CHAK
tink tink
PHEW, I'M TIRED.
bam bam bam
Uomasa's lady always wants to chat for a long time.
Sigh...
I'M STARTING TO GET A LITTLE HUNGRY.
Just a little.
tmp
IF I REMEMBER CORRECTLY, THERE IS SOME LEFT-OVER SUSHI FROM YESTERDAY.
I WONDER IF IT'S STILL GOOD...
tmp
tmp
tmp
HUH?

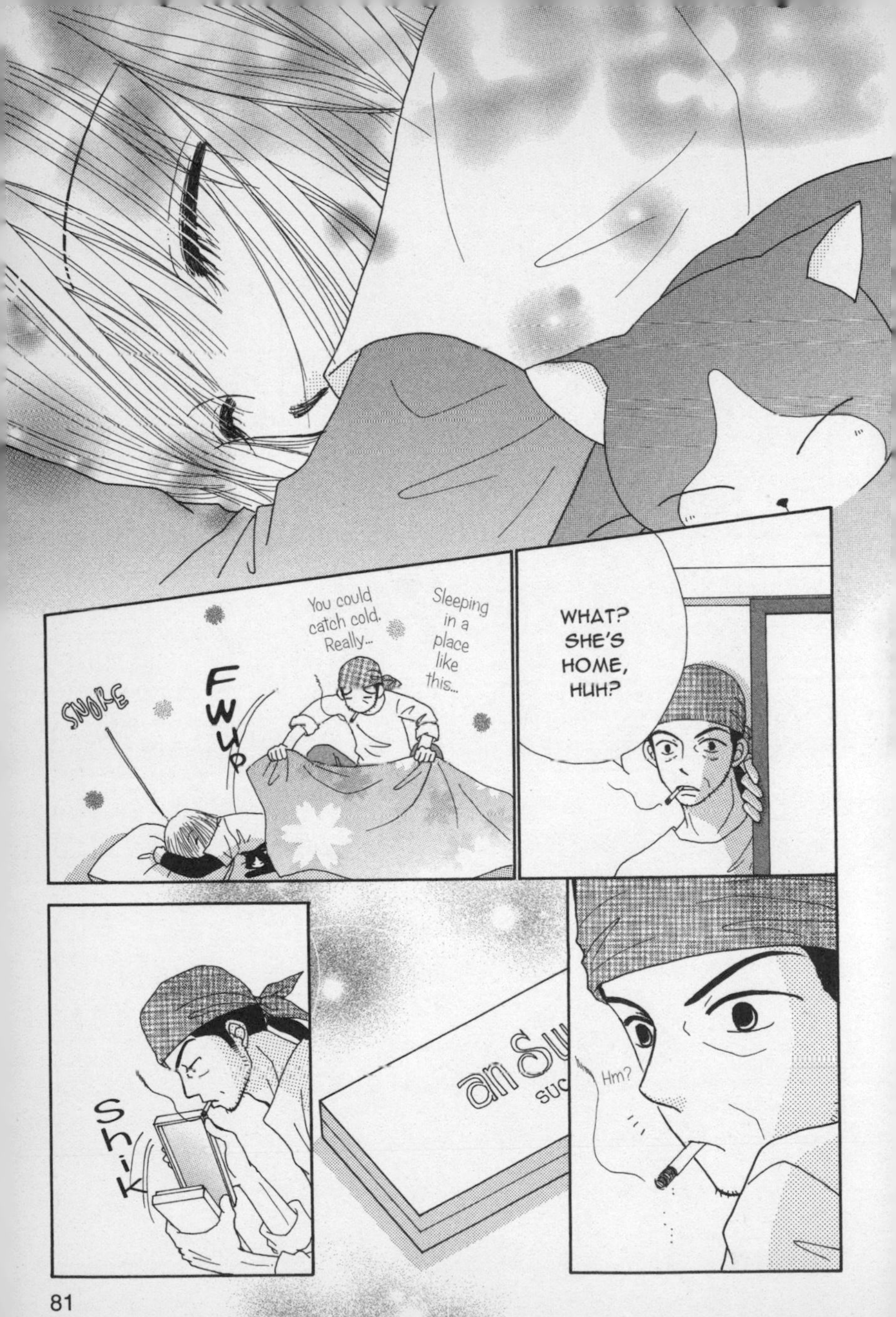
WHAT? SHE'S HOME, HUH?
Sleeping in a place like this...
You could catch cold. Really...
FWUP
SNORE
Hm?
an Su
SUC
Shik

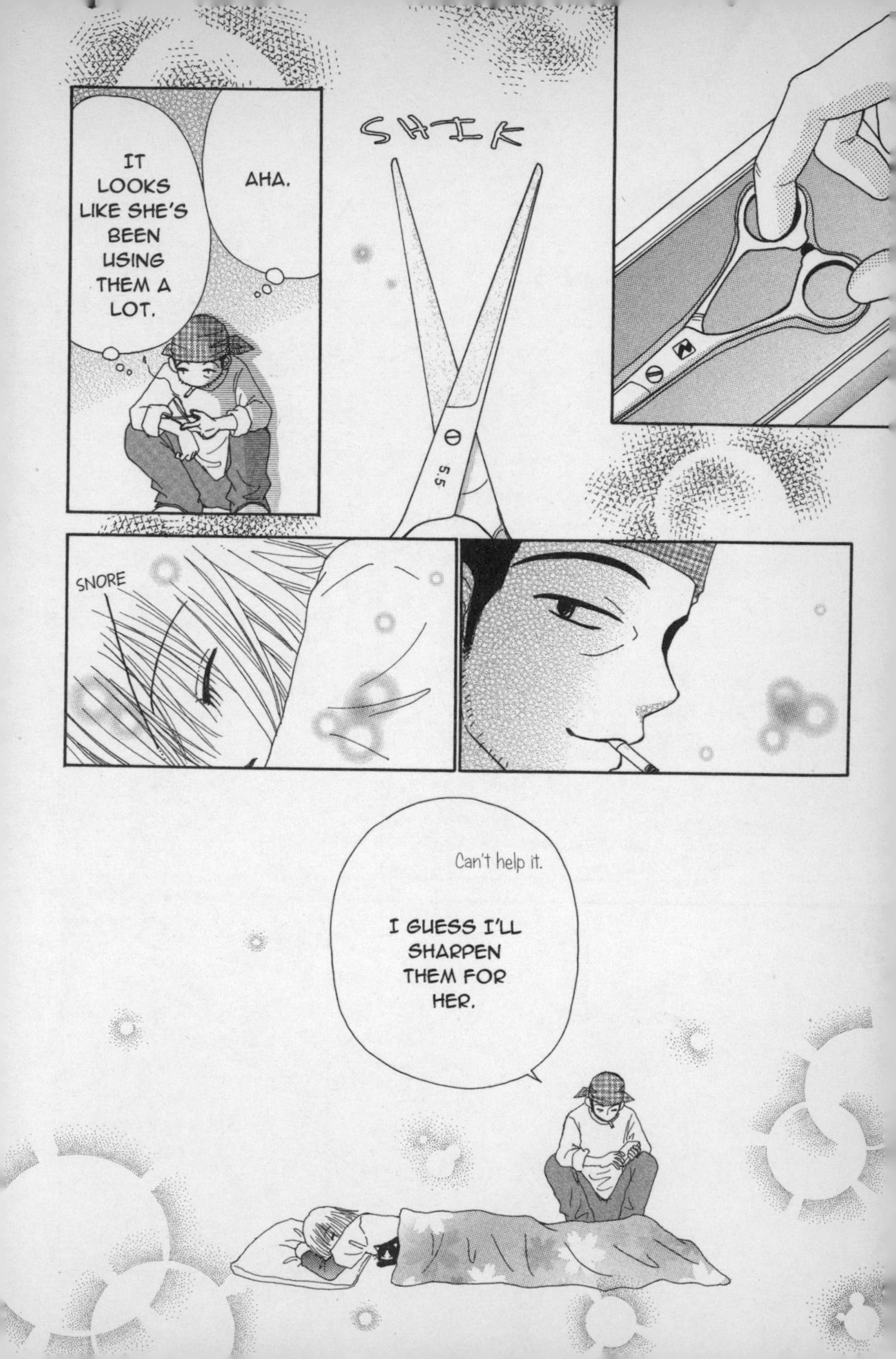
SHIK
5.5
AHA.
IT LOOKS LIKE SHE'S BEEN USING THEM A LOT.
SNORE
Can't help it.
I GUESS I'LL SHARPEN THEM FOR HER.

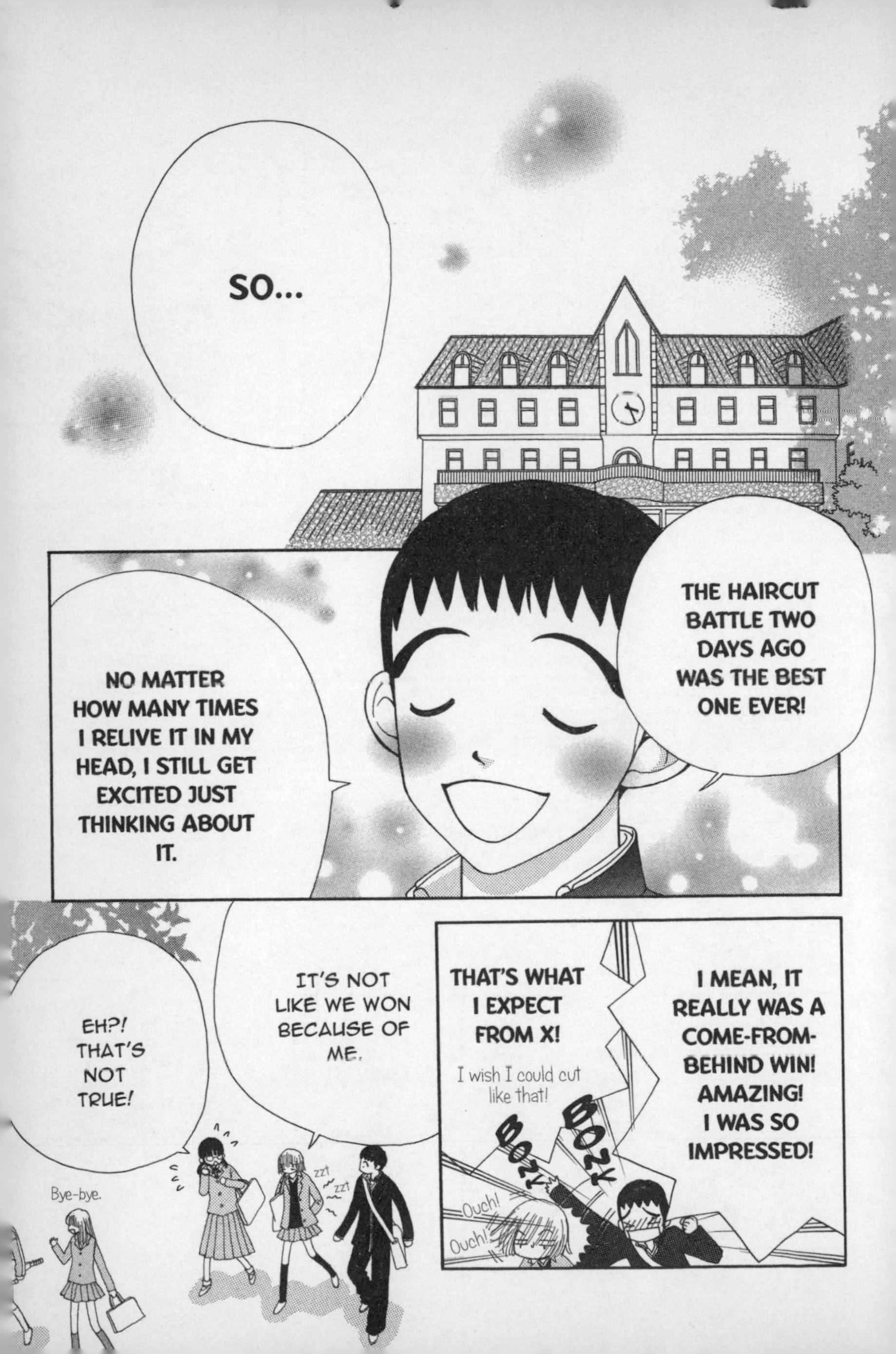
SO...
THE HAIRCUT BATTLE TWO DAYS AGO WAS THE BEST ONE EVER!
NO MATTER HOW MANY TIMES I RELIVE IT IN MY HEAD, I STILL GET EXCITED JUST THINKING ABOUT IT.
I MEAN, IT REALLY WAS A COME-FROM-BEHIND WIN! AMAZING! I WAS SO IMPRESSED!
THAT'S WHAT I EXPECT FROM X!
I wish I could cut like that!
BONK
BONK
Ouch!
Ouch!
IT'S NOT LIKE WE WON BECAUSE OF ME.
EH?! THAT'S NOT TRUE!
zzt
zzt
Bye-bye.

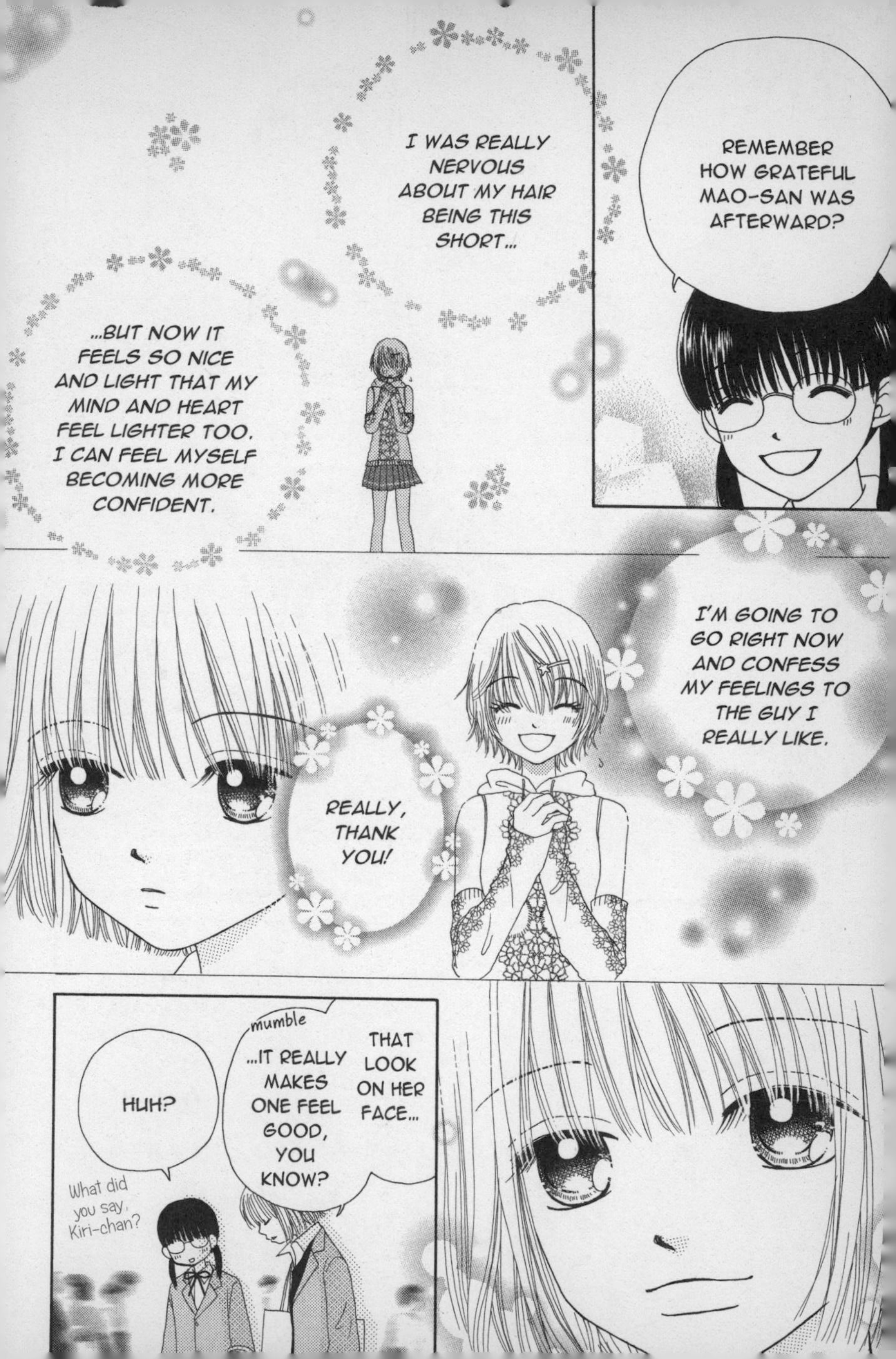
REMEMBER HOW GRATEFUL MAO-SAN WAS AFTERWARD?
I WAS REALLY NERVOUS ABOUT MY HAIR BEING THIS SHORT...
...BUT NOW IT FEELS SO NICE AND LIGHT THAT MY MIND AND HEART FEEL LIGHTER TOO. I CAN FEEL MYSELF BECOMING MORE CONFIDENT.
I'M GOING TO GO RIGHT NOW AND CONFESS MY FEELINGS TO THE GUY I REALLY LIKE.
REALLY, THANK YOU!
THAT LOOK ON HER FACE...
mumble
...IT REALLY MAKES ONE FEEL GOOD, YOU KNOW?
HUH?
What did you say, Kiri-chan?

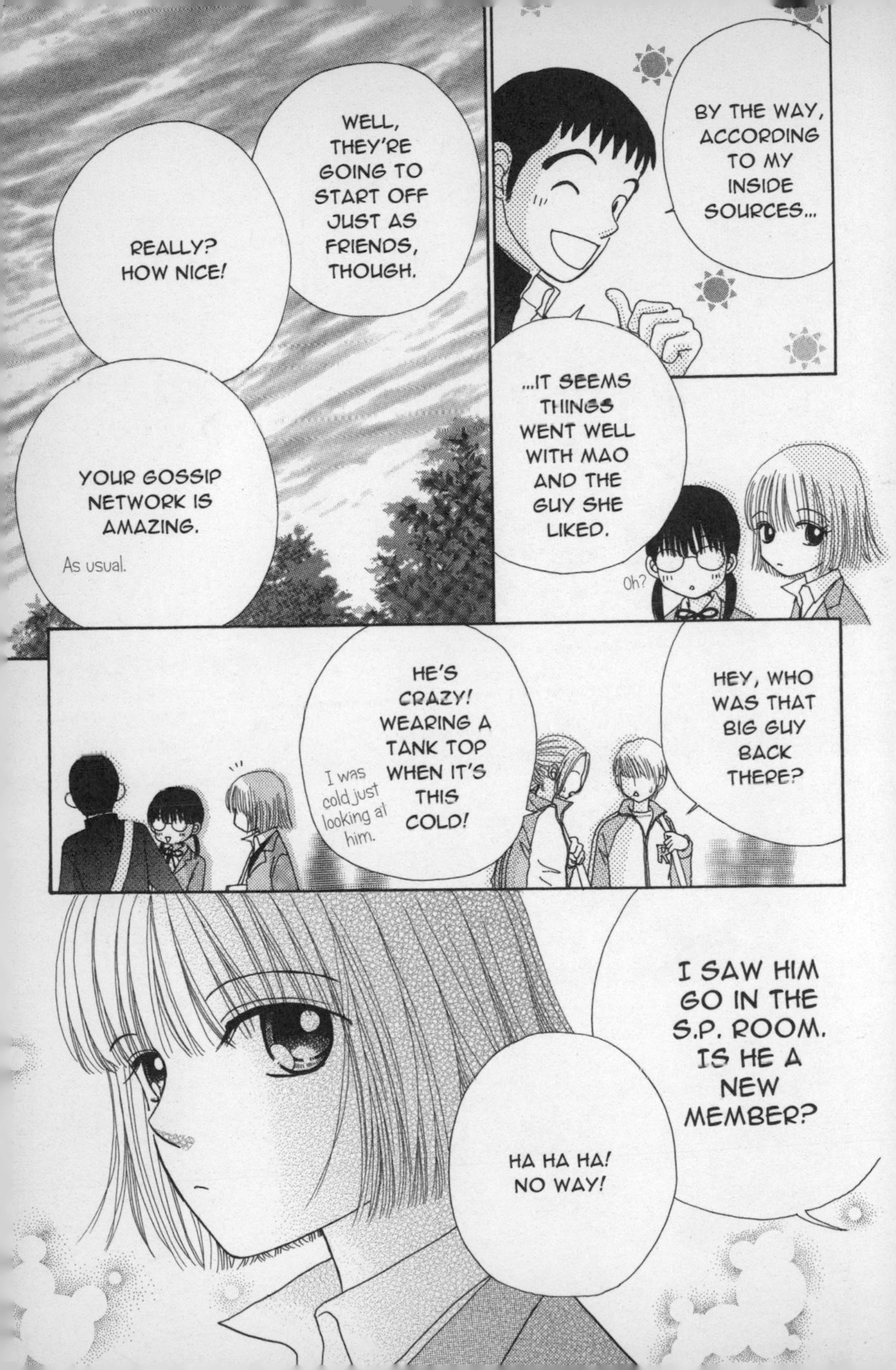

BY THE WAY, ACCORDING TO MY INSIDE SOURCES...
...IT SEEMS THINGS WENT WELL WITH MAO AND THE GUY SHE LIKED.
Oh?
WELL, THEY'RE GOING TO START OFF JUST AS FRIENDS, THOUGH.
REALLY? HOW NICE!
YOUR GOSSIP NETWORK IS AMAZING.
As usual.
HEY, WHO WAS THAT BIG GUY BACK THERE?
HE'S CRAZY! WEARING A TANK TOP WHEN IT'S THIS COLD!
I was cold just looking at him.
I SAW HIM GO IN THE S.P. ROOM. IS HE A NEW MEMBER?
HA HA HA! NO WAY!

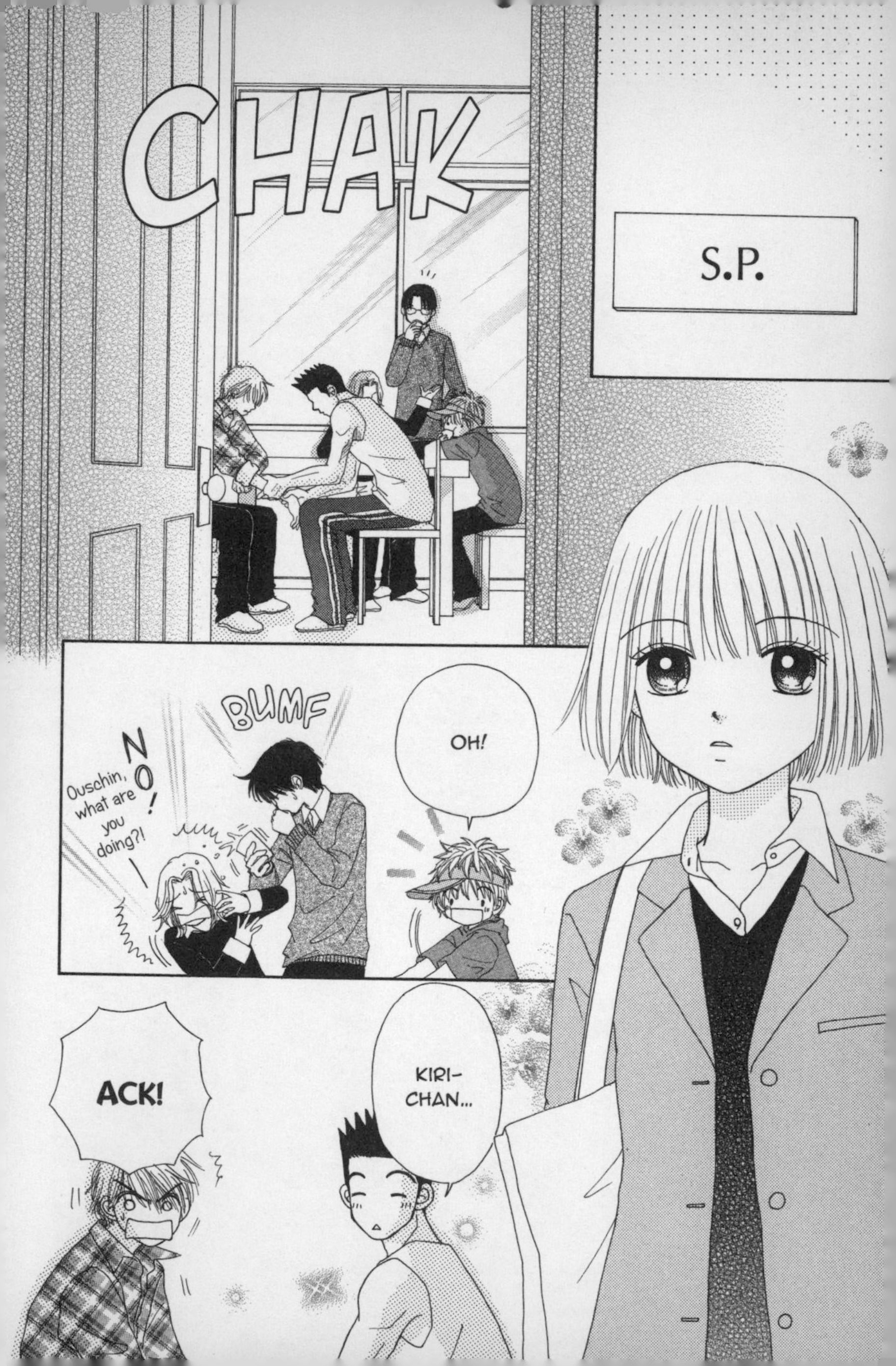
S.P.
CHAK
OH!
BUMF
NO!
Ouschin, what are you doing?!
KIRI-CHAN...
ACK!

READ THIS WAY

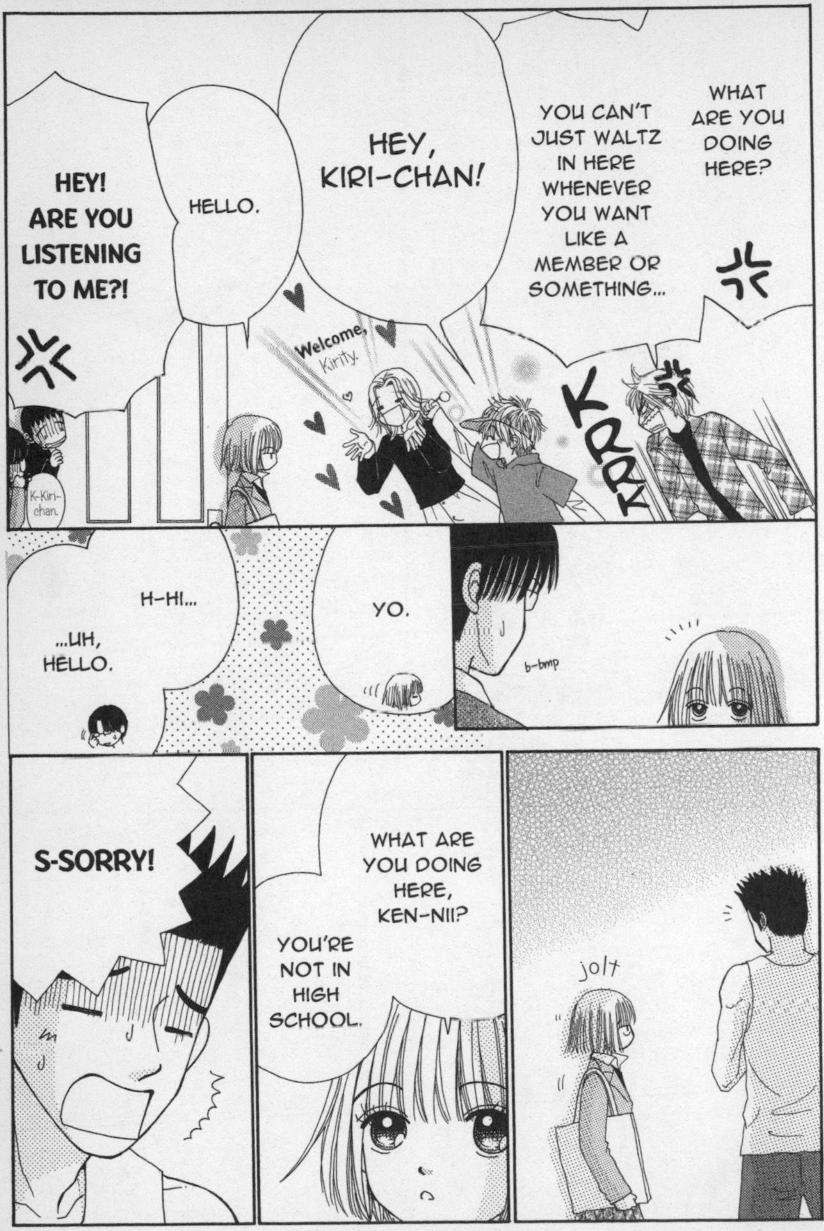
WHAT ARE YOU DOING HERE?
YOU CAN'T JUST WALTZ IN HERE WHENEVER YOU WANT LIKE A MEMBER OR SOMETHING...
KRRRK
HEY, KIRI-CHAN!
Welcome, Kirity.
HELLO.
HEY! ARE YOU LISTENING TO ME?!
K-Kiri-chan.
b-bmp
YO.
H-HI...
...UH, HELLO.
jolt
WHAT ARE YOU DOING HERE, KEN-NII?
YOU'RE NOT IN HIGH SCHOOL.
S-SORRY!

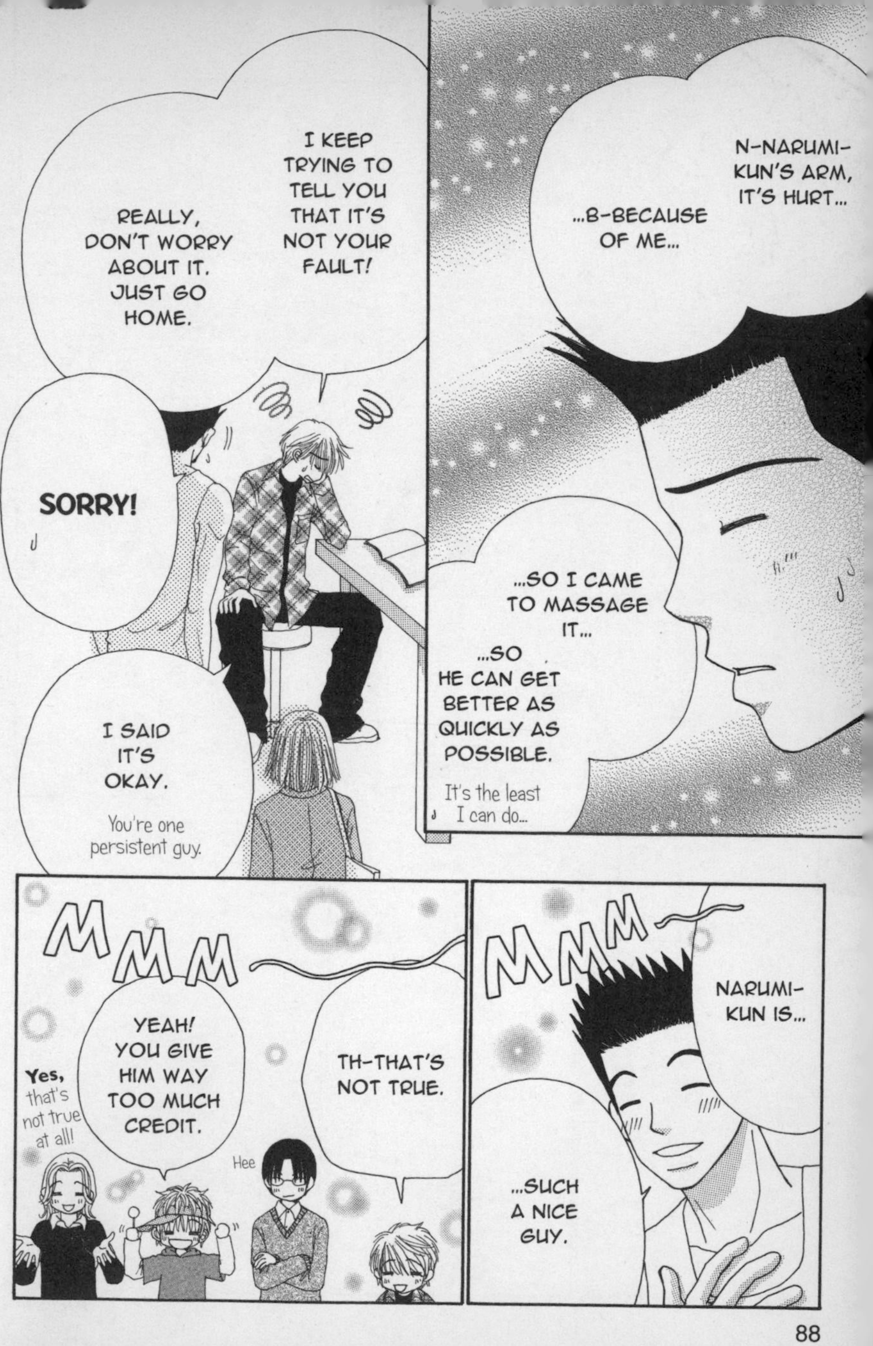
N-NARUMI-KUN'S ARM, IT'S HURT...
...B-BECAUSE OF ME...
...SO I CAME TO MASSAGE IT...
...SO HE CAN GET BETTER AS QUICKLY AS POSSIBLE.
It's the least I can do...
I KEEP TRYING TO TELL YOU THAT IT'S NOT YOUR FAULT!
REALLY, DON'T WORRY ABOUT IT. JUST GO HOME.
SORRY!
I SAID IT'S OKAY.
You're one persistent guy.
MMM~
NARUMI-KUN IS...
...SUCH A NICE GUY.
MMM~
TH-THAT'S NOT TRUE.
YEAH! YOU GIVE HIM WAY TOO MUCH CREDIT.
Hee
Yes, that's not true at all!

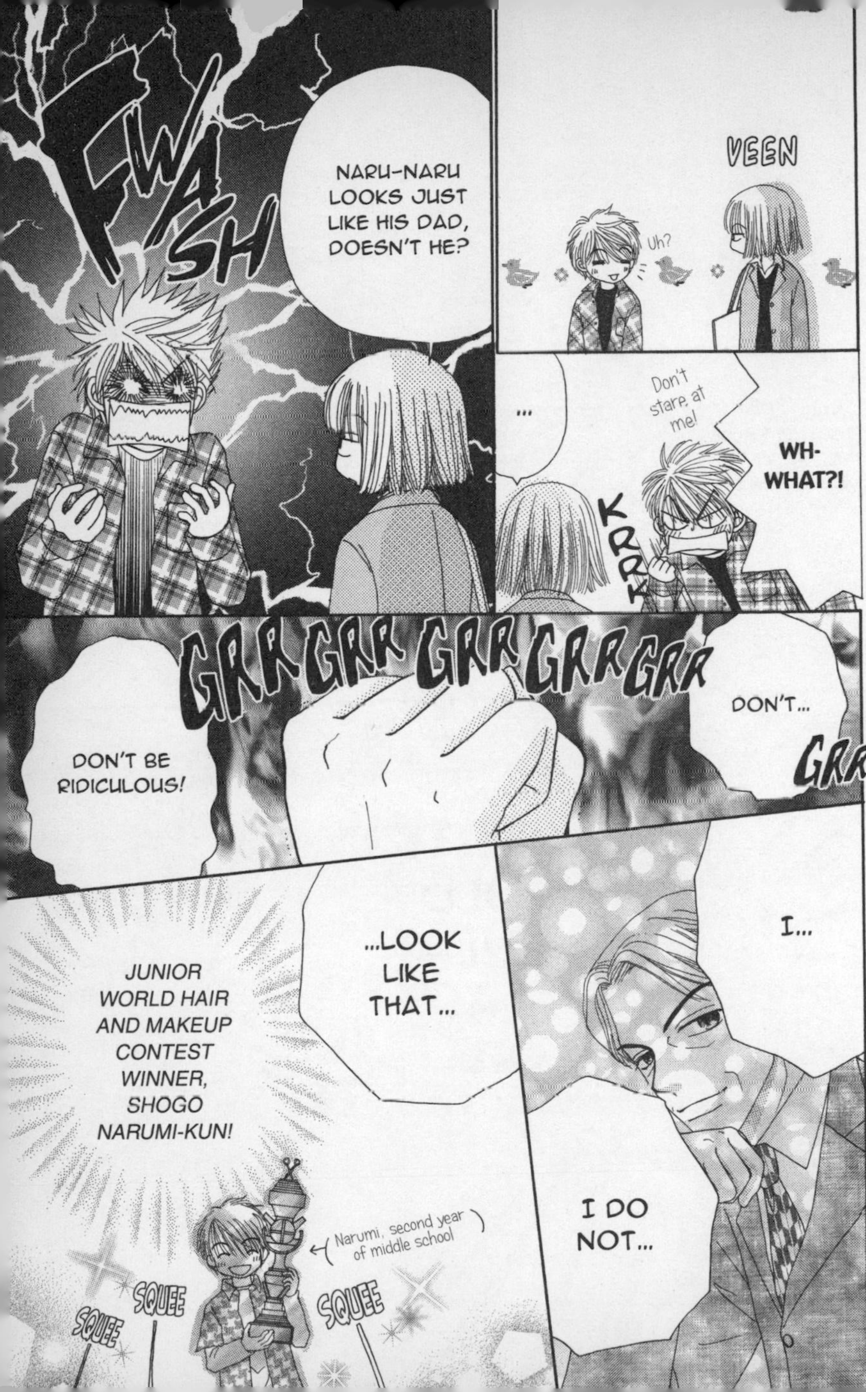
VEEN
Uh?
...
Don't stare at me!
WH-WHAT?!
KRRRK
FWASH
NARU-NARU LOOKS JUST LIKE HIS DAD, DOESN'T HE?
DON'T...
GRR
GRR GRR GRR GRR GRR
DON'T BE RIDICULOUS!
I...
I DO NOT...
...LOOK LIKE THAT...
JUNIOR WORLD HAIR AND MAKEUP CONTEST WINNER, SHOGO NARUMI-KUN!
(Narumi, second year of middle school)
SQUEE
SQUEE
SQUEE

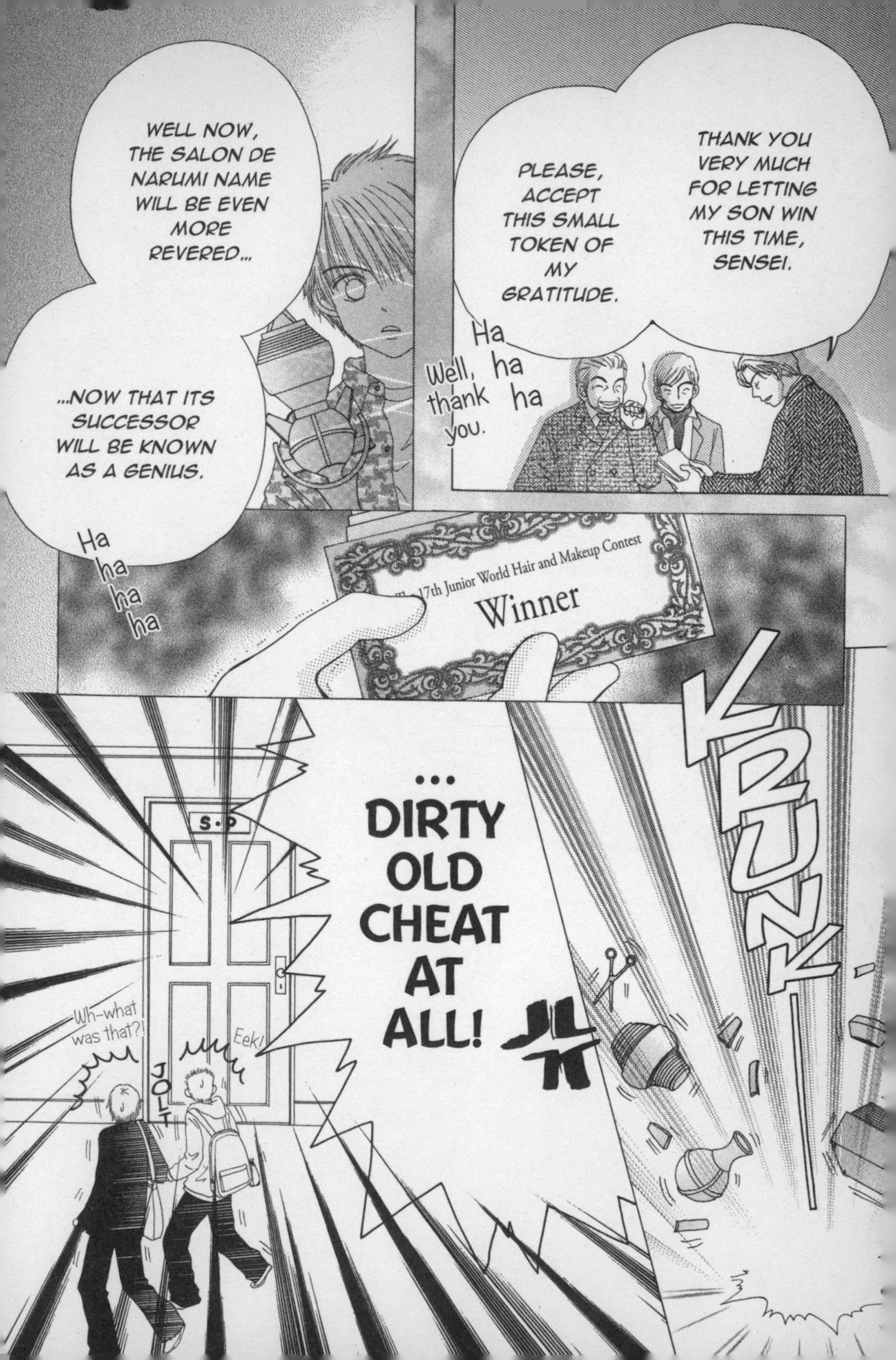
THANK YOU VERY MUCH FOR LETTING MY SON WIN THIS TIME, SENSEI.
PLEASE, ACCEPT THIS SMALL TOKEN OF MY GRATITUDE.
Ha ha ha
Well, thank you.
WELL NOW, THE SALON DE NARUMI NAME WILL BE EVEN MORE REVERED...
...NOW THAT ITS SUCCESSOR WILL BE KNOWN AS A GENIUS.
Ha ha ha ha
17th Junior World Hair and Makeup Contest
Winner
KRUNK
... DIRTY OLD CHEAT AT ALL!
S・P
Eek!
Wh-what was that?!
JOLT

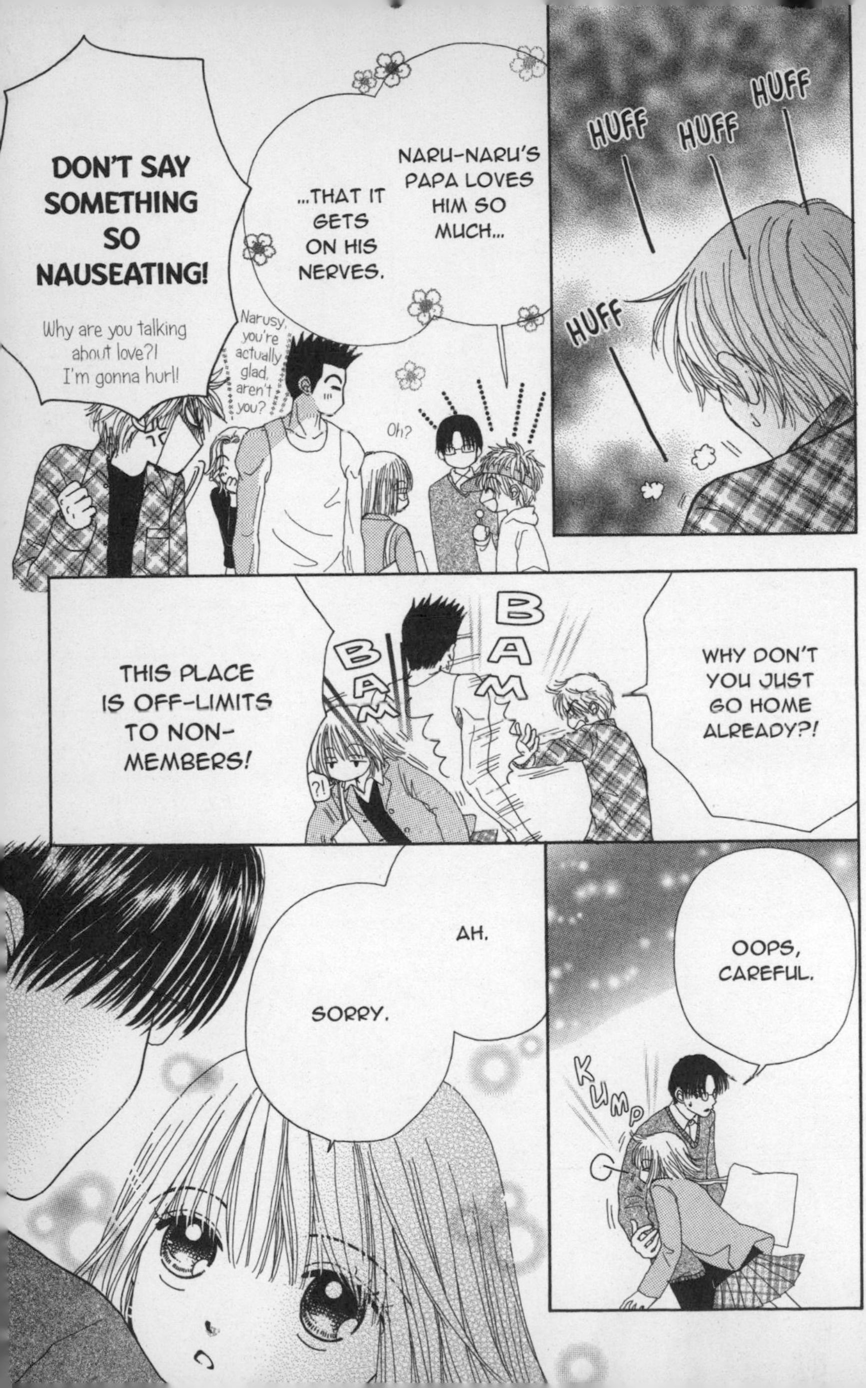
HUFF
HUFF
HUFF
HUFF
NARU-NARU'S PAPA LOVES HIM SO MUCH...
...THAT IT GETS ON HIS NERVES.
Oh?
Narusy, you're actually glad, aren't you?
DON'T SAY SOMETHING SO NAUSEATING!
Why are you talking about love?! I'm gonna hurl!
WHY DON'T YOU JUST GO HOME ALREADY?!
BAM
BAM
?!
THIS PLACE IS OFF-LIMITS TO NON-MEMBERS!
OOPS, CAREFUL.
KUMP
AH.
SORRY.

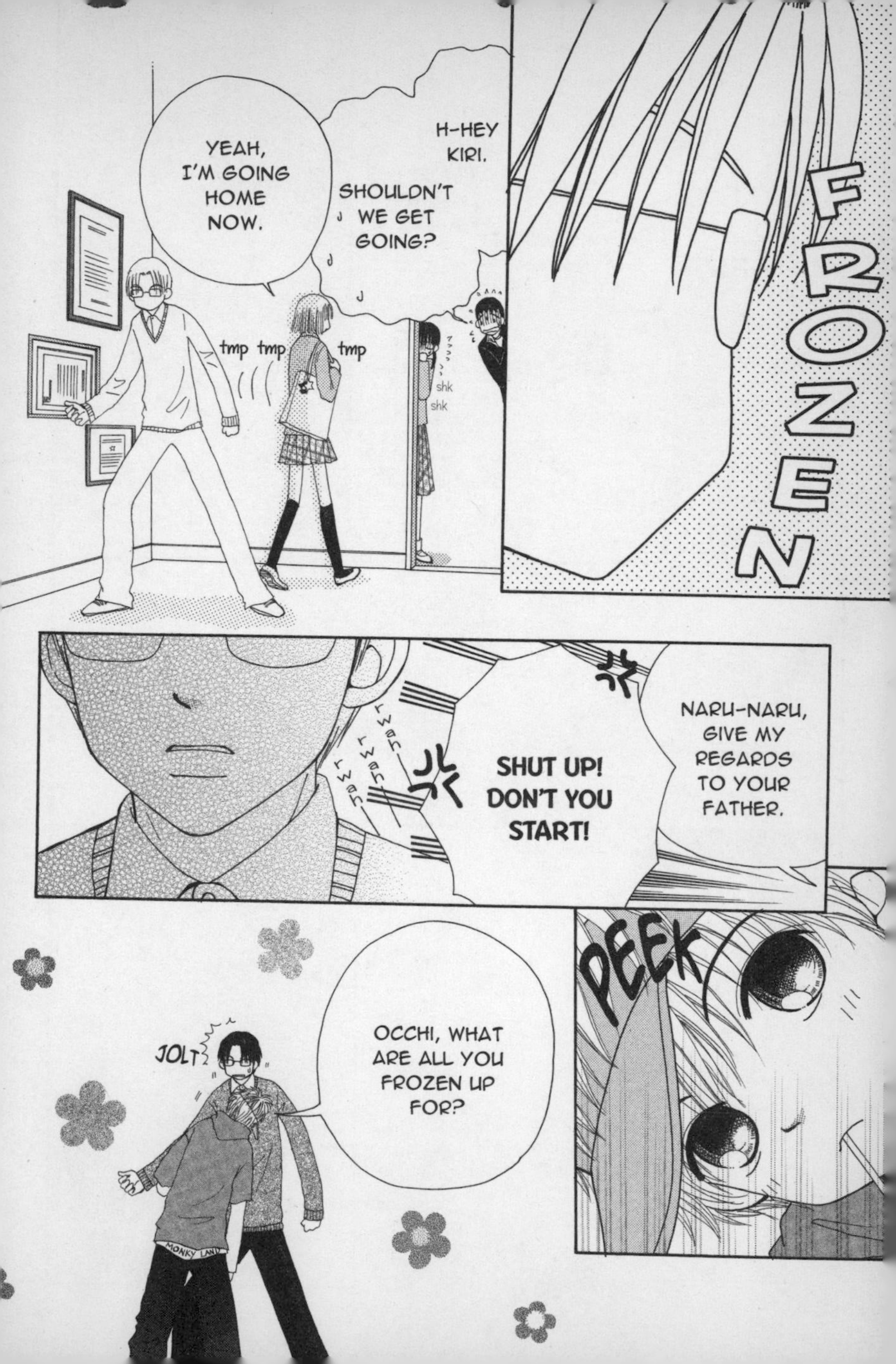
FROZEN
H-HEY KIRI.
SHOULDN'T WE GET GOING?
YEAH, I'M GOING HOME NOW.
tmp tmp tmp
shk shk
NARU-NARU, GIVE MY REGARDS TO YOUR FATHER.
SHUT UP! DON'T YOU START!
rwah rwah rwah
PEEK
OCCHI, WHAT ARE ALL YOU FROZEN UP FOR?
JOLT
MONKY LAND

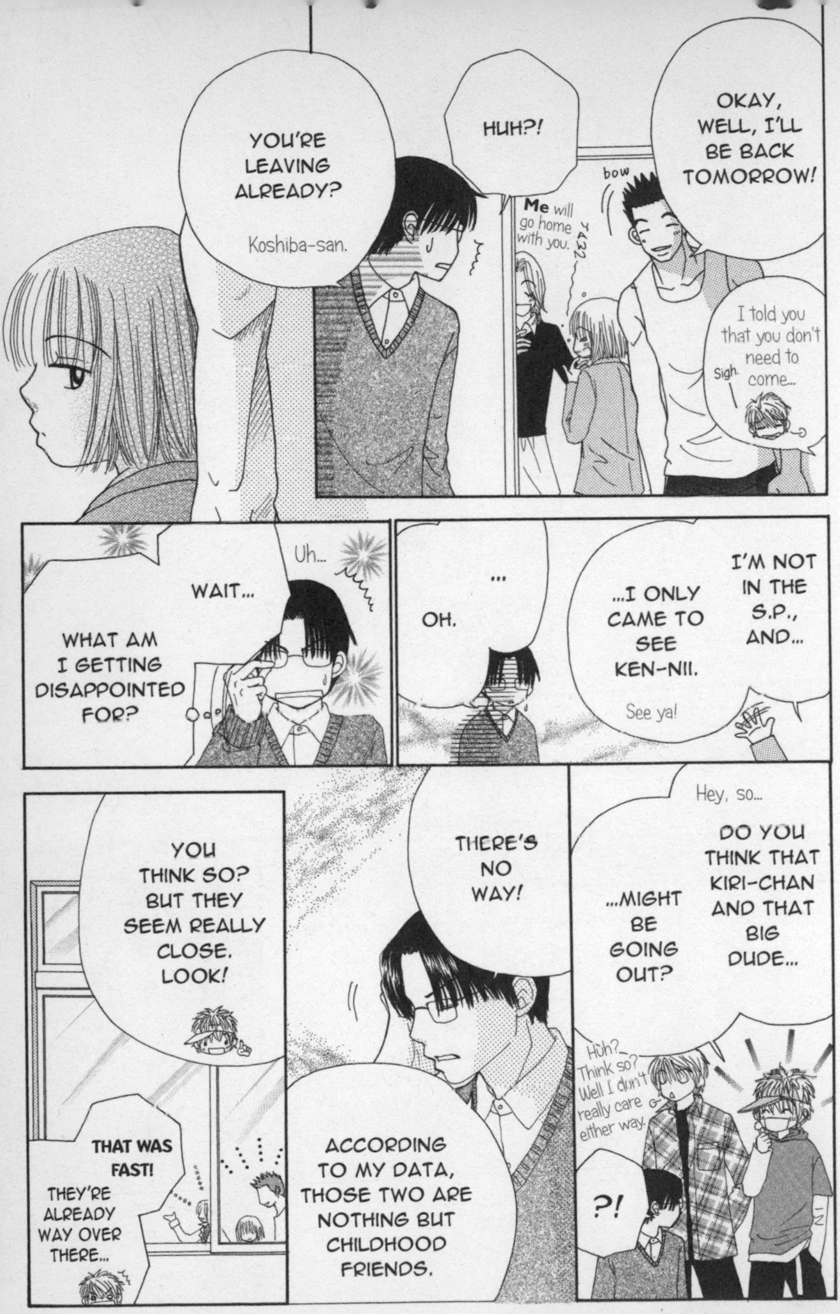
OKAY, WELL, I'LL BE BACK TOMORROW!
bow
I told you that you don't need to come...
Sigh.
Me will go home with you.
HUH?!
YOU'RE LEAVING ALREADY?
Koshiba-san.
I'M NOT IN THE S.P., AND...
...I ONLY CAME TO SEE KEN-NII.
See ya!
...
OH.
Uh...
WAIT...
WHAT AM I GETTING DISAPPOINTED FOR?
Hey, so...
DO YOU THINK THAT KIRI-CHAN AND THAT BIG DUDE...
...MIGHT BE GOING OUT?
Huh? Think so? Well I don't really care either way.
?!
THERE'S NO WAY!
ACCORDING TO MY DATA, THOSE TWO ARE NOTHING BUT CHILDHOOD FRIENDS.
YOU THINK SO? BUT THEY SEEM REALLY CLOSE. LOOK!
THAT WAS FAST!
THEY'RE ALREADY WAY OVER THERE...

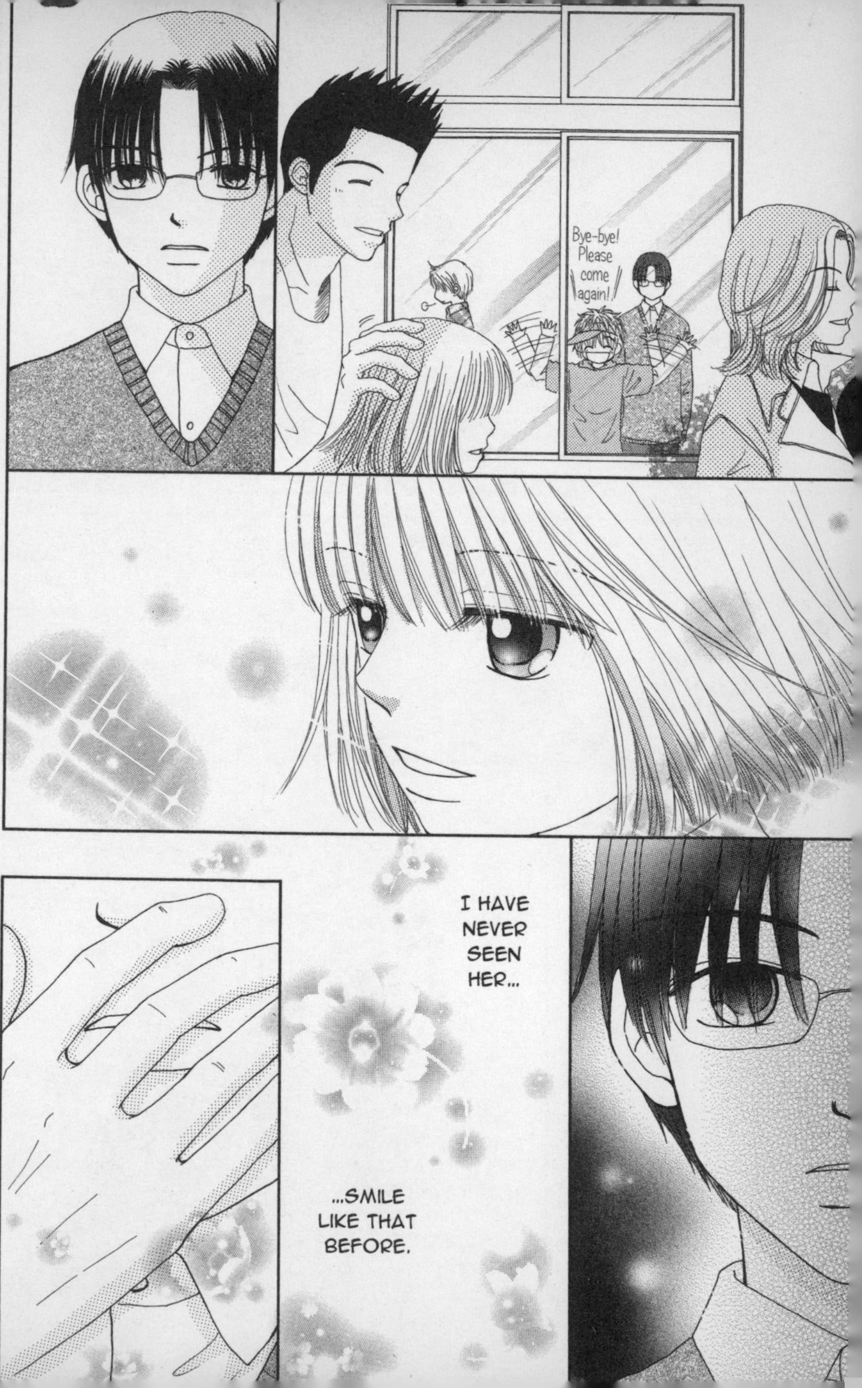
Bye-bye! Please come again!
I HAVE NEVER SEEN HER...
...SMILE LIKE THAT BEFORE.

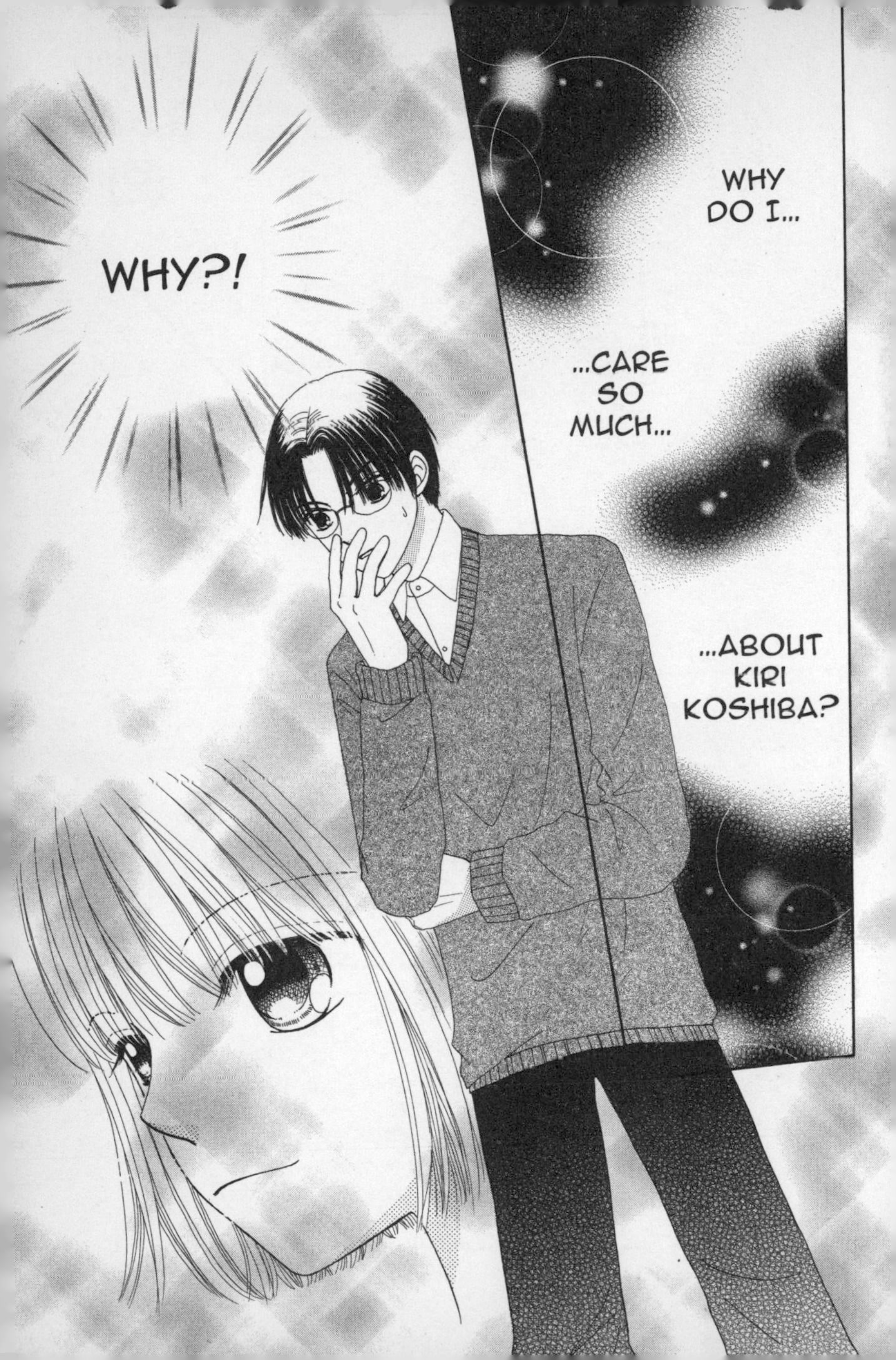
WHY DO I...
...CARE SO MUCH...
...ABOUT KIRI KOSHIBA?
WHY?!

Manga Theater ②

drop-dead
The dream I had right before my deadline...
Ugh. Ugh.
What is that? It feels so heavy.
EEK
No way!
THMP!
The dresser...
The dresser is on top of me...!
Me
KLMP
Nothing like that has ever happened before, and it hasn't happened since.
Why are all three cats on top of me?
Man, they're heavy!
Did they come to wake me? Or is it because they need food...?
Huh?
You're already awake? It's only been ten minutes.
...
cat food

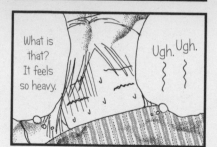

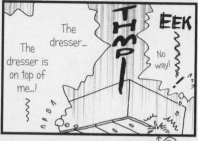

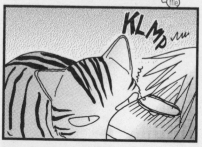

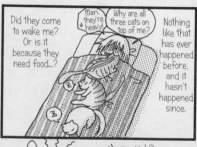

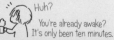

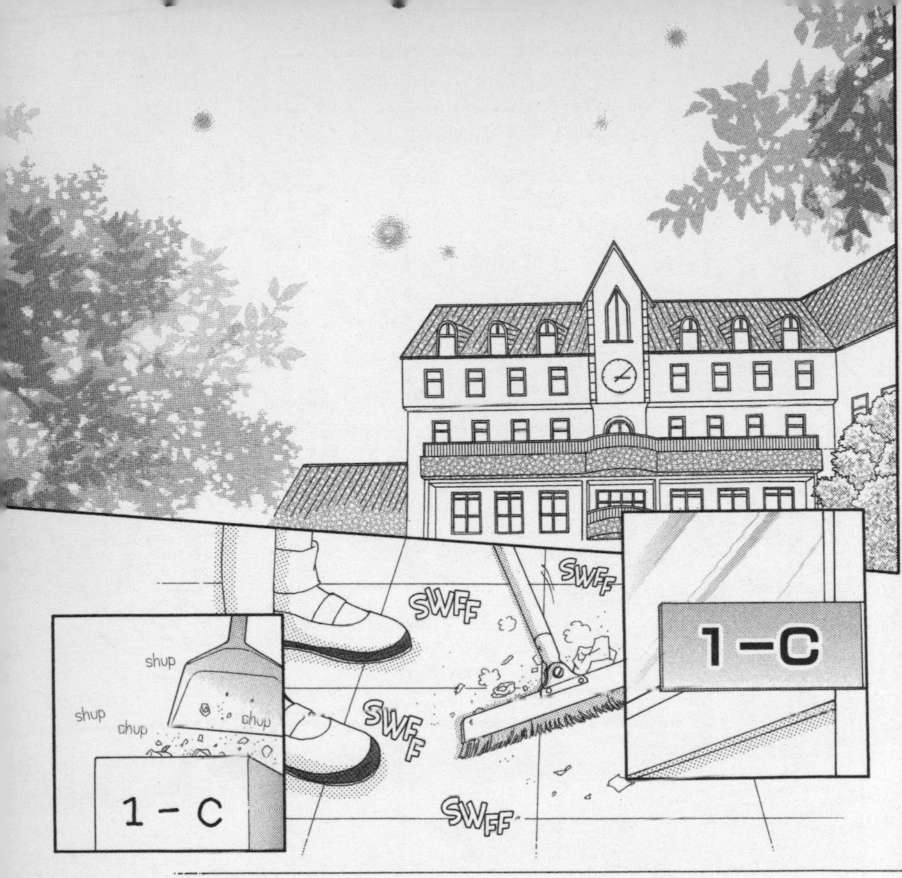
1-C
SWFF
SWFF
SWFF
SWFF
shup
shup
chup
shup
1 - C

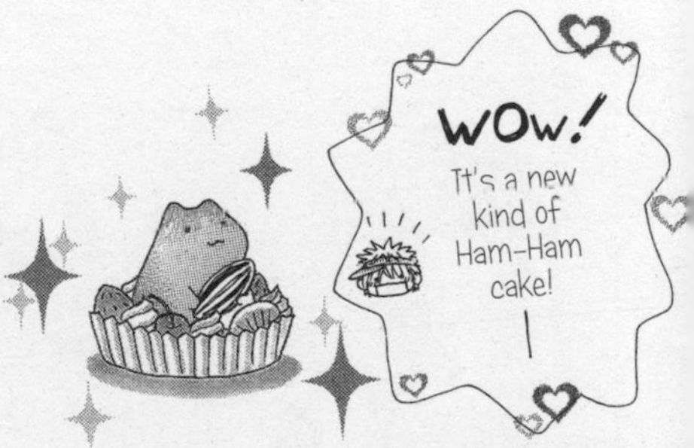
WOW!
It's a new kind of Ham-Ham cake!

(It doesn't look good to me—it's Ham-Ham cake.
How can you eat that when you have a hamster for a pet, Kei...?)

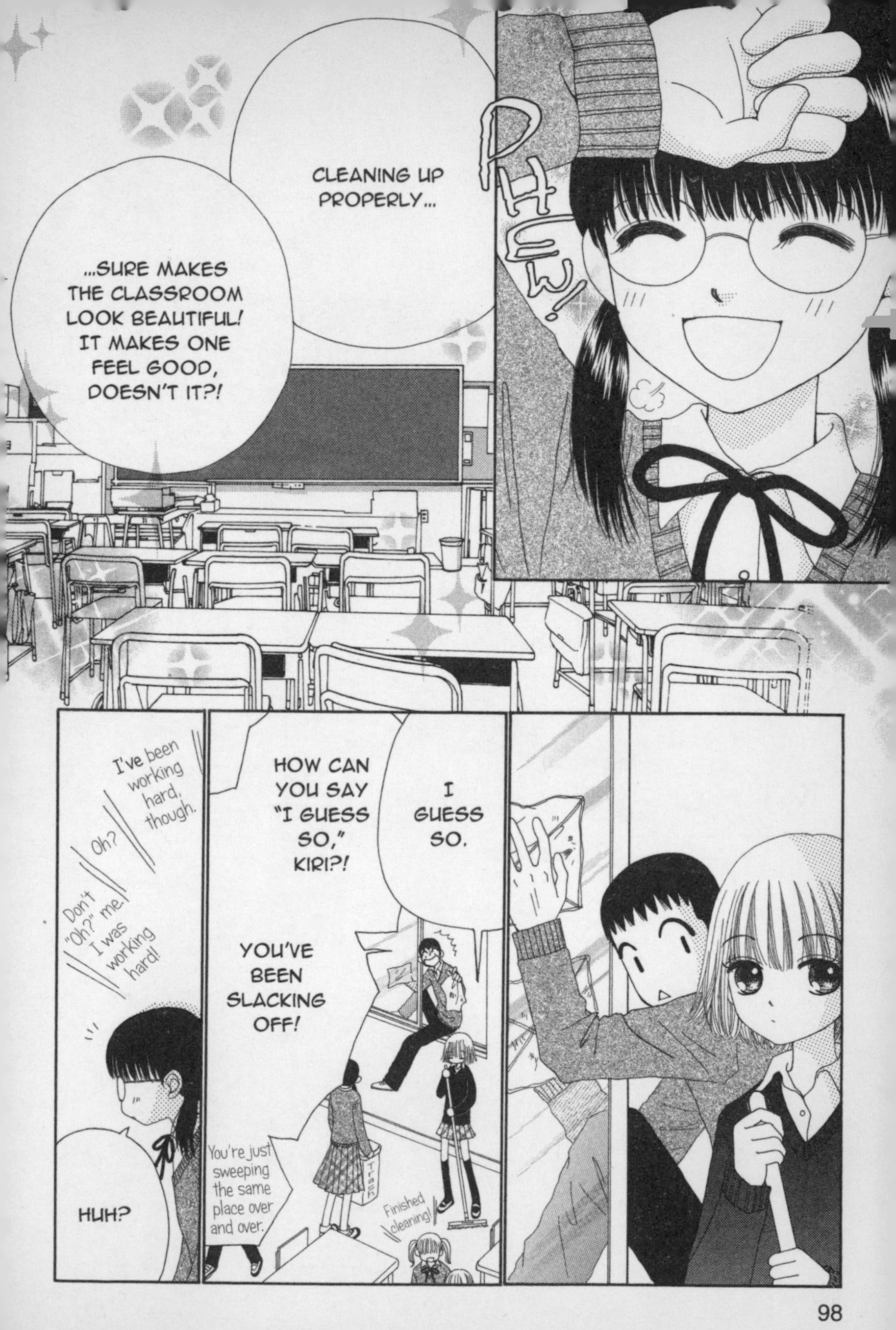
PHEW!
CLEANING UP PROPERLY...
...SURE MAKES THE CLASSROOM LOOK BEAUTIFUL! IT MAKES ONE FEEL GOOD, DOESN'T IT?!
I GUESS SO.
HOW CAN YOU SAY "I GUESS SO," KIRI?!
YOU'VE BEEN SLACKING OFF!
Finished cleaning!
You're just sweeping the same place over and over.
I've been working hard, though.
Oh?
Don't "Oh?" me. I was working hard!
HUH?

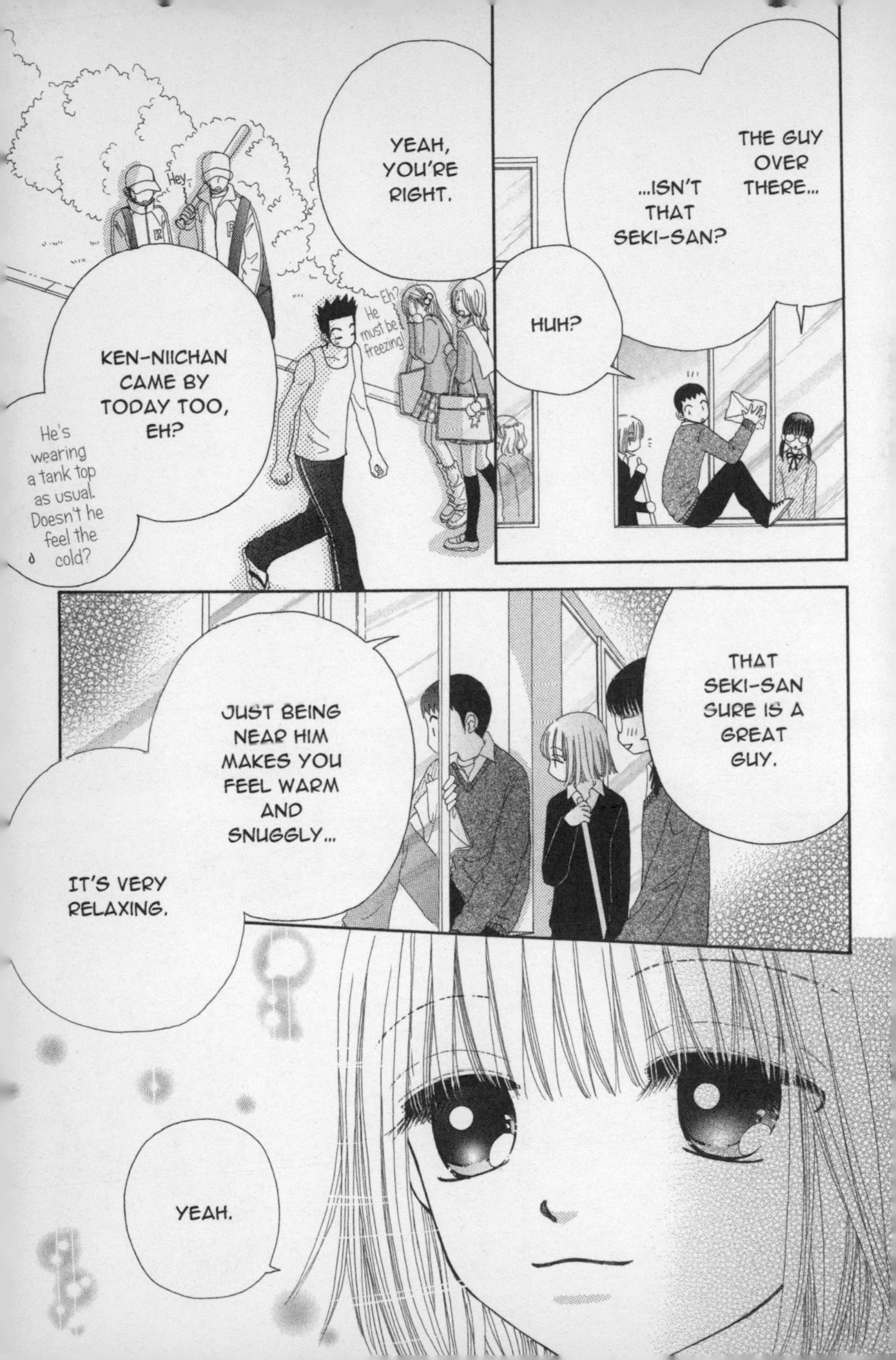
THE GUY OVER THERE... ...ISN'T THAT SEKI-SAN?
HUH?
YEAH, YOU'RE RIGHT.
Eh? He must be freezing.
Hey...
KEN-NIICHAN CAME BY TODAY TOO, EH?
He's wearing a tank top as usual. Doesn't he feel the cold?
THAT SEKI-SAN SURE IS A GREAT GUY.
JUST BEING NEAR HIM MAKES YOU FEEL WARM AND SNUGGLY...
IT'S VERY RELAXING.
YEAH.

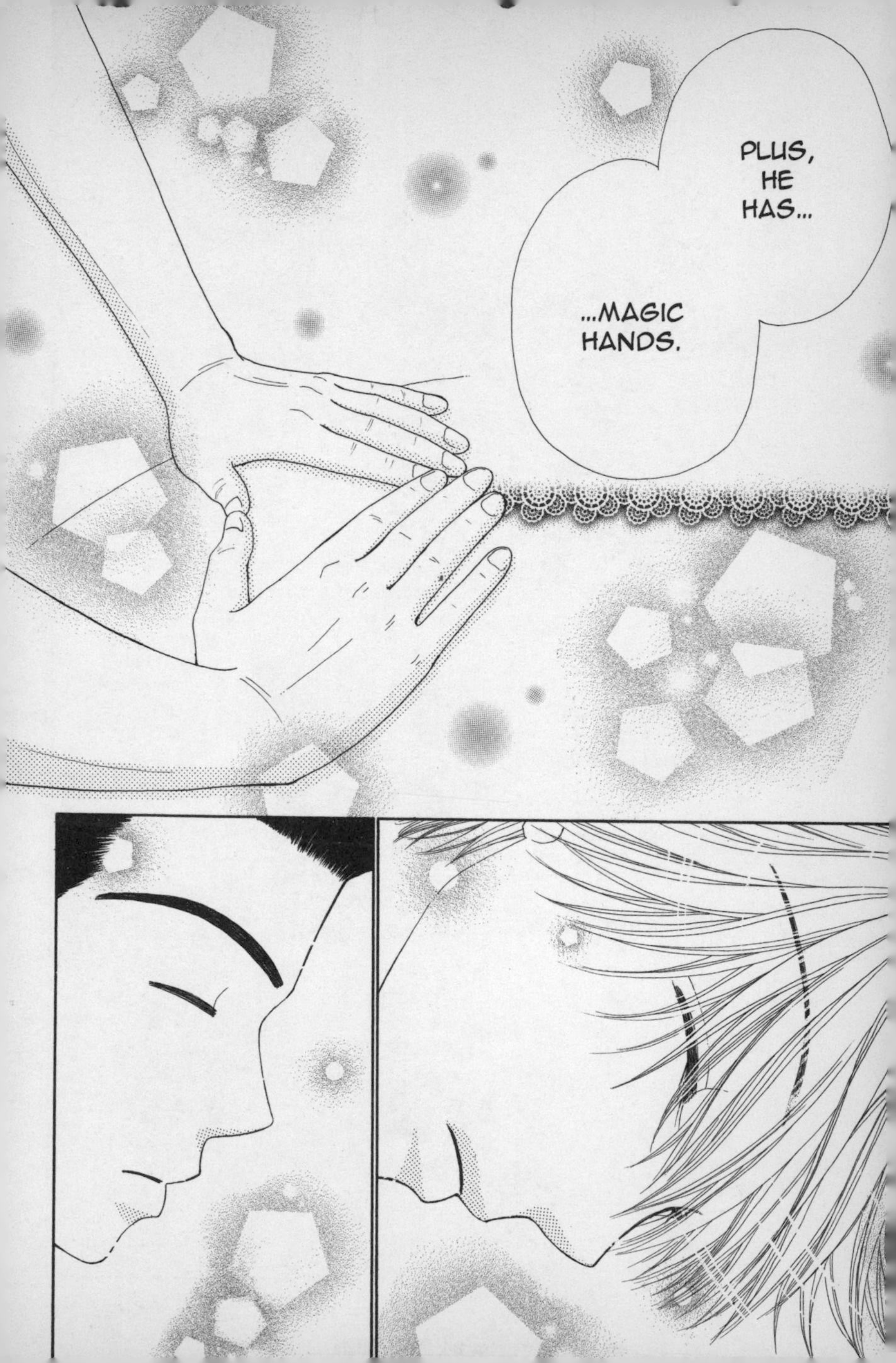
PLUS, HE HAS...
...MAGIC HANDS.

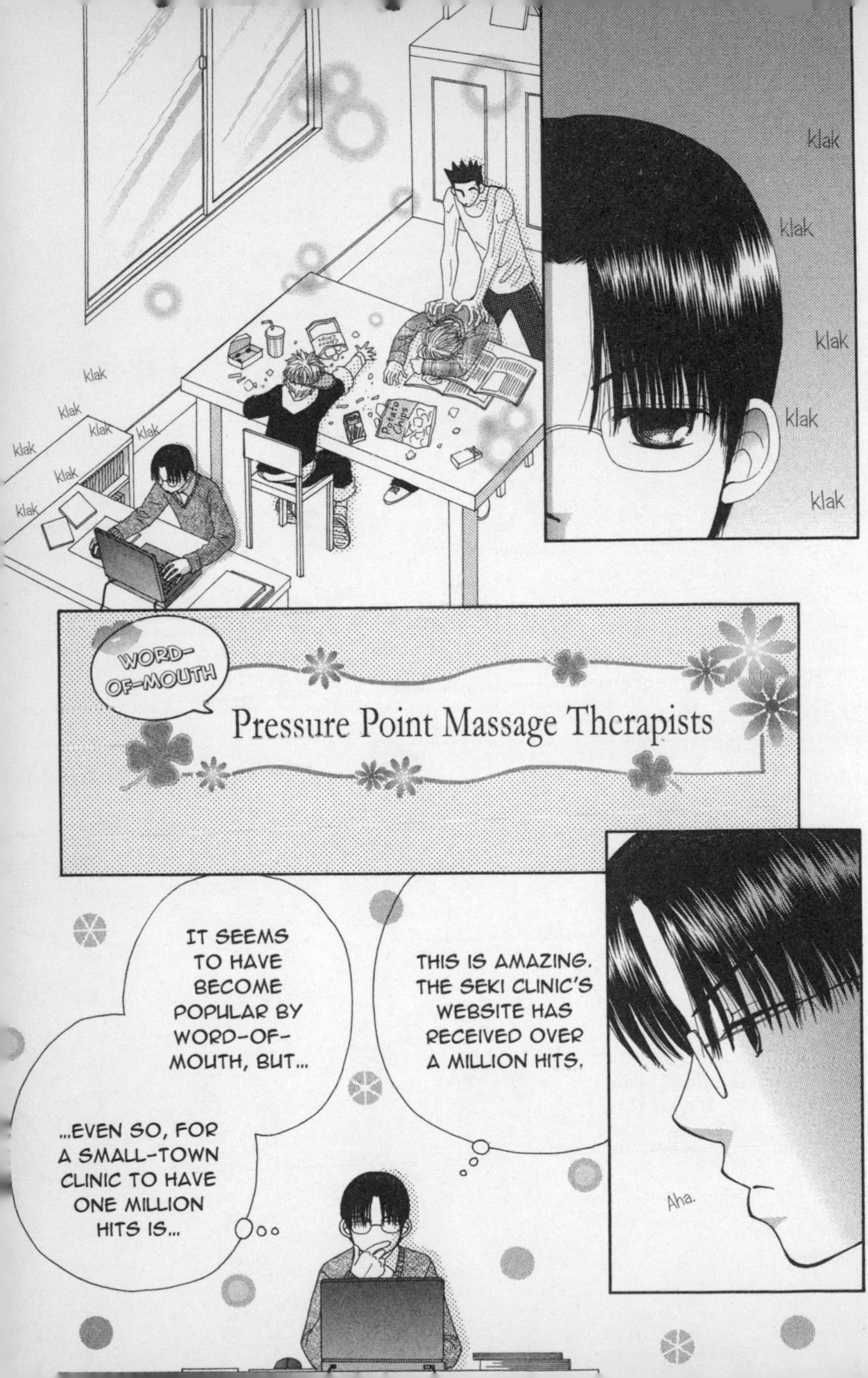
klak
klak
klak
klak
klak
klak
klak
klak
klak
klak
klak
WORD-OF-MOUTH
Pressure Point Massage Therapists
Aha.
THIS IS AMAZING. THE SEKI CLINIC'S WEBSITE HAS RECEIVED OVER A MILLION HITS.
IT SEEMS TO HAVE BECOME POPULAR BY WORD-OF-MOUTH, BUT...
...EVEN SO, FOR A SMALL-TOWN CLINIC TO HAVE ONE MILLION HITS IS...

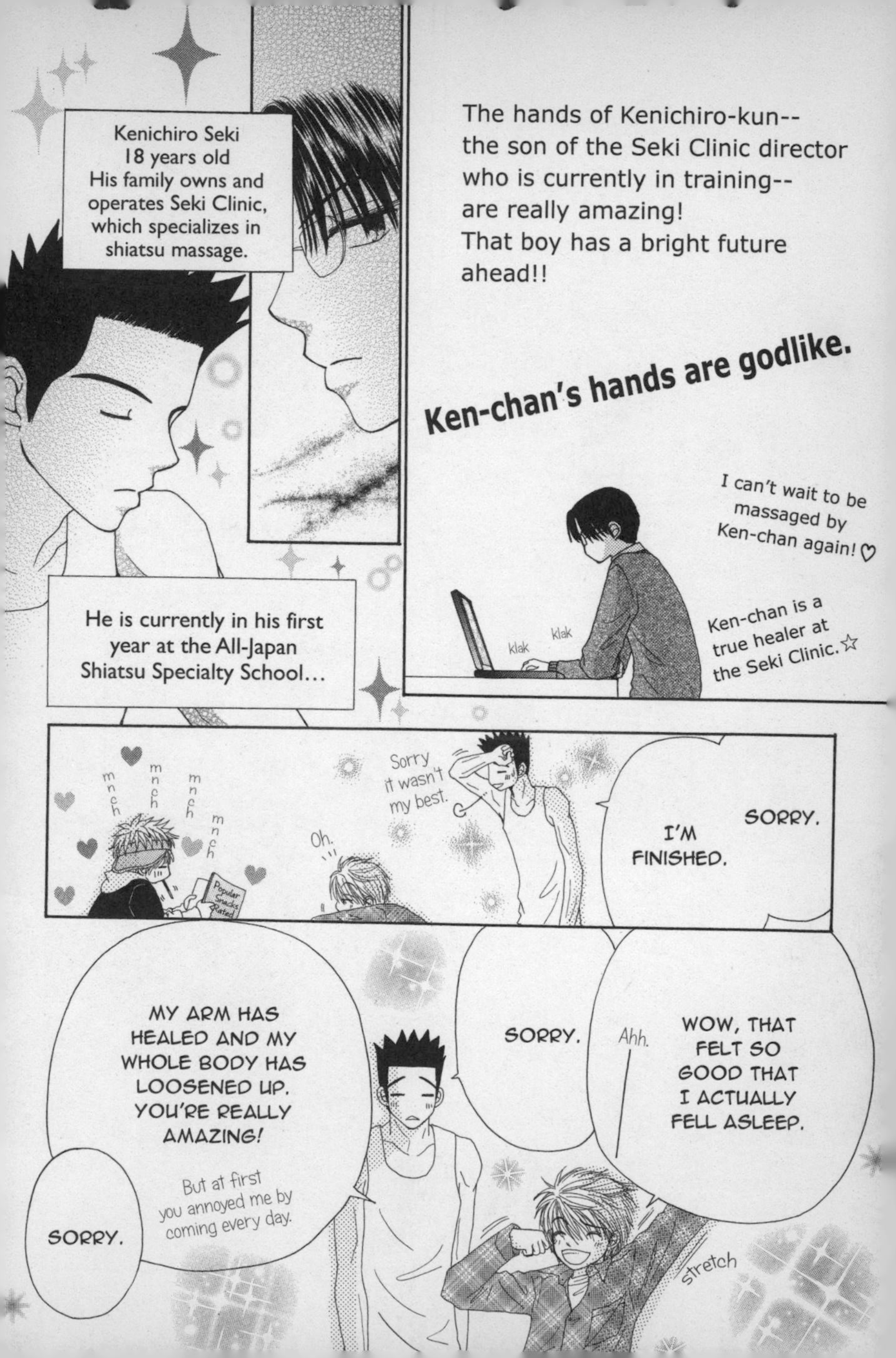

The hands of Kenichiro-kun--
the son of the Seki Clinic director
who is currently in training--
are really amazing!
That boy has a bright future ahead!!
Ken-chan's hands are godlike.
I can't wait to be massaged by Ken-chan again! ♡
Ken-chan is a true healer at the Seki Clinic. ☆
klak
klak
Kenichiro Seki
18 years old
His family owns and operates Seki Clinic, which specializes in shiatsu massage.
He is currently in his first year at the All-Japan Shiatsu Specialty School...
SORRY.
I'M FINISHED.
Sorry it wasn't my best.
Oh.
mnch
mnch
mnch
mnch
Popular Snacks Rated
WOW, THAT FELT SO GOOD THAT I ACTUALLY FELL ASLEEP.
Ahh.
SORRY.
MY ARM HAS HEALED AND MY WHOLE BODY HAS LOOSENED UP. YOU'RE REALLY AMAZING!
But at first you annoyed me by coming every day.
SORRY.
stretch

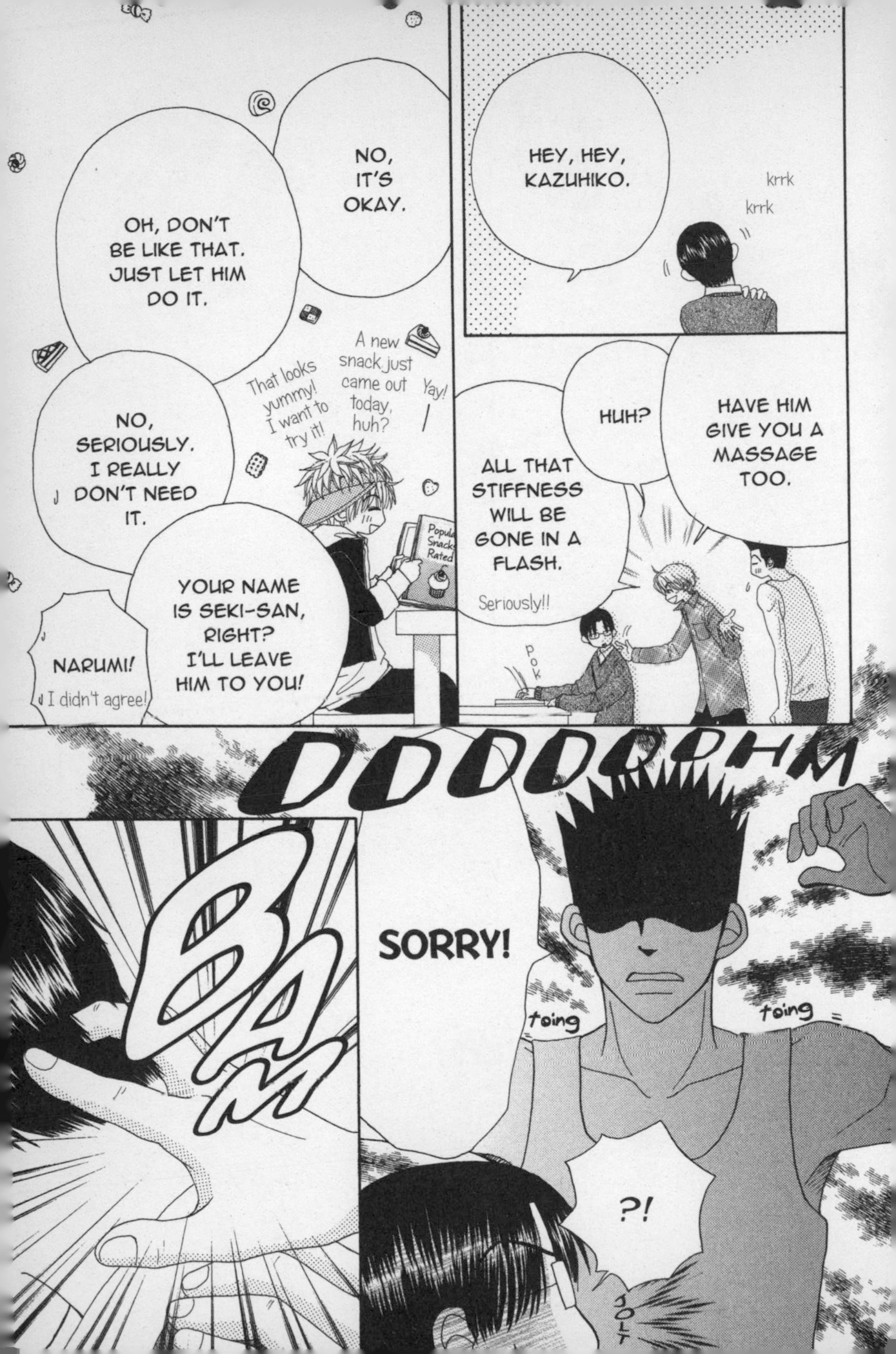
HEY, HEY, KAZUHIKO.
krrk
krrk
HAVE HIM GIVE YOU A MASSAGE TOO.
HUH?
ALL THAT STIFFNESS WILL BE GONE IN A FLASH.
Seriously!!
Pok
NO, IT'S OKAY.
OH, DON'T BE LIKE THAT. JUST LET HIM DO IT.
A new snack just came out today, huh?
Yay!
That looks yummy! I want to try it!
NO, SERIOUSLY. I REALLY DON'T NEED IT.
YOUR NAME IS SEKI-SAN, RIGHT? I'LL LEAVE HIM TO YOU!
NARUMI!
I didn't agree!
DDDDRRHM
SORRY!
toing
toing
?!
JOLT
BAM

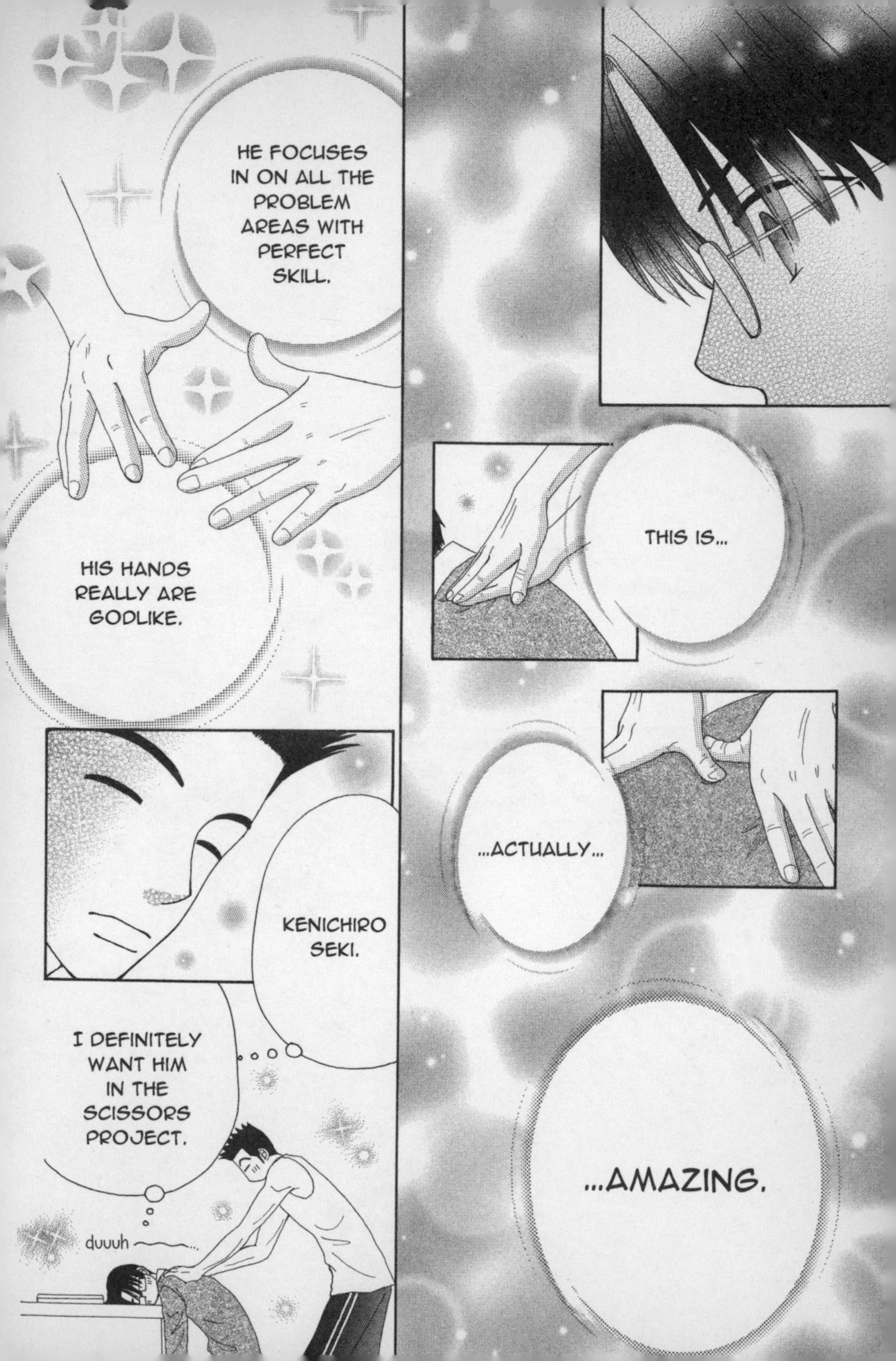
THIS IS...
...ACTUALLY...
...AMAZING.
HE FOCUSES IN ON ALL THE PROBLEM AREAS WITH PERFECT SKILL.
HIS HANDS REALLY ARE GODLIKE.
KENICHIRO SEKI.
I DEFINITELY WANT HIM IN THE SCISSORS PROJECT.
duuuh ~...

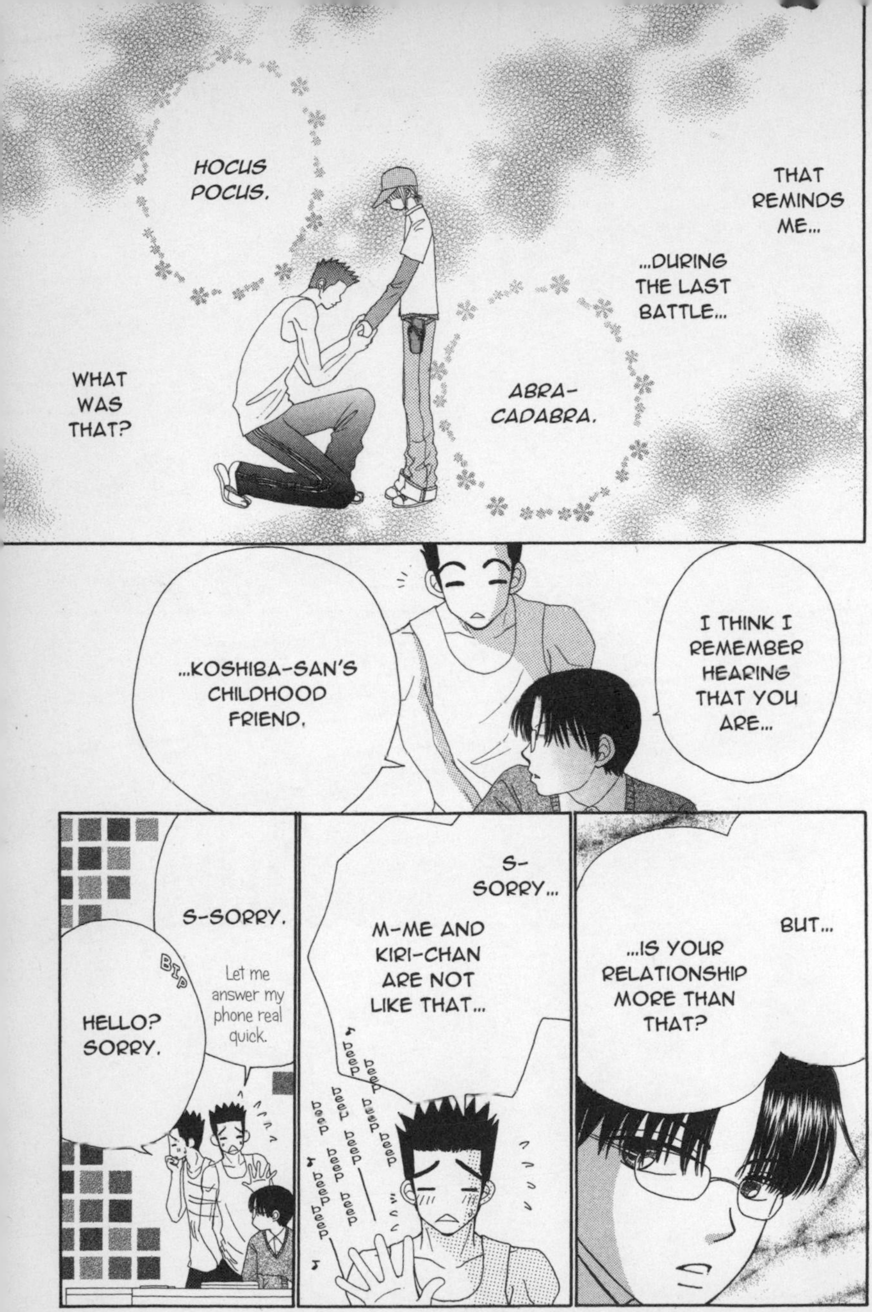
THAT REMINDS ME...
...DURING THE LAST BATTLE...
ABRA-CADABRA.
HOCUS POCUS.
WHAT WAS THAT?
I THINK I REMEMBER HEARING THAT YOU ARE...
...KOSHIBA-SAN'S CHILDHOOD FRIEND.
BUT...
...IS YOUR RELATIONSHIP MORE THAN THAT?
S-SORRY...
M-ME AND KIRI-CHAN ARE NOT LIKE THAT...
beep beep beep beep beep beep beep beep beep beep beep beep
S-SORRY.
Let me answer my phone real quick.
BIP
HELLO? SORRY.

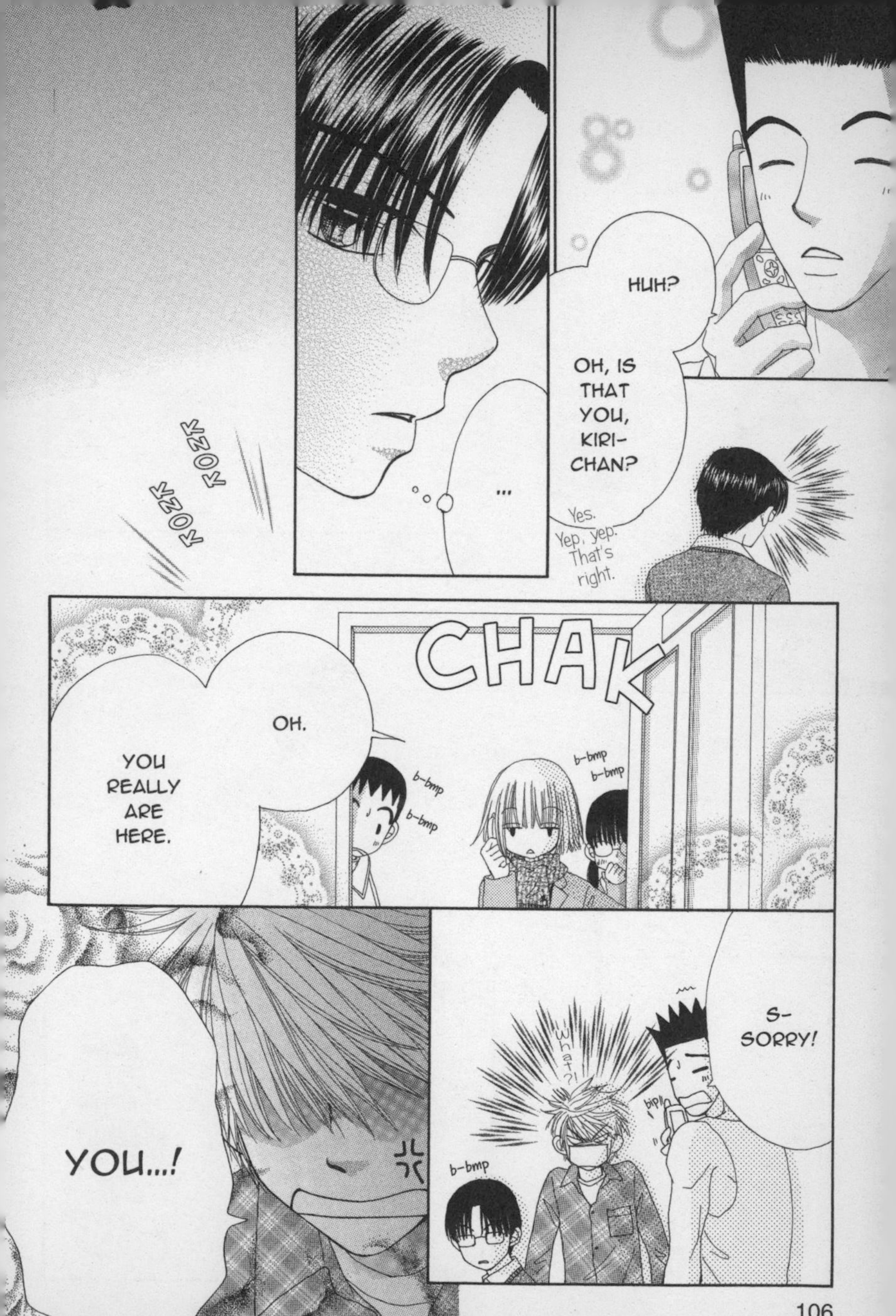
HUH?
OH, IS THAT YOU, KIRI-CHAN?
Yes. Yep, yep. That's right.
...
KNOK KNOK
CHAK
OH.
YOU REALLY ARE HERE.
b-bmp b-bmp
b-bmp b-bmp
S-SORRY!
What?!
bip
b-bmp
YOU...!

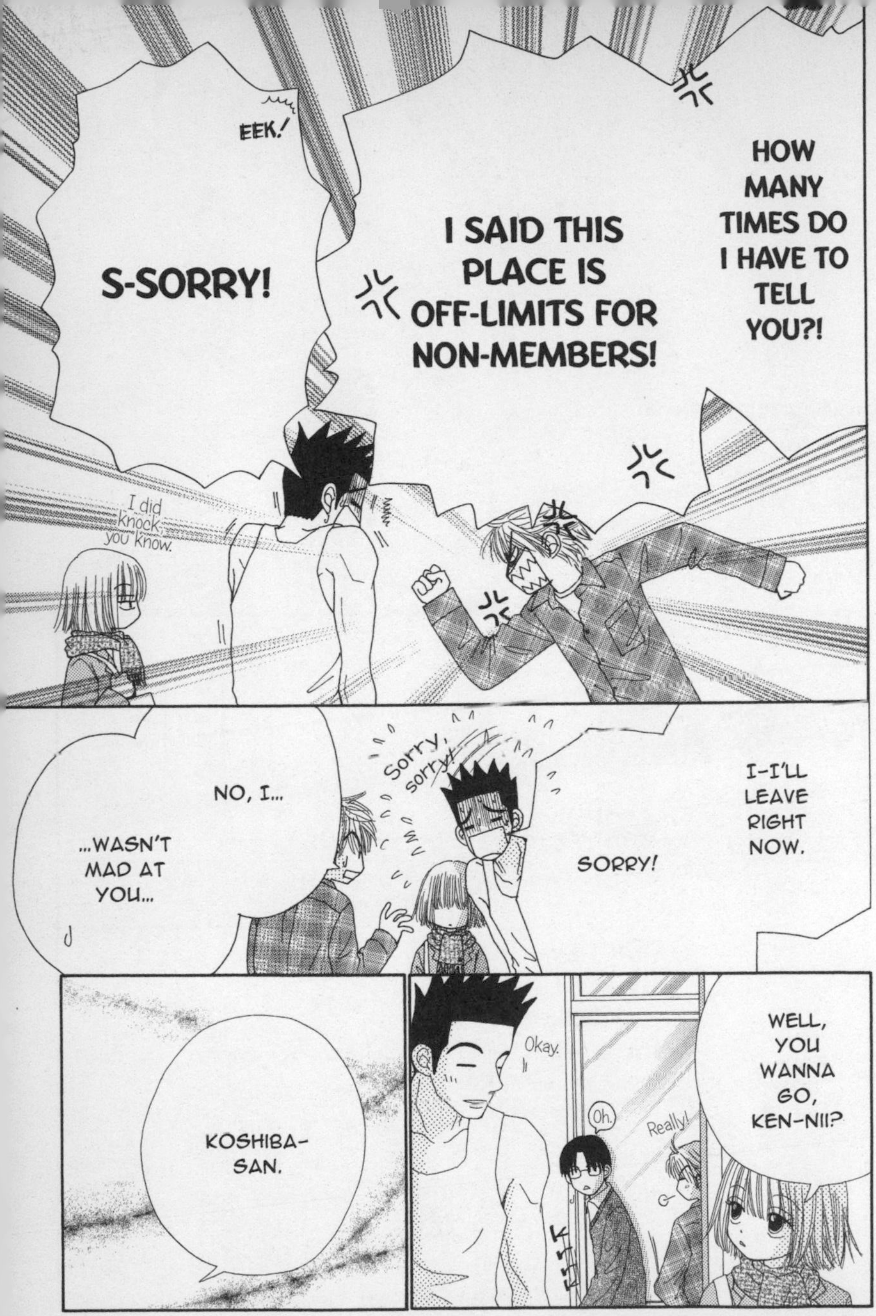
HOW MANY TIMES DO I HAVE TO TELL YOU?!
I SAID THIS PLACE IS OFF-LIMITS FOR NON-MEMBERS!
EEK!
S-SORRY!
I did knock, you know.
I-I'LL LEAVE RIGHT NOW.
SORRY!
Sorry, sorry!
NO, I...
...WASN'T MAD AT YOU...
WELL, YOU WANNA GO, KEN-NII?
Really!
Oh.
Okay.
KOSHIBA-SAN.

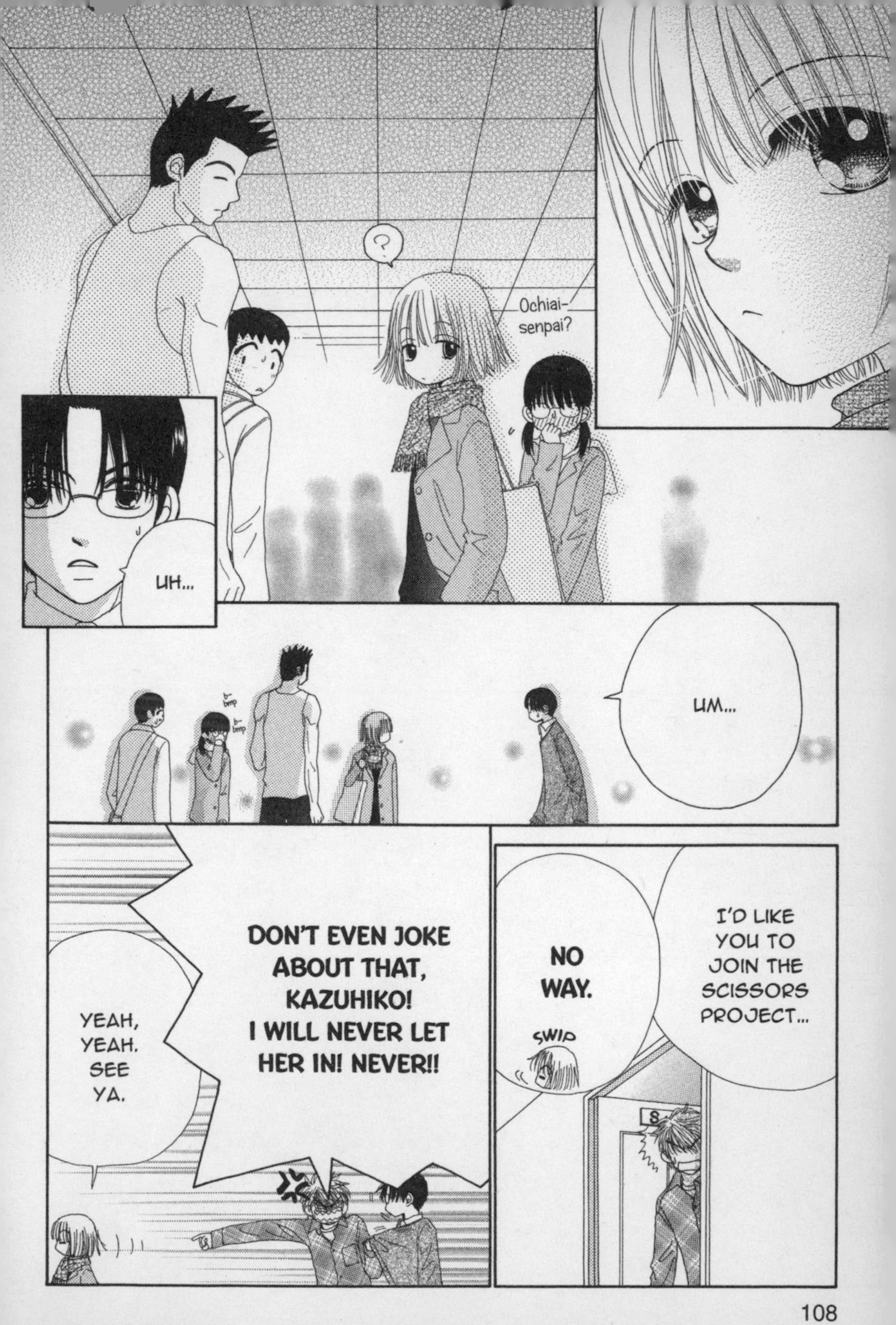
?
Ochiai-senpai?
UH...
b-bump b-bump
UM...
I'D LIKE YOU TO JOIN THE SCISSORS PROJECT...
NO WAY.
SWIP
DON'T EVEN JOKE ABOUT THAT, KAZUHIKO! I WILL NEVER LET HER IN! NEVER!!
YEAH, YEAH. SEE YA.

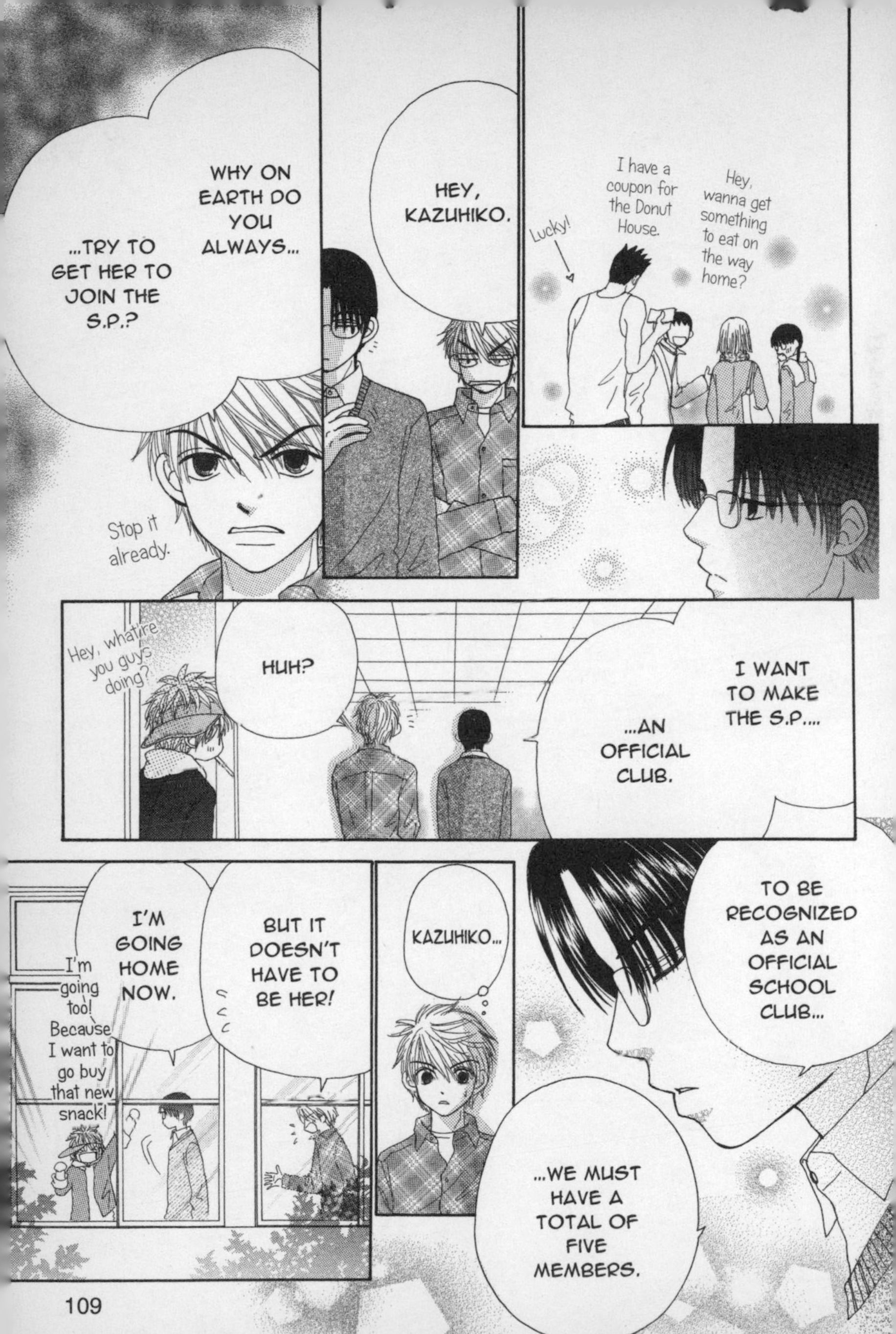

Hey, wanna get something to eat on the way home?
I have a coupon for the Donut House.
Lucky!
HEY, KAZUHIKO.
WHY ON EARTH DO YOU ALWAYS...
...TRY TO GET HER TO JOIN THE S.P.?
Stop it already.
I WANT TO MAKE THE S.P....
...AN OFFICIAL CLUB.
HUH?
Hey, what're you guys doing?
TO BE RECOGNIZED AS AN OFFICIAL SCHOOL CLUB...
...WE MUST HAVE A TOTAL OF FIVE MEMBERS.
KAZUHIKO...
BUT IT DOESN'T HAVE TO BE HER!
I'M GOING HOME NOW.
I'm going too! Because I want to go buy that new snack!

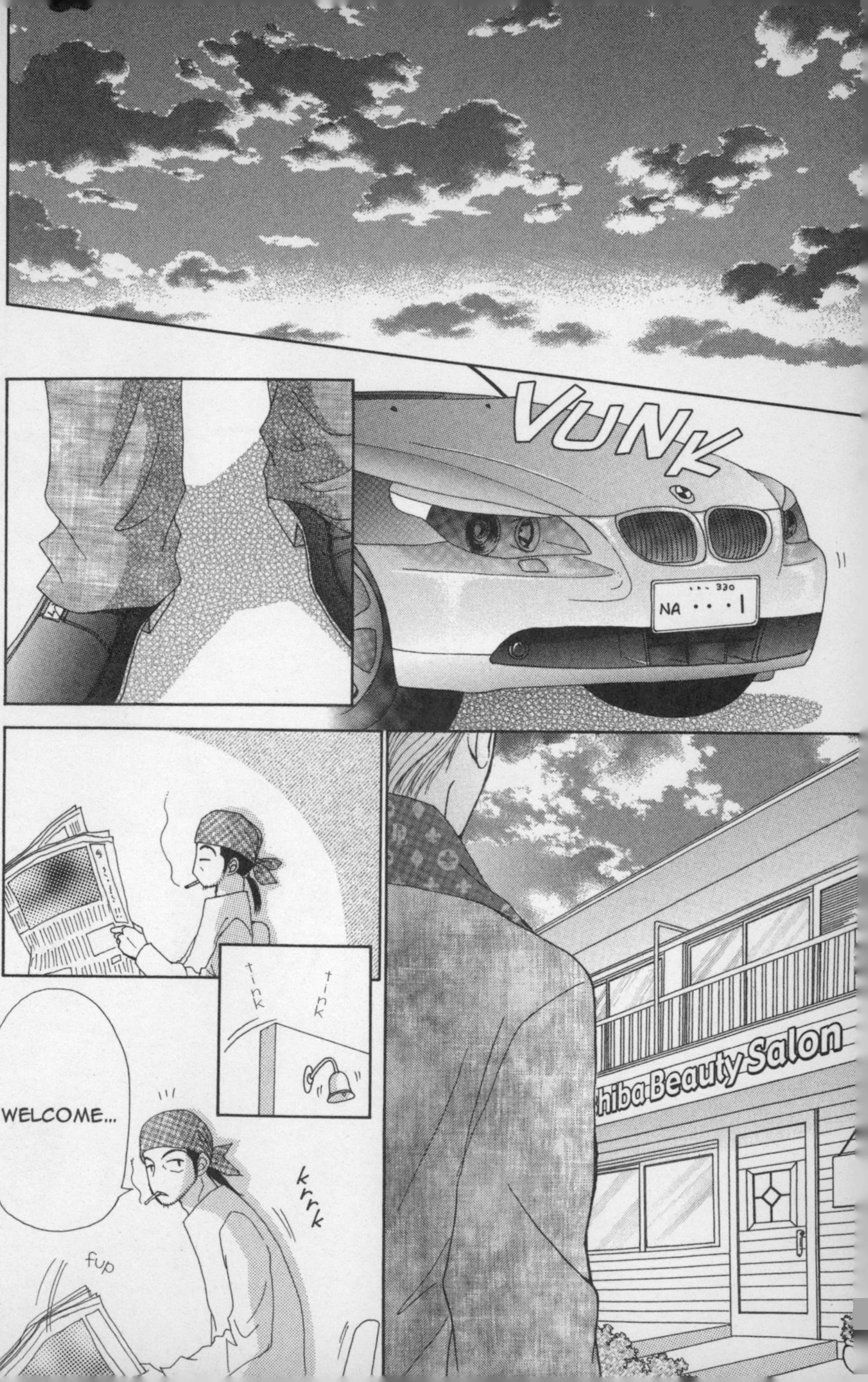
VUNK
NA ・・・1
hiba Beauty Salon
tink
tink
WELCOME...
krrk
fup

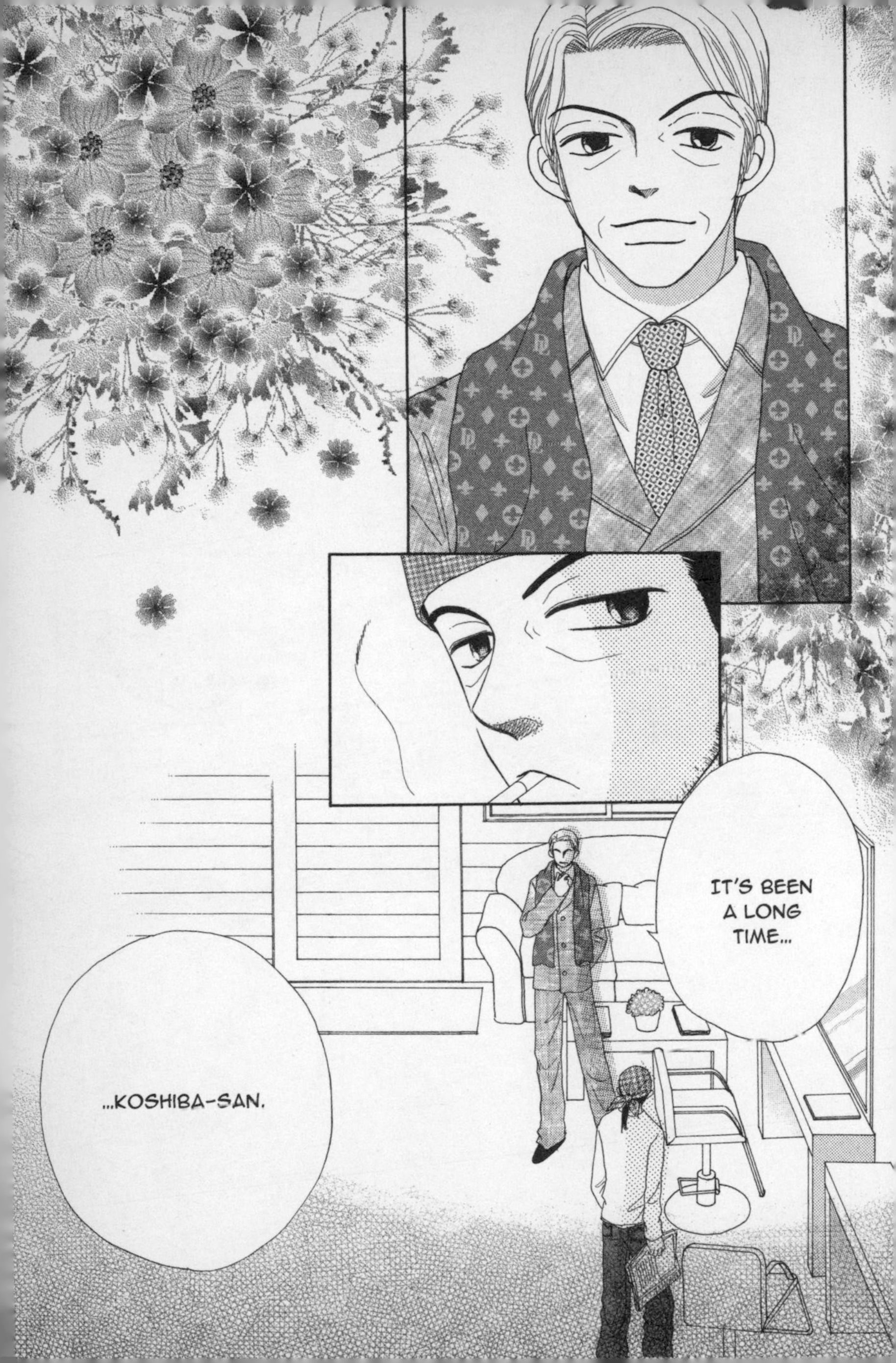
IT'S BEEN A LONG TIME...
...KOSHIBA-SAN.

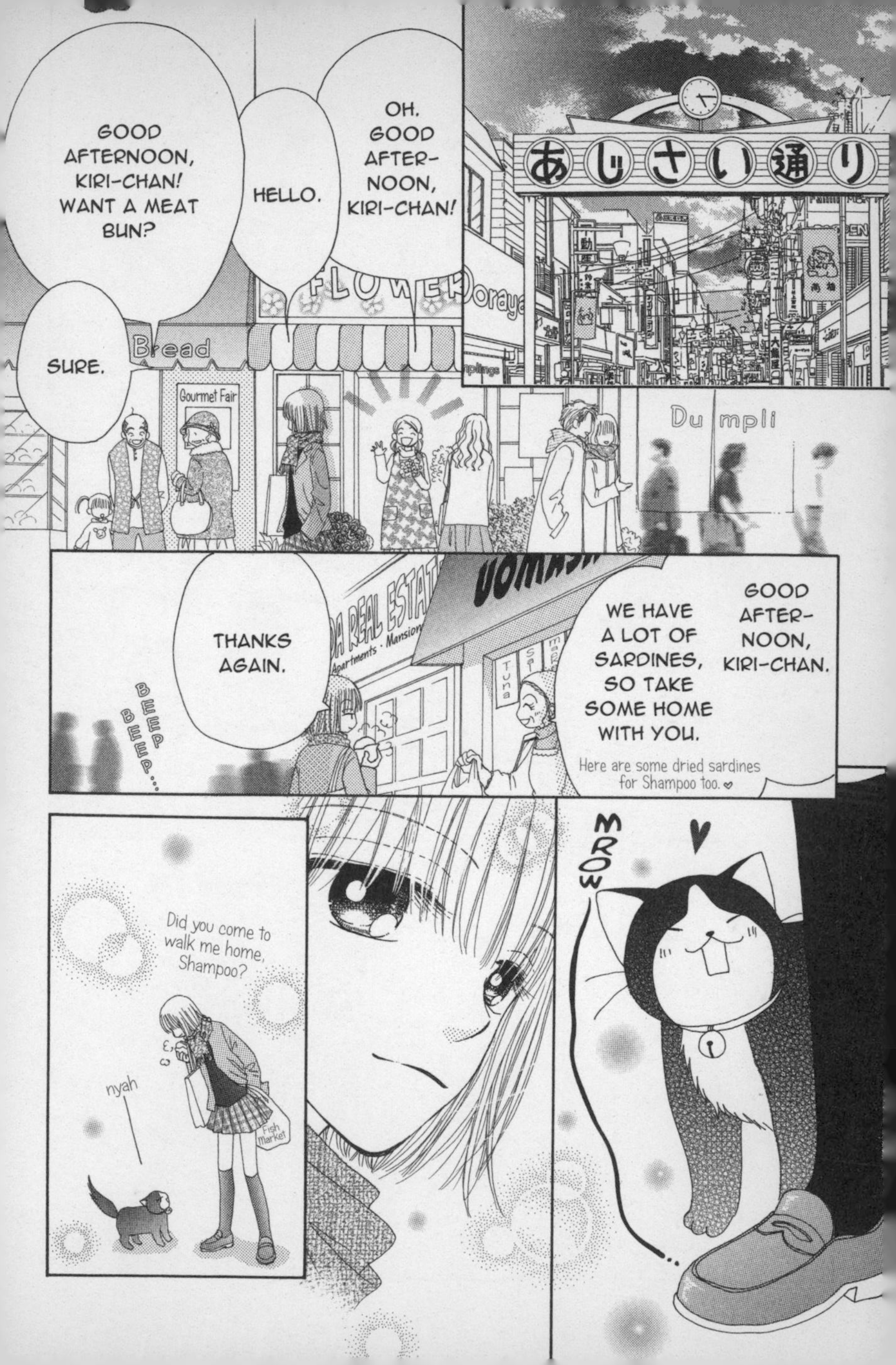

あじさい通り
OH. GOOD AFTER-NOON, KIRI-CHAN!
HELLO.
GOOD AFTERNOON, KIRI-CHAN! WANT A MEAT BUN?
SURE.
Bread
Gourmet Fair
GOOD AFTER-NOON, KIRI-CHAN.
WE HAVE A LOT OF SARDINES, SO TAKE SOME HOME WITH YOU.
Here are some dried sardines for Shampoo too. ♥
Tuna
THANKS AGAIN.
BEEP BEEP...
MROW ♥ ...
Did you come to walk me home, Shampoo?
nyah
Fish Market

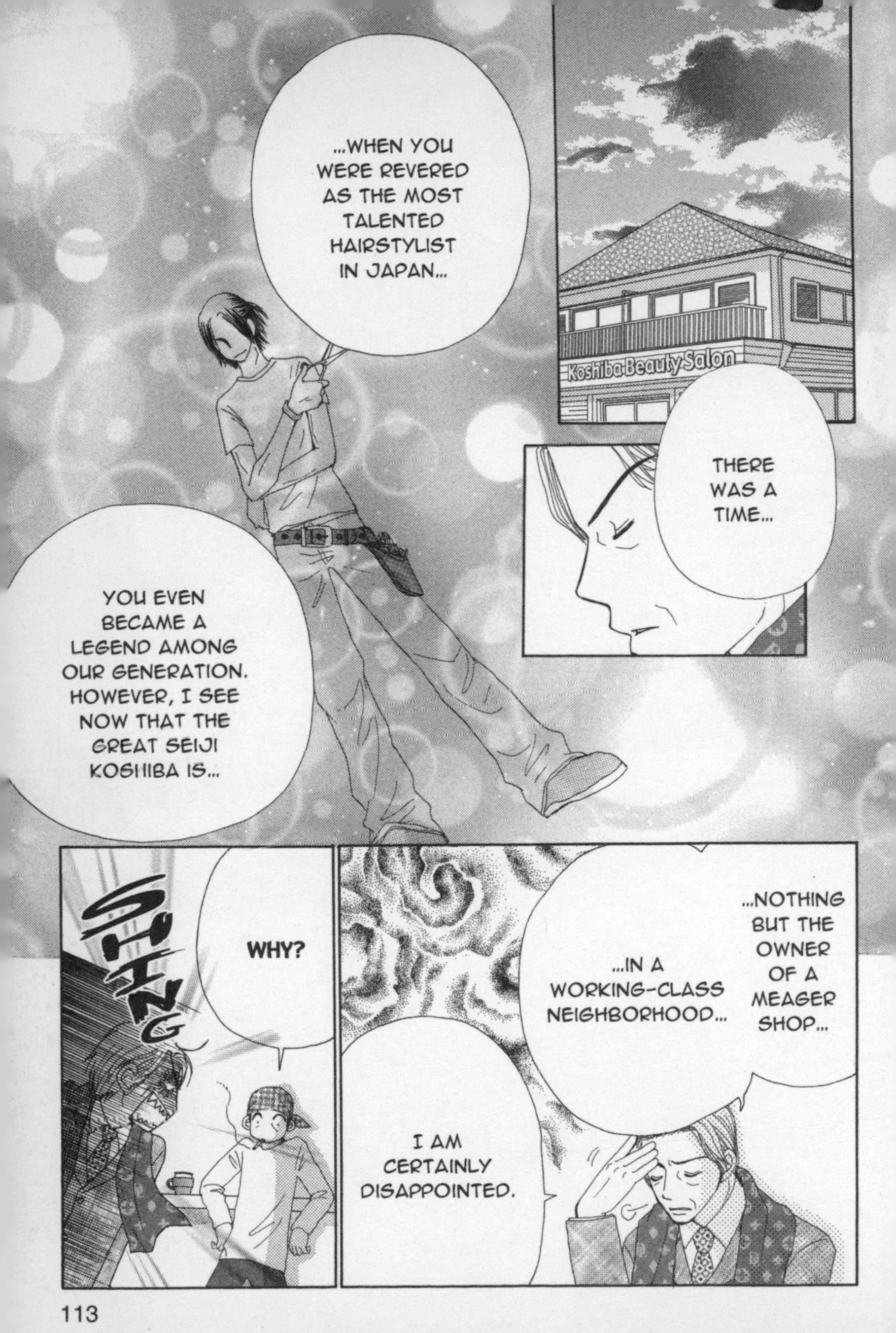
Koshiba Beauty Salon
THERE WAS A TIME...
...WHEN YOU WERE REVERED AS THE MOST TALENTED HAIRSTYLIST IN JAPAN...
YOU EVEN BECAME A LEGEND AMONG OUR GENERATION. HOWEVER, I SEE NOW THAT THE GREAT SEIJI KOSHIBA IS...
...NOTHING BUT THE OWNER OF A MEAGER SHOP...
...IN A WORKING-CLASS NEIGHBORHOOD...
I AM CERTAINLY DISAPPOINTED.
SHING
WHY?

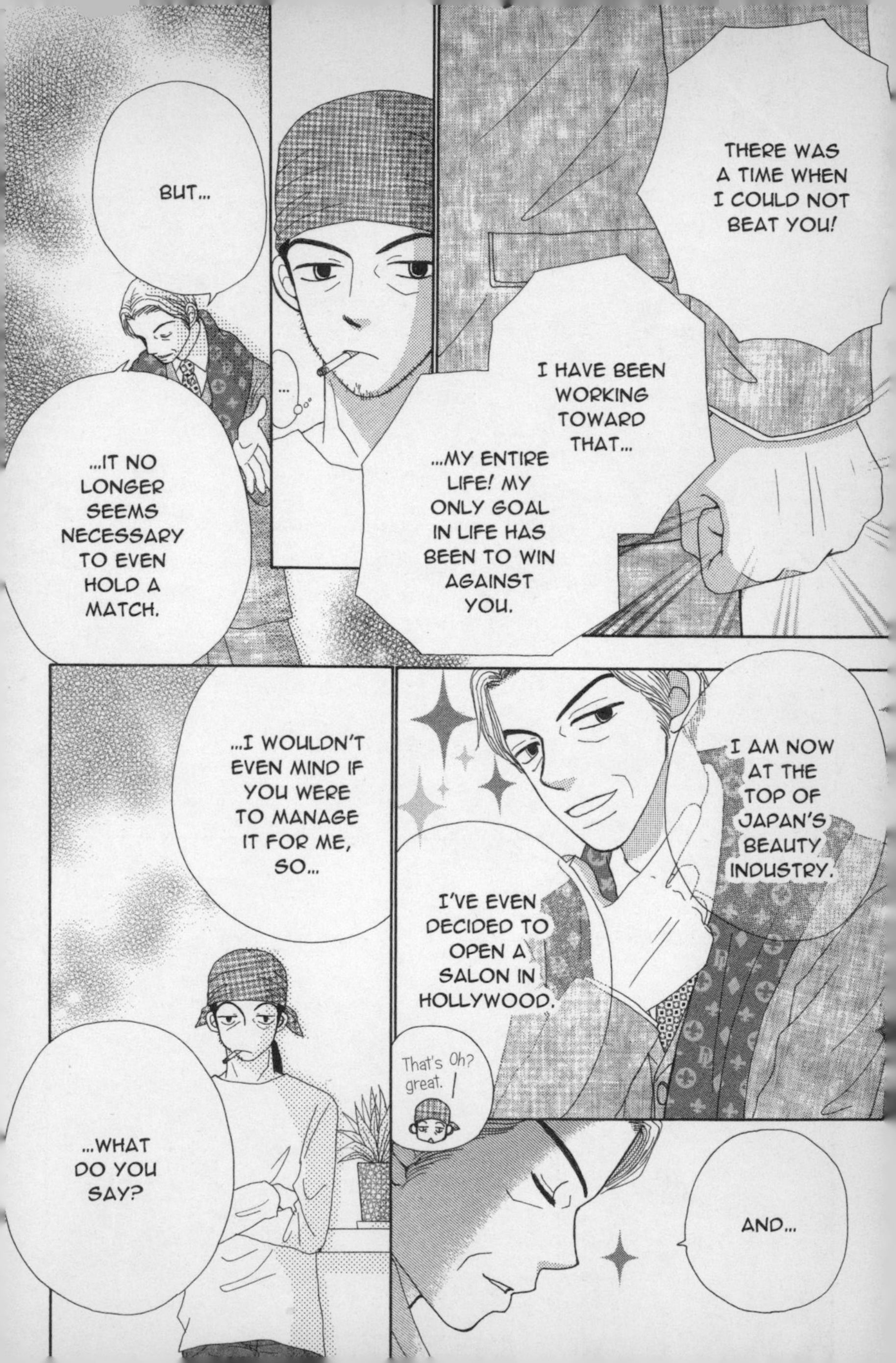
THERE WAS A TIME WHEN I COULD NOT BEAT YOU!
I HAVE BEEN WORKING TOWARD THAT...
...MY ENTIRE LIFE! MY ONLY GOAL IN LIFE HAS BEEN TO WIN AGAINST YOU.
...
BUT...
...IT NO LONGER SEEMS NECESSARY TO EVEN HOLD A MATCH.
I AM NOW AT THE TOP OF JAPAN'S BEAUTY INDUSTRY.
I'VE EVEN DECIDED TO OPEN A SALON IN HOLLYWOOD.
Oh?
That's great.
AND...
...I WOULDN'T EVEN MIND IF YOU WERE TO MANAGE IT FOR ME, SO...
...WHAT DO YOU SAY?

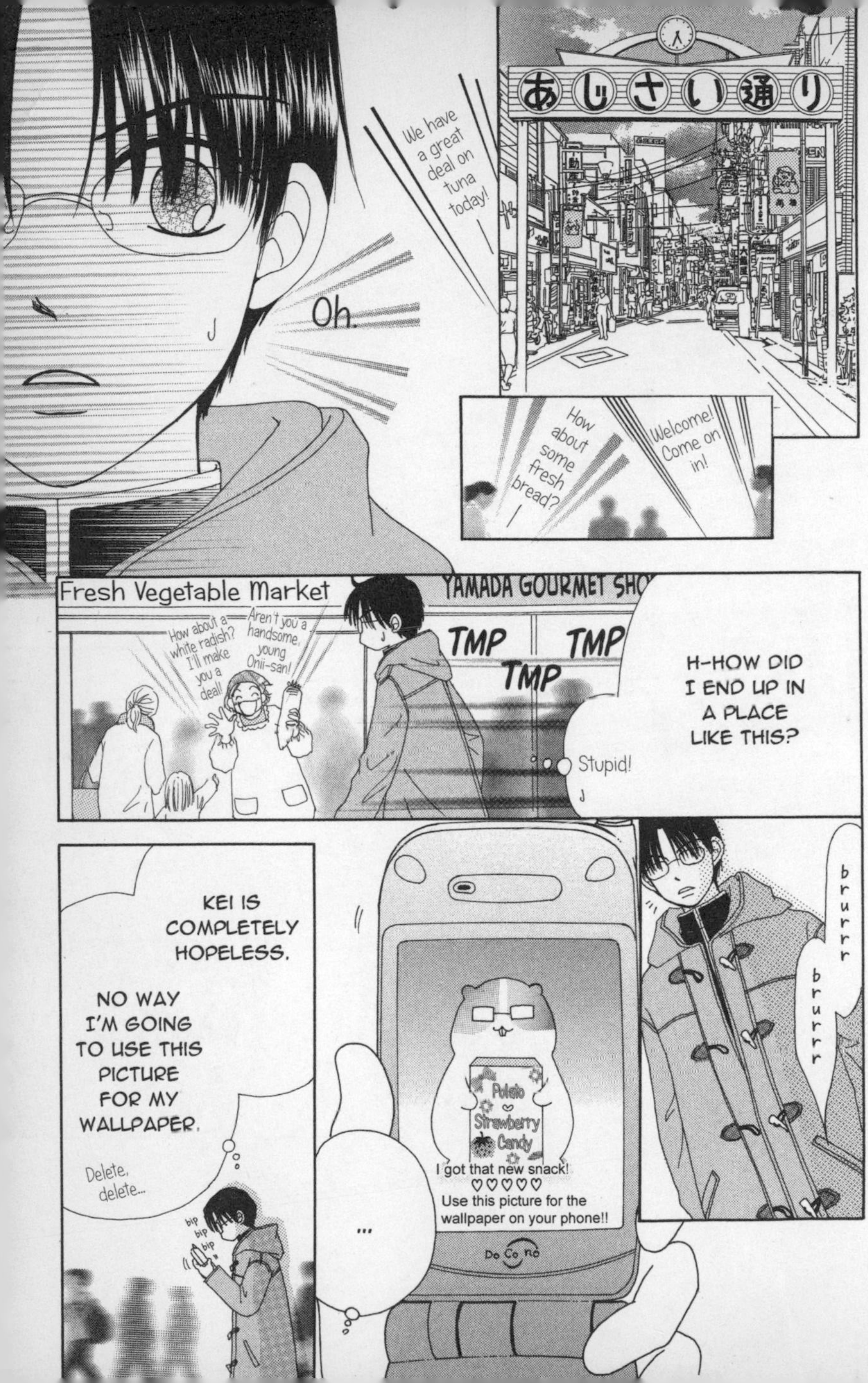
あじさい通り
We have a great deal on tuna today!
Welcome! Come on in!
How about some fresh bread?
Oh.
H-HOW DID I END UP IN A PLACE LIKE THIS?
Stupid!
TMP
TMP
TMP
YAMADA GOURMET SHO
Aren't you a handsome, young Onii-san!
How about a white radish? I'll make you a deal!
Fresh Vegetable Market
brurrr
brurrr
I got that new snack! ♡♡♡♡♡
Use this picture for the wallpaper on your phone!!
Potato
Strawberry
Candy
...
KEI IS COMPLETELY HOPELESS.
NO WAY I'M GOING TO USE THIS PICTURE FOR MY WALLPAPER.
Delete, delete...
bip
bip
bip

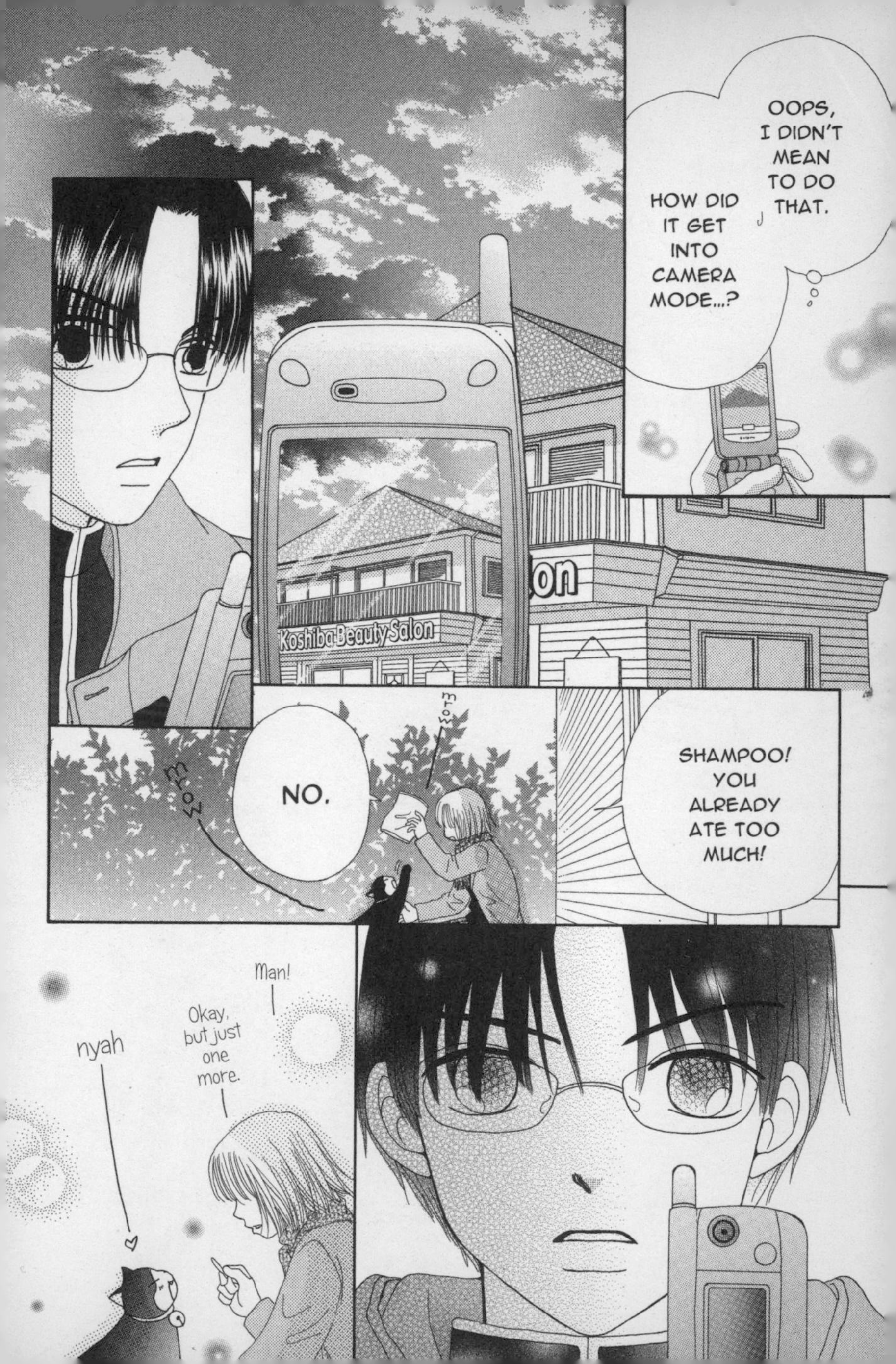
OOPS, I DIDN'T MEAN TO DO THAT.
HOW DID IT GET INTO CAMERA MODE...?
Koshiba Beauty Salon
SHAMPOO! YOU ALREADY ATE TOO MUCH!
mrow
NO.
mrow
Man!
Okay, but just one more.
nyah

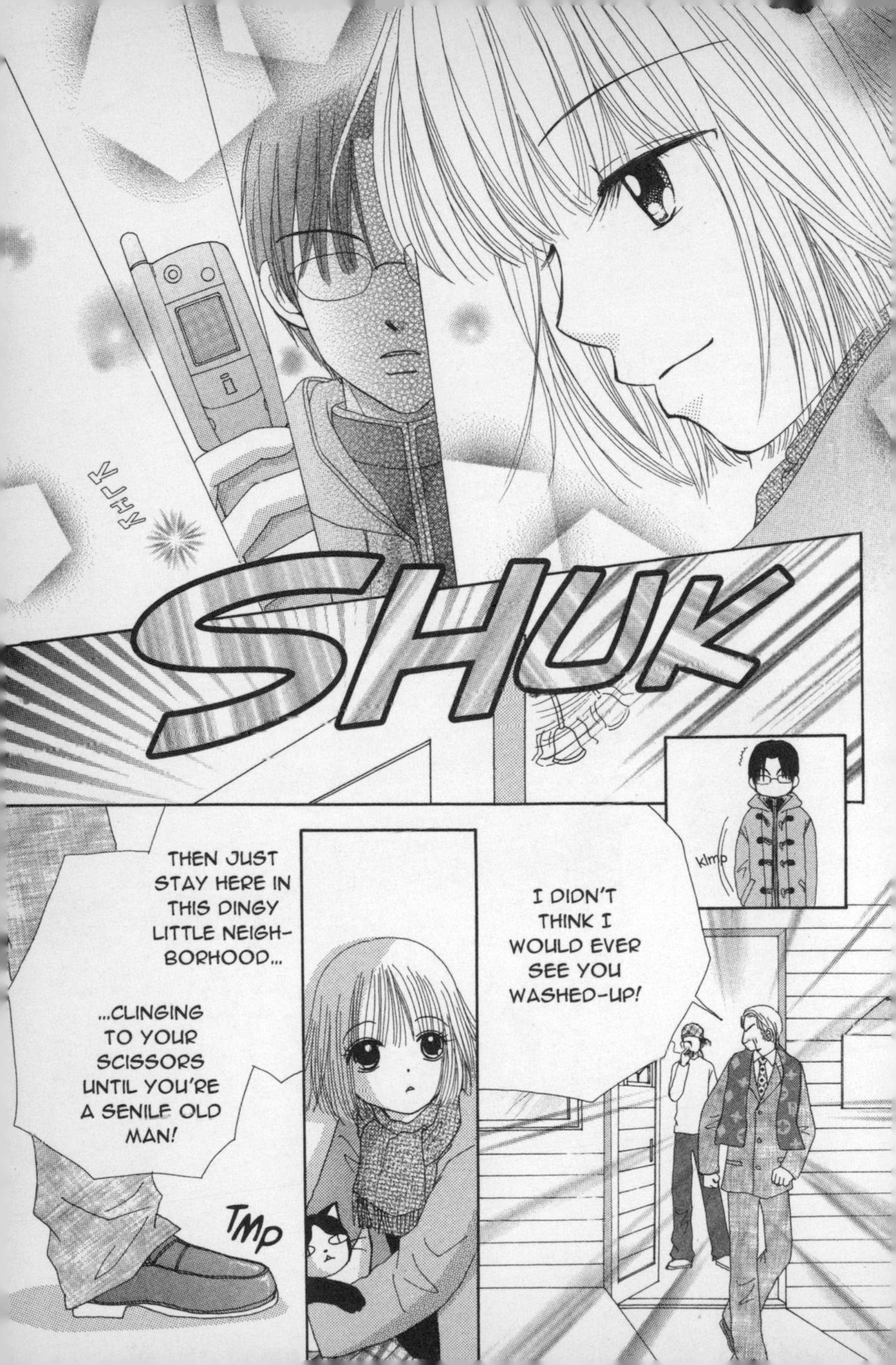
SHUK
klmp
I DIDN'T THINK I WOULD EVER SEE YOU WASHED-UP!
THEN JUST STAY HERE IN THIS DINGY LITTLE NEIGHBORHOOD...
...CLINGING TO YOUR SCISSORS UNTIL YOU'RE A SENILE OLD MAN!
TMP

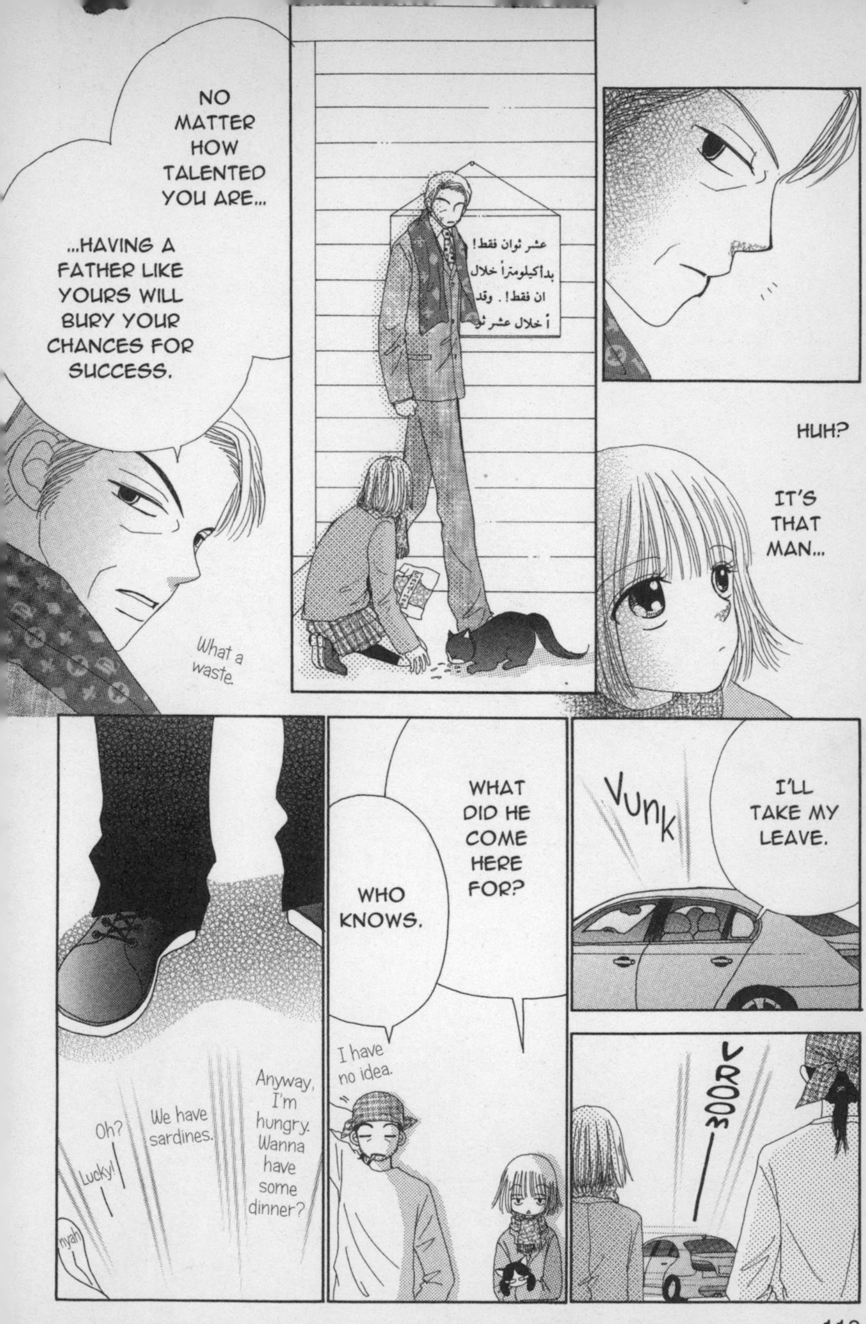

HUH?
IT'S THAT MAN...
عشر ثوان فقط!
بدأكيلومتراً خلال
ان فقط!. وقد
أ خلال عشر ثو
NO MATTER HOW TALENTED YOU ARE...
...HAVING A FATHER LIKE YOURS WILL BURY YOUR CHANCES FOR SUCCESS.
What a waste.
I'LL TAKE MY LEAVE.
Vunk
VROOM—
WHAT DID HE COME HERE FOR?
WHO KNOWS.
I have no idea.
Anyway, I'm hungry. Wanna have some dinner?
We have sardines.
Oh?
Lucky!
nyah

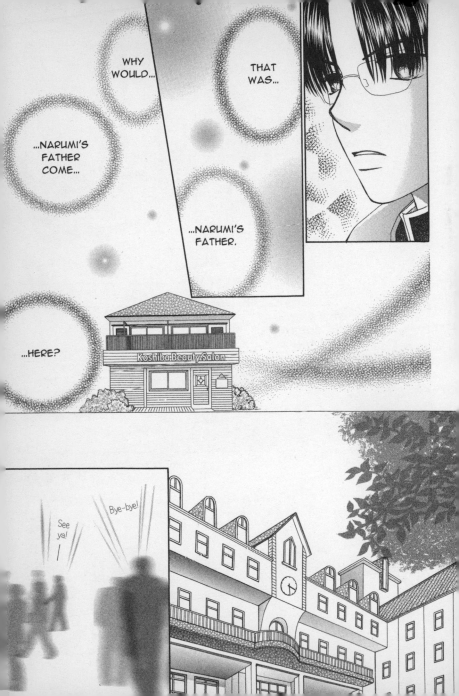

WHY WOULD...

THAT WAS...

...NARUMI'S FATHER COME...

...NARUMI'S FATHER.

...HERE?

Koshiba Beauty Salon

See ya!

Bye-bye!

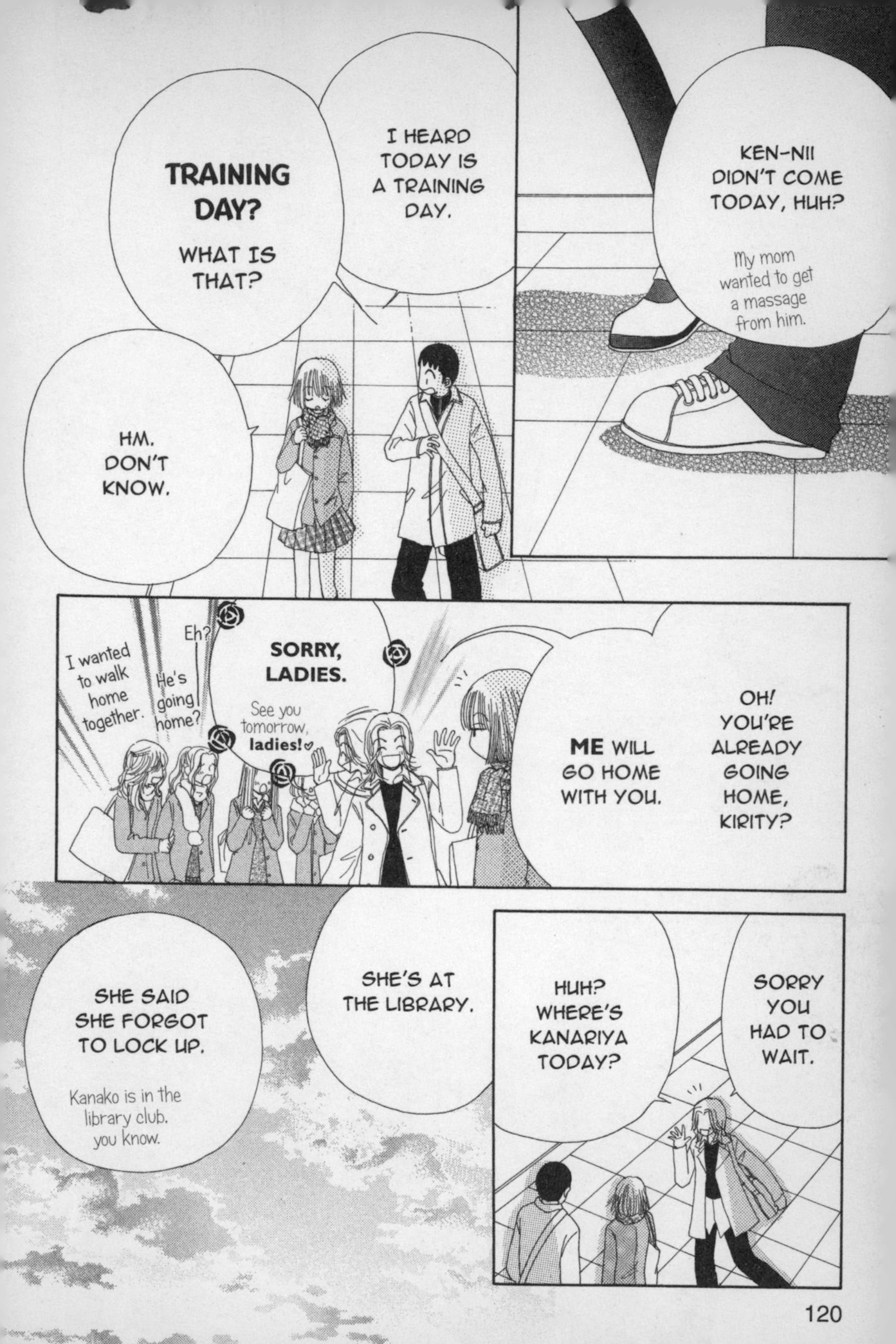
KEN-NII DIDN'T COME TODAY, HUH?
My mom wanted to get a massage from him.
I HEARD TODAY IS A TRAINING DAY.
TRAINING DAY? WHAT IS THAT?
HM. DON'T KNOW.
OH! YOU'RE ALREADY GOING HOME, KIRITY?
ME WILL GO HOME WITH YOU.
SORRY, LADIES.
See you tomorrow, ladies!♥
Eh?
He's going home?
I wanted to walk home together.
SORRY YOU HAD TO WAIT.
HUH? WHERE'S KANARIYA TODAY?
SHE'S AT THE LIBRARY.
SHE SAID SHE FORGOT TO LOCK UP.
Kanako is in the library club, you know.

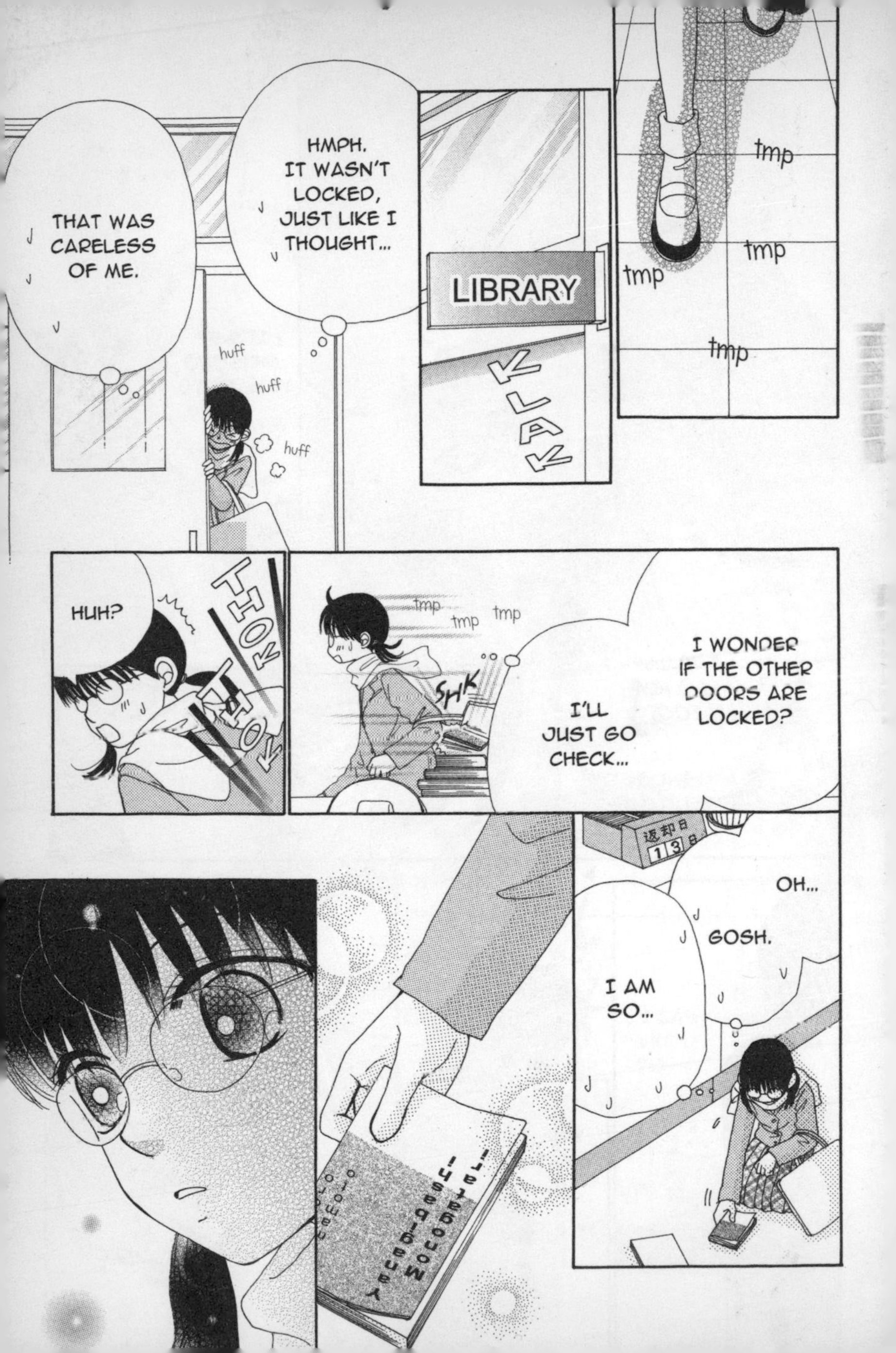
tmp
tmp
tmp
tmp
LIBRARY
KLAK
HMPH. IT WASN'T LOCKED, JUST LIKE I THOUGHT...
THAT WAS CARELESS OF ME.
huff
huff
huff
I WONDER IF THE OTHER DOORS ARE LOCKED?
I'LL JUST GO CHECK...
tmp
tmp
tmp
SHK
THOK
HUH?
OH...
GOSH.
I AM SO...

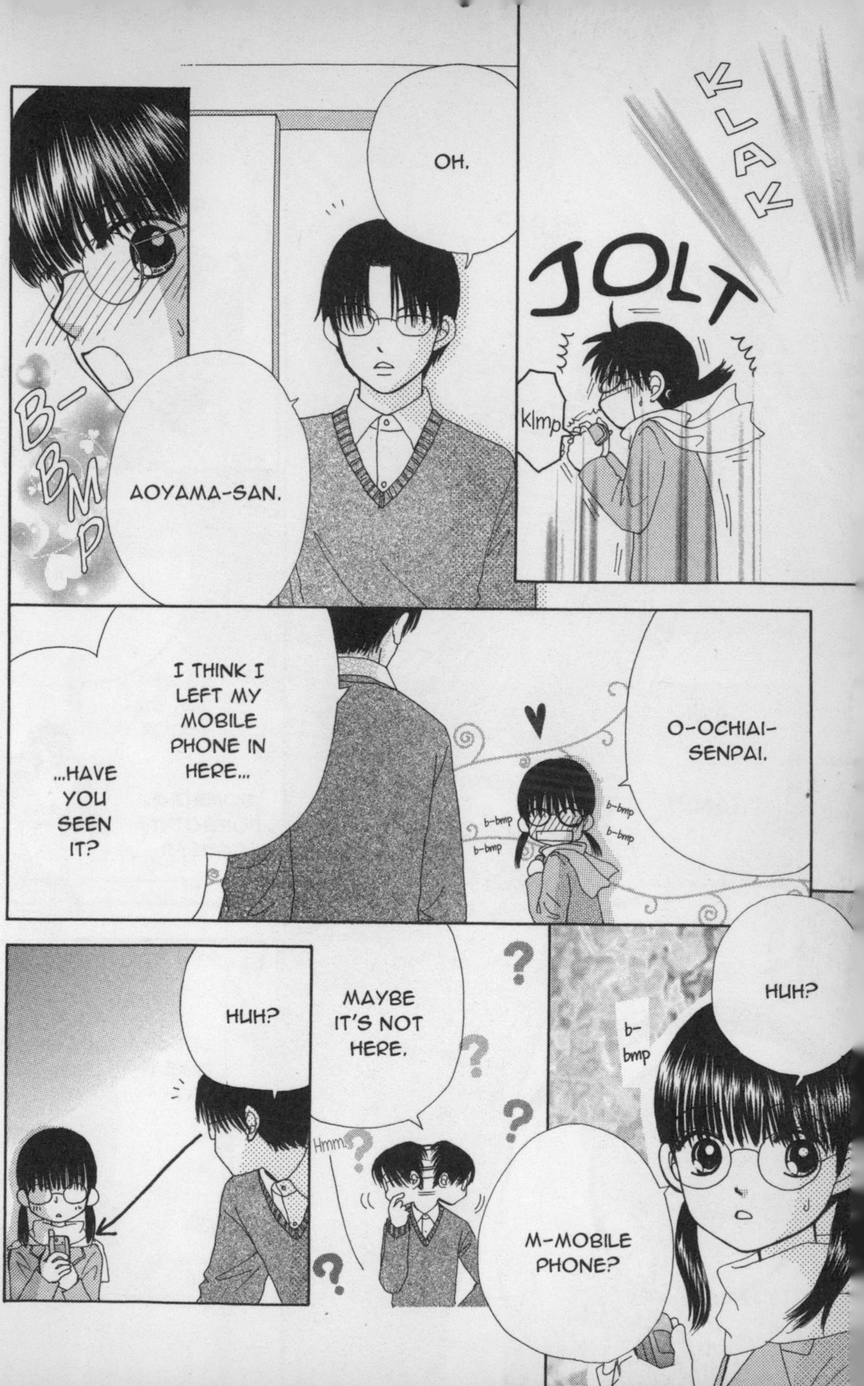
KLAK
JOLT
klmp
OH.
AOYAMA-SAN.
B-BMP
O-OCHIAI-SENPAI.
b-bmp
b-bmp
b-bmp
b-bmp
I THINK I LEFT MY MOBILE PHONE IN HERE...
...HAVE YOU SEEN IT?
HUH?
b-bmp
M-MOBILE PHONE?
MAYBE IT'S NOT HERE.
Hmm.
HUH?

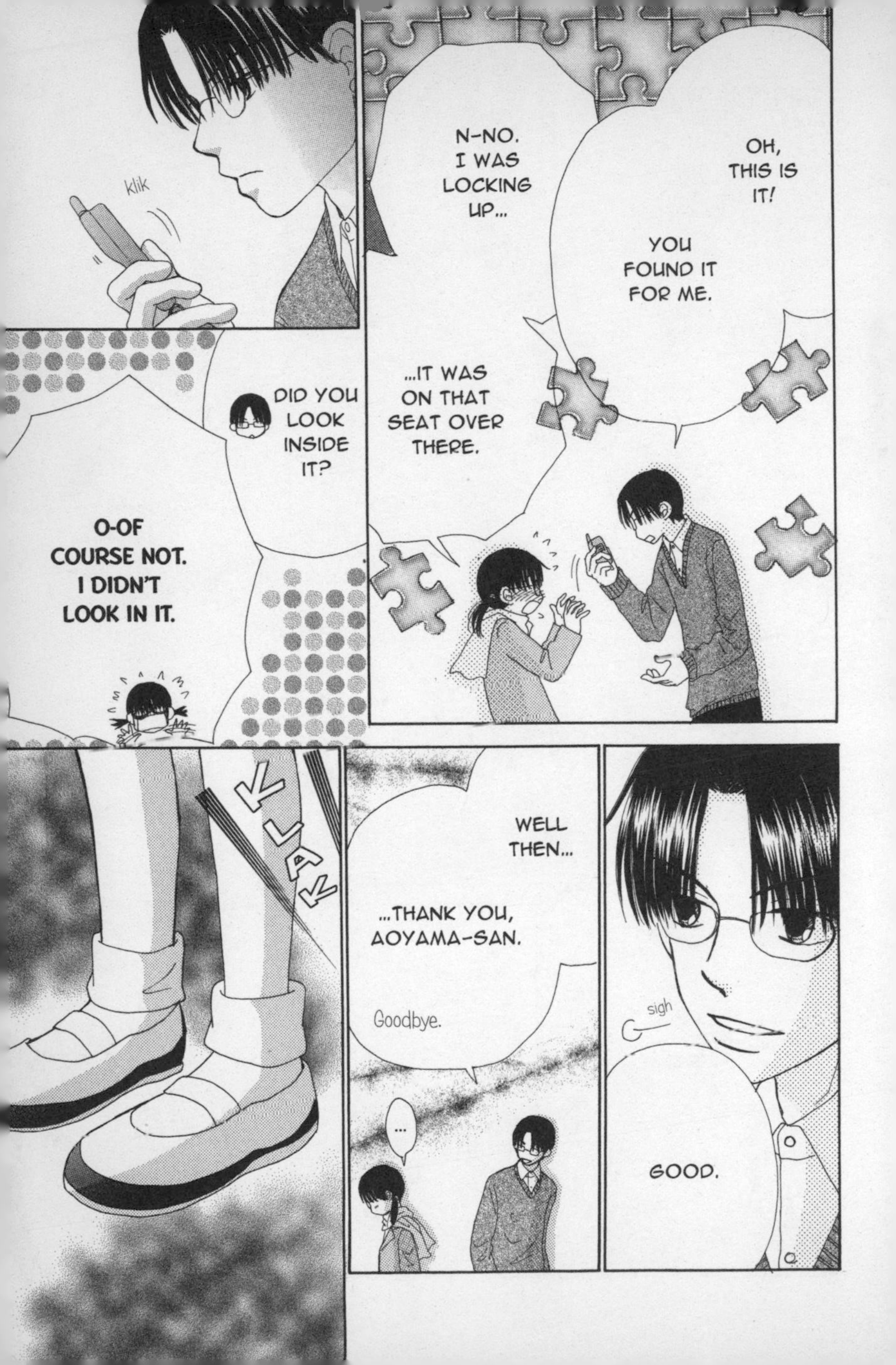
OH, THIS IS IT!
YOU FOUND IT FOR ME.
N-NO. I WAS LOCKING UP...
...IT WAS ON THAT SEAT OVER THERE.
klik
DID YOU LOOK INSIDE IT?
O-OF COURSE NOT. I DIDN'T LOOK IN IT.
sigh
GOOD.
WELL THEN...
...THANK YOU, AOYAMA-SAN.
Goodbye.
...
KLAK

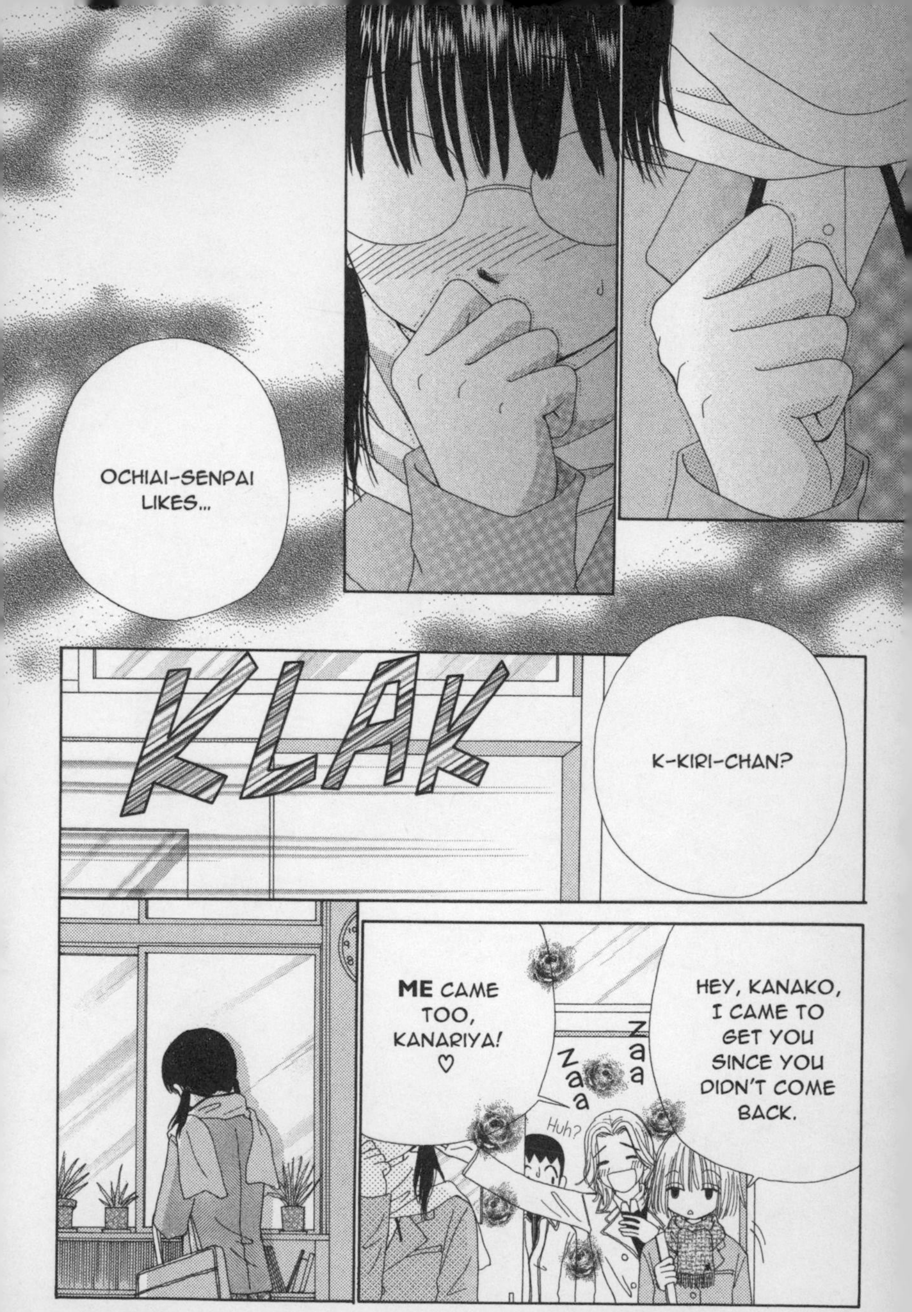
OCHIAI-SENPAI LIKES...
K-KIRI-CHAN?
KLAK
HEY, KANAKO, I CAME TO GET YOU SINCE YOU DIDN'T COME BACK.
ME CAME TOO, KANARIYA! ♡
Zaa
Zaa
Huh?

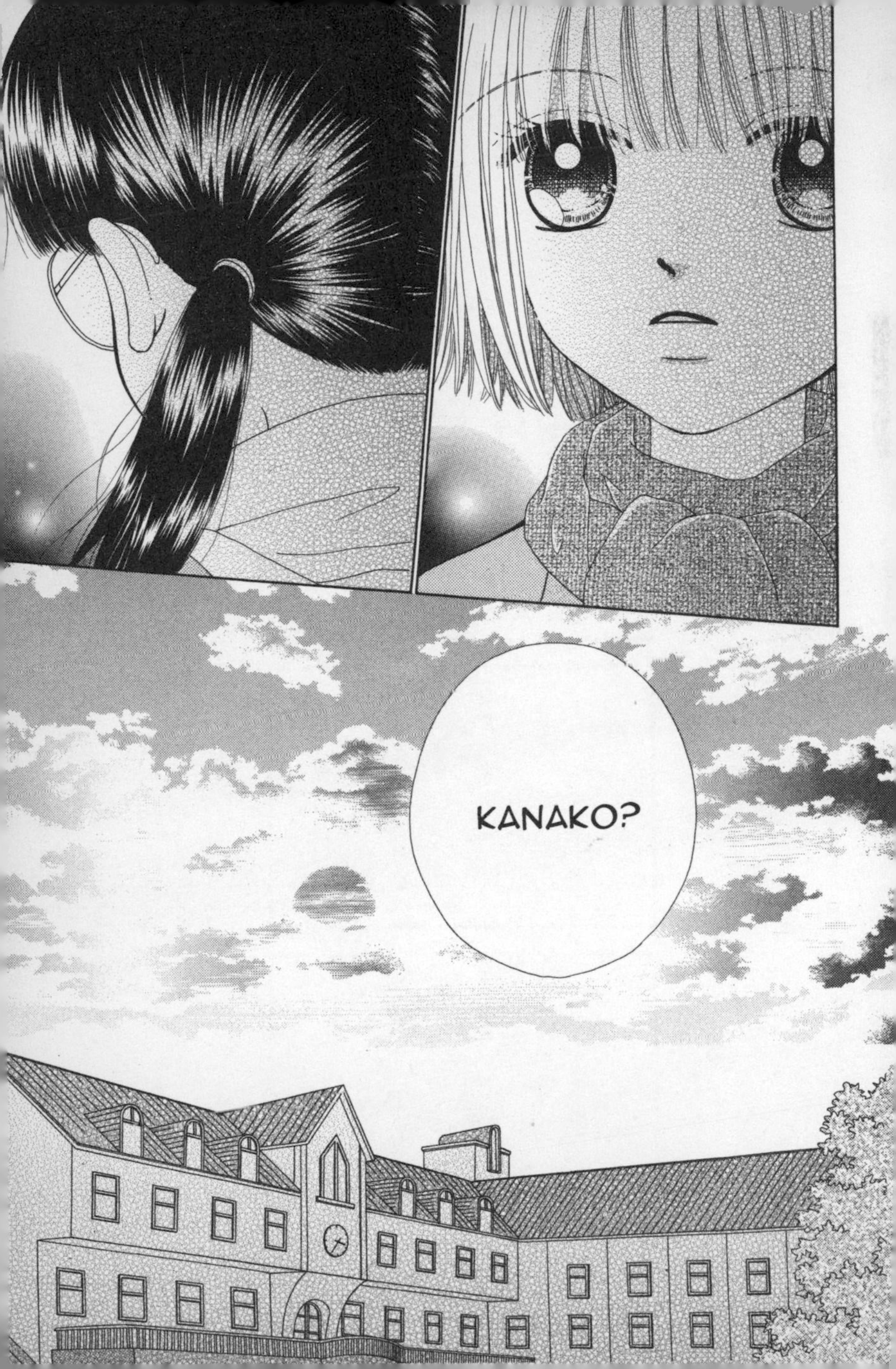
KANAKO?

MANGA THEATER ③

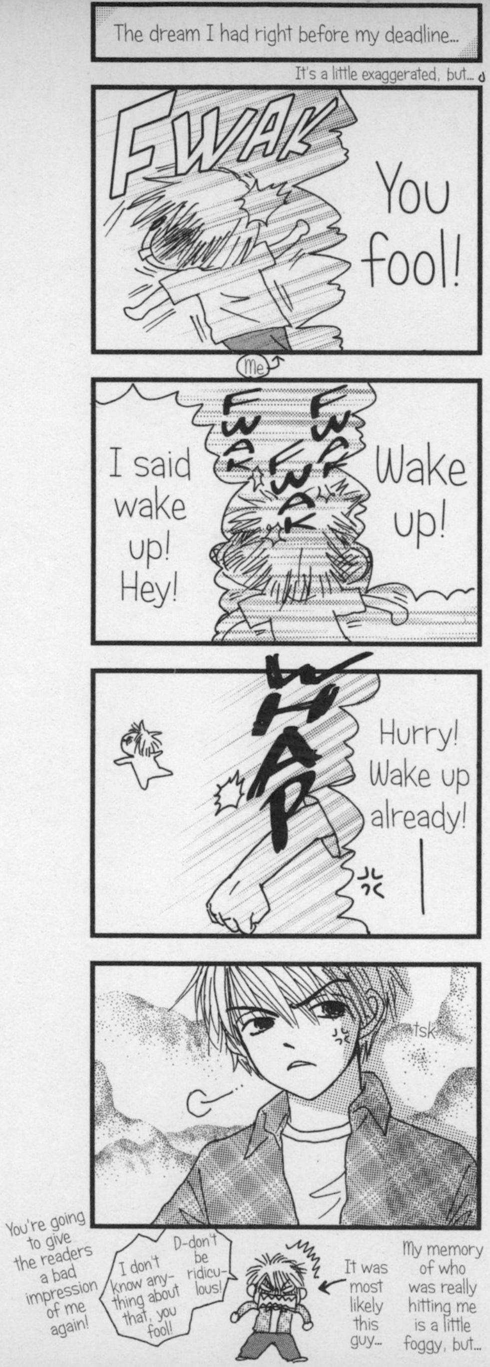
The dream I had right before my deadline...
It's a little exaggerated, but...
FWAK
You fool!
Me
Wake up!
FWAK
FWAK
FWAK
I said wake up! Hey!
WHAP
Hurry! Wake up already!
tsk
My memory of who was really hitting me is a little foggy, but...
It was most likely this guy...
D-don't be ridicu-lous!
I don't know any-thing about that, you fool!
You're going to give the readers a bad impression of me again!

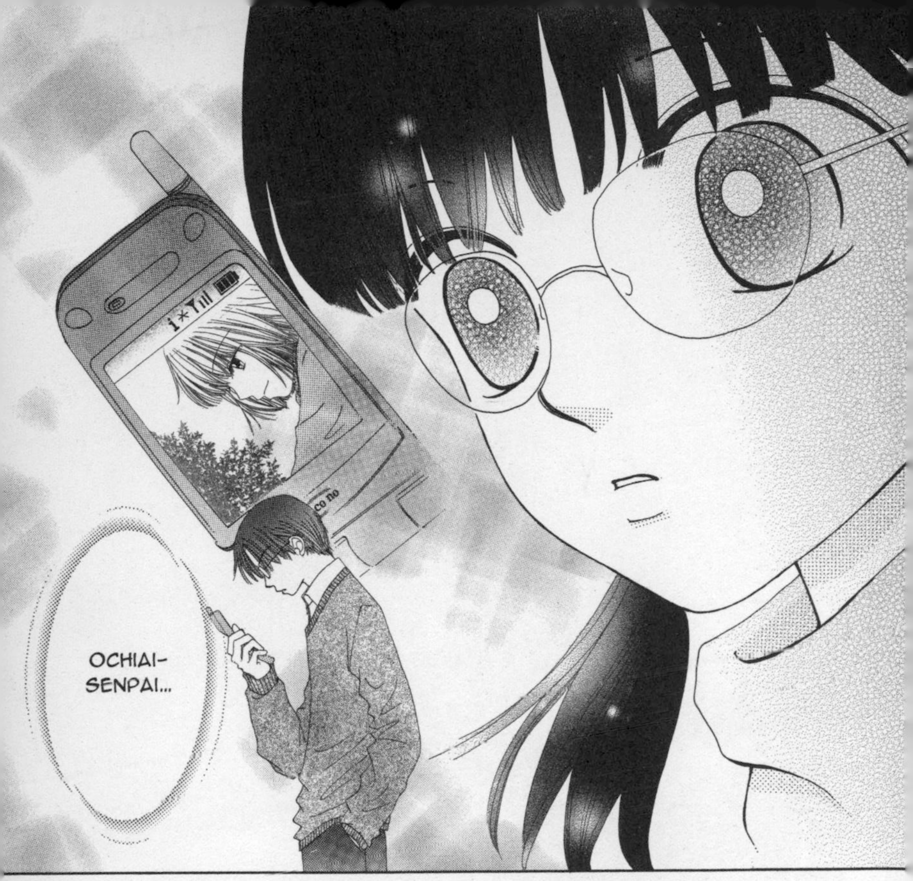
OCHIAI-
SENPAI...

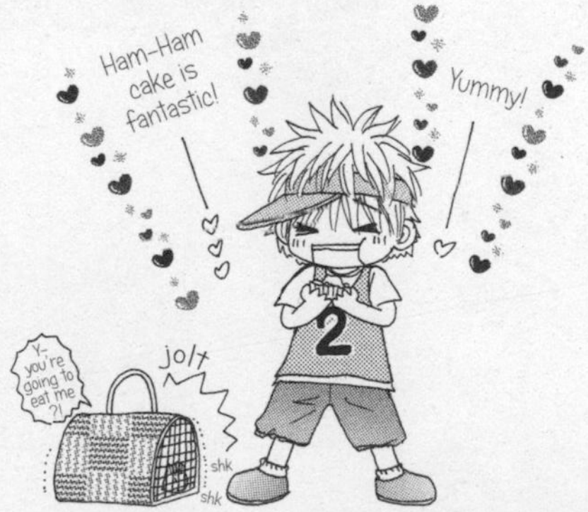
Yummy!
Ham-Ham cake is fantastic!
jolt
Y-you're going to eat me?!
shk
shk

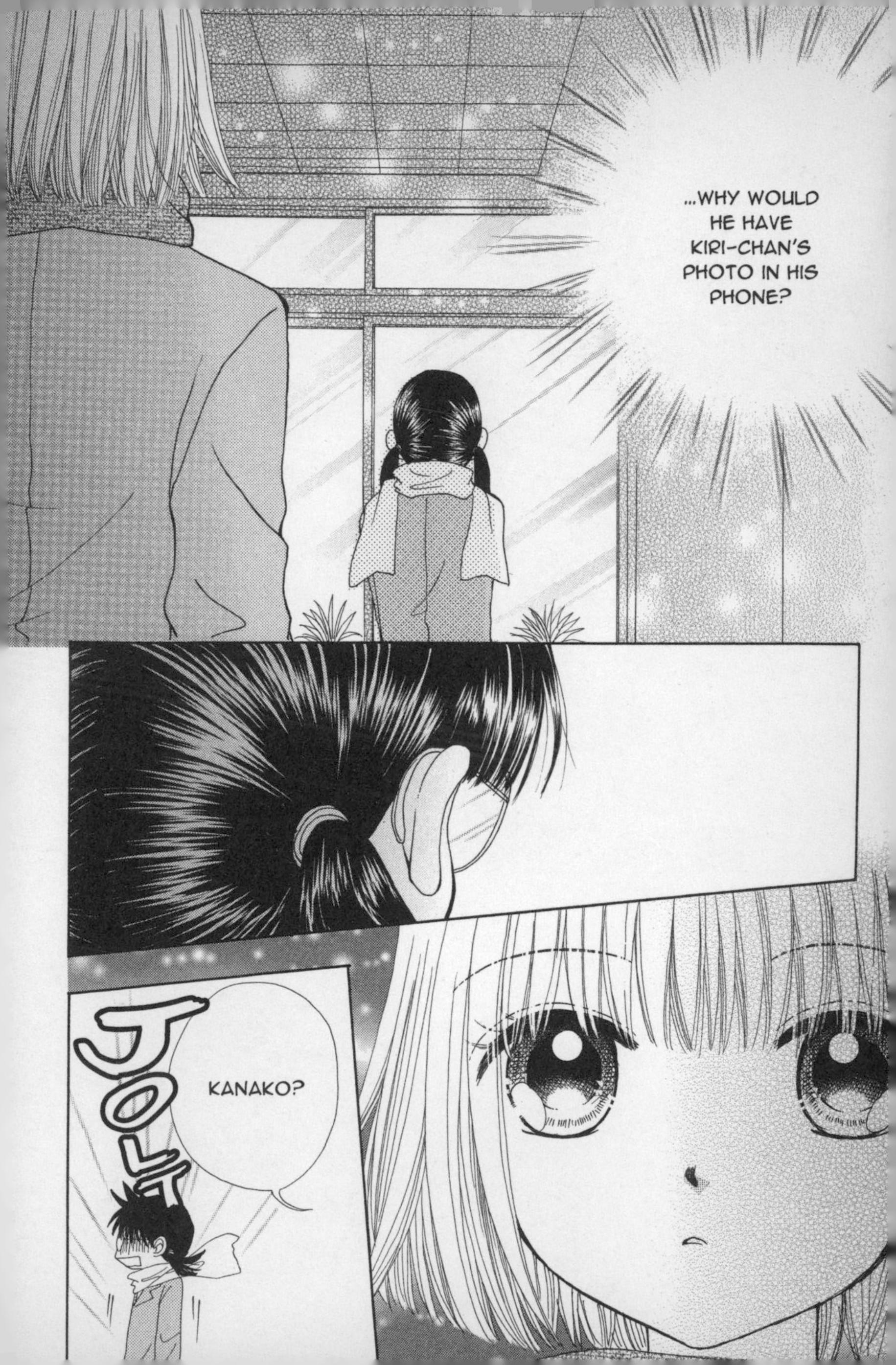
...WHY WOULD HE HAVE KIRI-CHAN'S PHOTO IN HIS PHONE?
KANAKO?
JOLT

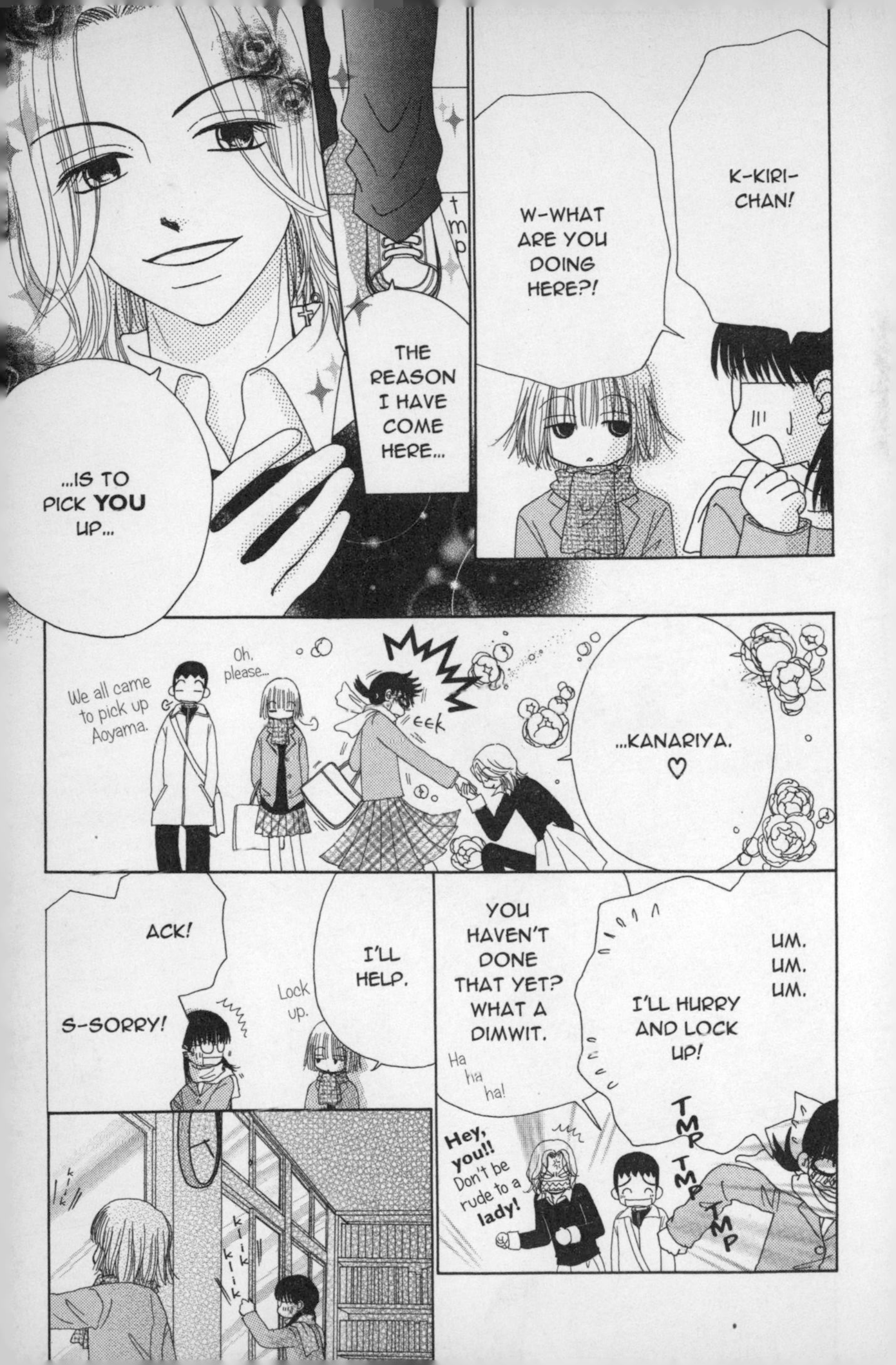
K-KIRI-CHAN!
W-WHAT ARE YOU DOING HERE?!
tmp
THE REASON I HAVE COME HERE...
...IS TO PICK YOU UP...
...KANARIYA. ♡
EEK
Oh, please...
We all came to pick up Aoyama.
UM. UM. UM.
I'LL HURRY AND LOCK UP!
YOU HAVEN'T DONE THAT YET? WHAT A DIMWIT.
Ha ha ha!
TMP TMP TMP
Hey, you!! Don't be rude to a lady!
I'LL HELP.
Lock up.
ACK!
S-SORRY!
klik
klik klik

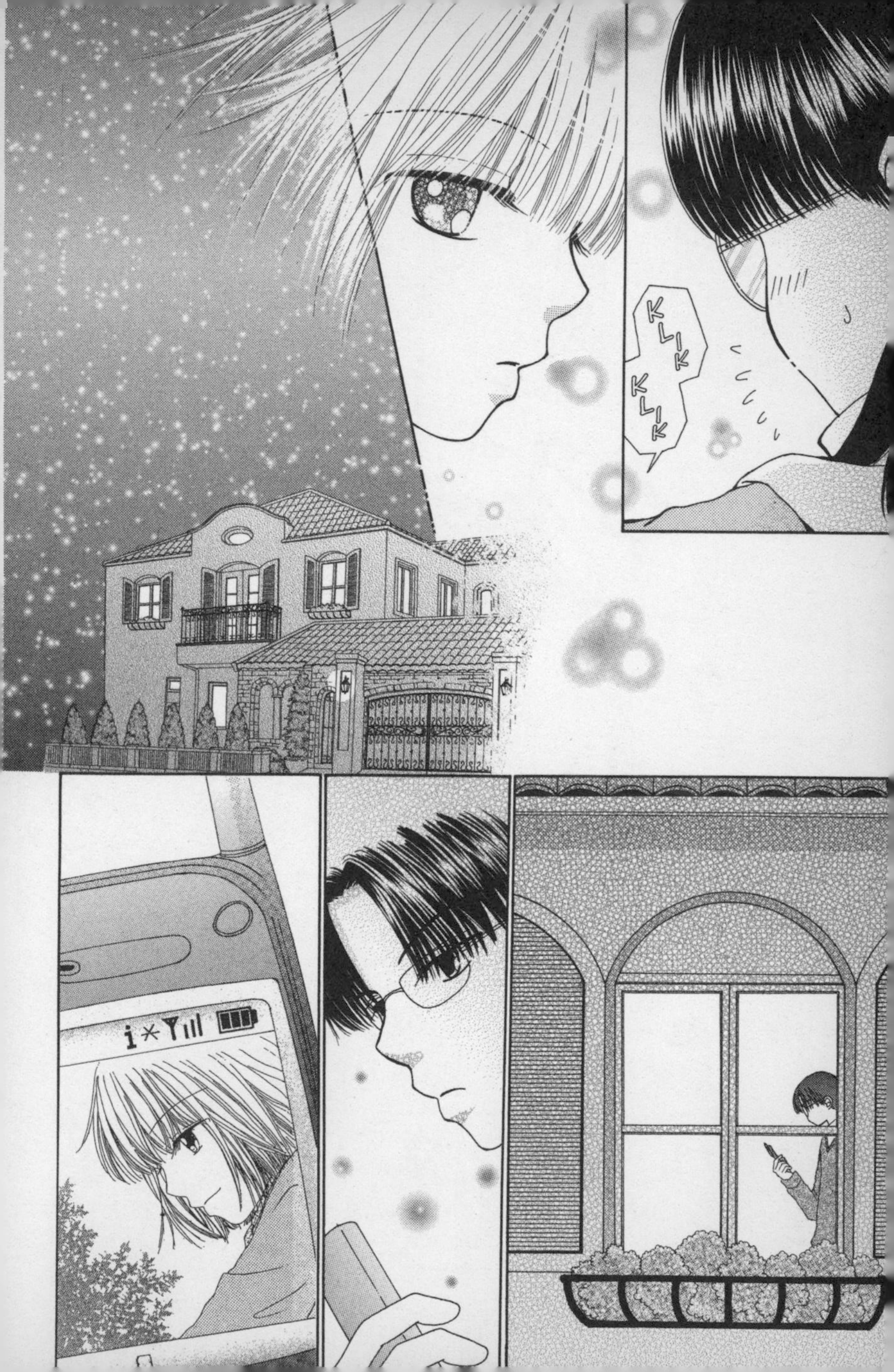
KLIK KLIK

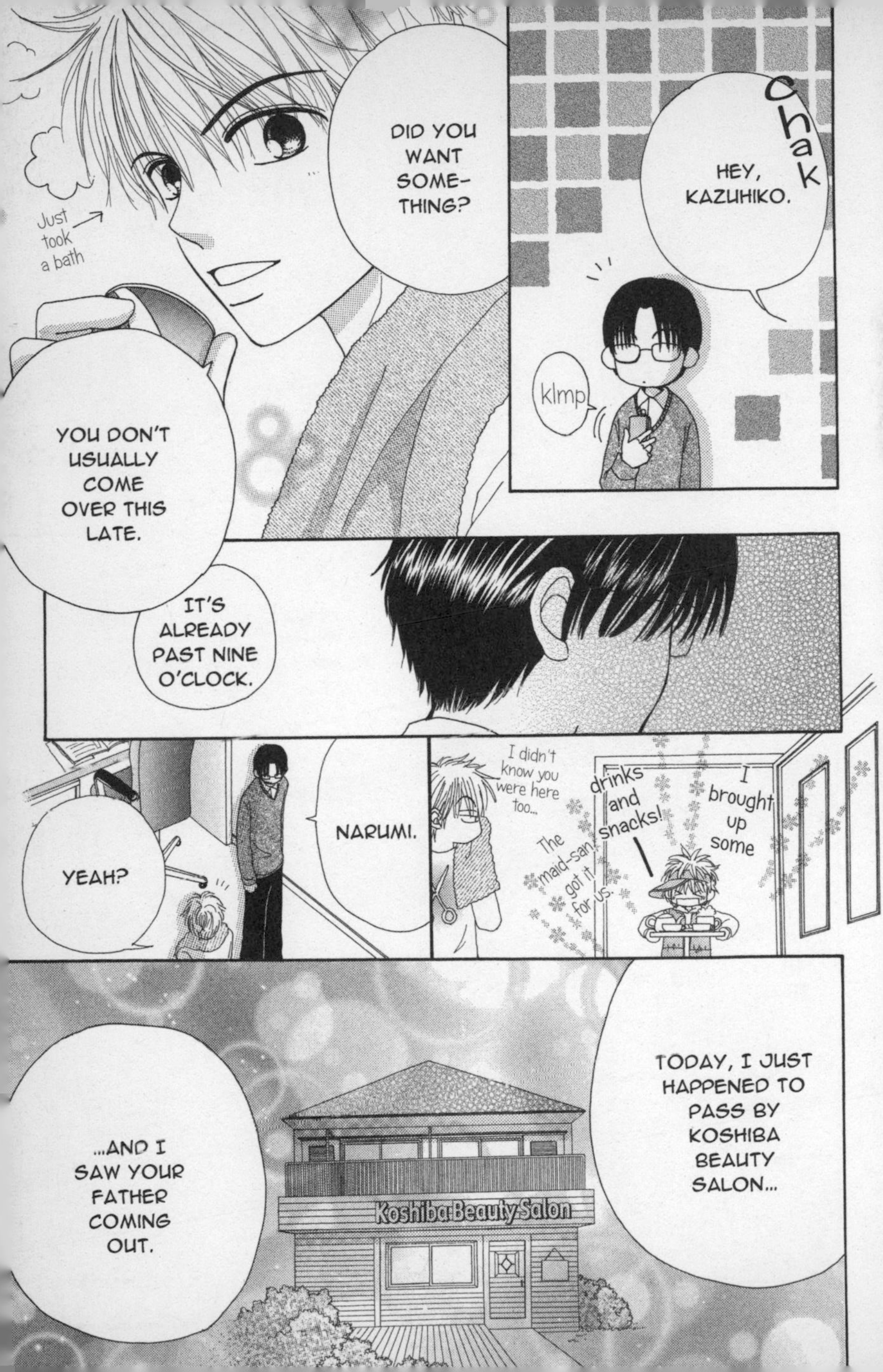
Chak
HEY, KAZUHIKO.
klmp
DID YOU WANT SOME-THING?
Just took a bath
YOU DON'T USUALLY COME OVER THIS LATE.
IT'S ALREADY PAST NINE O'CLOCK.
I brought up some drinks and snacks!
The maid-san got it for us.
I didn't know you were here too...
NARUMI.
YEAH?
TODAY, I JUST HAPPENED TO PASS BY KOSHIBA BEAUTY SALON...
Koshiba Beauty Salon
...AND I SAW YOUR FATHER COMING OUT.

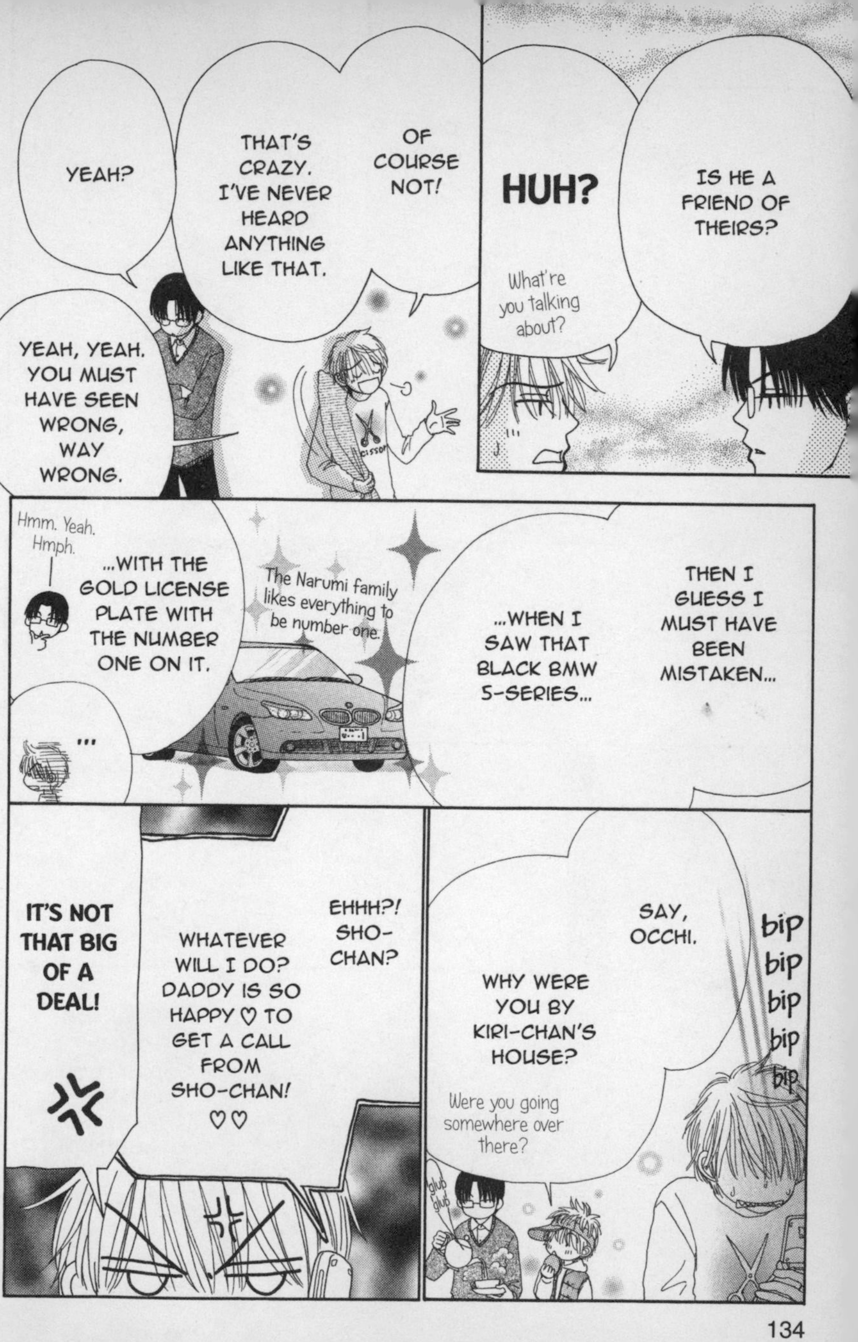
IS HE A FRIEND OF THEIRS?
HUH?
What're you talking about?
OF COURSE NOT!
THAT'S CRAZY. I'VE NEVER HEARD ANYTHING LIKE THAT.
YEAH?
YEAH, YEAH. YOU MUST HAVE SEEN WRONG, WAY WRONG.
THEN I GUESS I MUST HAVE BEEN MISTAKEN...
...WHEN I SAW THAT BLACK BMW 5-SERIES...
The Narumi family likes everything to be number one.
...WITH THE GOLD LICENSE PLATE WITH THE NUMBER ONE ON IT.
Hmm. Yeah. Hmph.
...
bip bip bip bip bip
SAY, OCCHI.
WHY WERE YOU BY KIRI-CHAN'S HOUSE?
Were you going somewhere over there?
glub glub
EHHH?! SHO-CHAN?
WHATEVER WILL I DO? DADDY IS SO HAPPY ♡ TO GET A CALL FROM SHO-CHAN! ♡♡
IT'S NOT THAT BIG OF A DEAL!

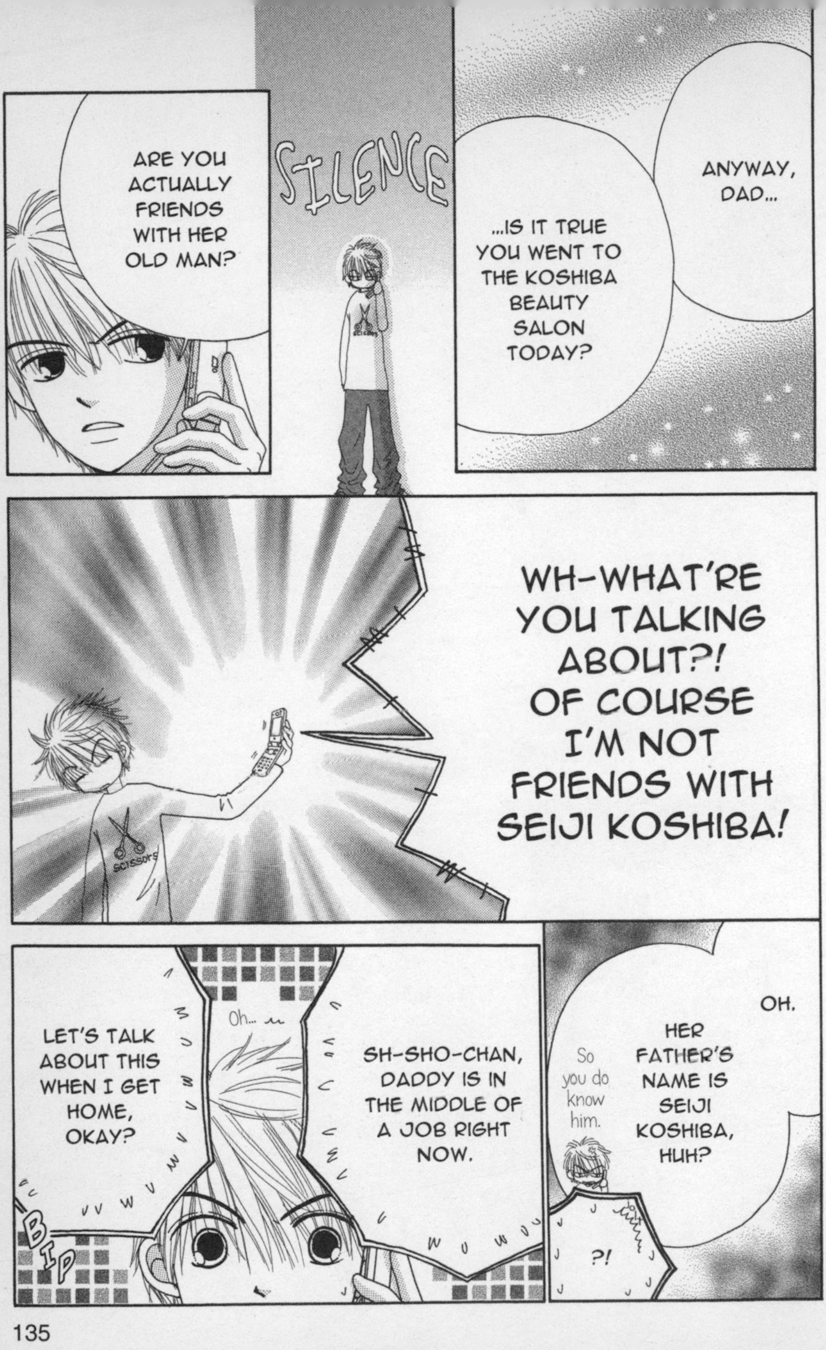
ANYWAY, DAD...
...IS IT TRUE YOU WENT TO THE KOSHIBA BEAUTY SALON TODAY?
SILENCE
ARE YOU ACTUALLY FRIENDS WITH HER OLD MAN?
WH-WHAT'RE YOU TALKING ABOUT?! OF COURSE I'M NOT FRIENDS WITH SEIJI KOSHIBA!
OH.
HER FATHER'S NAME IS SEIJI KOSHIBA, HUH?
So you do know him.
?!
Oh...
SH-SHO-CHAN, DADDY IS IN THE MIDDLE OF A JOB RIGHT NOW.
LET'S TALK ABOUT THIS WHEN I GET HOME, OKAY?
BIP

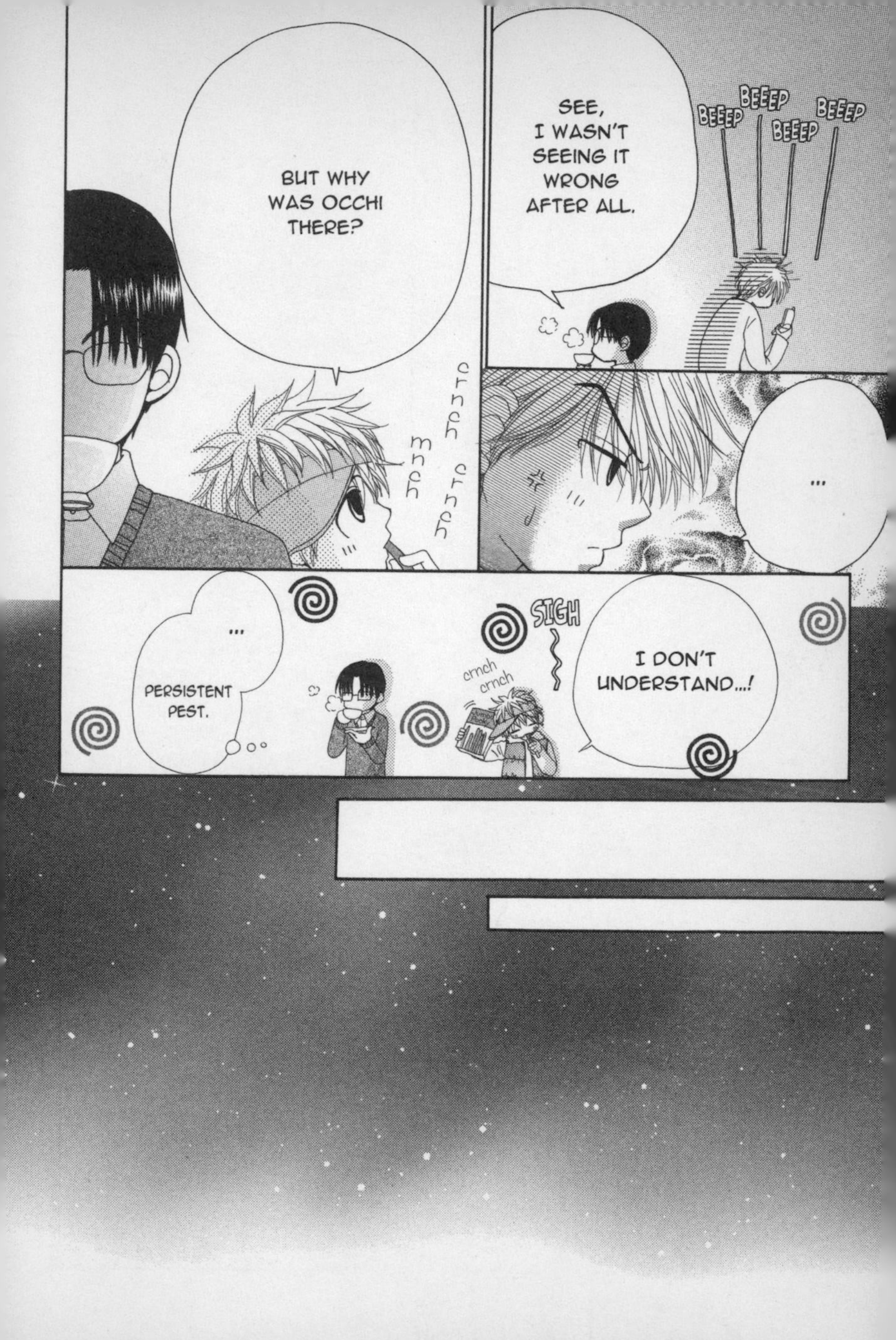

SEE, I WASN'T SEEING IT WRONG AFTER ALL.
BEEEP
BEEEP
BEEEP
BEEEP
...
BUT WHY WAS OCCHI THERE?
crnch crnch
mnch
I DON'T UNDERSTAND...!
SIGH
crnch crnch
... PERSISTENT PEST.

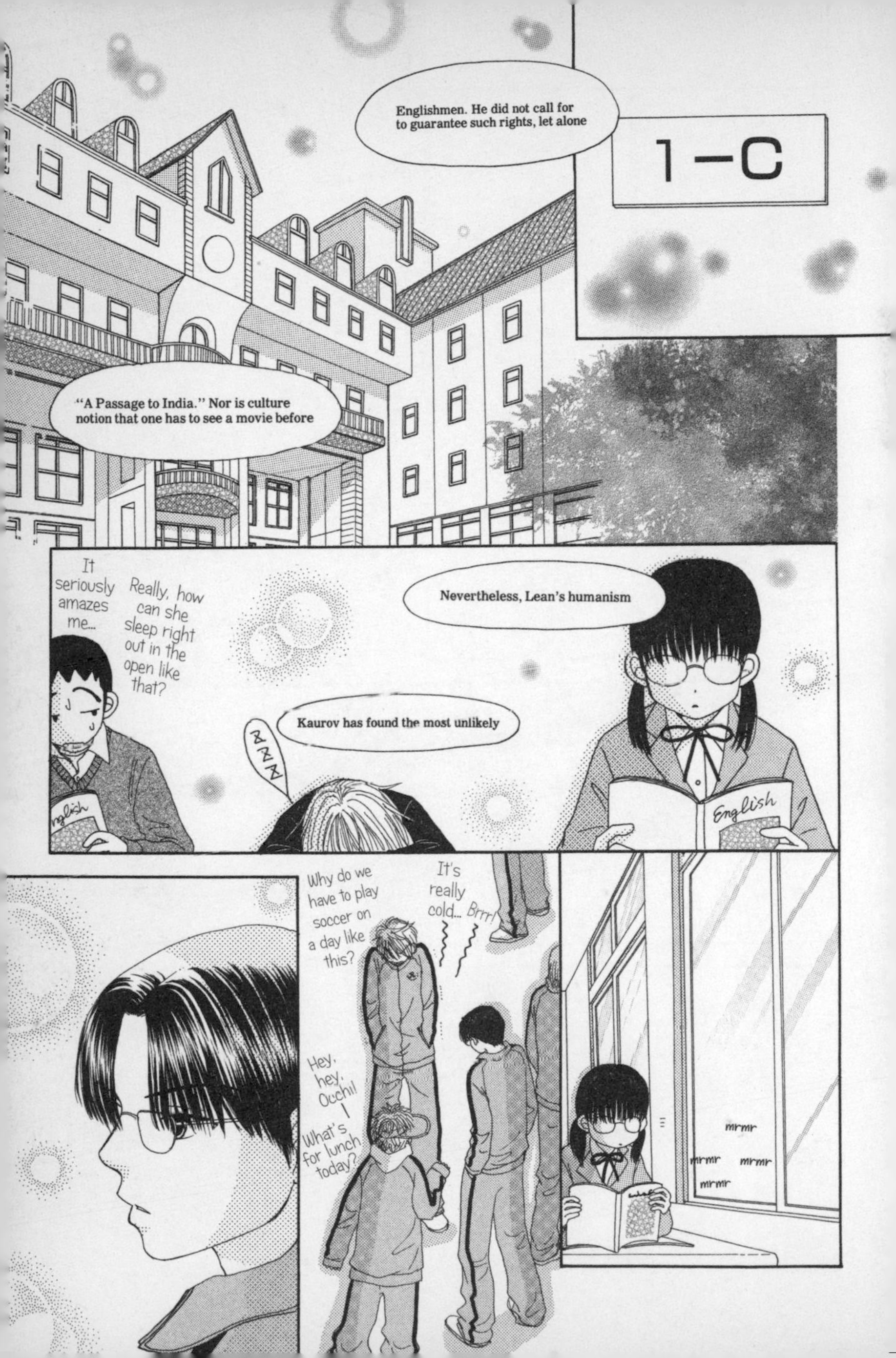

1-C
Englishmen. He did not call for to guarantee such rights, let alone
"A Passage to India." Nor is culture notion that one has to see a movie before
Nevertheless, Lean's humanism
Kaurov has found the most unlikely
ZZZ
Really, how can she sleep right out in the open like that?
It seriously amazes me...
mrmr
mrmr
mrmr
mrmr
It's really cold... Brrr!
Why do we have to play soccer on a day like this?
Hey, hey, Occhi! What's for lunch today?

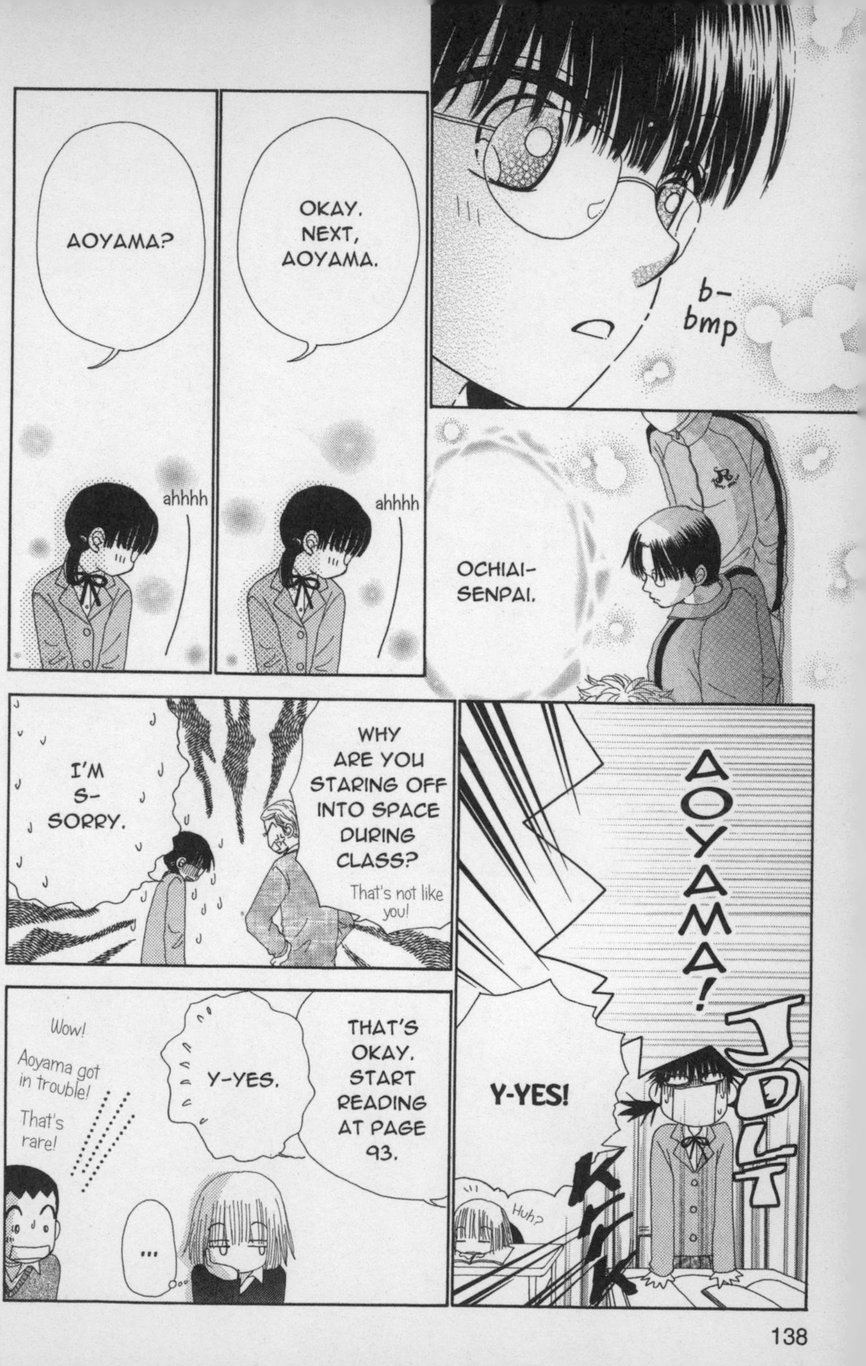
b-bmp
OCHIAI-SENPAI.
OKAY. NEXT, AOYAMA.
ahhhh
AOYAMA?
ahhhh
AOYAMA!
JOLT
Y-YES!
KKK
Huh?
WHY ARE YOU STARING OFF INTO SPACE DURING CLASS?
That's not like you!
I'M S-SORRY.
THAT'S OKAY. START READING AT PAGE 93.
Y-YES.
Wow!
Aoyama got in trouble!
That's rare!
...

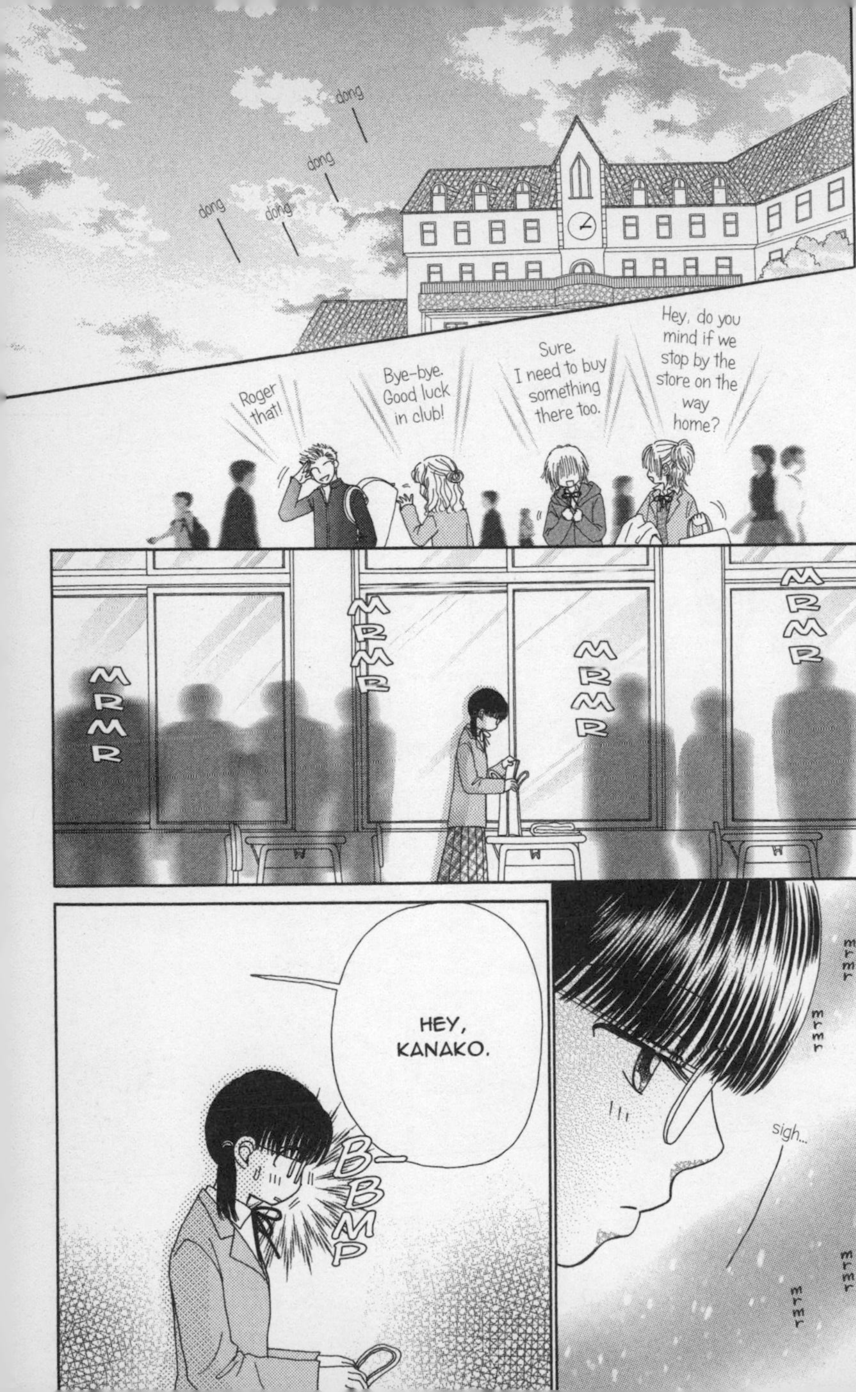
dong
dong
dong
dong
Hey, do you mind if we stop by the store on the way home?
Sure. I need to buy something there too.
Bye-bye. Good luck in club!
Roger that!
MRMR
MRMR
MRMR
MRMR
mrmr
mrmr
!!!
sigh...
mrmr
mrmr
HEY, KANAKO.
B-BMP

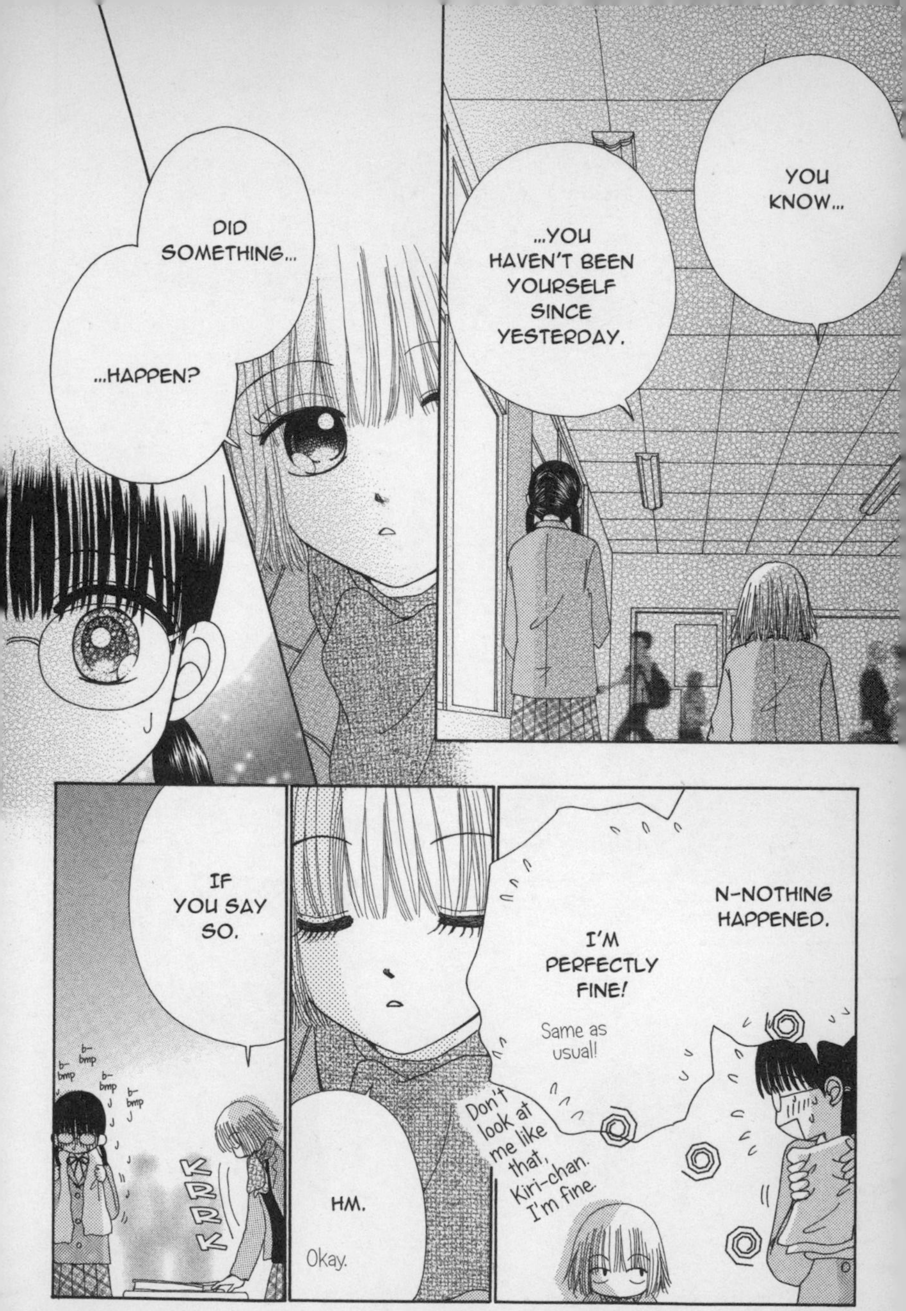
YOU KNOW...
...YOU HAVEN'T BEEN YOURSELF SINCE YESTERDAY.
DID SOMETHING...
...HAPPEN?
N-NOTHING HAPPENED.
I'M PERFECTLY FINE!
Same as usual!
Don't look at me like that, Kiri-chan. I'm fine.
HM.
Okay.
IF YOU SAY SO.
b-bmp
b-bmp
b-bmp
b-bmp
KRRK

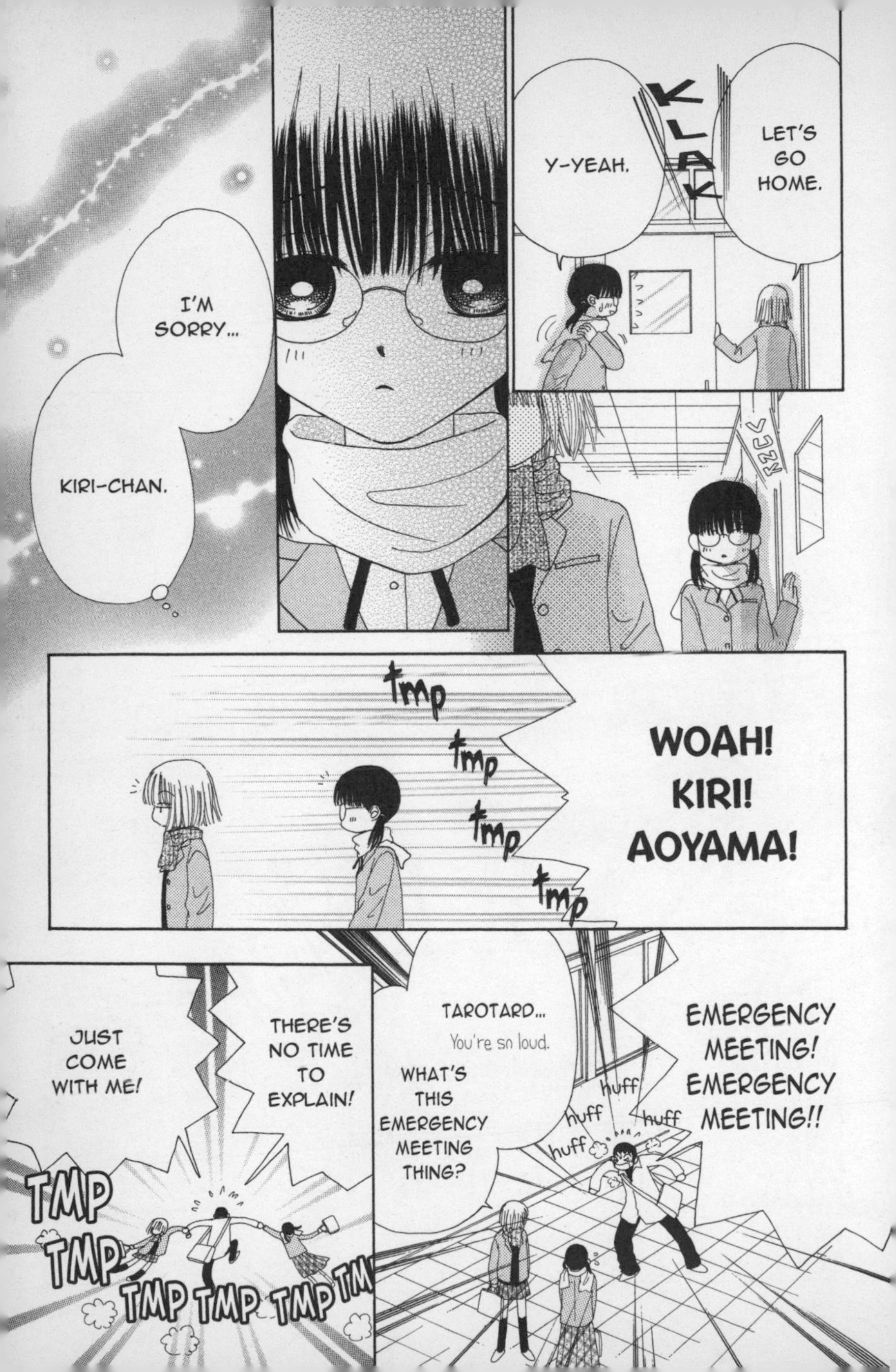
LET'S GO HOME.
KLAK
Y-YEAH.
I'M SORRY...
KIRI-CHAN.
tmp
tmp
tmp
tmp
WOAH! KIRI! AOYAMA!
EMERGENCY MEETING! EMERGENCY MEETING!!
huff
huff
huff
huff
TAROTARD...
You're so loud.
WHAT'S THIS EMERGENCY MEETING THING?
THERE'S NO TIME TO EXPLAIN!
JUST COME WITH ME!
TMP TMP TMP TMP TMP TM

EVERYONE...

S.P.

...AN OFFICIAL SCHOOL CLUB.

...AS OF TODAY, THE SCISSORS PROJECT IS NOW...

TA DAH

LET'S REVEAL WHO WAS JUST VOTED IN AS PRESIDENT.

Ochiai	5
Narumi	1
Iori Minamoto	1
Abstained	1

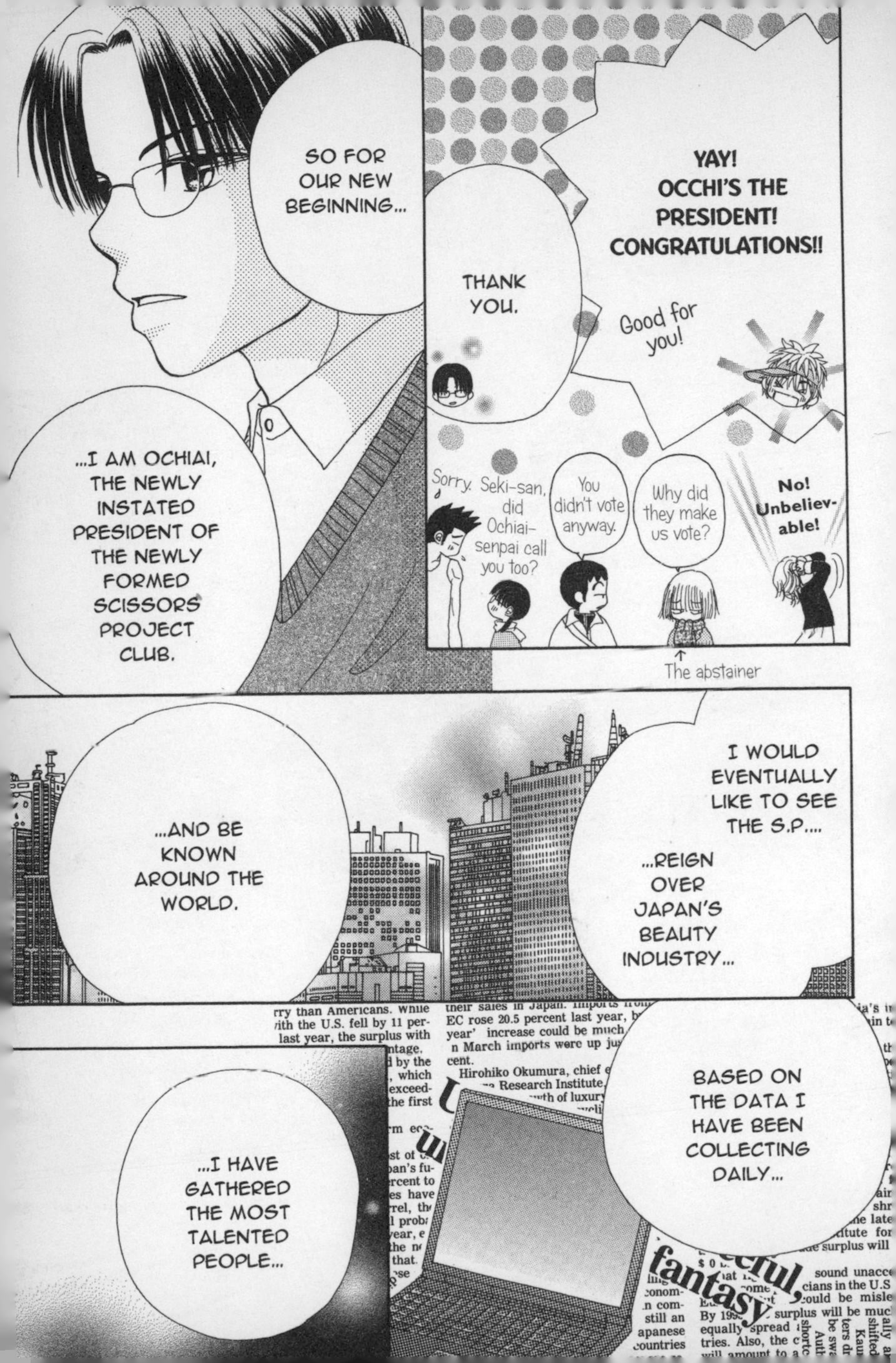
YAY! OCCHI'S THE PRESIDENT! CONGRATULATIONS!!
Good for you!
THANK YOU.
No! Unbeliev-able!
Why did they make us vote?
You didn't vote anyway.
Sorry. Seki-san, did Ochiai-senpai call you too?
The abstainer
SO FOR OUR NEW BEGINNING...
...I AM OCHIAI, THE NEWLY INSTATED PRESIDENT OF THE NEWLY FORMED SCISSORS PROJECT CLUB.
I WOULD EVENTUALLY LIKE TO SEE THE S.P....
...REIGN OVER JAPAN'S BEAUTY INDUSTRY...
...AND BE KNOWN AROUND THE WORLD.
BASED ON THE DATA I HAVE BEEN COLLECTING DAILY...
...I HAVE GATHERED THE MOST TALENTED PEOPLE...

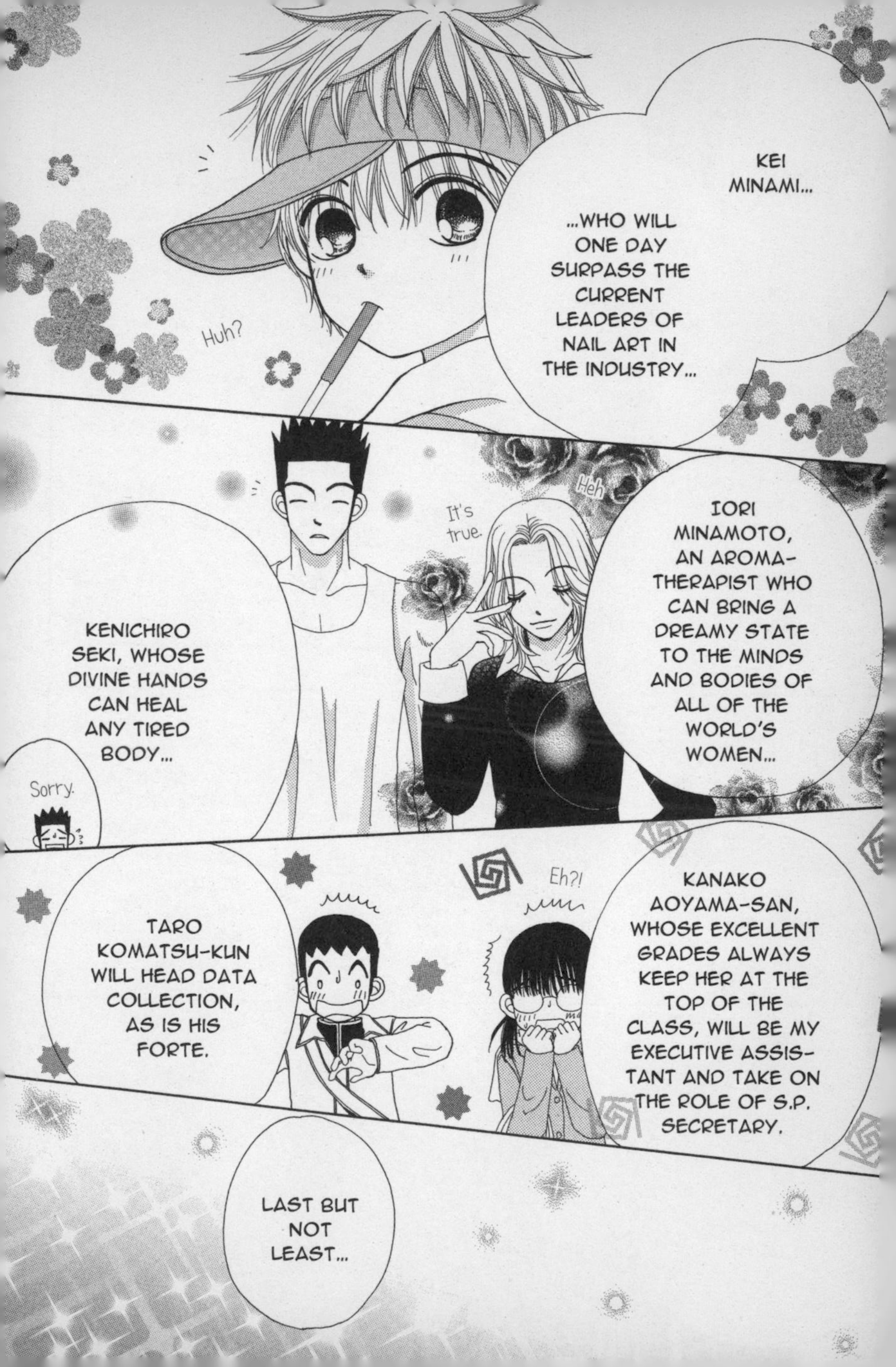
KEI MINAMI...
...WHO WILL ONE DAY SURPASS THE CURRENT LEADERS OF NAIL ART IN THE INDUSTRY...
Huh?
IORI MINAMOTO, AN AROMA-THERAPIST WHO CAN BRING A DREAMY STATE TO THE MINDS AND BODIES OF ALL OF THE WORLD'S WOMEN...
Heh
It's true.
KENICHIRO SEKI, WHOSE DIVINE HANDS CAN HEAL ANY TIRED BODY...
Sorry.
KANAKO AOYAMA-SAN, WHOSE EXCELLENT GRADES ALWAYS KEEP HER AT THE TOP OF THE CLASS, WILL BE MY EXECUTIVE ASSIS-TANT AND TAKE ON THE ROLE OF S.P. SECRETARY.
Eh?!
TARO KOMATSU-KUN WILL HEAD DATA COLLECTION, AS IS HIS FORTE.
LAST BUT NOT LEAST...

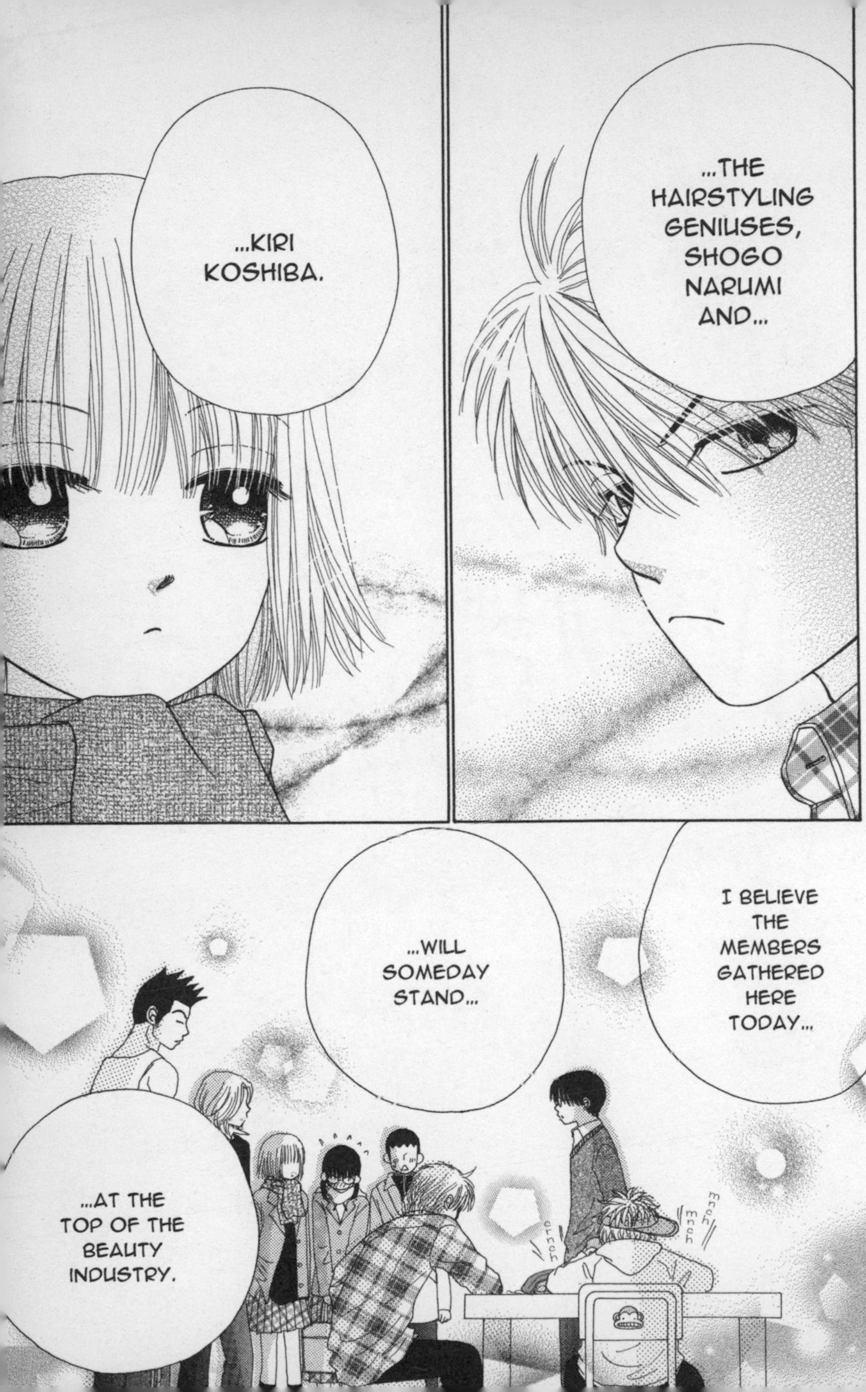
...THE HAIRSTYLING GENIUSES, SHOGO NARUMI AND...
...KIRI KOSHIBA.
I BELIEVE THE MEMBERS GATHERED HERE TODAY...
...WILL SOMEDAY STAND...
mnch mnch
crnch
...AT THE TOP OF THE BEAUTY INDUSTRY.

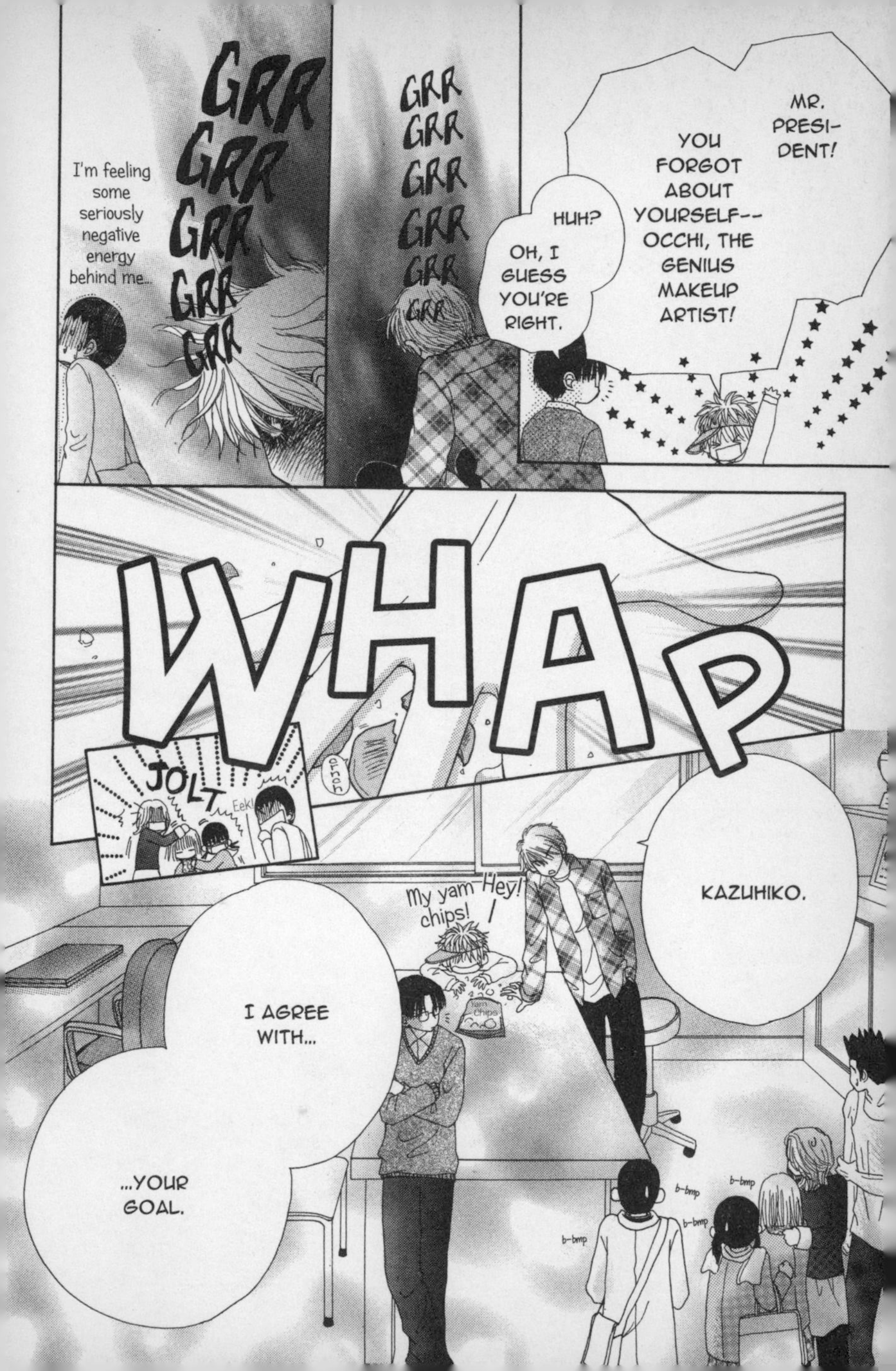
MR. PRESI-DENT!
YOU FORGOT ABOUT YOURSELF-- OCCHI, THE GENIUS MAKEUP ARTIST!
HUH?
OH, I GUESS YOU'RE RIGHT.
GRR GRR GRR GRR GRR GRR
I'm feeling some seriously negative energy behind me...
GRR GRR GRR GRR GRR GRR
WHAP
crunch
JOLT
Eek!
KAZUHIKO.
Hey!
My yam chips!
Yam Chips
I AGREE WITH...
...YOUR GOAL.
b-bmp
b-bmp
b-bmp
b-bmp

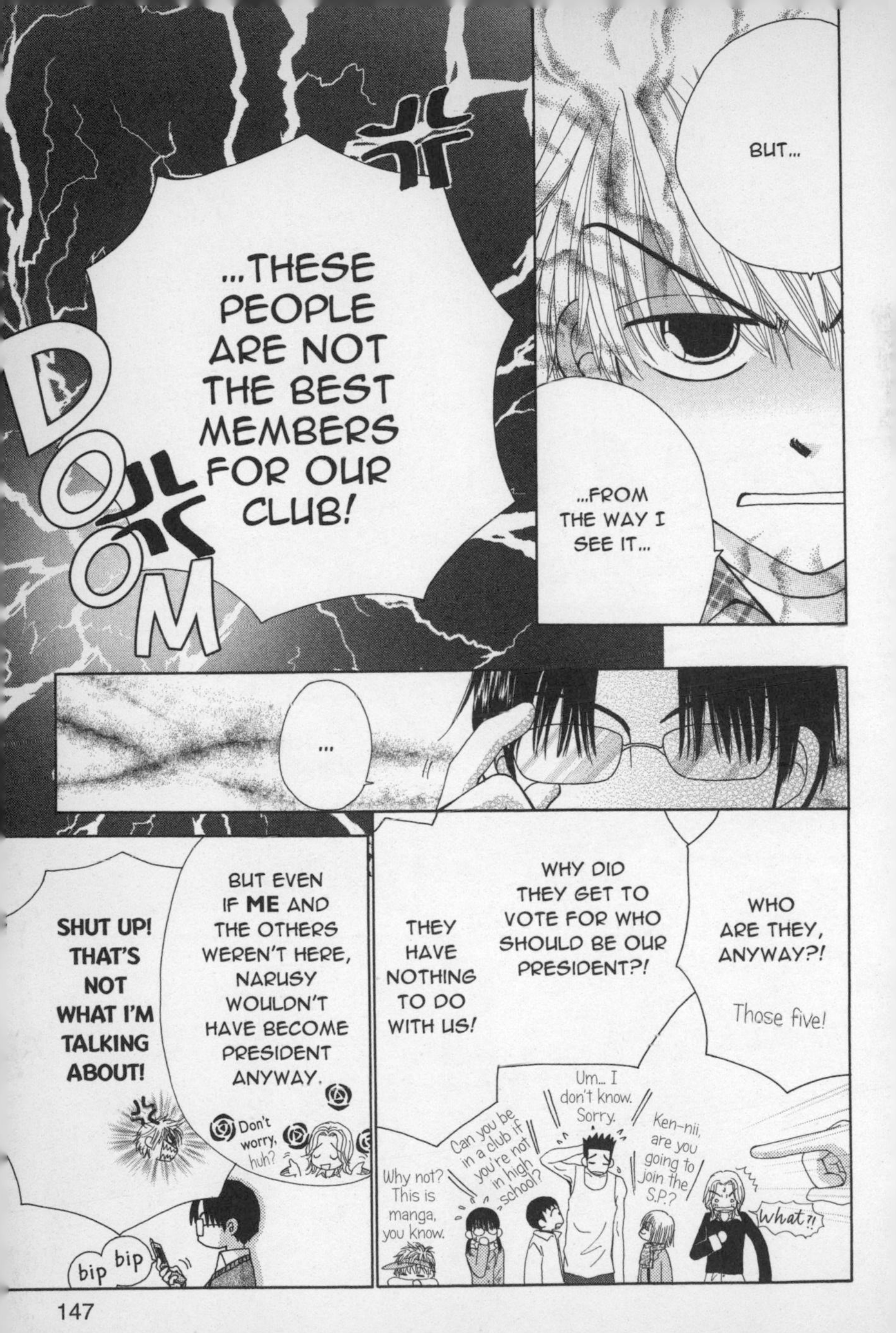

BUT...
...FROM THE WAY I SEE IT...
...THESE PEOPLE ARE NOT THE BEST MEMBERS FOR OUR CLUB!
DOOM
...
WHO ARE THEY, ANYWAY?!
Those five!
WHY DID THEY GET TO VOTE FOR WHO SHOULD BE OUR PRESIDENT?!
THEY HAVE NOTHING TO DO WITH US!
What?!
Ken-nii, are you going to join the S.P.?
Um... I don't know. Sorry.
Can you be in a club if you're not in high school?
Why not? This is manga, you know.
BUT EVEN IF ME AND THE OTHERS WEREN'T HERE, NARUSY WOULDN'T HAVE BECOME PRESIDENT ANYWAY.
SHUT UP! THAT'S NOT WHAT I'M TALKING ABOUT!
Don't worry, huh?
bip bip

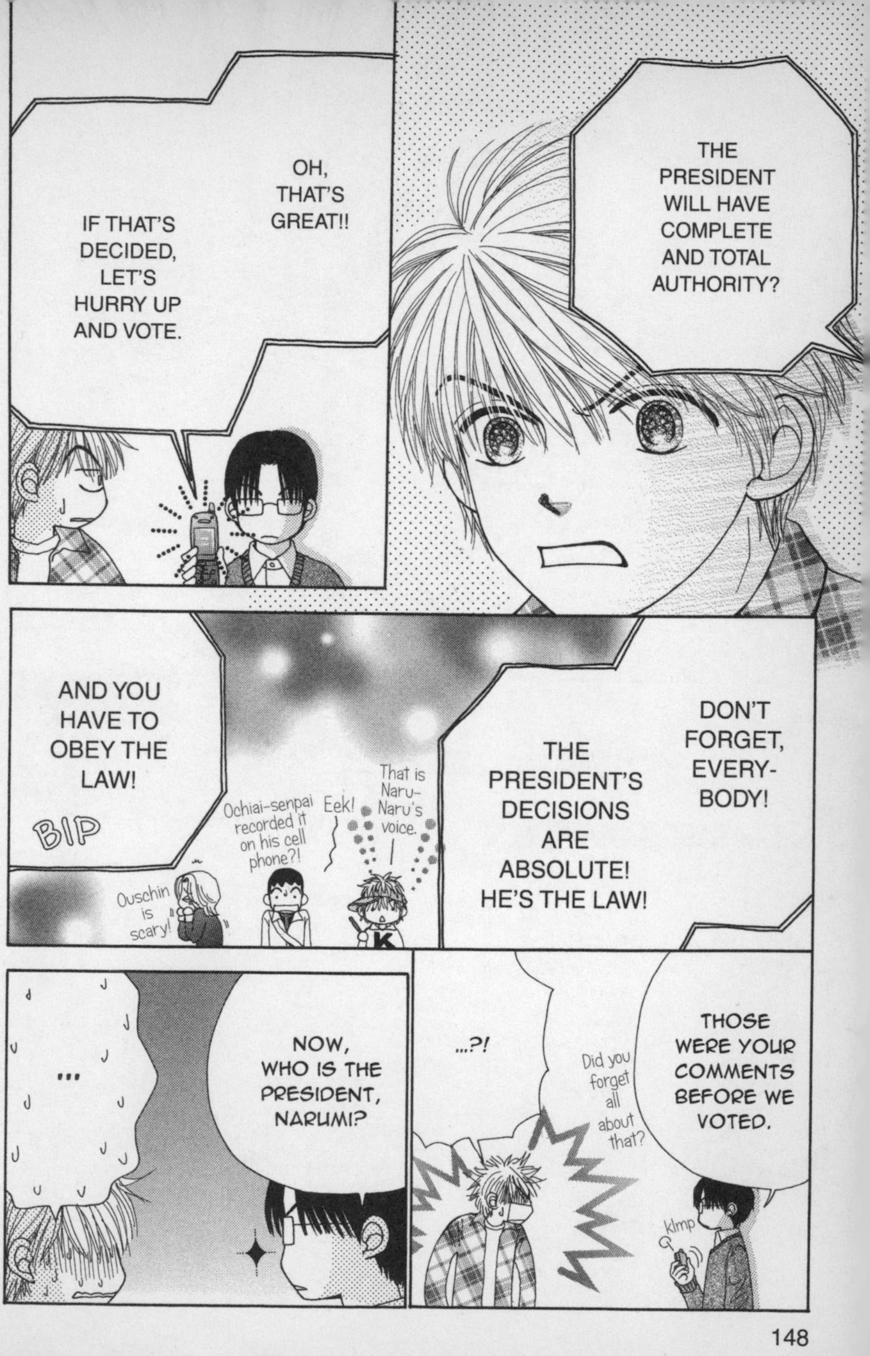
THE PRESIDENT WILL HAVE COMPLETE AND TOTAL AUTHORITY?
OH, THAT'S GREAT!!
IF THAT'S DECIDED, LET'S HURRY UP AND VOTE.
DON'T FORGET, EVERYBODY!
THE PRESIDENT'S DECISIONS ARE ABSOLUTE! HE'S THE LAW!
AND YOU HAVE TO OBEY THE LAW!
BIP
That is Naru-Naru's voice.
Eek!
Ochiai-senpai recorded it on his cell phone?!
Ouschin is scary!
THOSE WERE YOUR COMMENTS BEFORE WE VOTED.
Did you forget all about that?
klmp
...?!
NOW, WHO IS THE PRESIDENT, NARUMI?
...

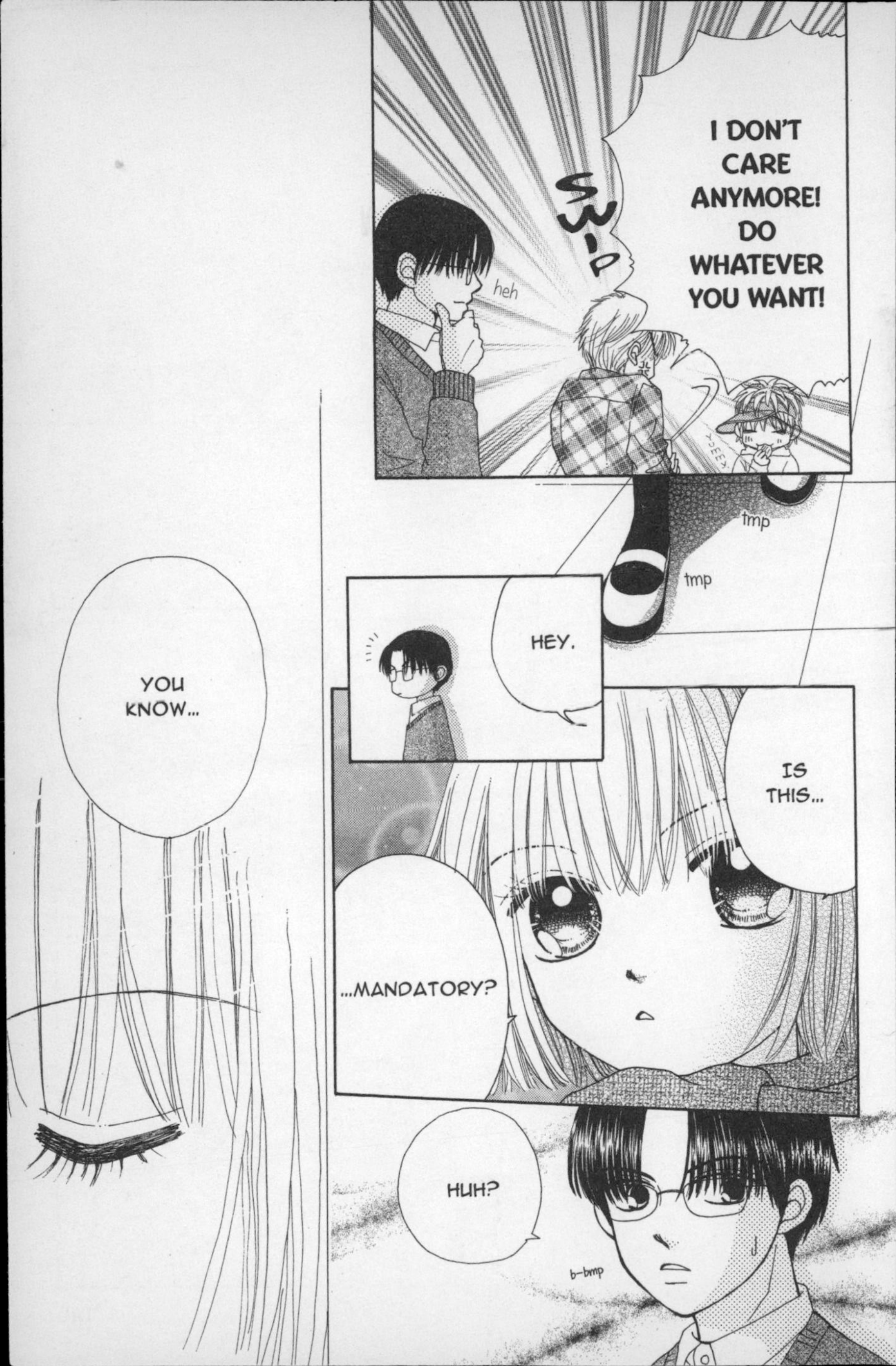
I DON'T CARE ANYMORE! DO WHATEVER YOU WANT!
SWIP
heh
tmp
tmp
HEY.
IS THIS...
...MANDATORY?
HUH?
b-bmp
YOU KNOW...

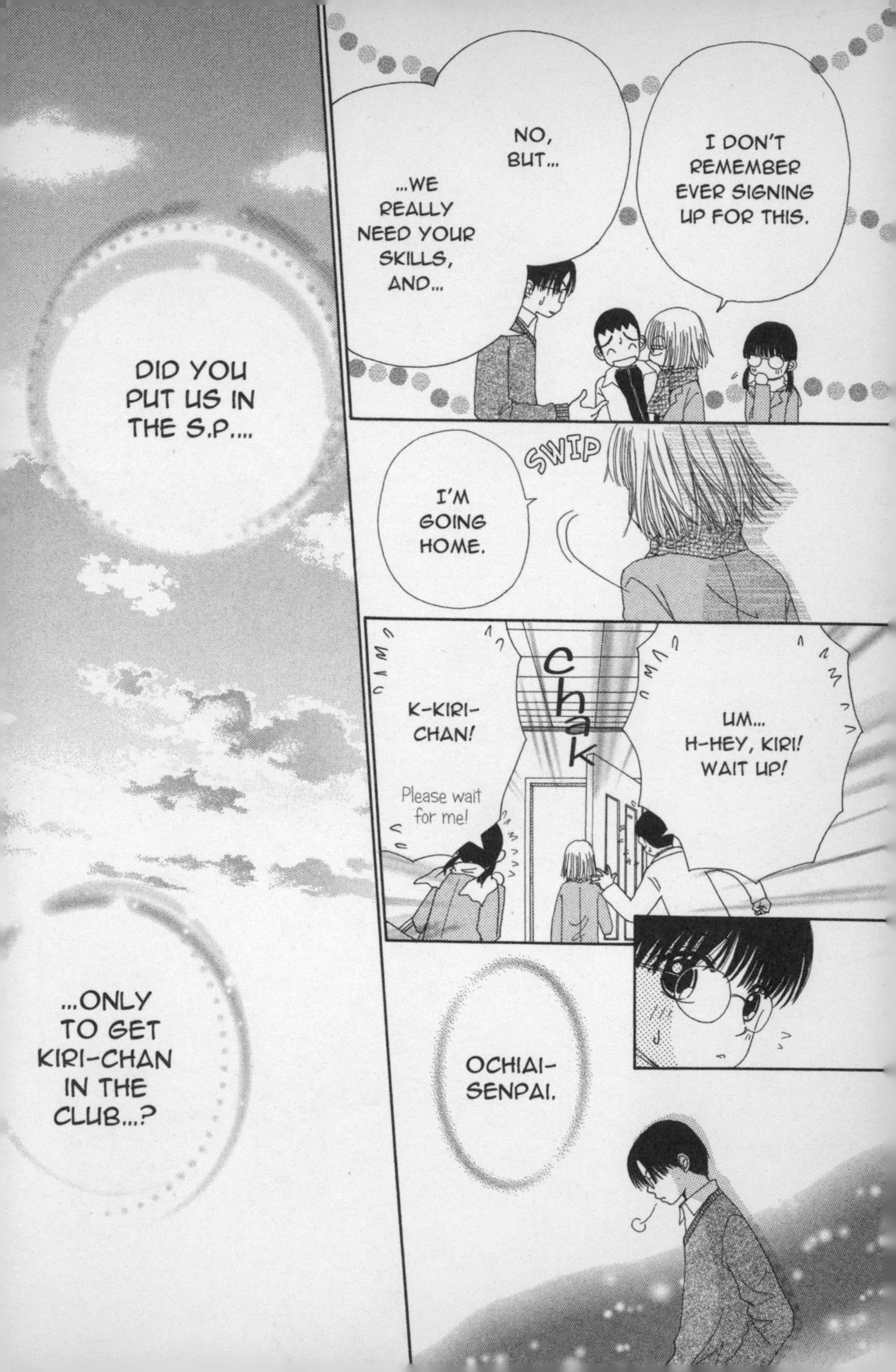
I DON'T REMEMBER EVER SIGNING UP FOR THIS.
NO, BUT...
...WE REALLY NEED YOUR SKILLS, AND...
SWIP
I'M GOING HOME.
UM... H-HEY, KIRI! WAIT UP!
Chak
K-KIRI-CHAN!
Please wait for me!
OCHIAI-SENPAI.
DID YOU PUT US IN THE S.P....
...ONLY TO GET KIRI-CHAN IN THE CLUB...?

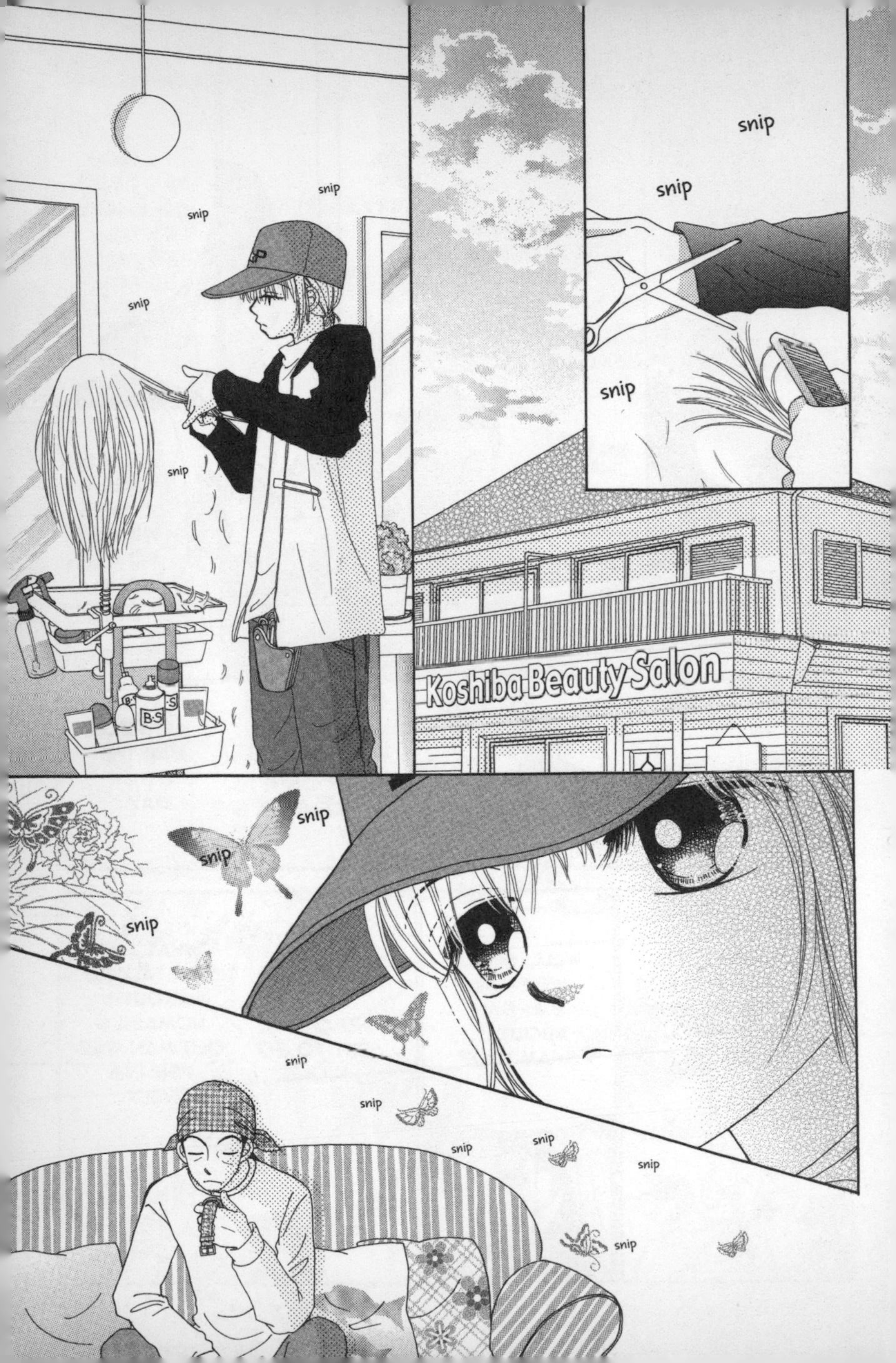
snip
snip
snip
Koshiba Beauty Salon
snip
snip
snip
snip
snip
snip
snip
snip
snip
snip
snip
snip
snip
snip

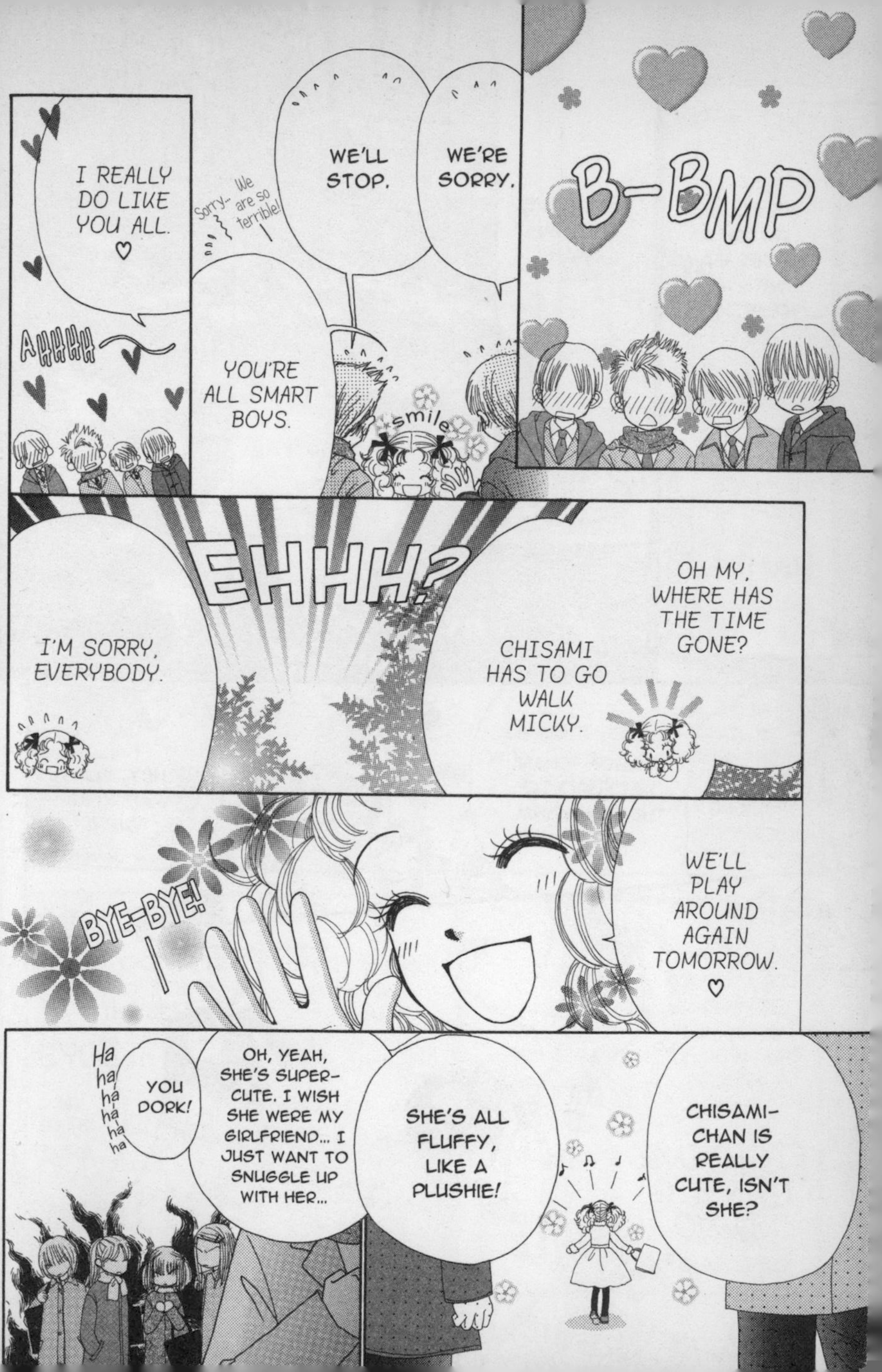
B-BMP
WE'RE SORRY.
WE'LL STOP.
Sorry... We are so terrible!
YOU'RE ALL SMART BOYS.
smile
I REALLY DO LIKE YOU ALL. ♡
AHHHH
OH MY, WHERE HAS THE TIME GONE?
CHISAMI HAS TO GO WALK MICKY.
EHHH?
I'M SORRY, EVERYBODY.
WE'LL PLAY AROUND AGAIN TOMORROW. ♡
BYE-BYE!
CHISAMI-CHAN IS REALLY CUTE, ISN'T SHE?
SHE'S ALL FLUFFY, LIKE A PLUSHIE!
OH, YEAH, SHE'S SUPER-CUTE. I WISH SHE WERE MY GIRLFRIEND... I JUST WANT TO SNUGGLE UP WITH HER...
YOU DORK!
Ha ha ha ha ha ha ha

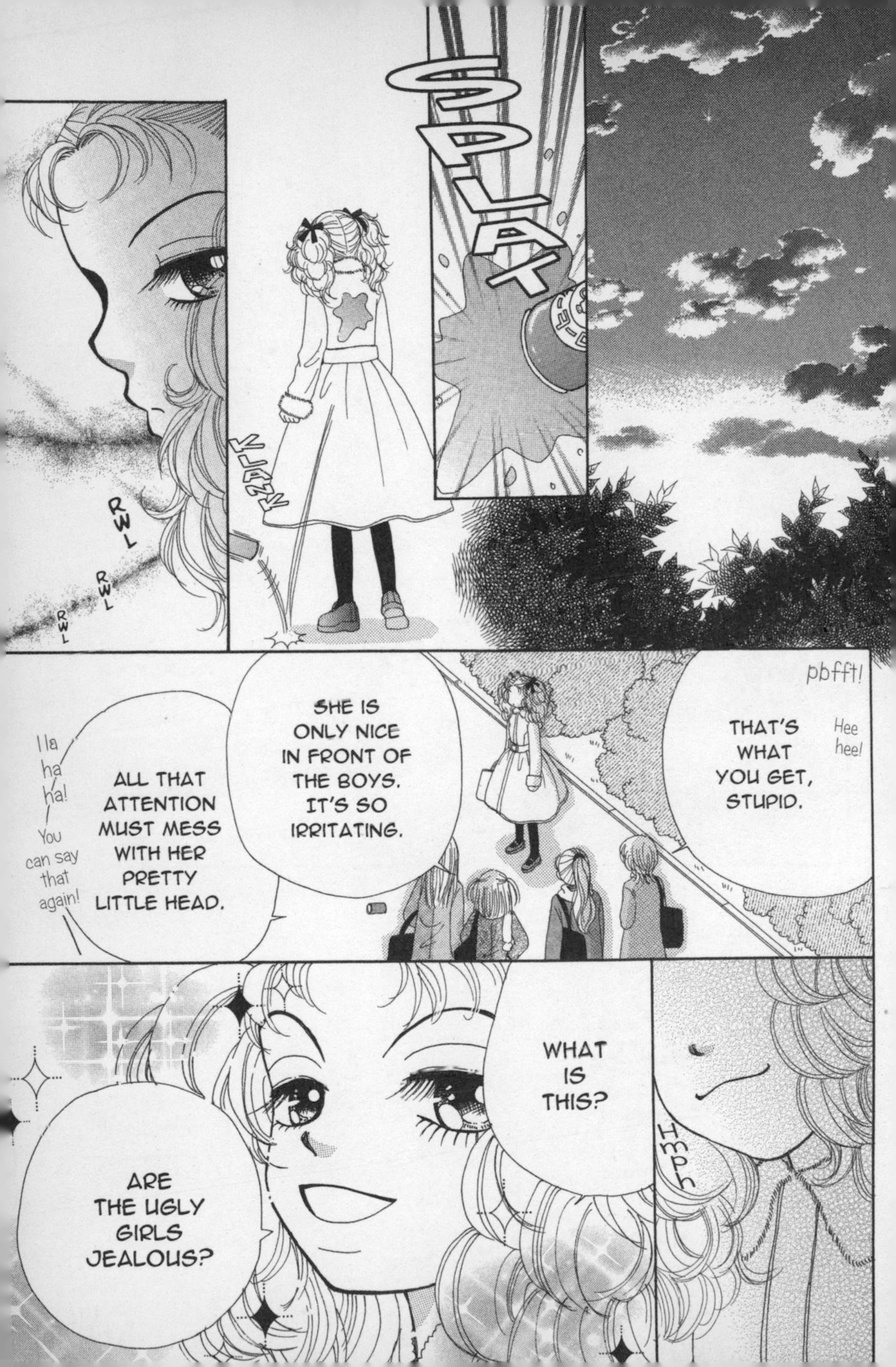
SPLAT
KLANK
RWL
RWL
RWL
pbfft!
THAT'S WHAT YOU GET, STUPID.
Hee hee!
SHE IS ONLY NICE IN FRONT OF THE BOYS. IT'S SO IRRITATING.
ALL THAT ATTENTION MUST MESS WITH HER PRETTY LITTLE HEAD.
Ha ha ha!
You can say that again!
Hmph
WHAT IS THIS?
ARE THE UGLY GIRLS JEALOUS?

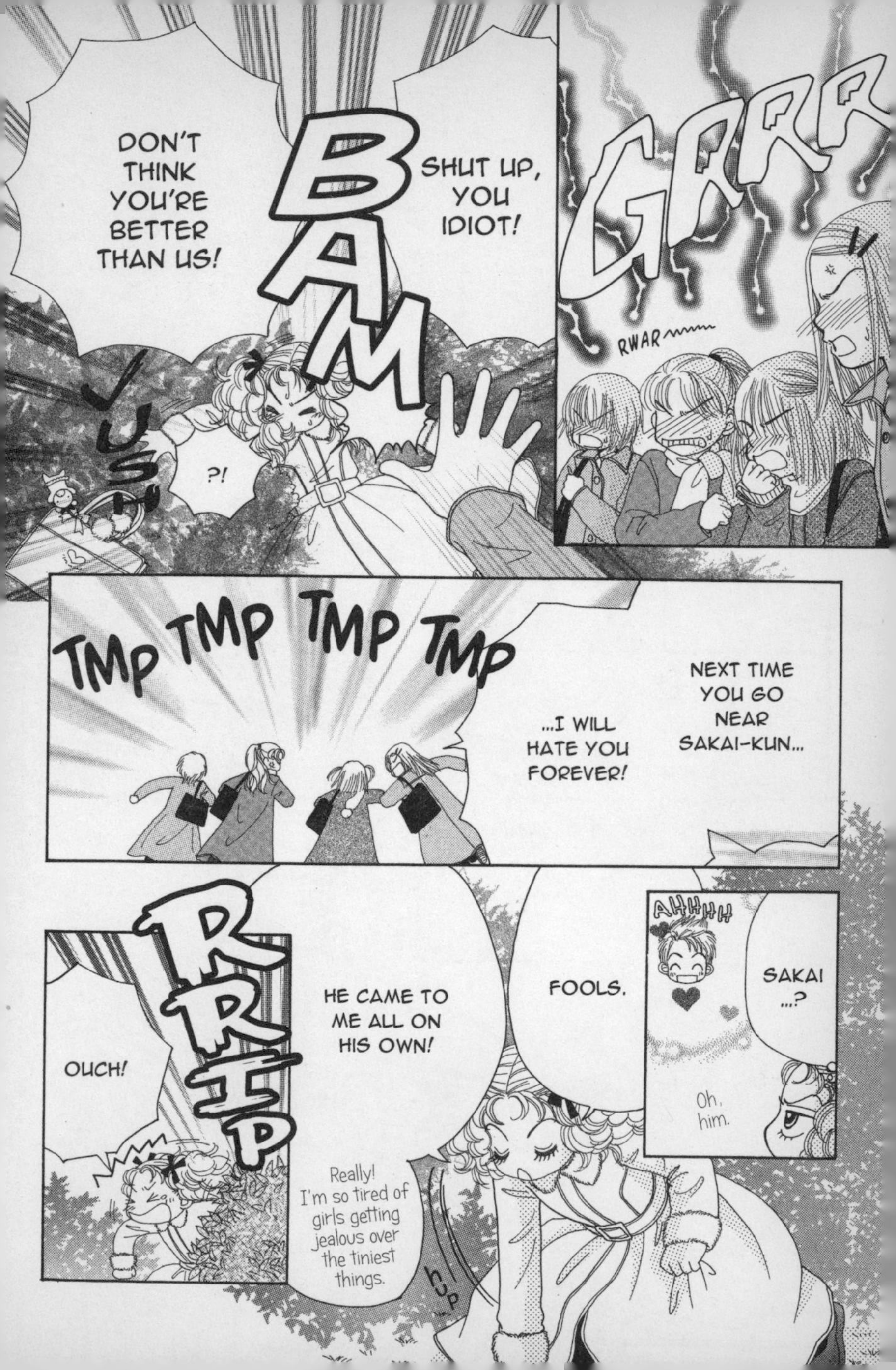
GRRR
RWAR
SHUT UP, YOU IDIOT!
DON'T THINK YOU'RE BETTER THAN US!
BAM
?!
JUSH
NEXT TIME YOU GO NEAR SAKAI-KUN...
...I WILL HATE YOU FOREVER!
TMP TMP TMP TMP
AHHHH
SAKAI ...?
Oh, him.
FOOLS.
HE CAME TO ME ALL ON HIS OWN!
Really! I'm so tired of girls getting jealous over the tiniest things.
HUP
RRIP
OUCH!

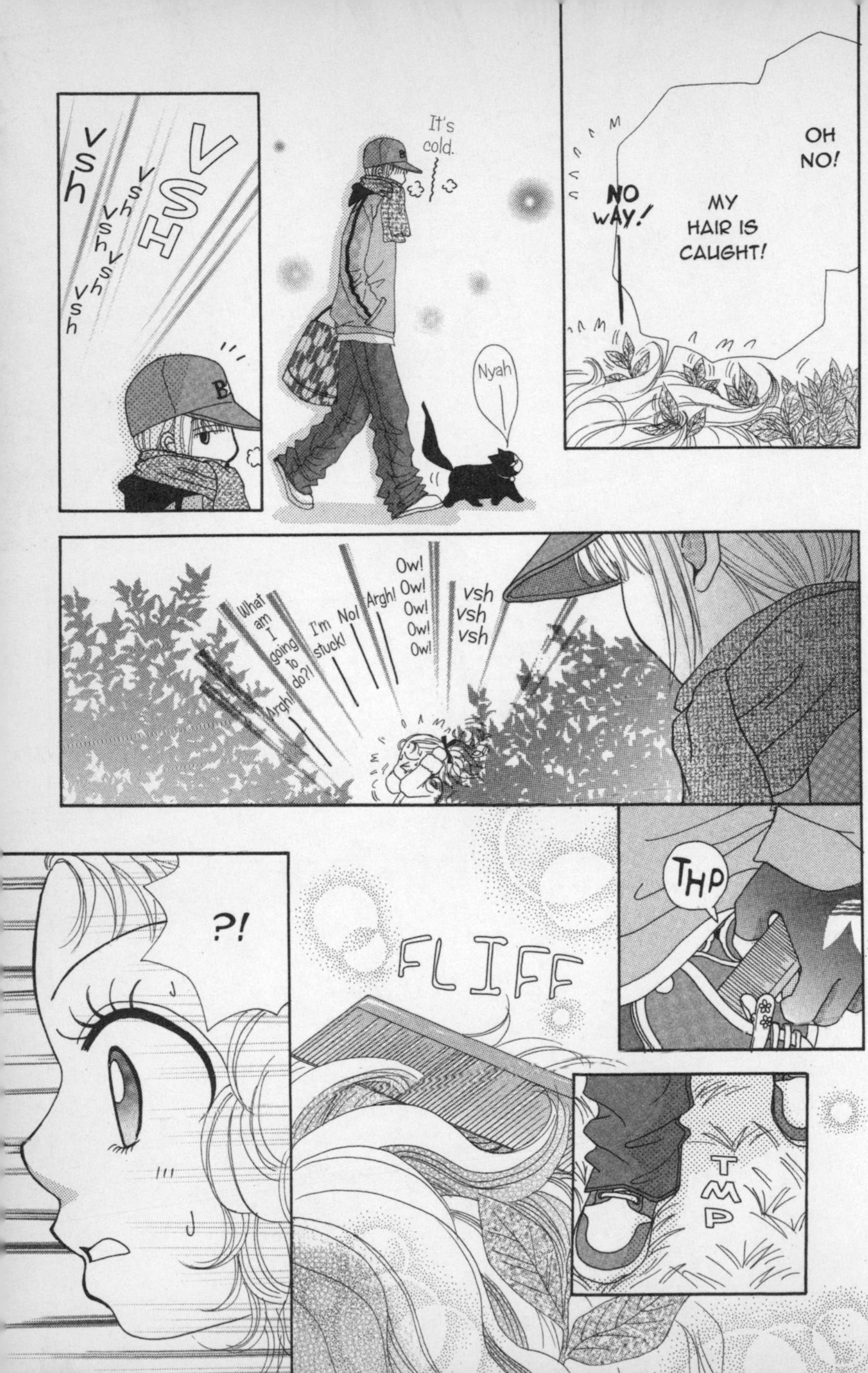
OH NO!
MY HAIR IS CAUGHT!
NO WAY!
It's cold.
Nyah
VSH
vsh vsh vsh vsh vsh
vsh vsh vsh
Ow! Ow! Ow! Ow! Ow!
Argh!
No!
I'm stuck!
What am I going to do?!
Argh!
THP
TMP
FLIFF
?!

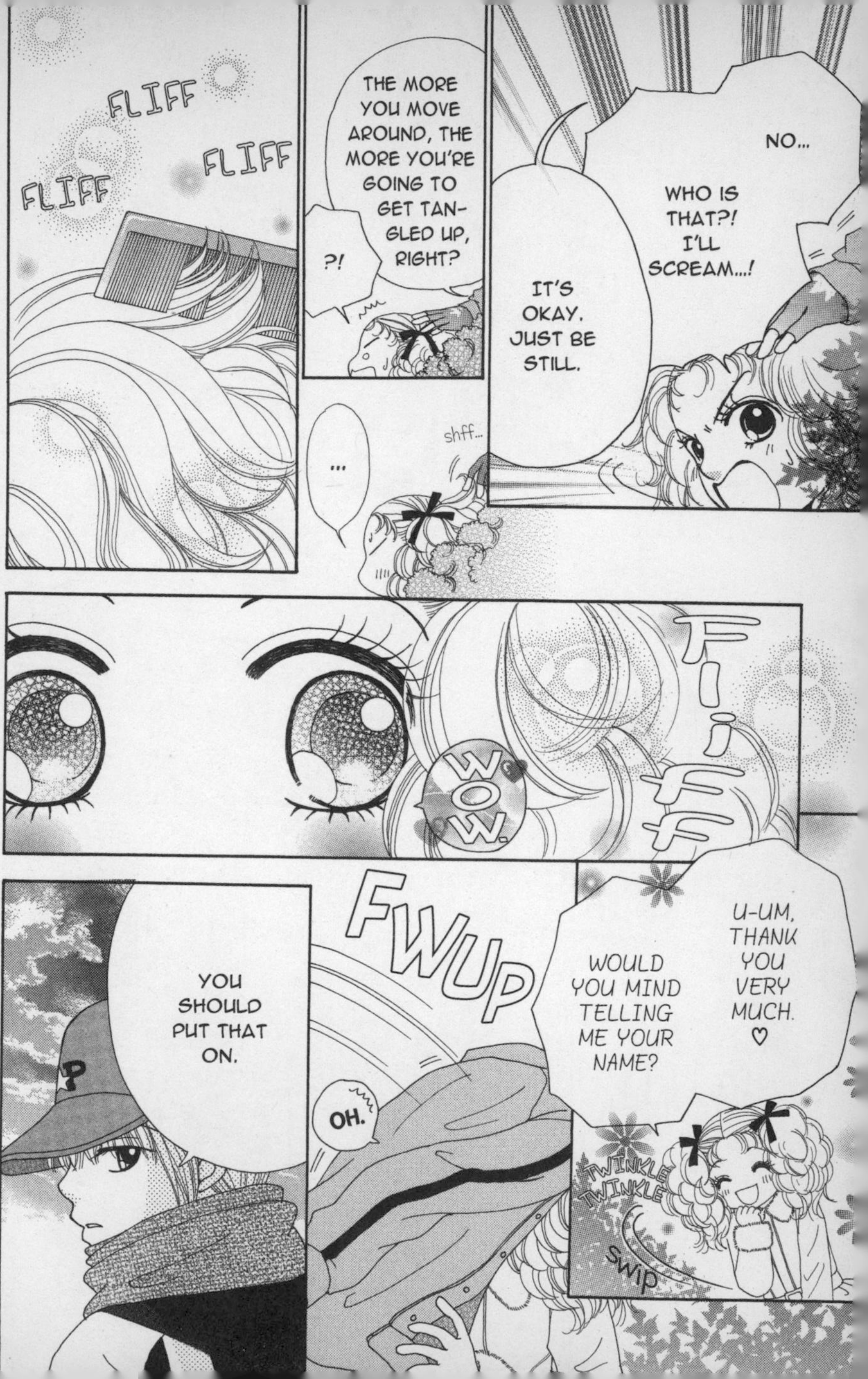
NO...
WHO IS THAT?! I'LL SCREAM...!
IT'S OKAY. JUST BE STILL.
THE MORE YOU MOVE AROUND, THE MORE YOU'RE GOING TO GET TAN-GLED UP, RIGHT?
?!
FLIFF
FLIFF
FLIFF
shff...
...
FIIFFF
WOW.
U-UM, THANK YOU VERY MUCH. ♡
WOULD YOU MIND TELLING ME YOUR NAME?
TWINKLE TWINKLE
swip
FWUP
OH.
YOU SHOULD PUT THAT ON.

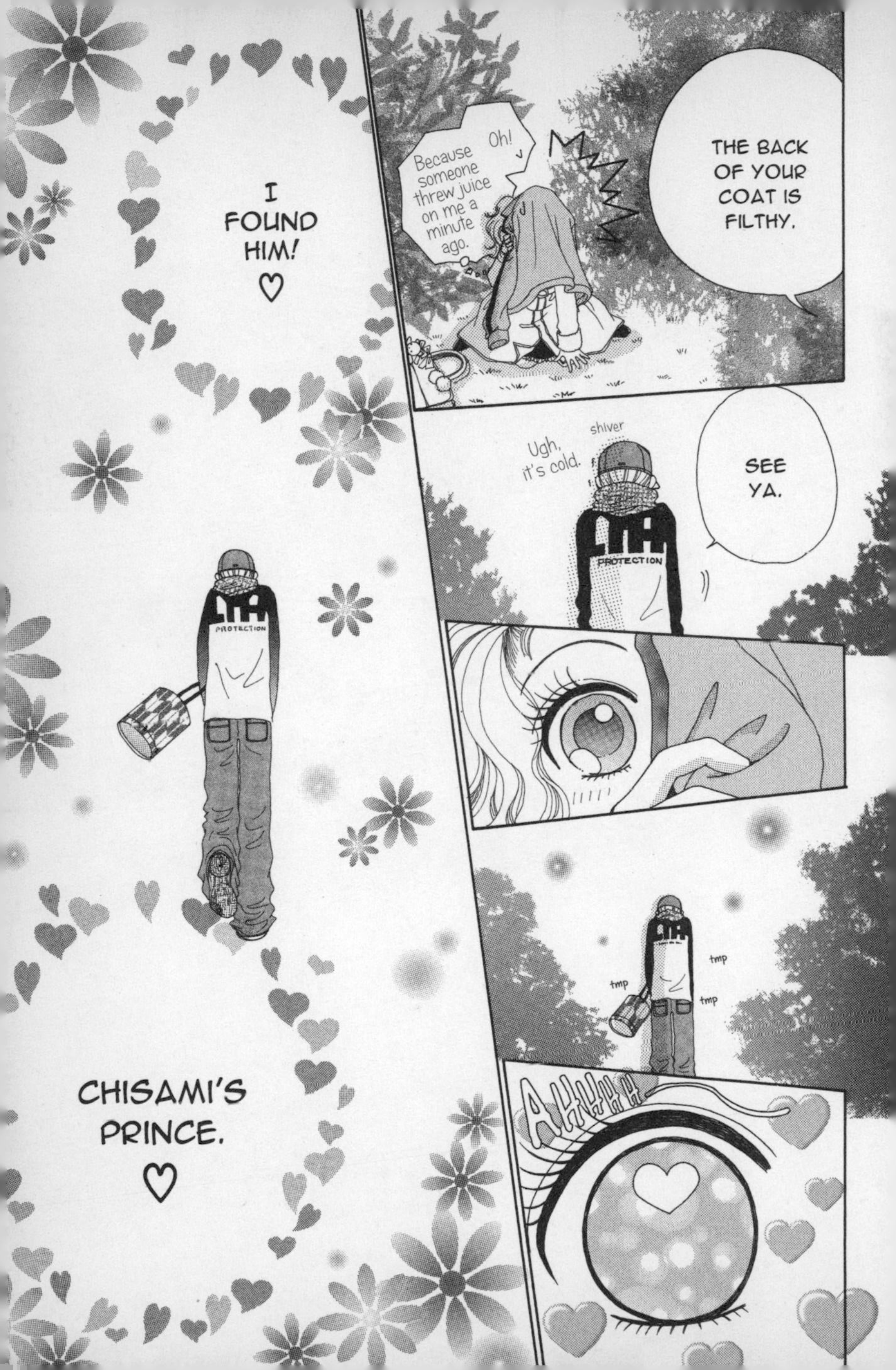
THE BACK OF YOUR COAT IS FILTHY.
Oh!
Because someone threw juice on me a minute ago.
SEE YA.
shiver
Ugh, it's cold.
tmp
tmp
tmp
AHHHH
I FOUND HIM! ♡
CHISAMI'S PRINCE. ♡

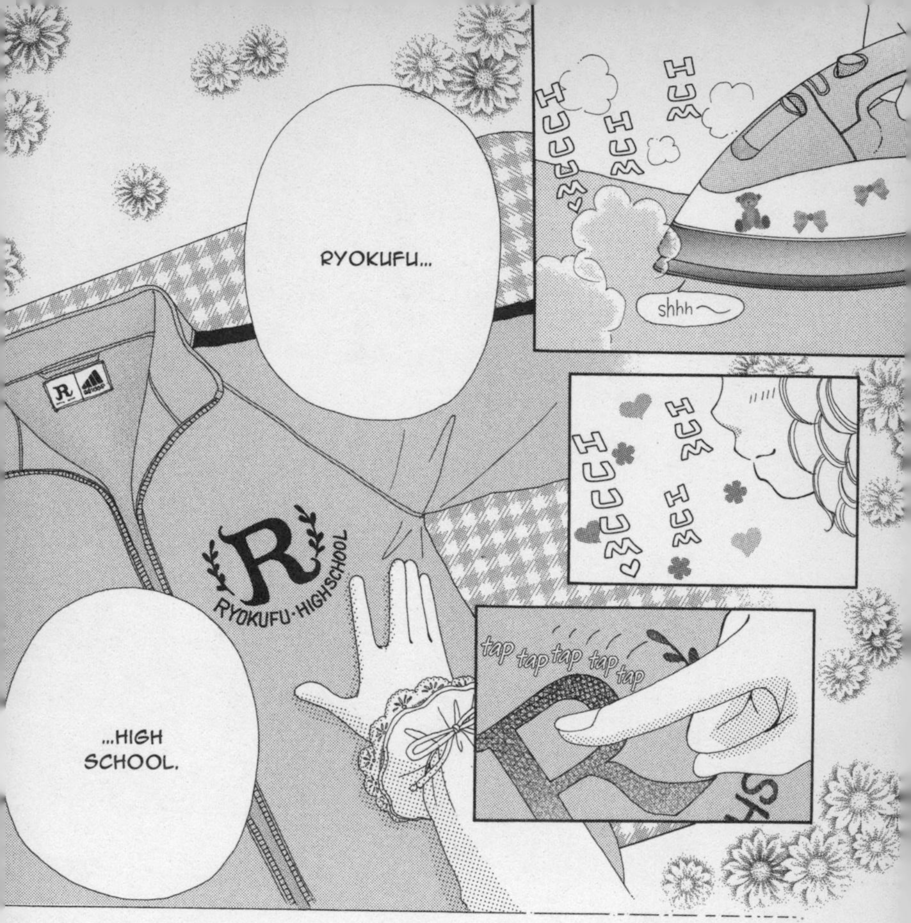
HUM
HUM
HUUUM♥
shhh~
HUM
HUM
HUUUM♥
tap tap tap tap tap
RYOKUFU...
RYOKUFU·HIGHSCHOOL
...HIGH SCHOOL.

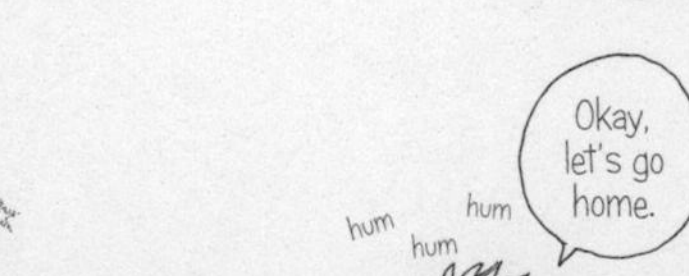
Okay, let's go home.
hum hum hum
HUH ?!
What happened to the Hamster Club?!
Hold on!
tmp tmp tmp

That's just the kind of guy Kei is.

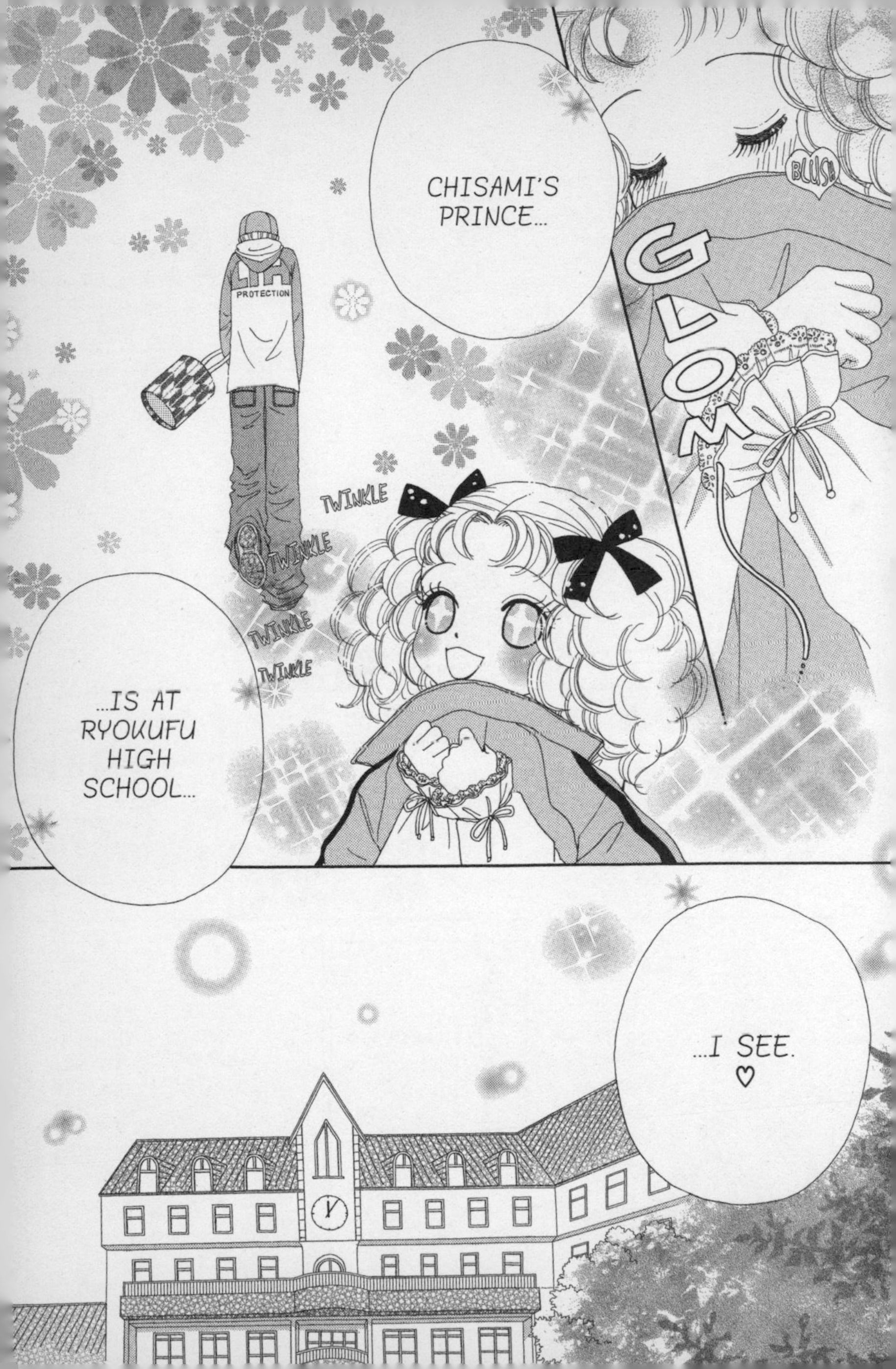
BLUSH
GLOM
CHISAMI'S PRINCE...
PROTECTION
TWINKLE
TWINKLE
TWINKLE
TWINKLE
...IS AT RYOKUFU HIGH SCHOOL...
...I SEE. ♡

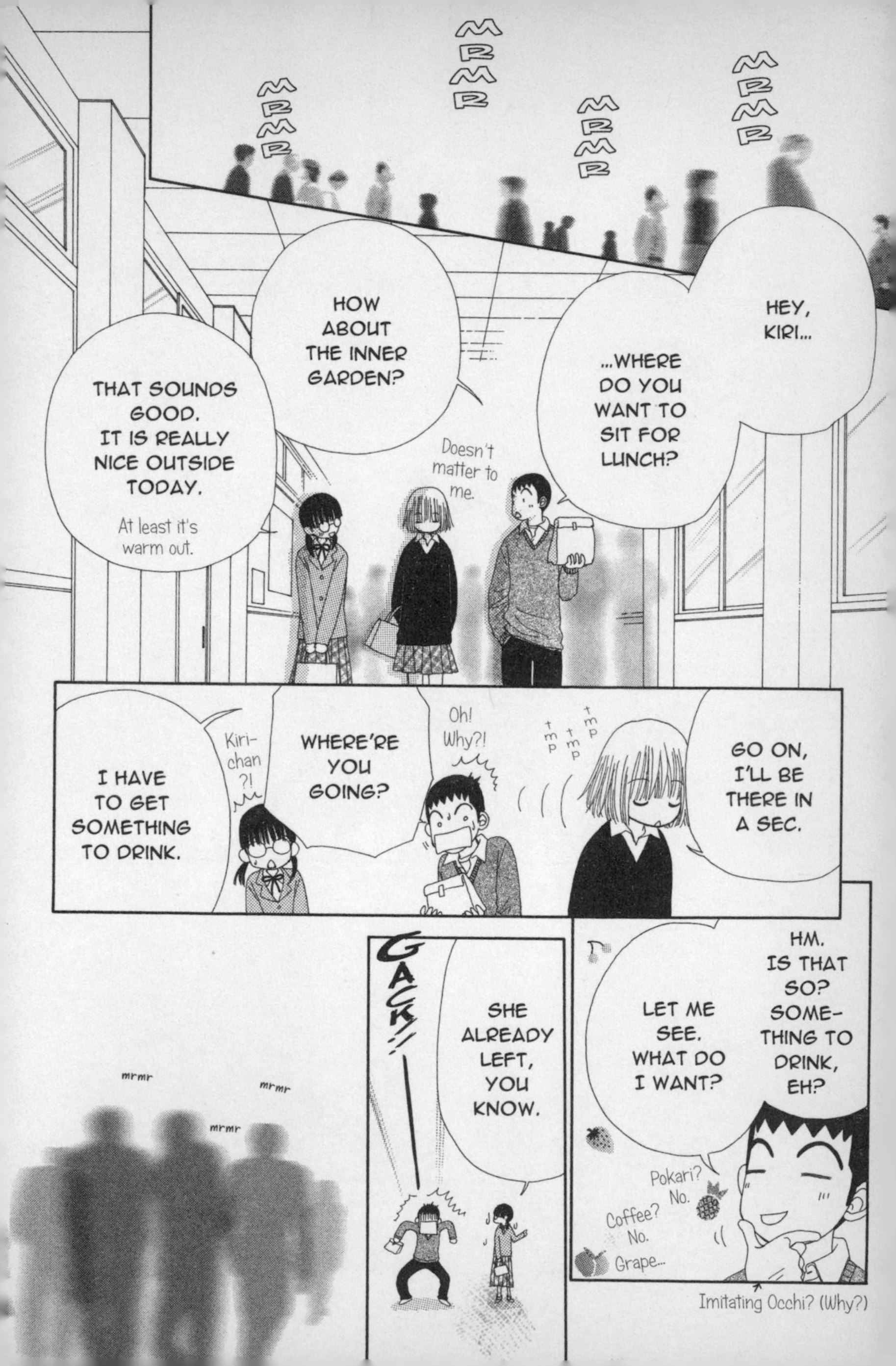
MRMR
MRMR
MRMR
MRMR
HEY, KIRI...
...WHERE DO YOU WANT TO SIT FOR LUNCH?
Doesn't matter to me.
HOW ABOUT THE INNER GARDEN?
THAT SOUNDS GOOD. IT IS REALLY NICE OUTSIDE TODAY.
At least it's warm out.
GO ON, I'LL BE THERE IN A SEC.
tmp tmp tmp
Oh! Why?!
WHERE'RE YOU GOING?
Kiri-chan ?!
I HAVE TO GET SOMETHING TO DRINK.
HM. IS THAT SO? SOMETHING TO DRINK, EH?
LET ME SEE. WHAT DO I WANT?
Pokari? No.
Coffee? No.
Grape...
Imitating Occchi? (Why?)
SHE ALREADY LEFT, YOU KNOW.
GACK!!
mrmr
mrmr
mrmr

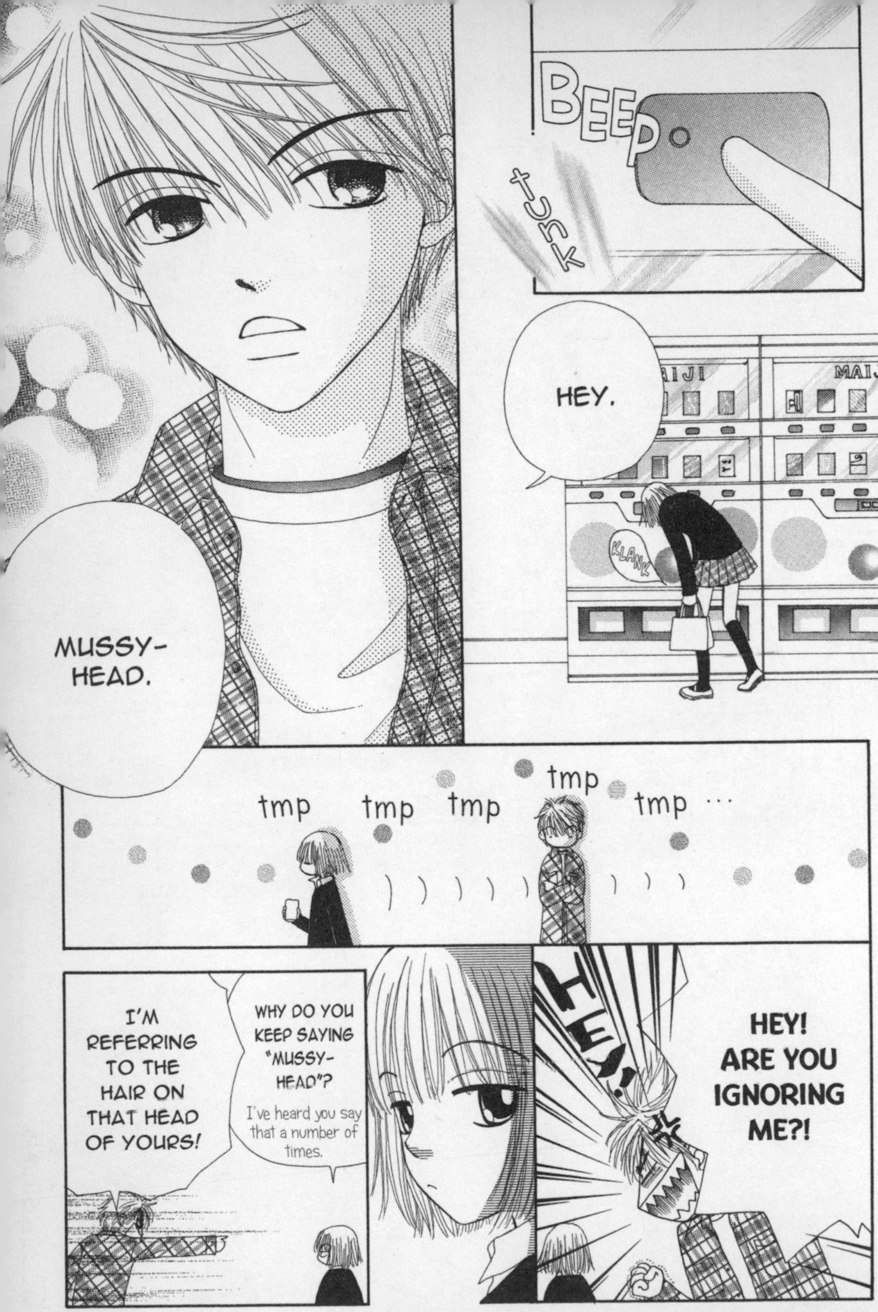
BEEP
tunk
HEY.
KLANK
MUSSY-HEAD.
tmp tmp tmp tmp tmp ...
HEY!
HEY! ARE YOU IGNORING ME?!
WHY DO YOU KEEP SAYING "MUSSY-HEAD"?
I've heard you say that a number of times.
I'M REFERRING TO THE HAIR ON THAT HEAD OF YOURS!

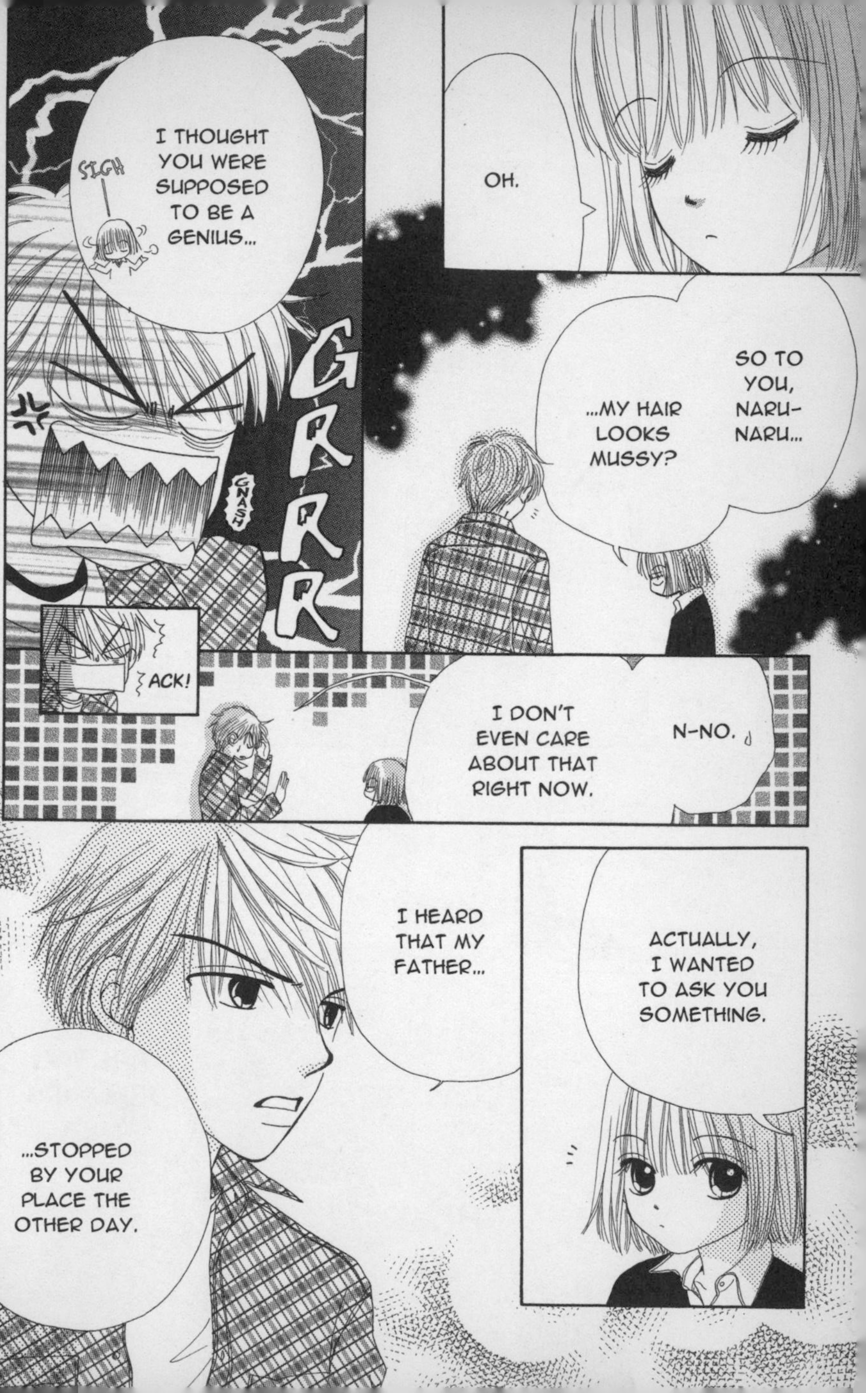
OH.
SO TO YOU, NARU-NARU...
...MY HAIR LOOKS MUSSY?
I THOUGHT YOU WERE SUPPOSED TO BE A GENIUS...
SIGH
GNASH
GRRR
ACK!
N-NO.
I DON'T EVEN CARE ABOUT THAT RIGHT NOW.
ACTUALLY, I WANTED TO ASK YOU SOMETHING.
I HEARD THAT MY FATHER...
...STOPPED BY YOUR PLACE THE OTHER DAY.

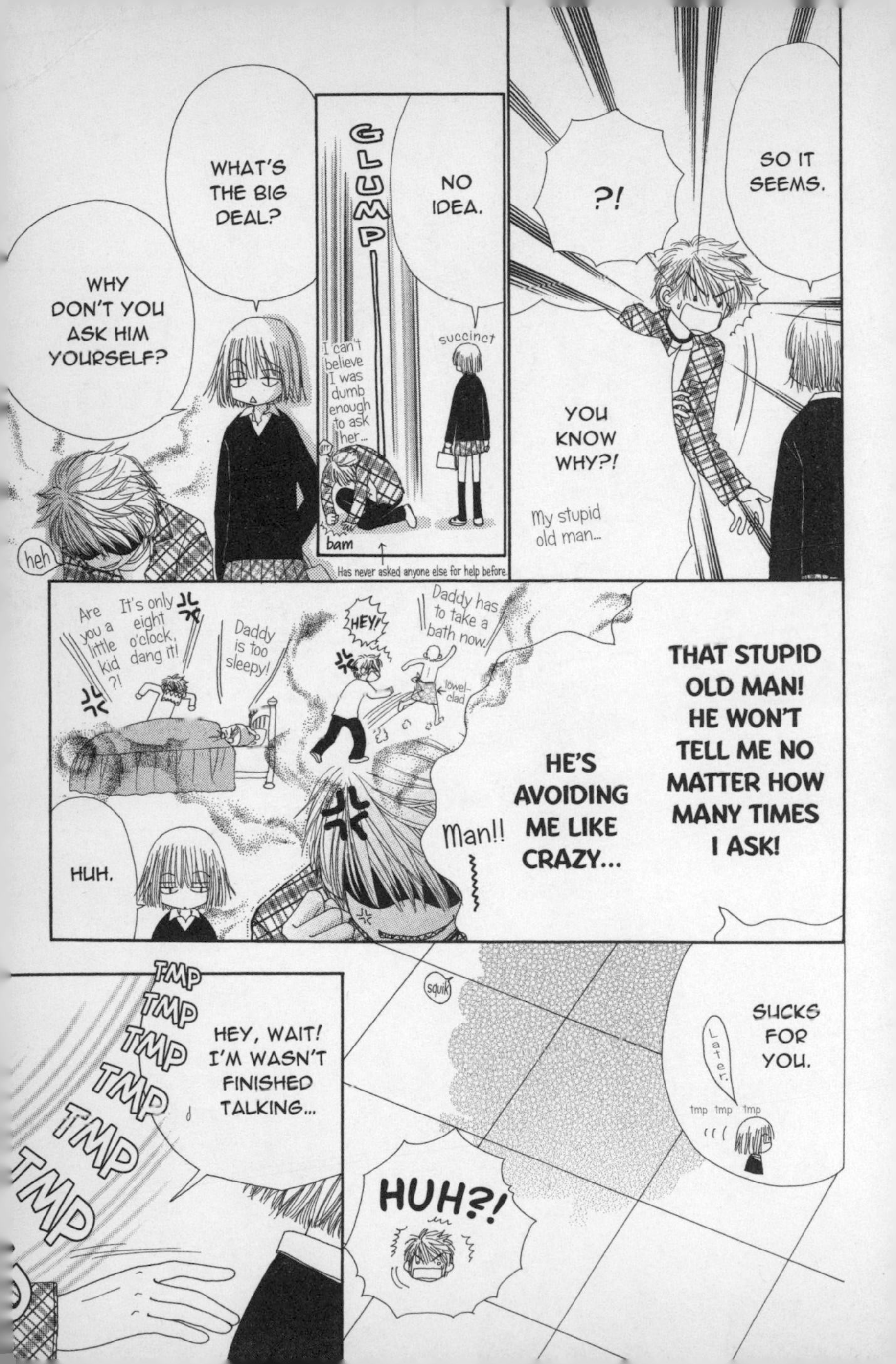
SO IT SEEMS.
?!
YOU KNOW WHY?!
My stupid old man...
NO IDEA.
GLUMP
succinct
I can't believe I was dumb enough to ask her...
bam
Has never asked anyone else for help before
WHAT'S THE BIG DEAL?
WHY DON'T YOU ASK HIM YOURSELF?
heh
THAT STUPID OLD MAN! HE WON'T TELL ME NO MATTER HOW MANY TIMES I ASK!
HE'S AVOIDING ME LIKE CRAZY...
Daddy has to take a bath now!
towel-clad
HEY!
Daddy is too sleepy!
It's only eight o'clock, dang it!
Are you a little kid?!
Man!!
HUH.
squik
SUCKS FOR YOU.
Later.
tmp tmp tmp
HUH?!
HEY, WAIT! I'M WASN'T FINISHED TALKING...
TMP TMP TMP TMP TMP TMP

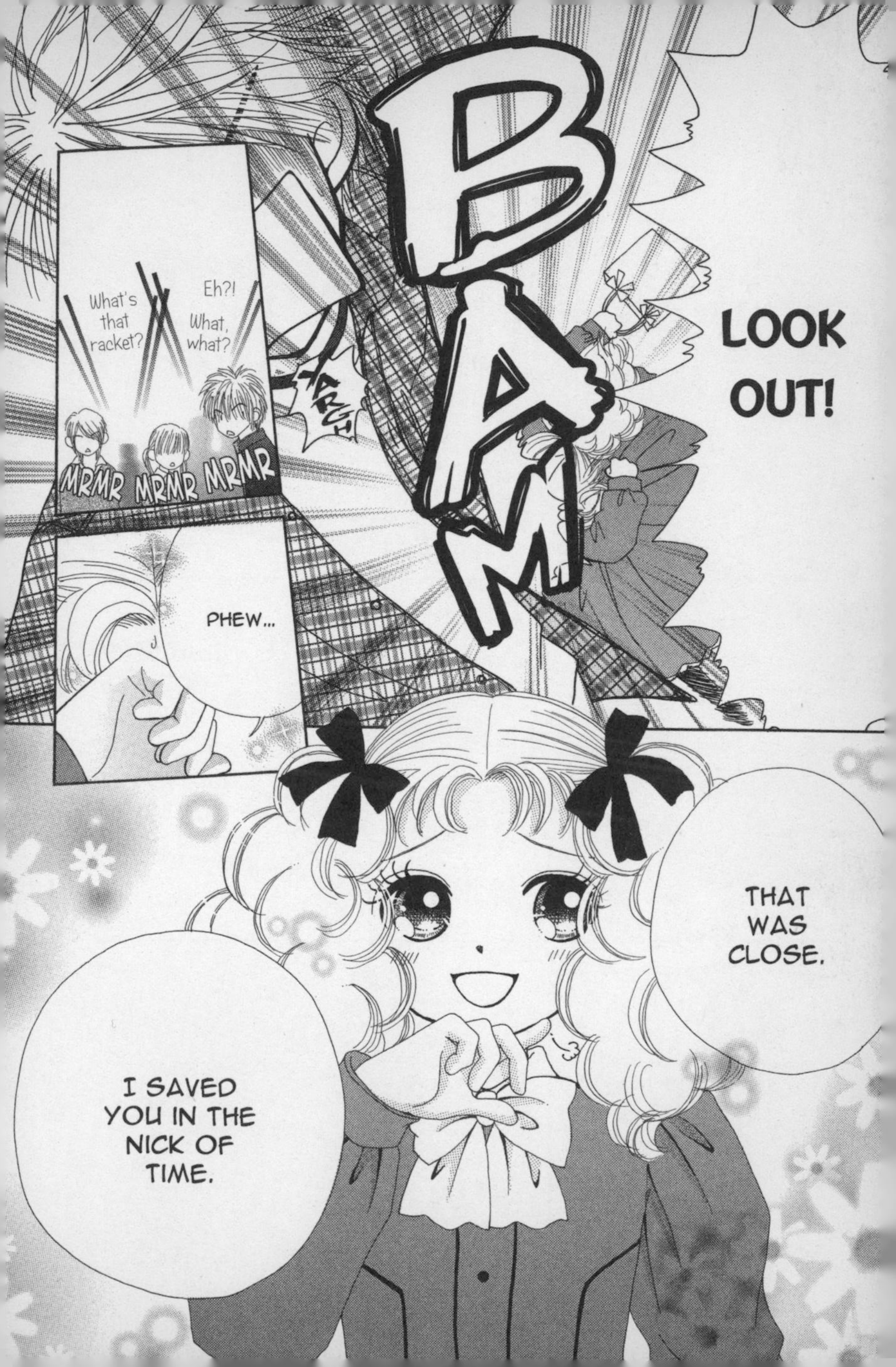
LOOK OUT!
BAM
ARGH
Eh?!
What, what?
What's that racket?
MRMR MRMR MRMR
PHEW...
THAT WAS CLOSE.
I SAVED YOU IN THE NICK OF TIME.

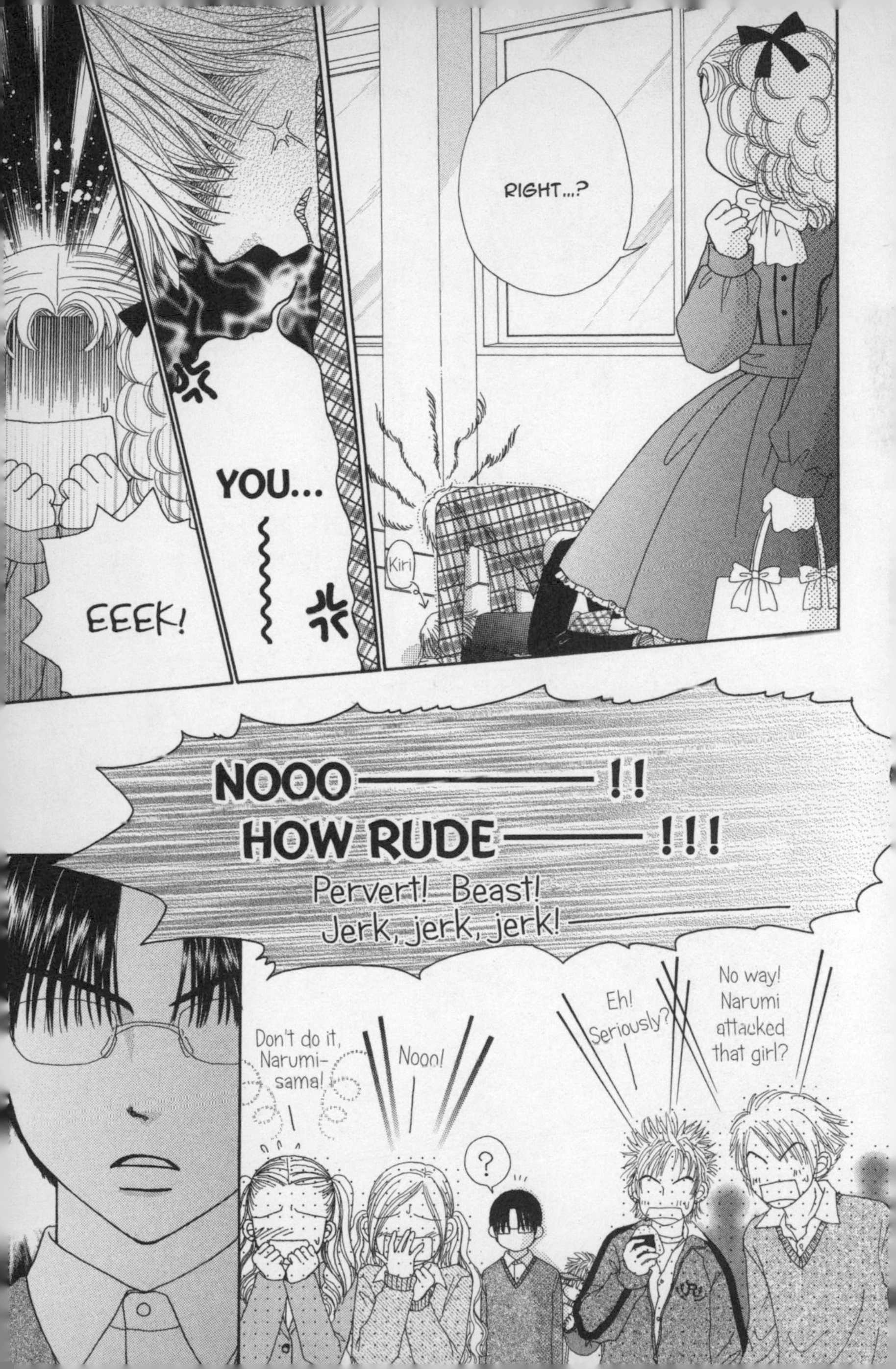
RIGHT...?
Kiri
YOU...
EEEK!
NOOO——!!
HOW RUDE——!!!
Pervert! Beast!
Jerk, jerk, jerk!——
No way! Narumi attacked that girl?
Eh! Seriously?
?
Nooo!
Don't do it, Narumi-sama!

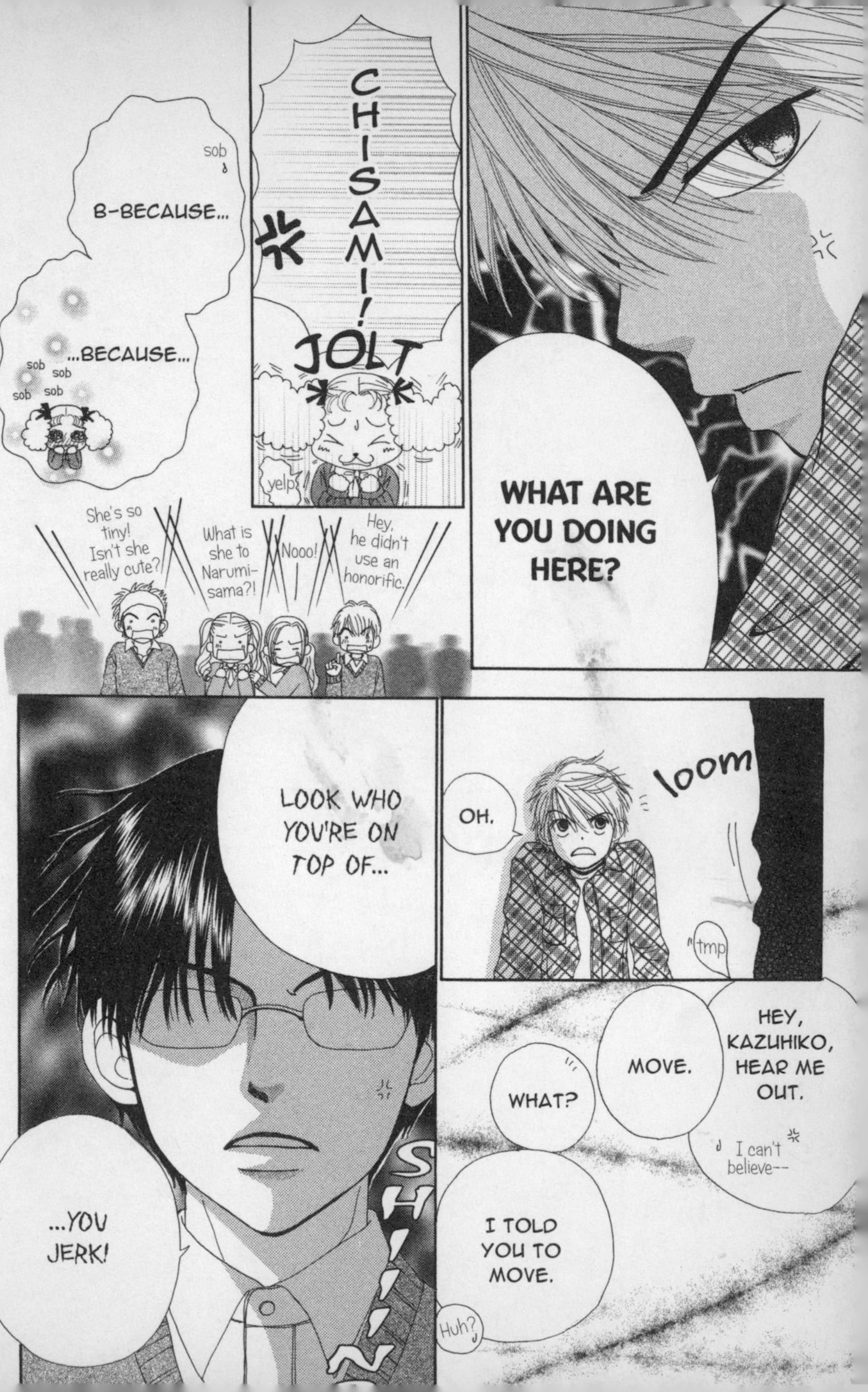
WHAT ARE YOU DOING HERE?
CHISAMI!
JOLT
yelp
sob
B-BECAUSE...
...BECAUSE...
sob sob sob sob
Hey, he didn't use an honorific.
Nooo!
What is she to Narumi-sama?!
She's so tiny! Isn't she really cute?
loom
OH.
tmp
HEY, KAZUHIKO, HEAR ME OUT.
I can't believe--
MOVE.
WHAT?
I TOLD YOU TO MOVE.
Huh?
LOOK WHO YOU'RE ON TOP OF...
...YOU JERK!

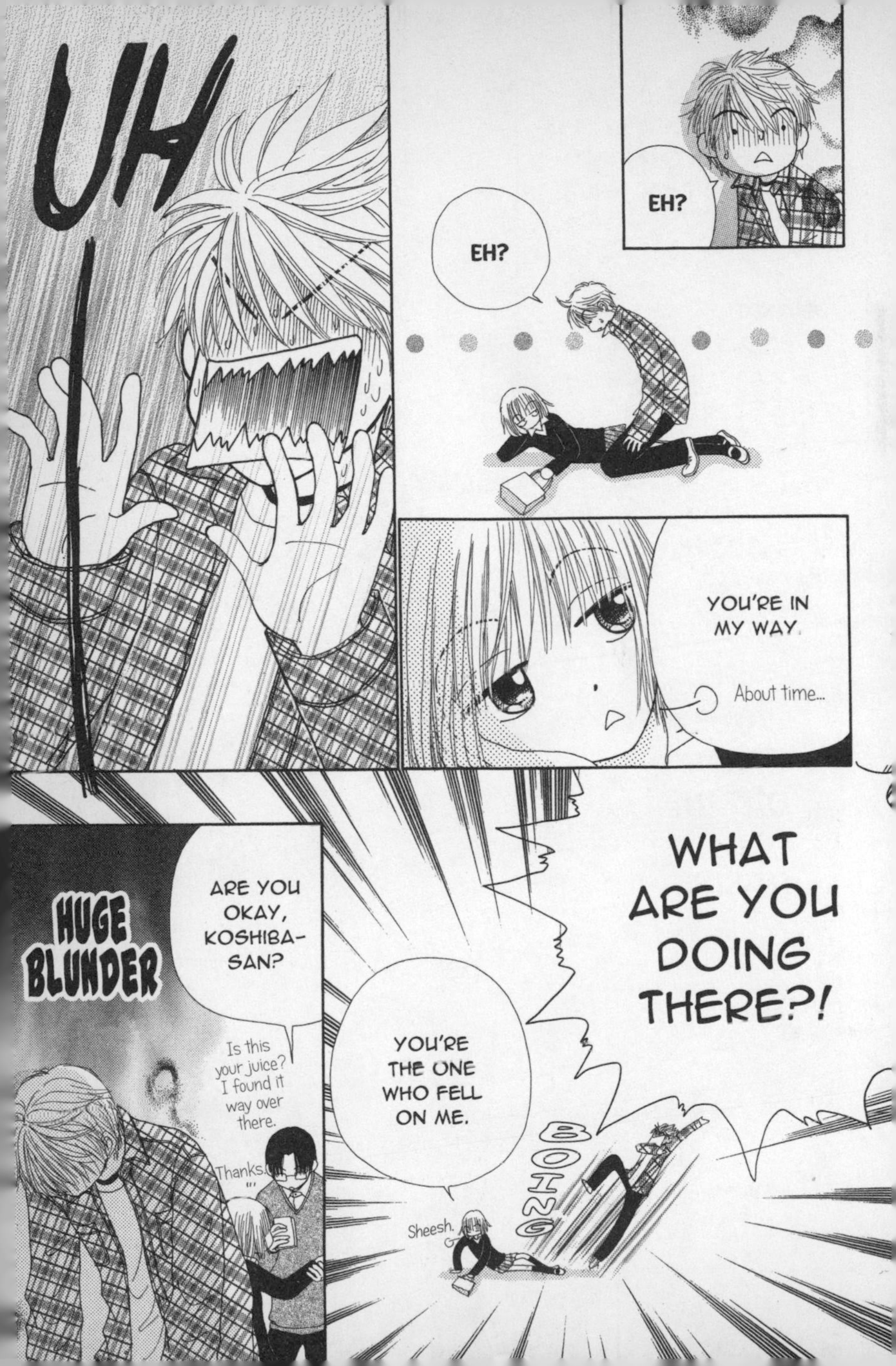
EH?
EH?
YOU'RE IN MY WAY.
About time...
UH
WHAT ARE YOU DOING THERE?!
YOU'RE THE ONE WHO FELL ON ME.
BOING
Sheesh.
HUGE BLUNDER
ARE YOU OKAY, KOSHIBA-SAN?
Is this your juice? I found it way over there.
Thanks.

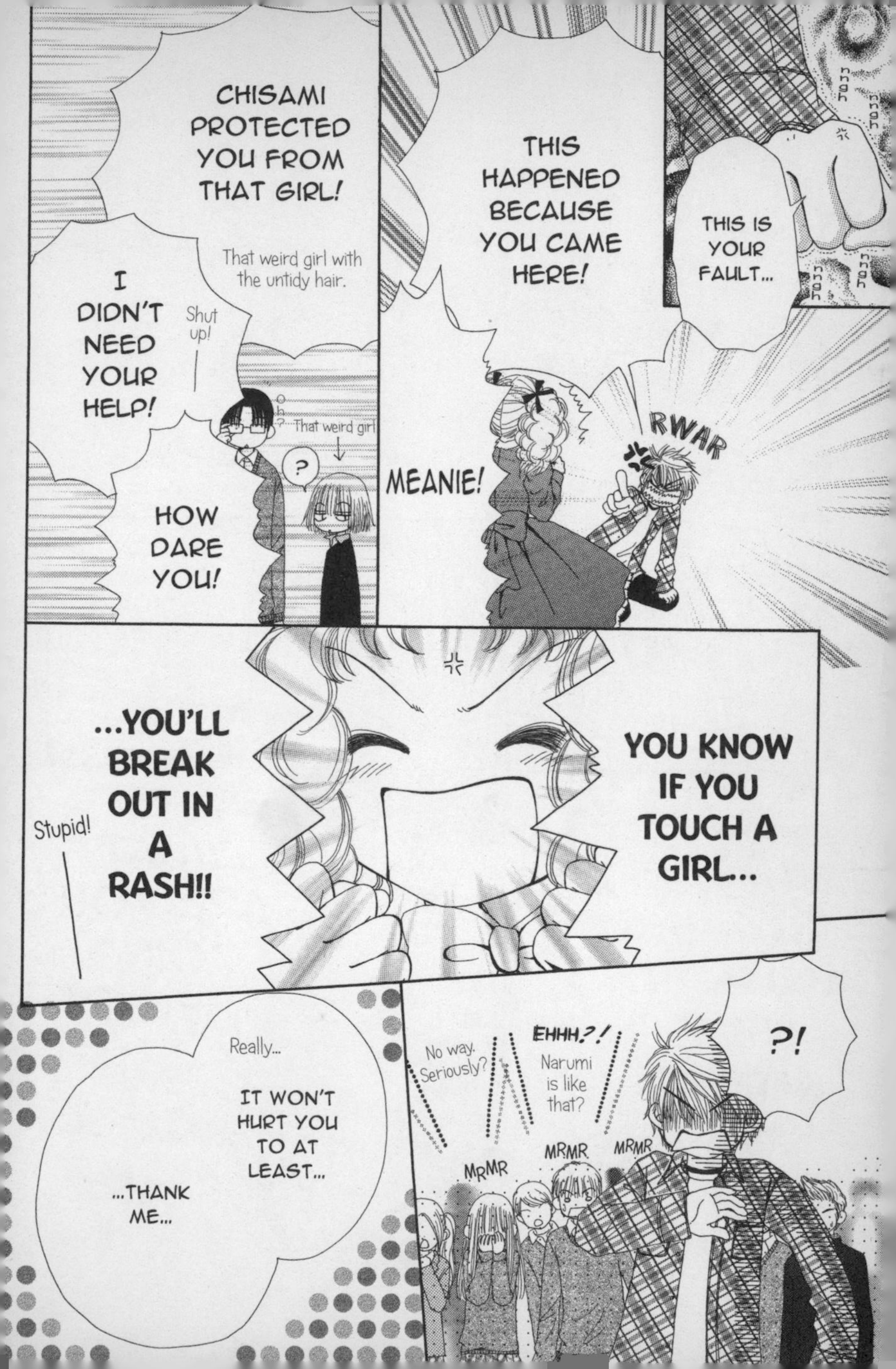
nngh nngh
THIS IS YOUR FAULT...
nngh nngh
THIS HAPPENED BECAUSE YOU CAME HERE!
RWAR
MEANIE!
CHISAMI PROTECTED YOU FROM THAT GIRL!
That weird girl with the untidy hair.
I DIDN'T NEED YOUR HELP!
Shut up!
Oh?
That weird girl
?
HOW DARE YOU!
YOU KNOW IF YOU TOUCH A GIRL...
...YOU'LL BREAK OUT IN A RASH!!
Stupid!
?!
EHHH?!
Narumi is like that?
No way. Seriously?
MRMR
MRMR
MRMR
Really...
IT WON'T HURT YOU TO AT LEAST...
...THANK ME...

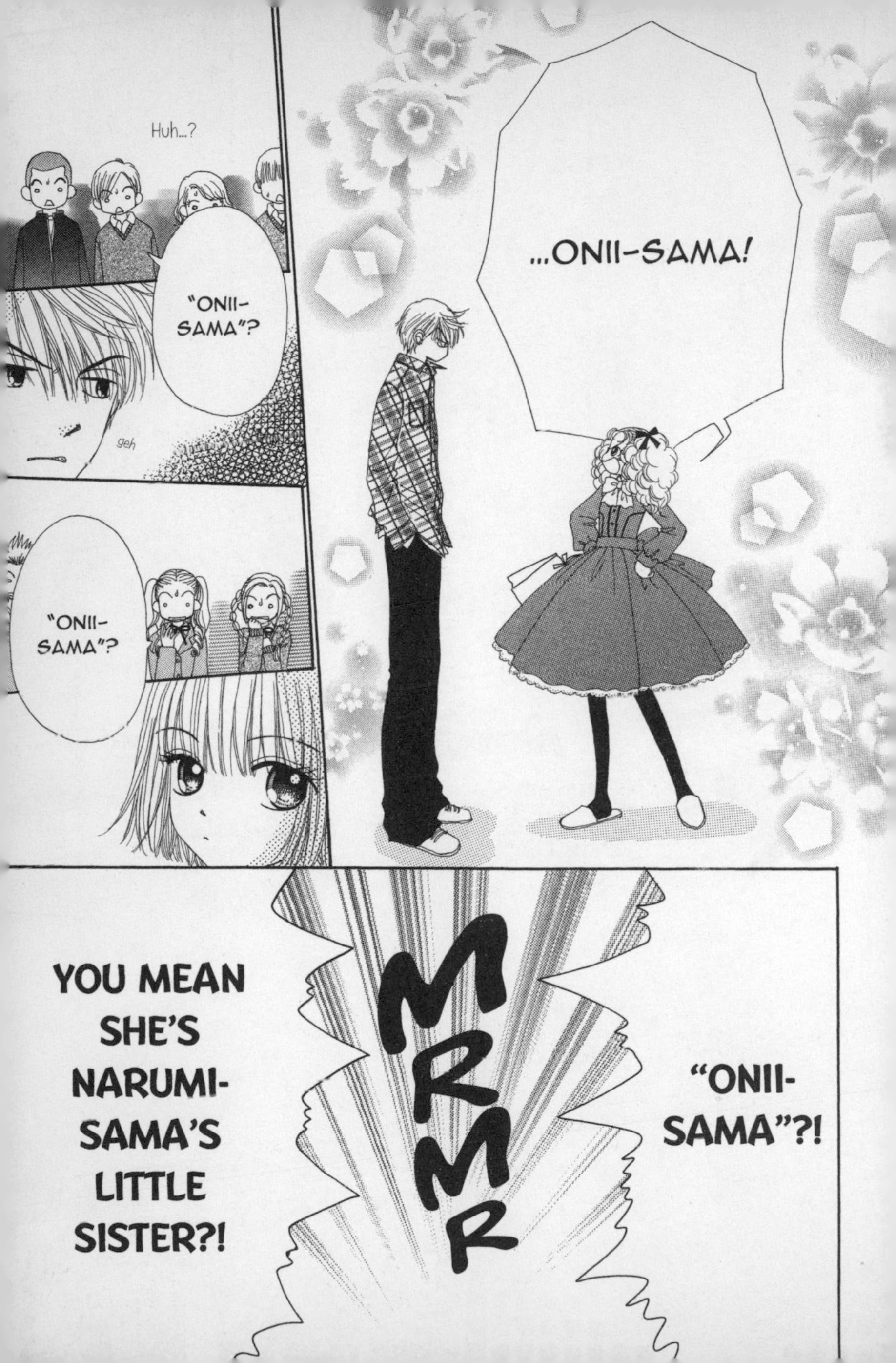
...ONII-SAMA!
Huh...?
"ONII-SAMA"?
geh
"ONII-SAMA"?
"ONII-SAMA"?!
MRMR
YOU MEAN SHE'S NARUMI-SAMA'S LITTLE SISTER?!

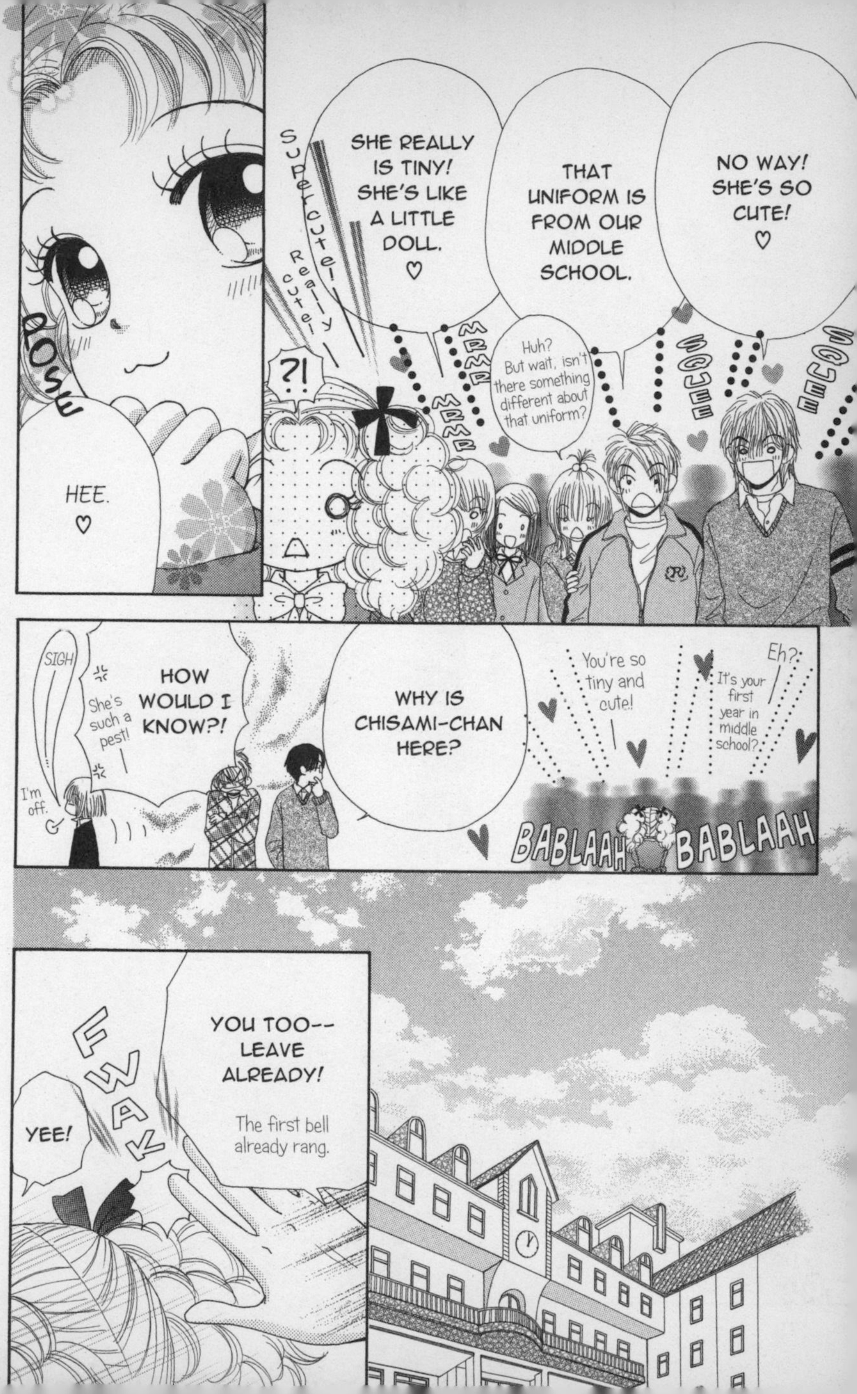
NO WAY! SHE'S SO CUTE! ♡
THAT UNIFORM IS FROM OUR MIDDLE SCHOOL.
SHE REALLY IS TINY! SHE'S LIKE A LITTLE DOLL. ♡
SQUEE
SQUEE
Huh? But wait, isn't there something different about that uniform?
MRMR
MRMR
Super cute!
Really cute!
?!
HEE. ♡
Eh?
It's your first year in middle school?
You're so tiny and cute!
BABLAAH
BABLAAH
WHY IS CHISAMI-CHAN HERE?
HOW WOULD I KNOW?!
She's such a pest!
SIGH
I'm off.
YOU TOO-- LEAVE ALREADY!
The first bell already rang.
FWAK
YEE!

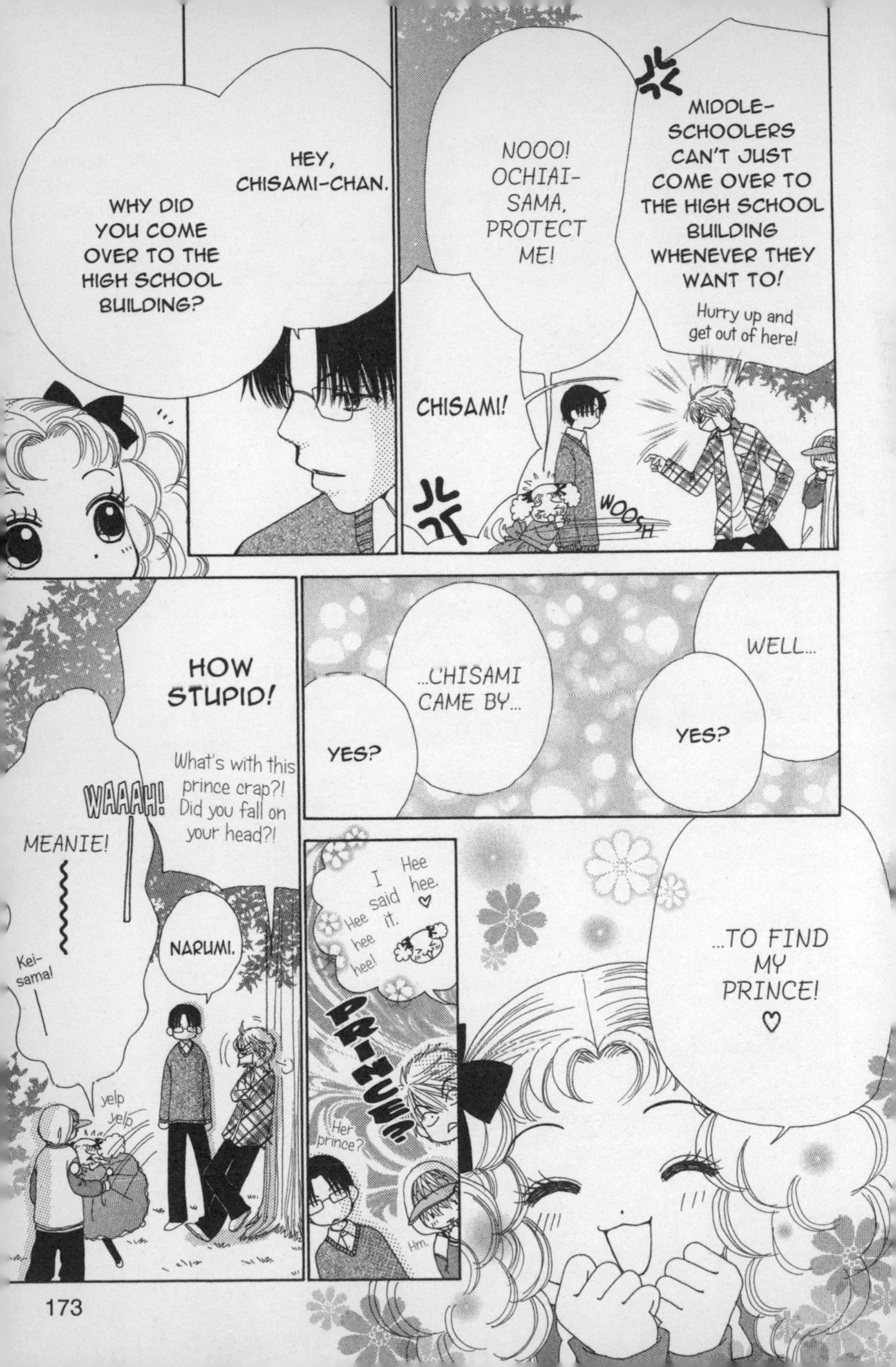
MIDDLE-SCHOOLERS CAN'T JUST COME OVER TO THE HIGH SCHOOL BUILDING WHENEVER THEY WANT TO!
Hurry up and get out of here!
NOOO! OCHIAI-SAMA, PROTECT ME!
CHISAMI!
WOOSH
HEY, CHISAMI-CHAN.
WHY DID YOU COME OVER TO THE HIGH SCHOOL BUILDING?
WELL...
YES?
...CHISAMI CAME BY...
YES?
...TO FIND MY PRINCE! ♡
I said it. Hee hee. ♡
Hee hee hee!
PRINCE?!
Her prince?
Hm.
HOW STUPID!
What's with this prince crap?! Did you fall on your head?!
WAAAH!
MEANIE!
Kei-sama!
NARUMI.
yelp yelp

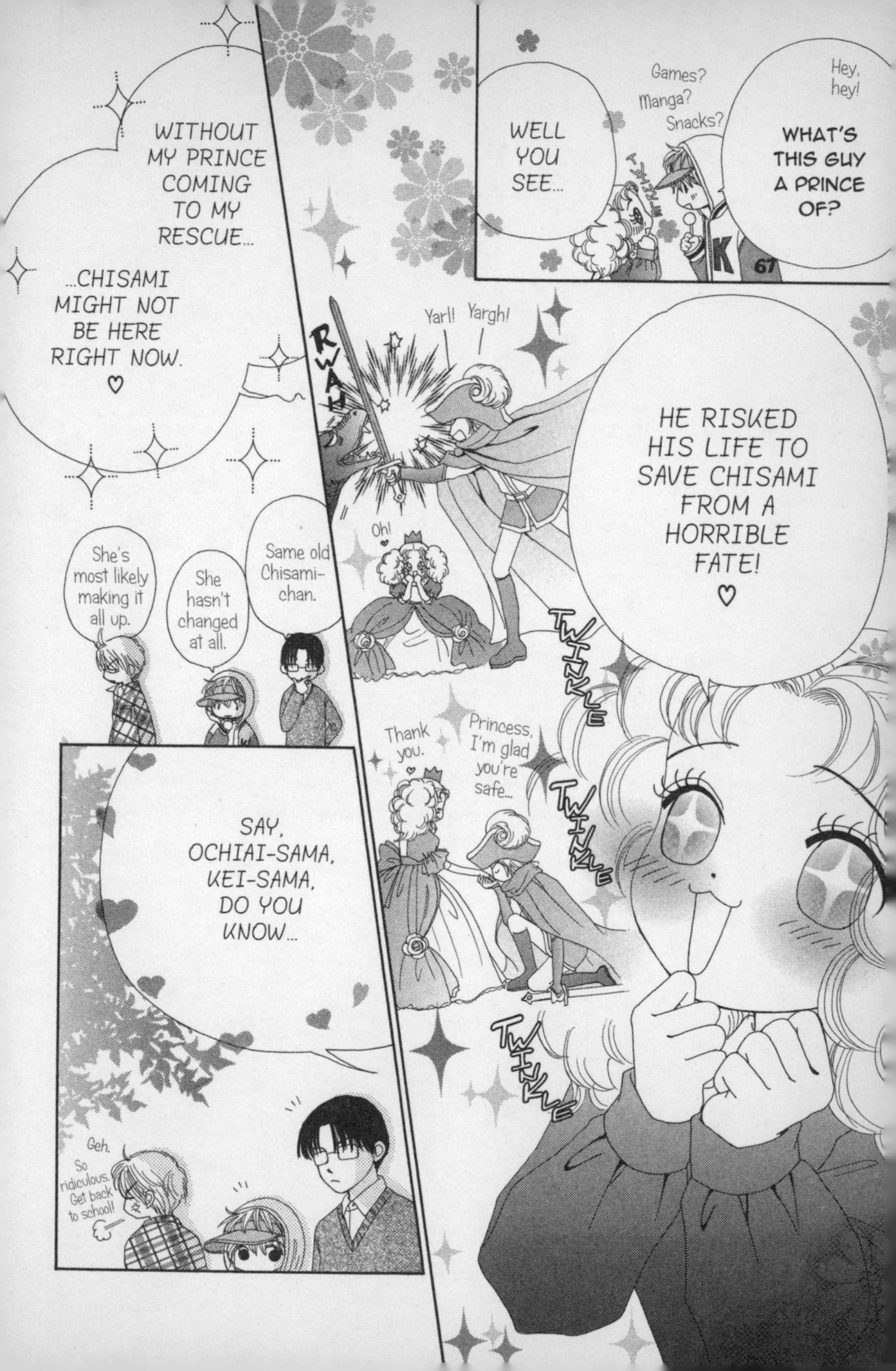
Hey, hey!
WHAT'S THIS GUY A PRINCE OF?
Games?
Manga?
Snacks?
WELL YOU SEE...
HE RISKED HIS LIFE TO SAVE CHISAMI FROM A HORRIBLE FATE! ♡
Yarl!
Yargh!
RWAH
Oh!
TWINKLE
TWINKLE
Princess, I'm glad you're safe...
Thank you.
TWINKLE
WITHOUT MY PRINCE COMING TO MY RESCUE...
...CHISAMI MIGHT NOT BE HERE RIGHT NOW. ♡
Same old Chisami-chan.
She hasn't changed at all.
She's most likely making it all up.
SAY, OCHIAI-SAMA, KEI-SAMA, DO YOU KNOW...
Geh.
So ridiculous. Get back to school!

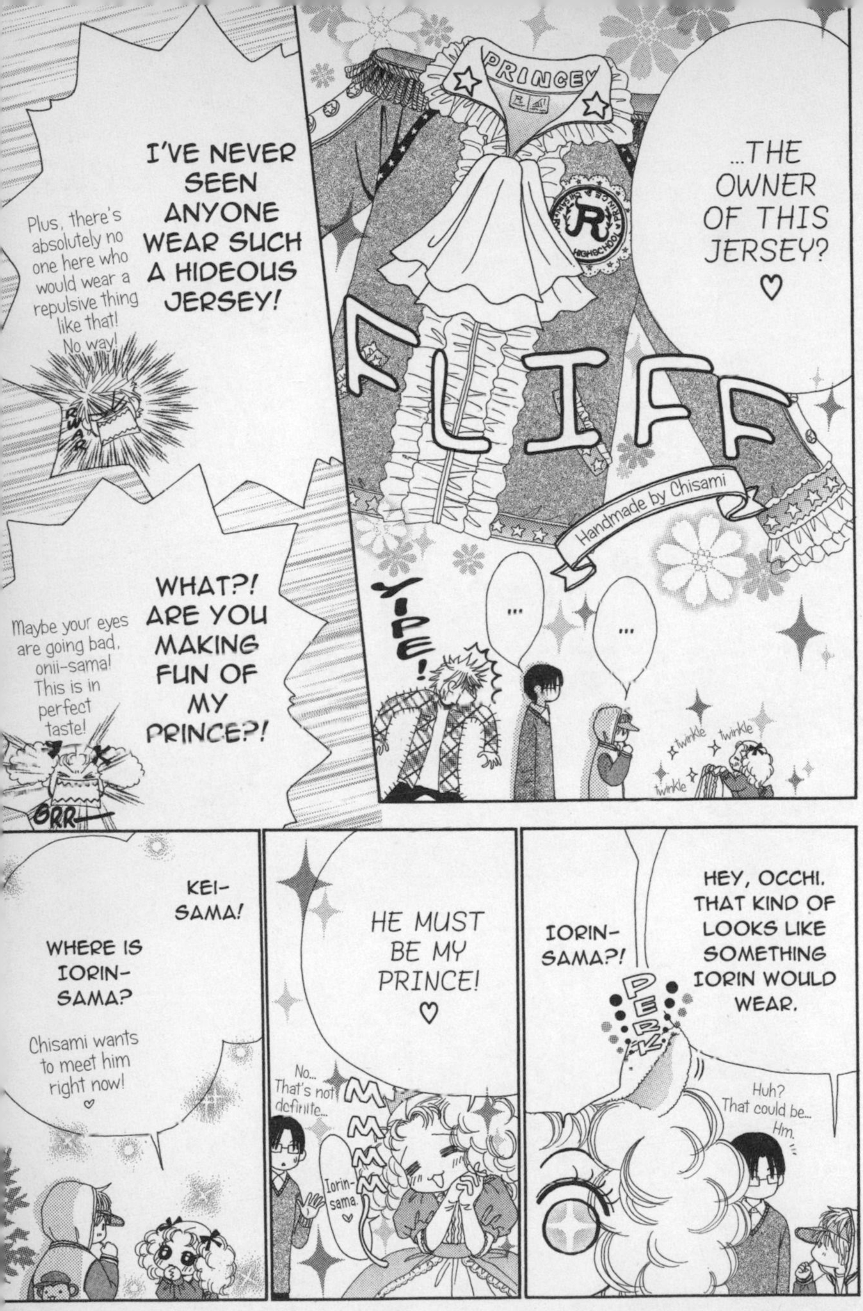
...THE OWNER OF THIS JERSEY? ♡
FLIFF
Handmade by Chisami
YIPE!
...
...
twinkle twinkle
twinkle
I'VE NEVER SEEN ANYONE WEAR SUCH A HIDEOUS JERSEY!
Plus, there's absolutely no one here who would wear a repulsive thing like that! No way!
RWAR
WHAT?! ARE YOU MAKING FUN OF MY PRINCE?!
Maybe your eyes are going bad, onii-sama! This is in perfect taste!
GRR
HEY, OCCHI. THAT KIND OF LOOKS LIKE SOMETHING IORIN WOULD WEAR.
IORIN-SAMA?!
PERK
Huh? That could be... Hm.
HE MUST BE MY PRINCE! ♡
No... That's not definite...
MMMM
Iorin-sama. ♡
KEI-SAMA!
WHERE IS IORIN-SAMA?
Chisami wants to meet him right now! ♡

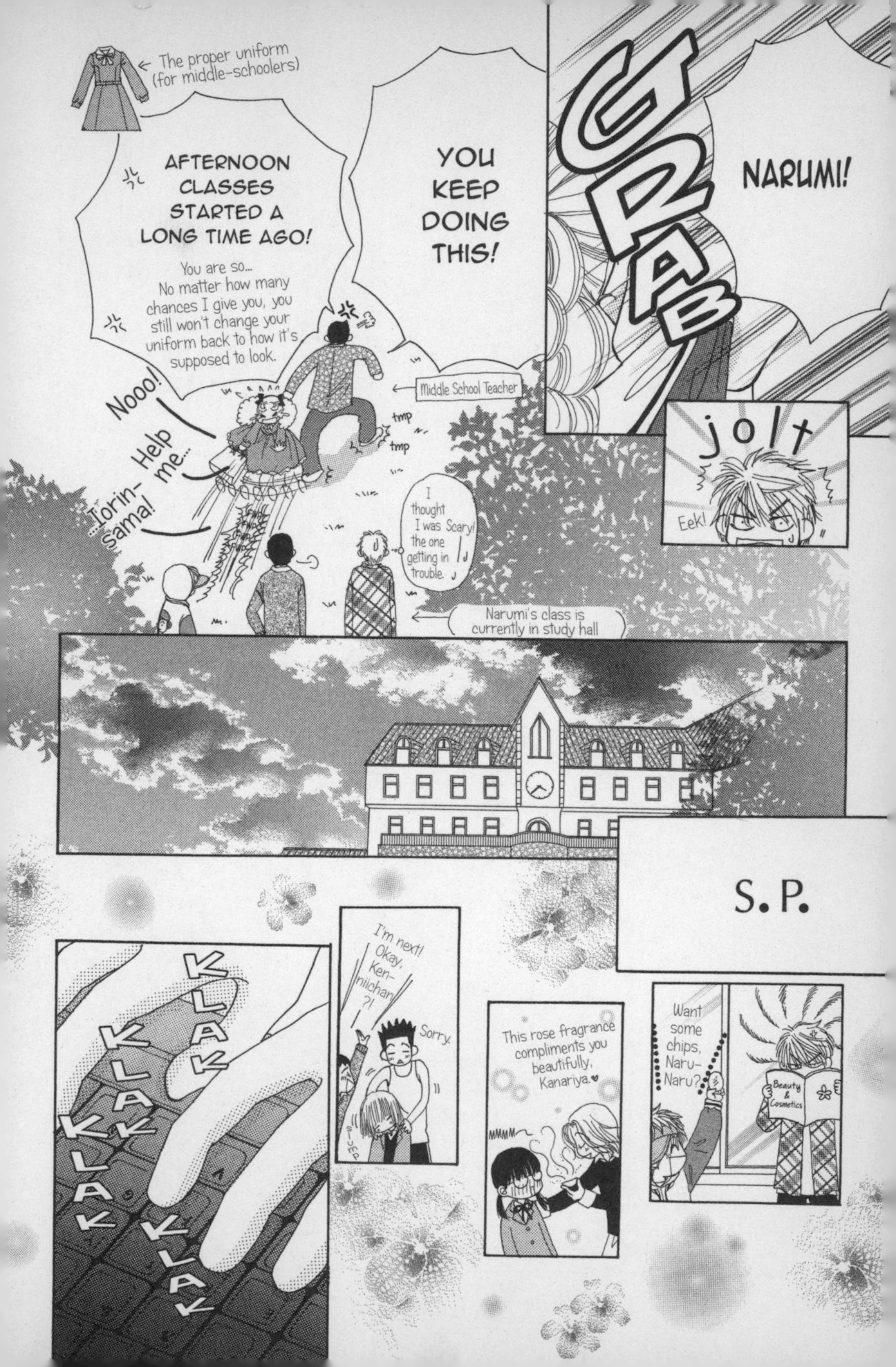
GRAB
NARUMI!
jolt
Eek!
YOU KEEP DOING THIS!
AFTERNOON CLASSES STARTED A LONG TIME AGO!
You are so... No matter how many chances I give you, you still won't change your uniform back to how it's supposed to look.
← The proper uniform (for middle-schoolers)
Middle School Teacher
tmp
tmp
Nooo!
Help me...
...Iorin-sama!
I thought I was the one getting in trouble.
Scary!
Narumi's class is currently in study hall
S.P.
Want some chips, Naru-Naru?
Beauty & Cosmetics
This rose fragrance compliments you beautifully, Kanariya.♥
MMMM
I'm next! Okay, Ken-niichan?!
Sorry.
SLUMP
KLAK
KLAK
KLAK
KLAK
KLAK
KLAK

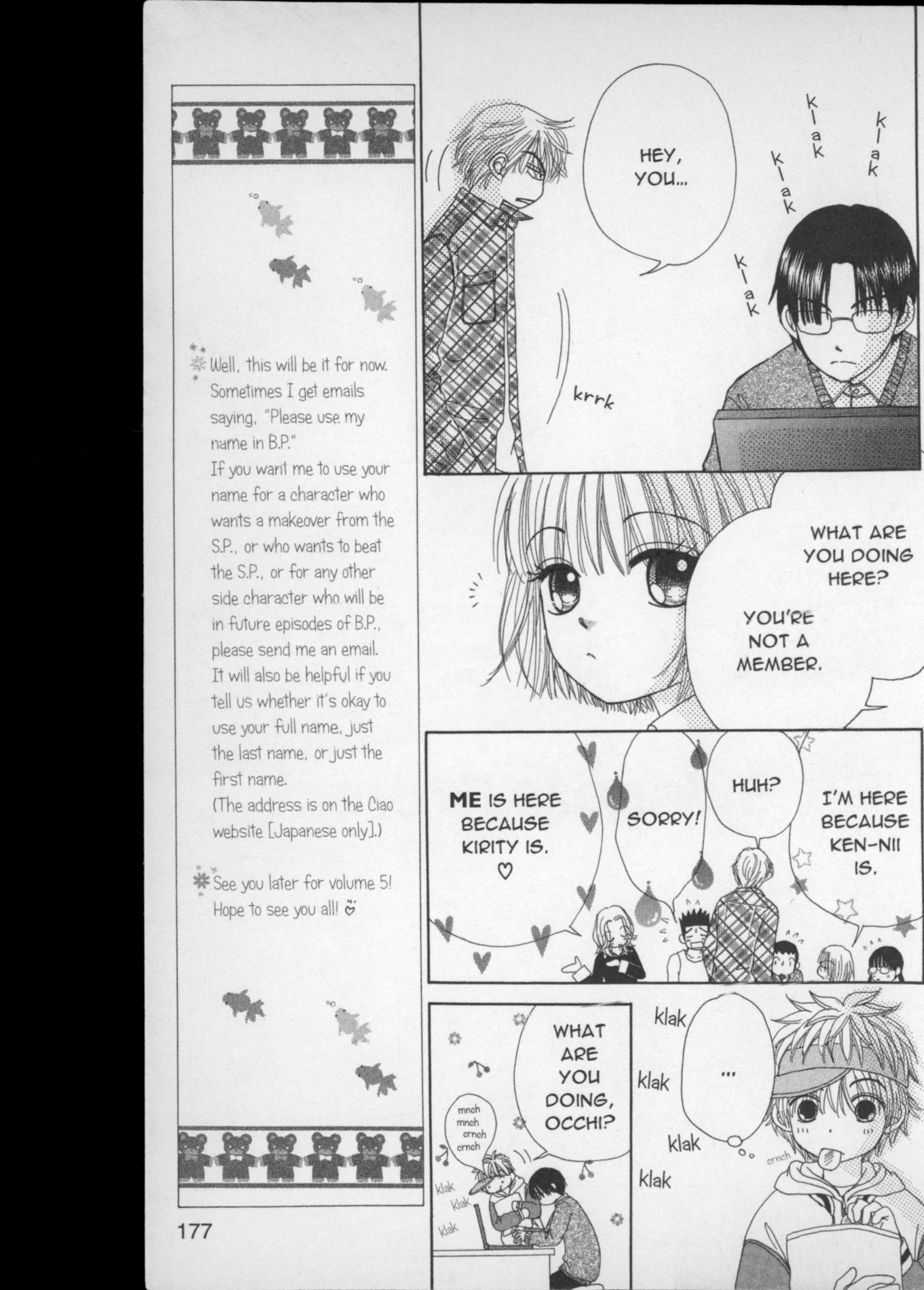

klak
klak
klak
klak
HEY, YOU...
krrk
WHAT ARE YOU DOING HERE?
YOU'RE NOT A MEMBER.
I'M HERE BECAUSE KEN-NII IS.
HUH?
SORRY!
ME IS HERE BECAUSE KIRITY IS. ♡
...
crnch
klak
klak
klak
klak
WHAT ARE YOU DOING, OCCHI?
mnch mnch crnch crnch
klak
klak
klak

✲ Well, this will be it for now. Sometimes I get emails saying, "Please use my name in B.P." If you want me to use your name for a character who wants a makeover from the S.P., or who wants to beat the S.P., or for any other side character who will be in future episodes of B.P., please send me an email. It will also be helpful if you tell us whether it's okay to use your full name, just the last name, or just the first name.
(The address is on the Ciao website [Japanese only].)

✲ See you later for volume 5! Hope to see you all! ♡

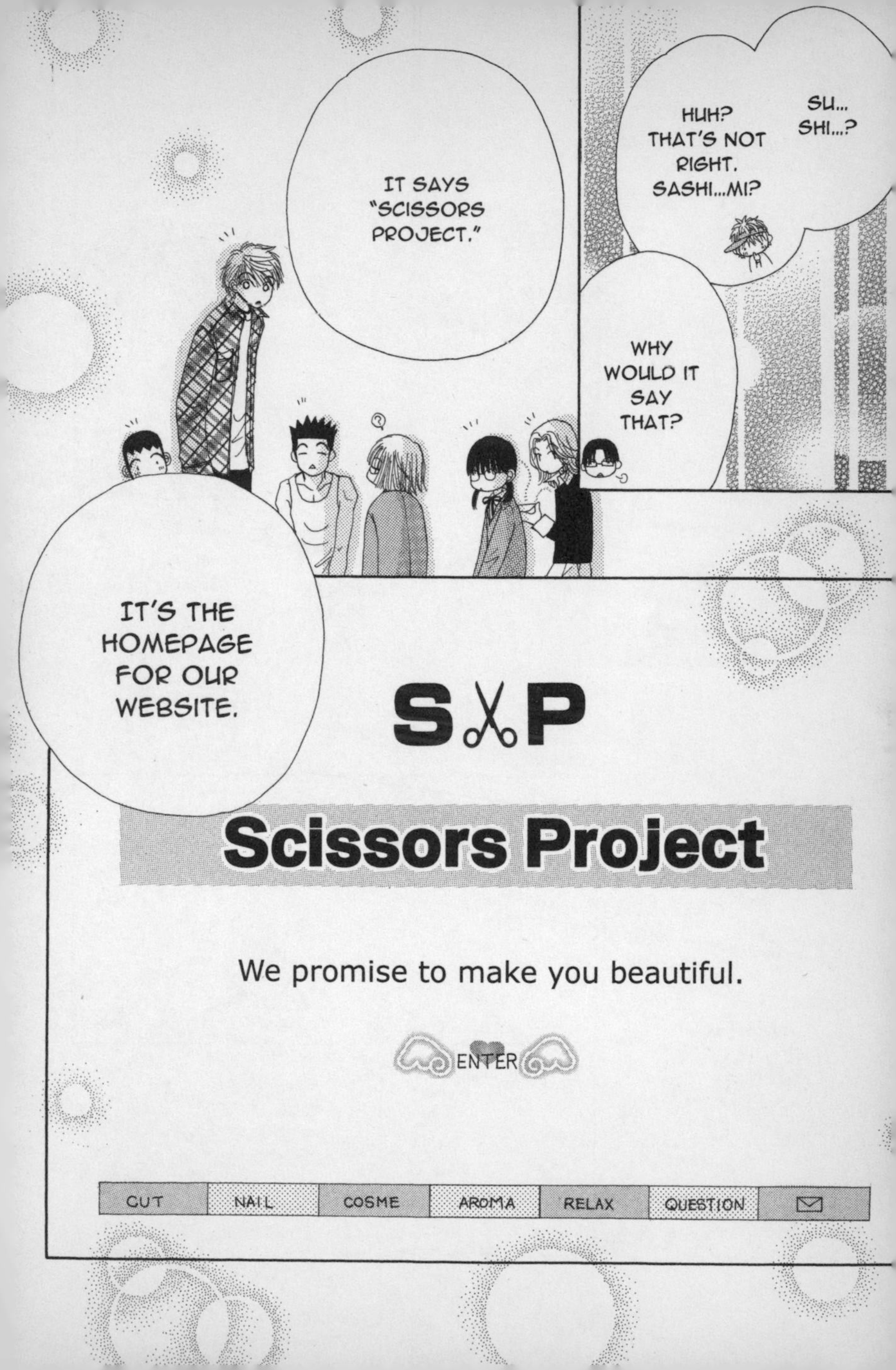
HUH? THAT'S NOT RIGHT. SASHI...MI?
SU... SHI...?
WHY WOULD IT SAY THAT?
IT SAYS "SCISSORS PROJECT."
IT'S THE HOMEPAGE FOR OUR WEBSITE.
S P
Scissors Project
We promise to make you beautiful.
ENTER
CUT
NAIL
COSME
AROMA
RELAX
QUESTION

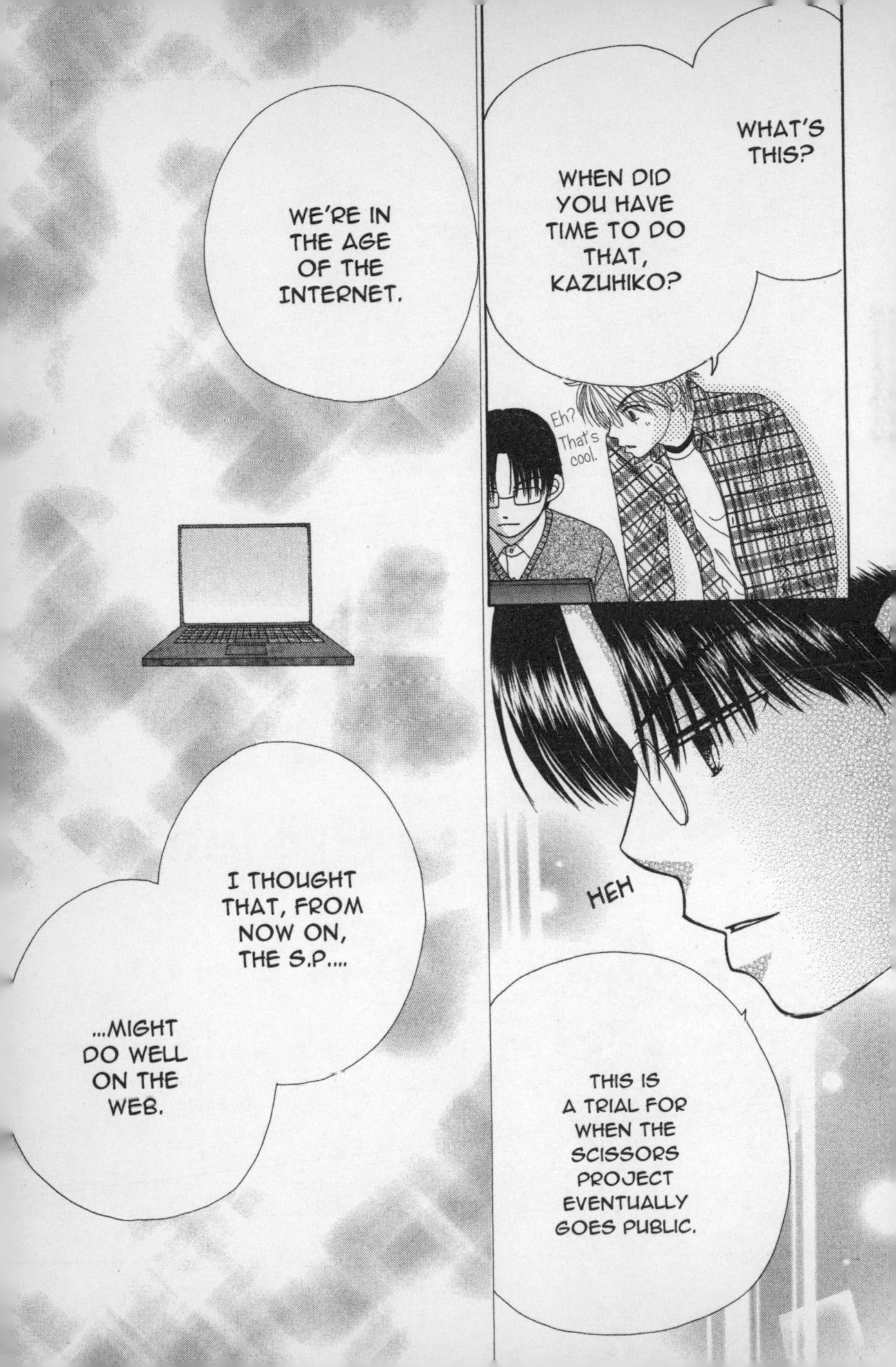
WHAT'S THIS?
WHEN DID YOU HAVE TIME TO DO THAT, KAZUHIKO?
Eh? That's cool.
HEH
THIS IS A TRIAL FOR WHEN THE SCISSORS PROJECT EVENTUALLY GOES PUBLIC.
WE'RE IN THE AGE OF THE INTERNET.
I THOUGHT THAT, FROM NOW ON, THE S.P....
...MIGHT DO WELL ON THE WEB.

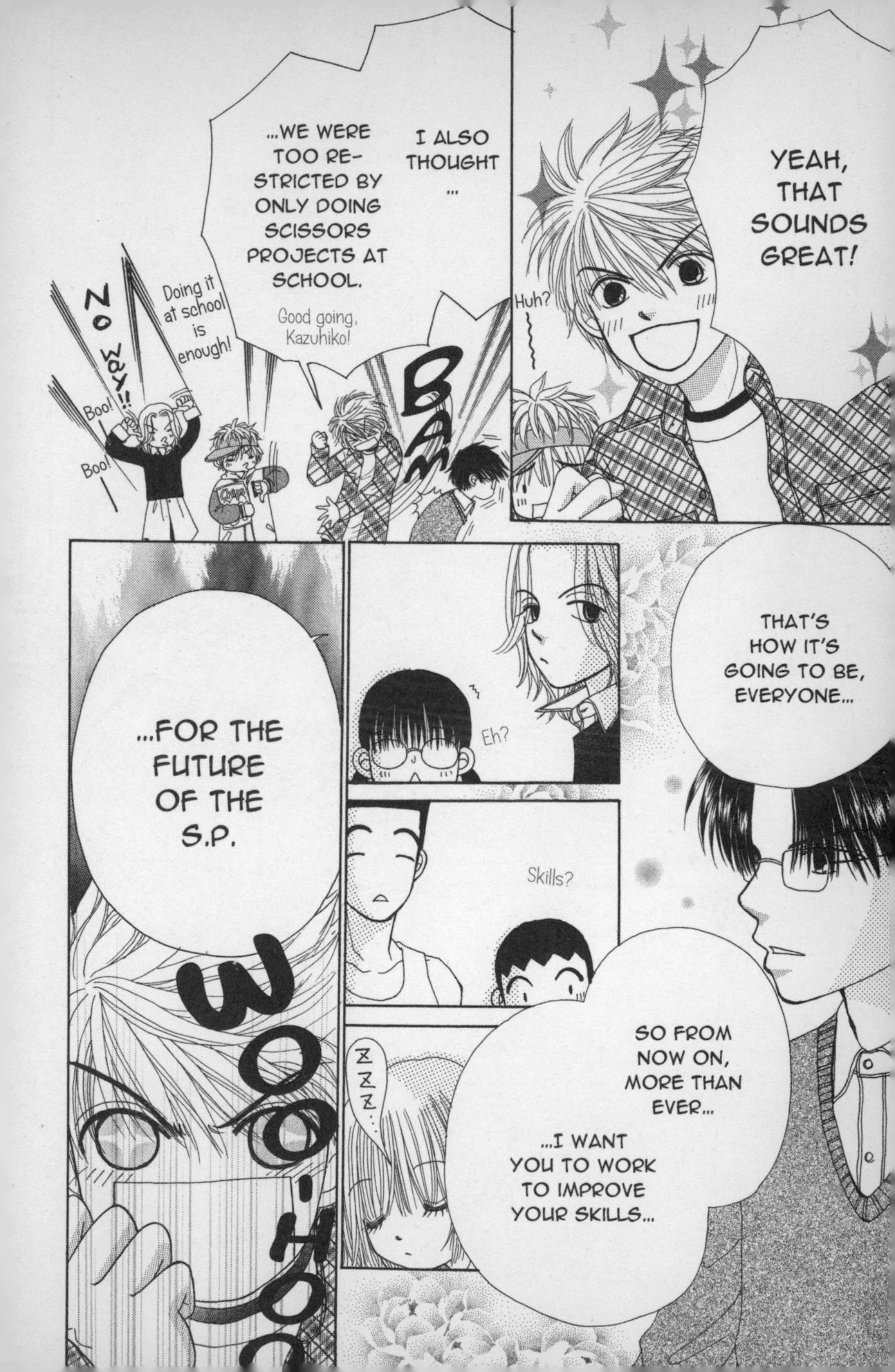
YEAH, THAT SOUNDS GREAT!
Huh?
I ALSO THOUGHT ...
...WE WERE TOO RE-STRICTED BY ONLY DOING SCISSORS PROJECTS AT SCHOOL.
Good going, Kazuhiko!
BAM
Doing it at school is enough!
No way!!
Boo!
Boo!
Chips
THAT'S HOW IT'S GOING TO BE, EVERYONE...
Eh?
Skills?
Z Z Z ...
SO FROM NOW ON, MORE THAN EVER...
...I WANT YOU TO WORK TO IMPROVE YOUR SKILLS...
...FOR THE FUTURE OF THE S.P.
WOO-HOO

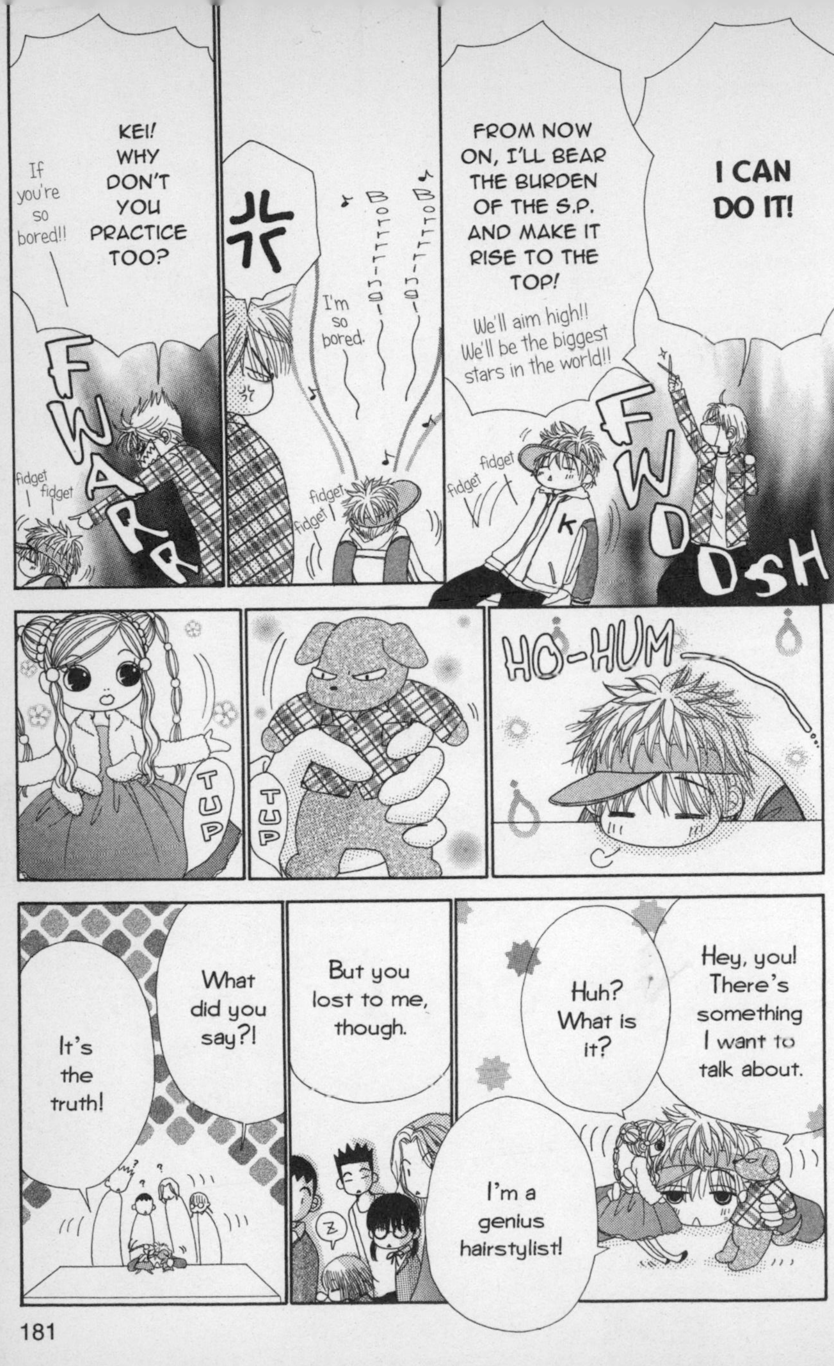
I CAN DO IT!
FROM NOW ON, I'LL BEAR THE BURDEN OF THE S.P. AND MAKE IT RISE TO THE TOP!
We'll aim high!! We'll be the biggest stars in the world!!
fidget fidget
FWDOSH
Borrring!
Borrring!
I'm so bored.
fidget fidget
KEI! WHY DON'T YOU PRACTICE TOO?
If you're so bored!!
FWARR
fidget fidget
HO-HUM
TUP
TUP
Hey, you! There's something I want to talk about.
Huh? What is it?
I'm a genius hairstylist!
But you lost to me, though.
What did you say?!
It's the truth!

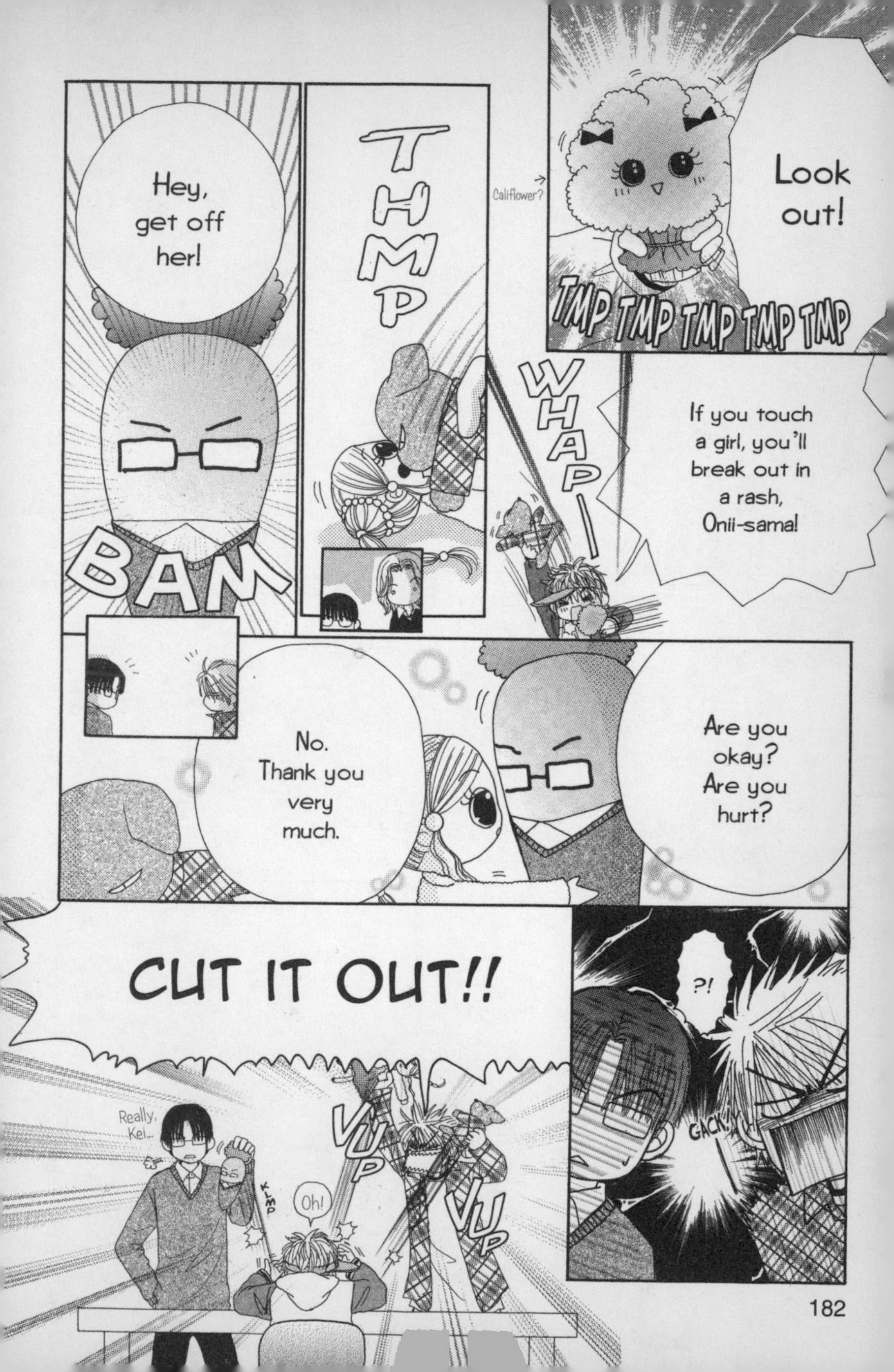
Califlower?
Look out!
TMP TMP TMP TMP TMP
If you touch a girl, you'll break out in a rash, Onii-sama!
WHAP
THMP
Hey, get off her!
BAM
Are you okay? Are you hurt?
No. Thank you very much.
?!
GACK!
CUT IT OUT!!
VUP
VUP
Oh!
Really, Kei...

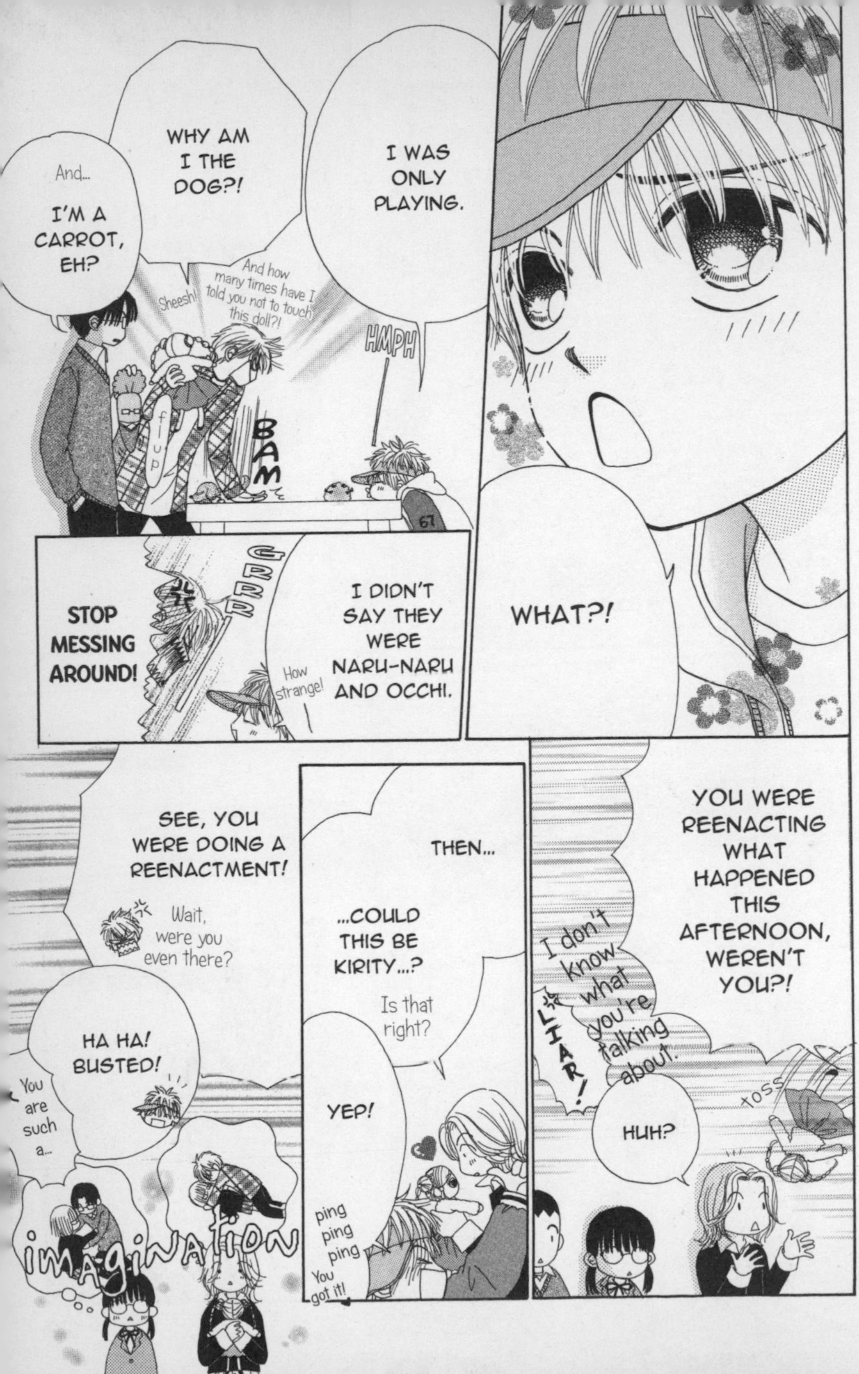
WHAT?!
I WAS ONLY PLAYING.
HMPH
WHY AM I THE DOG?!
And how many times have I told you not to touch this doll?!
Sheesh!
And...
I'M A CARROT, EH?
BAM
flup
I DIDN'T SAY THEY WERE NARU-NARU AND OCCHI.
GRRR
How strange!
STOP MESSING AROUND!
YOU WERE REENACTING WHAT HAPPENED THIS AFTERNOON, WEREN'T YOU?!
I don't know what you're talking about.
LIAR!
HUH?
toss
THEN...
...COULD THIS BE KIRITY...?
Is that right?
YEP!
ping ping ping
You got it!
SEE, YOU WERE DOING A REENACTMENT!
Wait, were you even there?
HA HA! BUSTED!
You are such a...
imagination

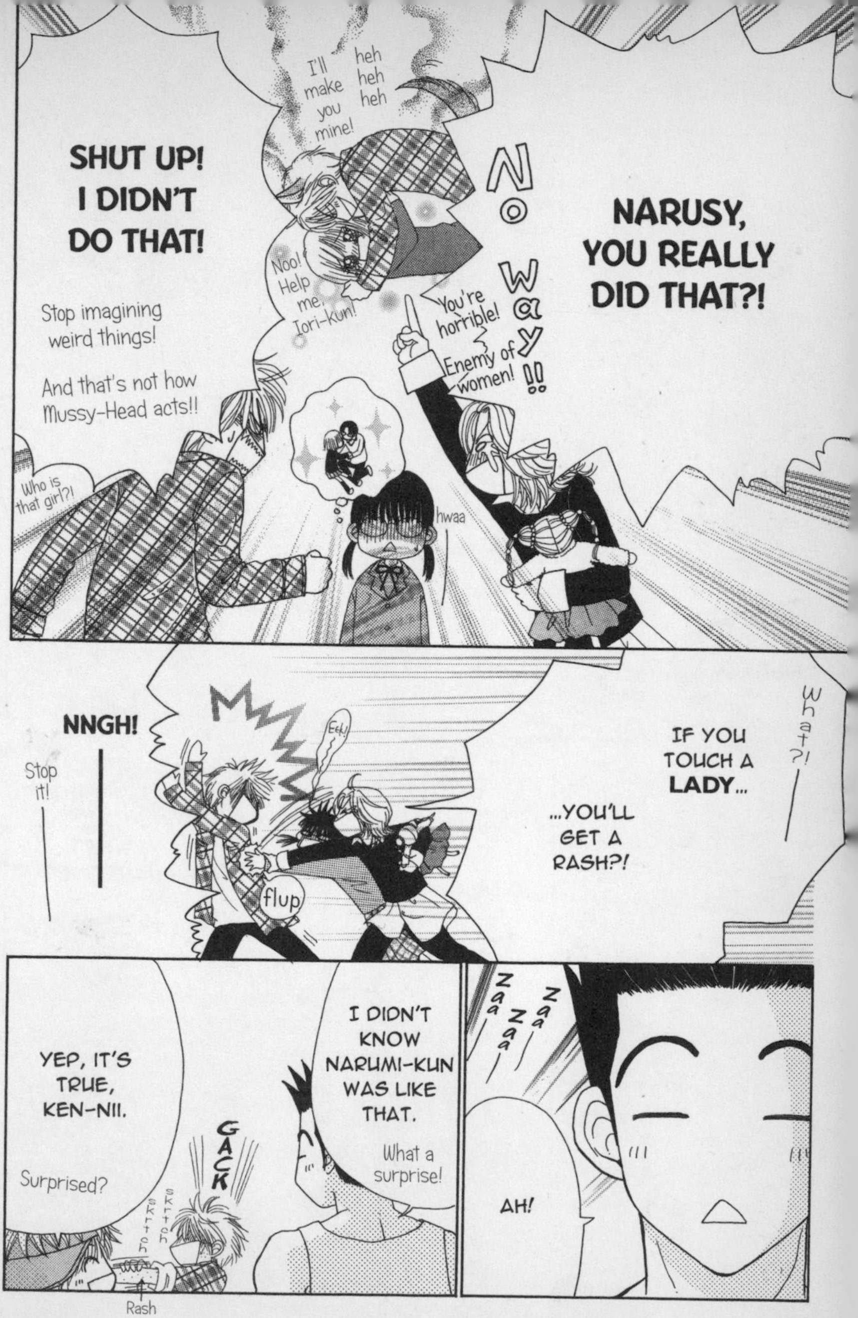
NARUSY, YOU REALLY DID THAT?!
No Way!!
You're horrible! Enemy of women!
heh heh heh
I'll make you mine!
Noo! Help me, Iori-kun!
hwaa
SHUT UP! I DIDN'T DO THAT!
Stop imagining weird things!
And that's not how Mussy-Head acts!!
Who is that girl?!
What?!
IF YOU TOUCH A LADY...
...YOU'LL GET A RASH?!
Eek!
flup
NNGH!
Stop it!
Zaa Zaa Zaa
AH!
I DIDN'T KNOW NARUMI-KUN WAS LIKE THAT.
What a surprise!
GACK
YEP, IT'S TRUE, KEN-NII.
Surprised?
skrtch skrtch
Rash

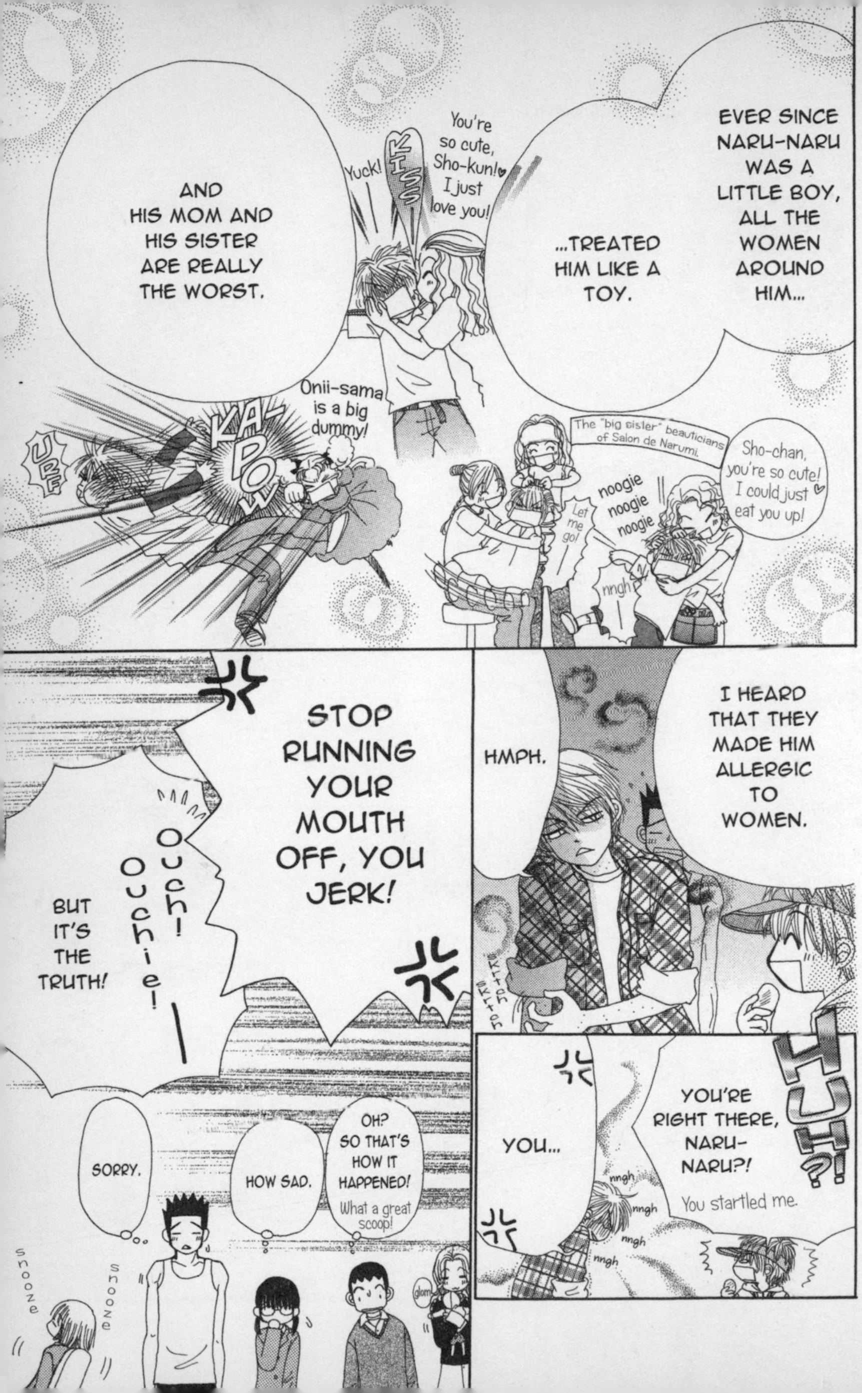
EVER SINCE NARU-NARU WAS A LITTLE BOY, ALL THE WOMEN AROUND HIM...
...TREATED HIM LIKE A TOY.
You're so cute, Sho-kun!♥ I just love you!
KISS
Yuck!
AND HIS MOM AND HIS SISTER ARE REALLY THE WORST.
The "big sister" beauticians of Salon de Narumi.
Sho-chan, you're so cute! I could just eat you up!♥
noogie noogie noogie
Let me go!
nngh
Onii-sama is a big dummy!
KA-POW
URF
I HEARD THAT THEY MADE HIM ALLERGIC TO WOMEN.
HMPH.
skritch skritch
HUH?!
YOU'RE RIGHT THERE, NARU-NARU?!
You startled me.
YOU...
nngh nngh nngh nngh
STOP RUNNING YOUR MOUTH OFF, YOU JERK!
Ouch! Ouch! Ouchie!
BUT IT'S THE TRUTH!
OH? SO THAT'S HOW IT HAPPENED!
What a great scoop!
HOW SAD.
SORRY.
glom
snooze snooze

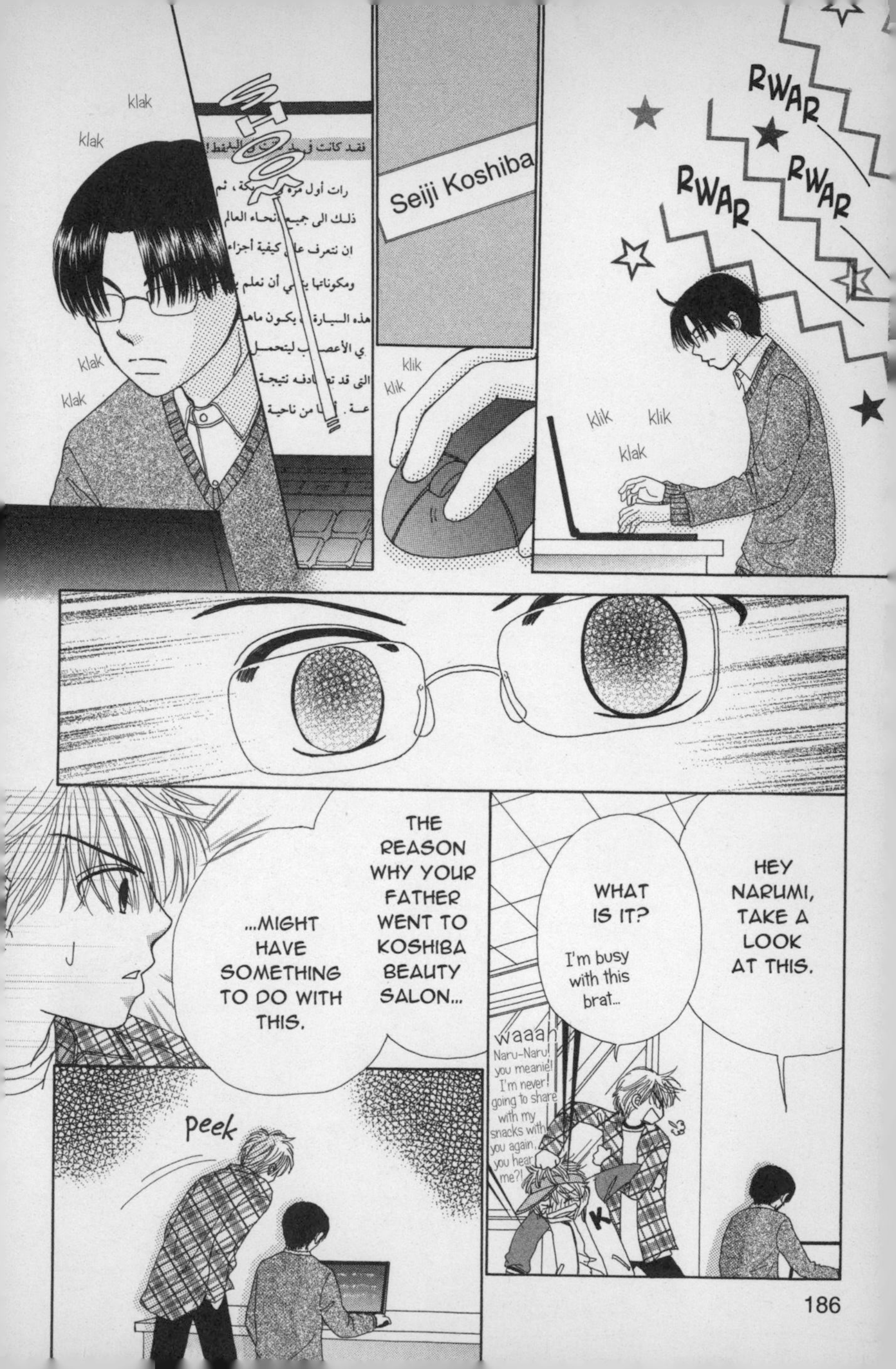
RWAR
RWAR
RWAR
klik
klik
klak
Seiji Koshiba
klik
klik
klak
klak
klak
klak
HEY NARUMI, TAKE A LOOK AT THIS.
WHAT IS IT?
I'm busy with this brat...
waaah
Naru-Naru! you meanie! I'm never going to share with my snacks with you again, you hear me?!
THE REASON WHY YOUR FATHER WENT TO KOSHIBA BEAUTY SALON...
...MIGHT HAVE SOMETHING TO DO WITH THIS.
peek

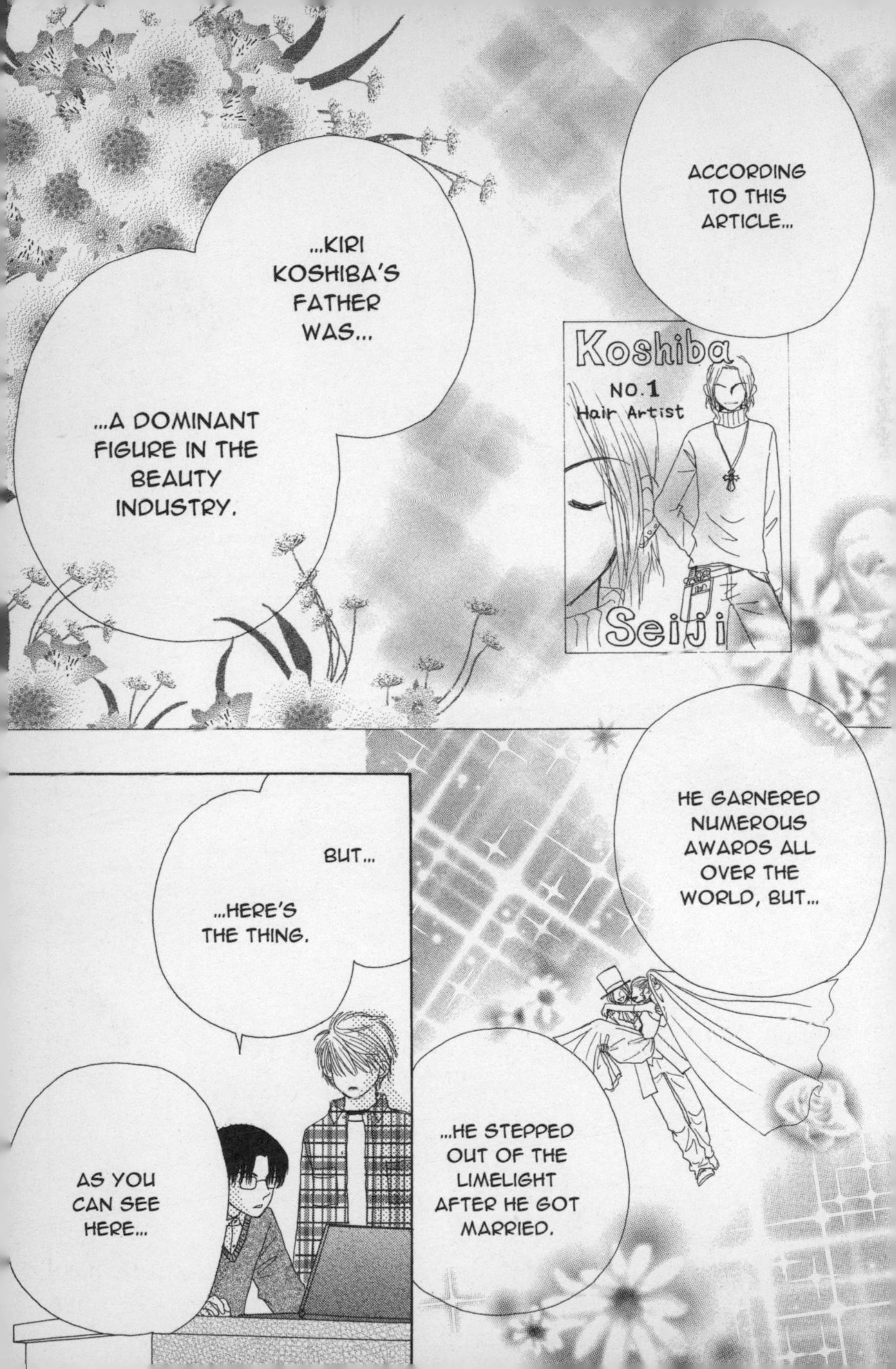
ACCORDING TO THIS ARTICLE...
Koshiba
NO.1 Hair Artist
Seiji
...KIRI KOSHIBA'S FATHER WAS...
...A DOMINANT FIGURE IN THE BEAUTY INDUSTRY.
HE GARNERED NUMEROUS AWARDS ALL OVER THE WORLD, BUT...
...HE STEPPED OUT OF THE LIMELIGHT AFTER HE GOT MARRIED.
BUT...
...HERE'S THE THING.
AS YOU CAN SEE HERE...

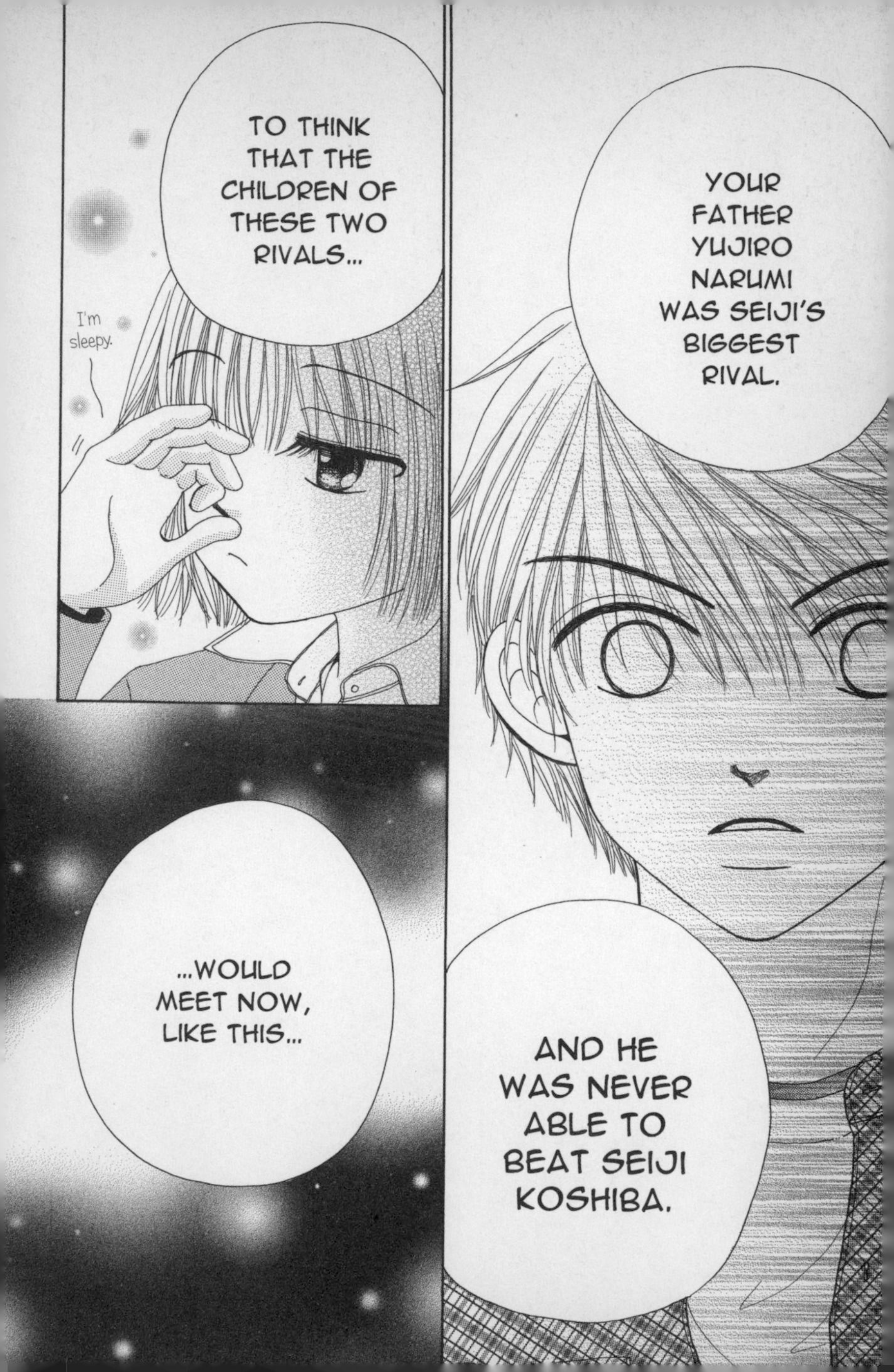
YOUR FATHER YUJIRO NARUMI WAS SEIJI'S BIGGEST RIVAL.
AND HE WAS NEVER ABLE TO BEAT SEIJI KOSHIBA.
TO THINK THAT THE CHILDREN OF THESE TWO RIVALS...
I'm sleepy.
...WOULD MEET NOW, LIKE THIS...

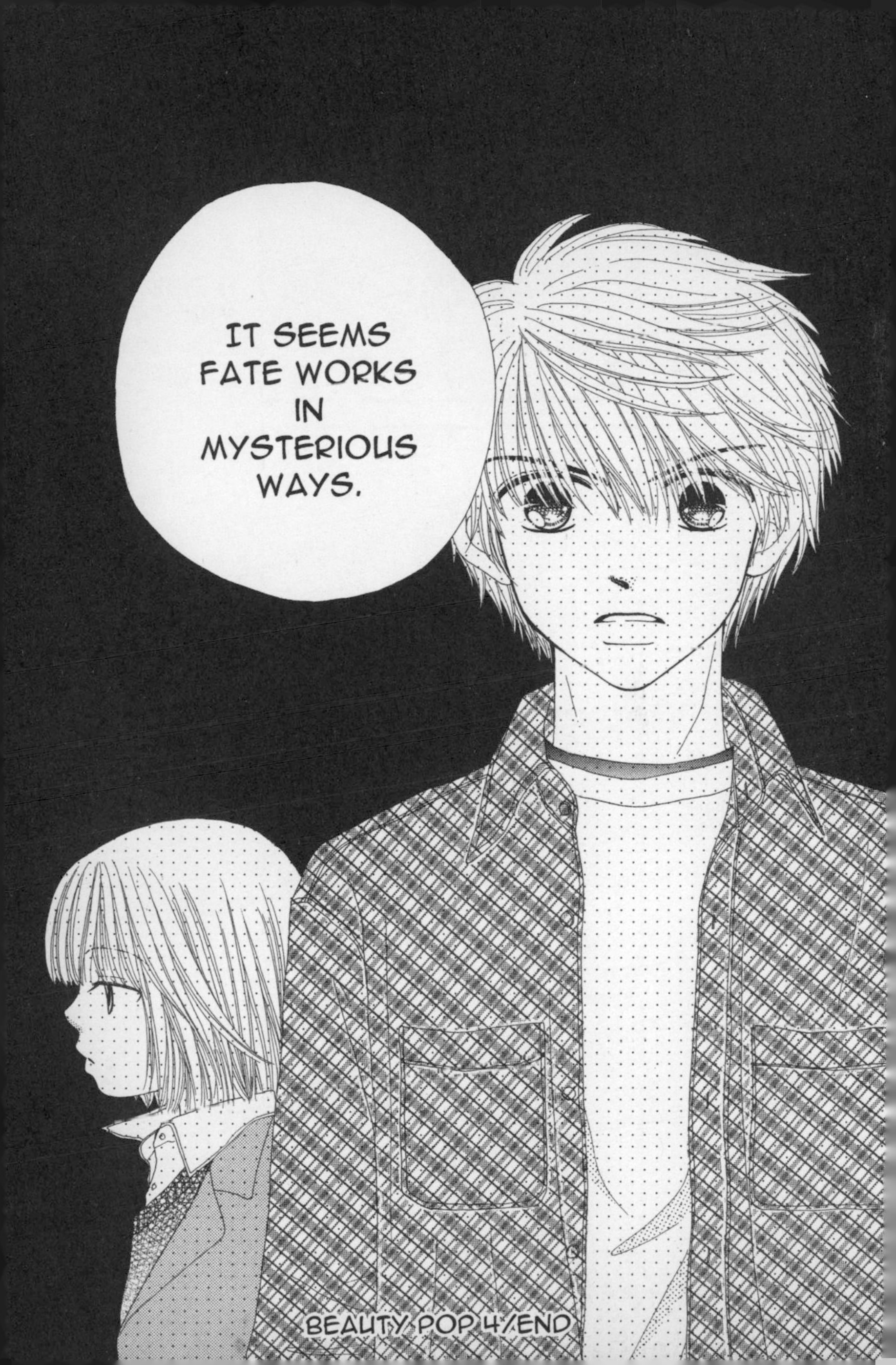
IT SEEMS FATE WORKS IN MYSTERIOUS WAYS.
BEAUTY POP 4/END

MANGA THEATER ④

Uncontrollably sleepy
The things I've done right before my deadline...
I drew a face inside a mouth.
(I still do it a lot...when I get so sleepy that my mind starts to wander...)
I wonder why?
Once, when I was as sleepy as I could possibly get, I kept saying "I'll just finish this page before I go to bed" and I thought I did my best, but...
...I flipped out when I saw that horrid drawing the next day.
Who's this?
Plus, I don't even remember drawing it...
What's this?
Occhi was wearing a girl's uniform.
Spare me.
I never want to go through this again.
That's not funny.
And Kiri was smiling really big.
Argh, that would never happen!
Why do you say that?
Sigh...
Am I the only one who does stuff like this?

RIGHT, "S.P."-SAN?

Honorifics

In Japan, people are usually addressed by their name followed by a suffix. The suffix shows familiarity or respect, depending on the relationship.

Male (familiar): first or last name + kun
Female (familiar): first or last name + chan
Upperclassman (polite): last name + senpai
Adult (polite): last name + san

+ sama: A deferential suffix that is also used by fan girls when referring to the object of their adoration.

+ sensei: A suffix used for respected professionals, such as teachers, doctors, and mangaka.

Yeee!
Narumi-senpai got mad.
NARU-CHAN'S FUSSY, ISN'T HE?
Because he's used to being treated like a prince.
PHFFT...
"Naru-chan"...

Author's Note

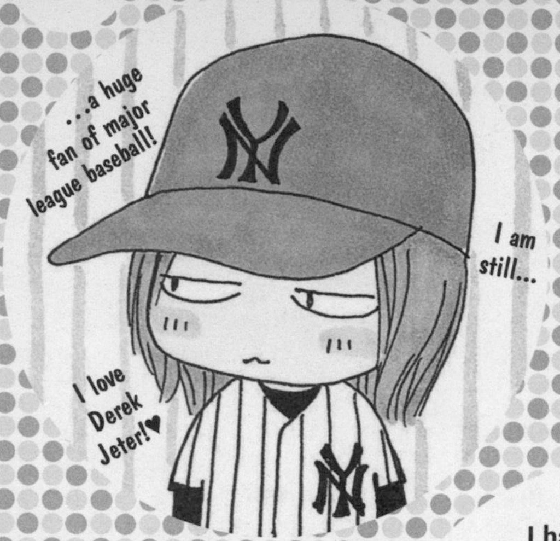
I am still...
...a huge fan of major league baseball!
I love Derek Jeter!♥

I have three cats and one dog at my house, but everything tends to revolve around the dog because she is more expressive. The cats don't seem to mind, or so I thought. But maybe, in reality, they really are lonely. Lately, when I go to bed, all three cats snuggle up next to me to sleep. I'm sorry, cat-chans.

Kiyoko Arai was born in Tokyo, and now resides in Chiba Prefecture. In 1999, she received the prestigious Shogakukan Manga Award for *Angel Lip*. The popular *Dr. Rin ni Kiitemite!* (Ask Dr. Rin!) was made into an animated TV show. *Beauty Pop* is her current series running in *Ciao* magazine.

Beauty Pop
Vol. 4
The Shojo Beat Manga Edition

STORY AND ART BY
KIYOKO ARAI

English Adaptation/Amanda Hubbard
Translation/Miho Nishida
Touch-up Art & Lettering/Inori Fukuda Trant
Design/Izumi Hirayama
Editor/Nancy Thistlethwaite

Editor in Chief, Books/Alvin Lu
Editor in Chief, Magazines/Marc Weidenbaum
VP of Publishing Licensing/Rika Inouye
VP of Sales/Gonzalo Ferreyra
Sr. VP of Marketing/Liza Coppola
Publisher/Hyoe Narita

Printed in Canada

Published by VIZ Media, LLC
P.O. Box 77010
San Francisco, CA 94107

Shojo Beat Manga Edition
10 9 8 7 6 5 4 3 2
First printing, June 2007
Second printing, July 2007

www.viz.com

store.viz.com

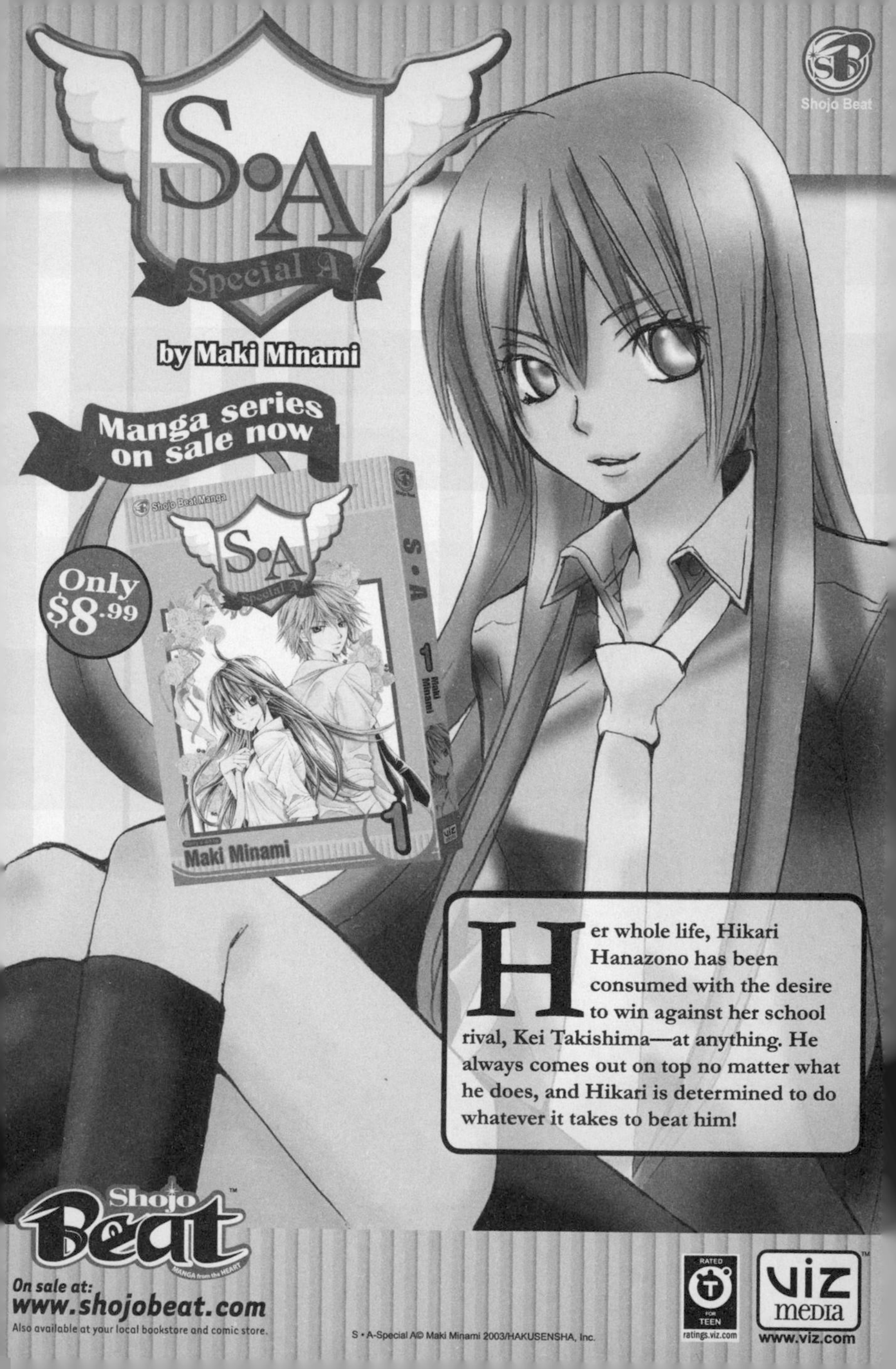

S•A
Special A
by Maki Minami
Manga series on sale now
Only $8.99
Shojo Beat Manga
S•A
Special A
Maki Minami
1
Her whole life, Hikari Hanazono has been consumed with the desire to win against her school rival, Kei Takishima—at anything. He always comes out on top no matter what he does, and Hikari is determined to do whatever it takes to beat him!
Shojo Beat
Shojo Beat
MANGA from the HEART
On sale at:
www.shojobeat.com
Also available at your local bookstore and comic store.
S • A-Special A© Maki Minami 2003/HAKUSENSHA, Inc.
RATED T FOR TEEN
ratings.viz.com
VIZ media
www.viz.com

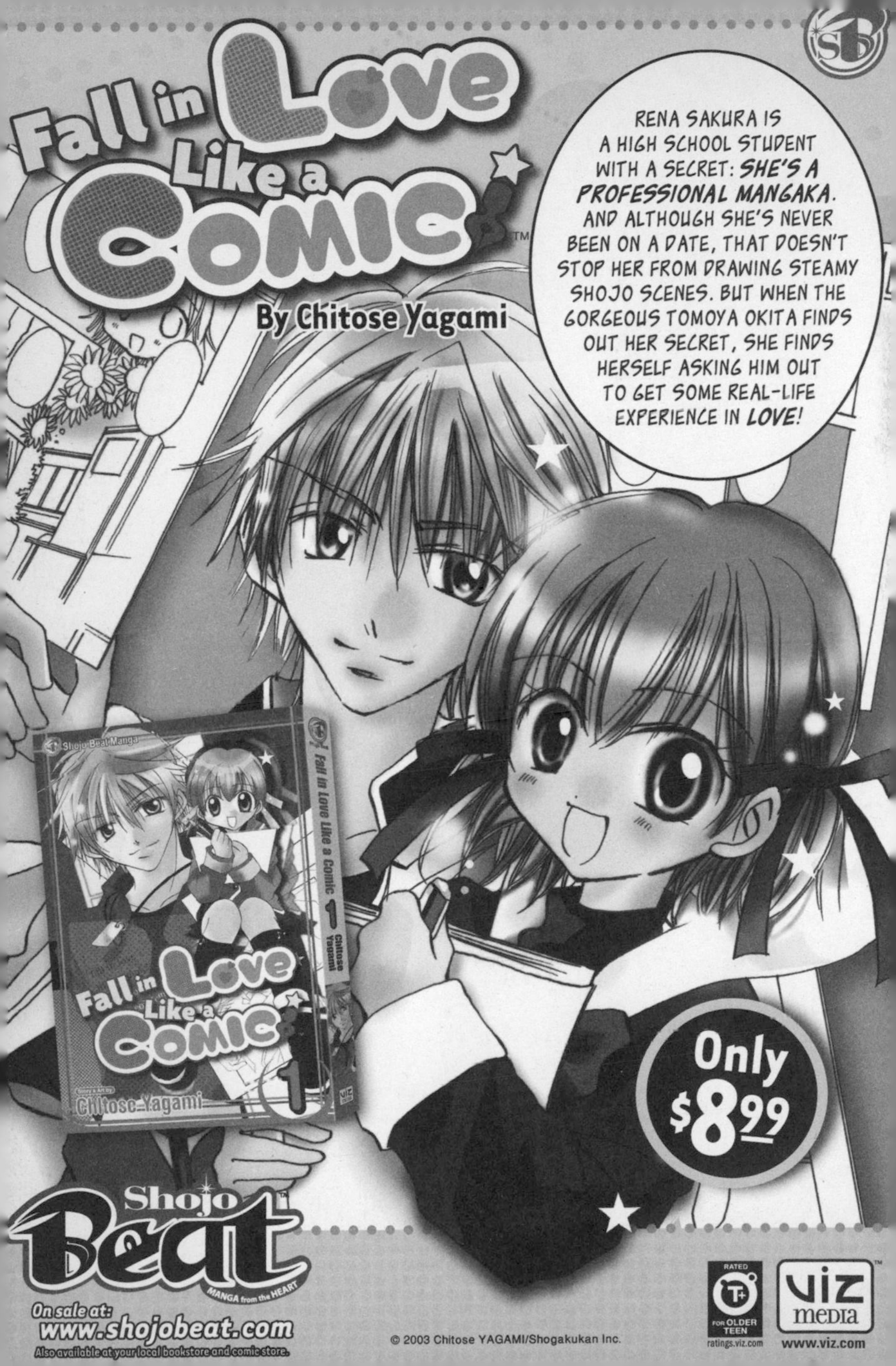

Fall in Love Like a Comic™
By Chitose Yagami
RENA SAKURA IS A HIGH SCHOOL STUDENT WITH A SECRET: SHE'S A PROFESSIONAL MANGAKA. AND ALTHOUGH SHE'S NEVER BEEN ON A DATE, THAT DOESN'T STOP HER FROM DRAWING STEAMY SHOJO SCENES. BUT WHEN THE GORGEOUS TOMOYA OKITA FINDS OUT HER SECRET, SHE FINDS HERSELF ASKING HIM OUT TO GET SOME REAL-LIFE EXPERIENCE IN LOVE!
Shojo Beat Manga
Fall in Love Like a Comic 1 Chitose Yagami
Fall in Love Like a Comic
Chitose Yagami
Only $8.99
Shojo Beat™
MANGA from the HEART
On sale at:
www.shojobeat.com
Also available at your local bookstore and comic store.
© 2003 Chitose YAGAMI/Shogakukan Inc.
RATED T+ FOR OLDER TEEN
ratings.viz.com
VIZ media
www.viz.com

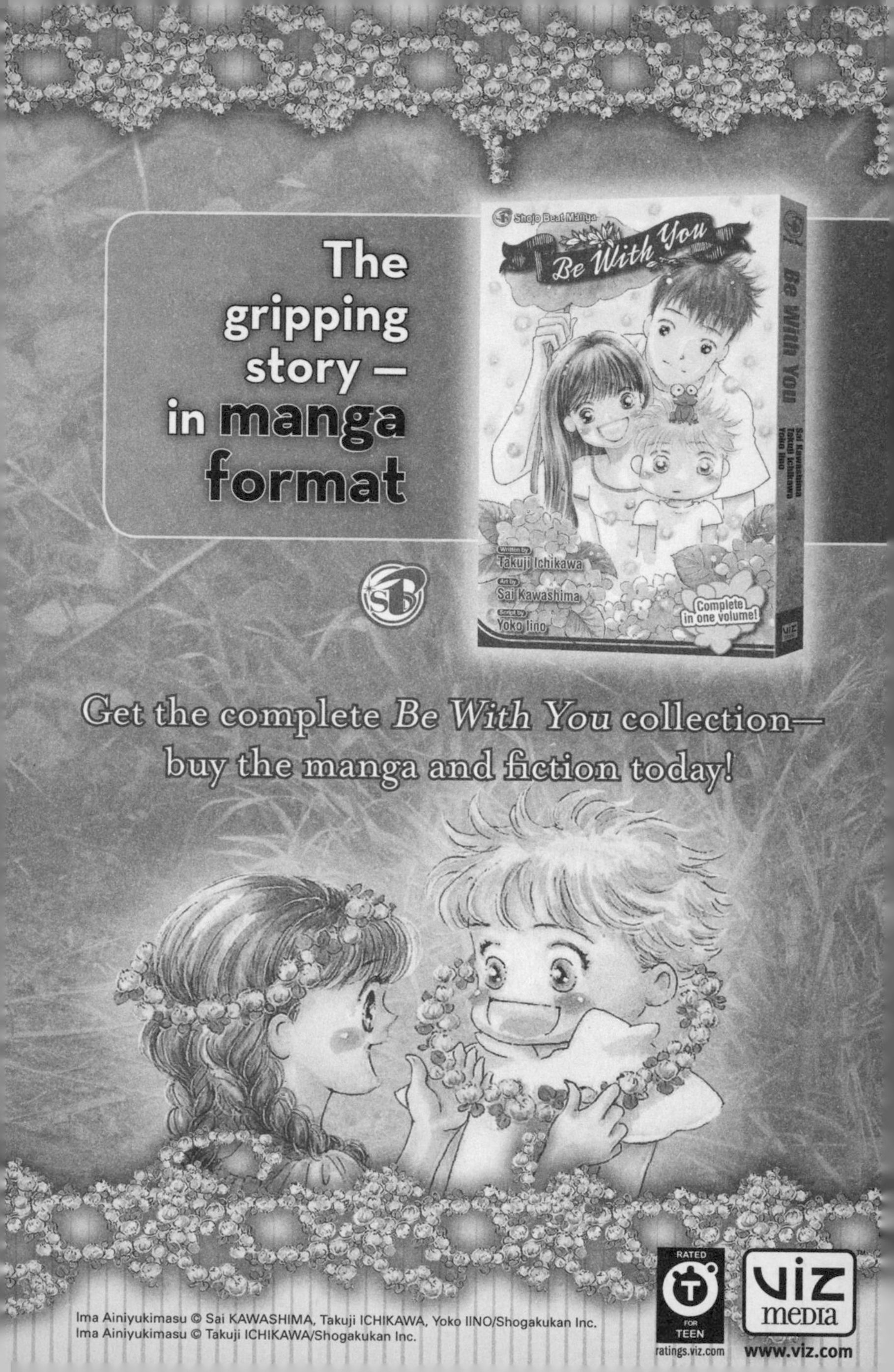
The gripping story — in manga format
Shojo Beat Manga
Be With You
Written by Takuji Ichikawa
Art by Sai Kawashima
Script by Yoko Iino
Complete in one volume!
Get the complete Be With You collection—
buy the manga and fiction today!
Ima Ainiyukimasu © Sai KAWASHIMA, Takuji ICHIKAWA, Yoko IINO/Shogakukan Inc.
Ima Ainiyukimasu © Takuji ICHIKAWA/Shogakukan Inc.
RATED T FOR TEEN
ratings.viz.com
VIZ MEDIA
www.viz.com

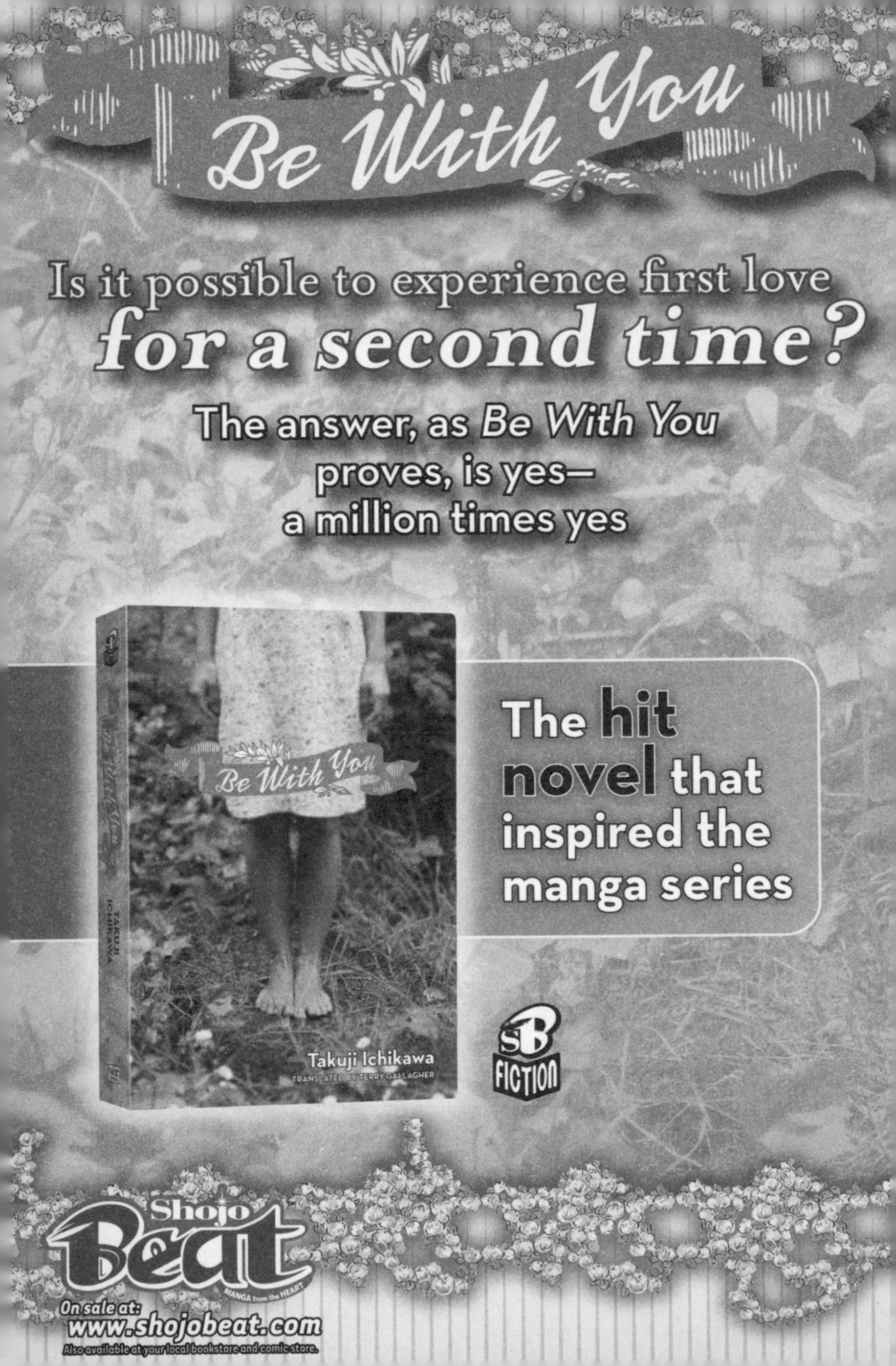
Be With You
Is it possible to experience first love
for a second time?
The answer, as Be With You
proves, is yes—
a million times yes
Be With You
Takuji Ichikawa
TRANSLATED BY TERRY GALLAGHER
The hit novel that inspired the manga series
SB FICTION
Shojo Beat
MANGA from the HEART
On sale at:
www.shojobeat.com
Also available at your local bookstore and comic store.

Tell us what you think about Shojo Beat Manga!

Our survey is now available online. Go to:

shojobeat.com/mangasurvey

Help us make our product offerings better!

THE REAL DRAMA BEGINS IN...